Hodder

Business

Hodder
VOCATIONAL
A-LEVEL

Business

■ SUSAN BLANCH (EDITOR)   ■ NEIL DENBY

Hodder & Stoughton
A MEMBER OF THE HODDER HEADLINE GROUP

Orders: please contact Bookpoint Ltd, 130 Milton Park, Abingdon, Oxon
OX14 4SB. Telephone: (44) 01235 827720, Fax: (44) 01235 400454. Lines
are open from 9.00 – 6.00, Monday to Saturday, with a 24 hour message
answering service. Email address: orders@bookpoint.co.uk

British Library Cataloguing in Publication Data
A catalogue record for this title is available from The British Library

ISBN 0 340 779 969

First published 2000
Impression number   10 9 8 7 6 5 4 3 2
Year   2005 2004 2003 2002 2001

Cover photo from the Telegraph Colour Library
Typeset by Dorchester Typesetting Group Ltd
Printed in Great Britain for Hodder & Stoughton Educational, a division of
Hodder Headline Plc, 338 Euston Road, London NW1 3BH by
J. W. Arrowsmith Ltd, Bristol

Contents

Acknowledgements

The authors and publisher would like to acknowledge the following for use of copyright material:

CORBIS, pp. 27, 36, 51, 74, 102, 298, 301.
Life File, pp. 12, 65, 159, 166, 169.
ONS, pp. 176, 177.
PA Photos, pp. 26, 82, 88, 109.
QCA, p. 37.
The Body Shop, p. 3.
The British Standards Institution, p. 55.
The Teaching Awards Trust (Lloyds TSB Group), p. 164.

The authors would like to thank Jennifer Denby and Darren Blanch for providing some of the illustrations for this book.

Every effort has been made to trace copyright holders but this has not always been possible in all cases; any omissions brought to our attention will be corrected in future printings.

Student Introduction

This book provides a comprehensive but straightforward text for Vocational A Level Business students. The six chapters of the book reflect the mandatory units of Vocational A Level Business:

Unit 1: Business at Work

Unit 2: The Competitive Business Environment

Unit 3: Marketing

Unit 4: Human Resources

Unit 5: Finance

Unit 6: Business Planning

Each chapter is divided into sections which follow the topics within each of the Vocational A Level units. The first five chapters are self-contained and can be read in any order. The first two chapters give a general overview of business and the business environment. Chapters 3, 4 and 5 look in detail at three of the main business functions. The final chapter is an integrative one which draws on the knowledge acquired by working through the other chapters.

Chapters and sections summarise learning objectives at the start. Each chapter provides a section on 'What you need to produce', giving a brief overview of the work required for your assessment of the unit. The text contains the following features:

● **Activities** – these provide a mixture of exercises for you to practise skills and apply knowledge you have acquired during your study. Key skills are identified in some activities. These indicate where you can collect evidence for your key skills qualification.

● **Top Tips** – items of interest or useful advice which add to your knowledge are highlighted throughout the text.

A note on assessment

The text has been written to provide you with a sound base from which to tackle the assessments. The Vocational A Level uses two forms of assessment:

● The **portfolio work** which consists of a report on topics covered in the unit, requiring some research and analysis. Portfolio assessed units are: Unit 1: Business at Work; Unit 3: Marketing; Unit 4: Human Resources and Unit 6: Business Planning. The aim in the chapters relating to this unit has been to make the assessment more straightforward, by breaking some of the required work into Assessment Activities within the text. The integrative chapter (chapter 6) has been written as a tool with which you can practise the practical application of your business planning skills.

● **External tests** which are set by the awarding bodies to test your knowledge on a unit. Externally tested units are: Unit 2: The Competitive Business Environment and Unit 5: Finance. The chapters relating to these units include self-tests at the end of each section, for you to practise answering test questions.

Note to Tutors

An overriding consideration in planning the text was to provide a student-friendly text which would help students work towards assessment in a planned and logical manner. The aim was to cover the knowledge required but, at the same time, give students a view of real businesses and business situations.

Activities give opportunities to develop learning and apply the skills and knowledge students require for assessments. Many of the Activities can be used as group exercises and discussion topics. Activities identify appropriate key skills. These indicate where it might be possible for students to obtain key skills evidence. Note that full information on key skills is not reproduced in the book but is available from the awarding body.

Chapter 6: Business Planning is designed for students to work through while building up the different sections of their final report. Students need to start work on their business planning assessment at an early stage in their programme. In Chapter 6, the text offers them a guide through the stages of business planning that can be followed while the other chapters are being studied. There are opportunities to link the Chapter 6 assessment to that of Chapter 3: Marketing.

There is a teacher's book to support this text (ISBN: 0340 779 950), which also has a range of additional activities and resources.

1

Business at Work

What this chapter is about

This chapter is about real businesses and how they operate. You will find out about different types of business, their objectives, structures and cultures. You will find out about the different functions within a business and how they contribute to its product or service. You will find out about the different processes used to create products and services and why quality is important. One way to approach the chapter is to consider that you are about to join a business or even set up in competition to it. ■

What you need to produce

You will need to produce a detailed business report on a medium-sized or large business. Your tutor will help you to select a suitable business on which to base your report. You will need to draw up a plan of action showing the tasks that will be carried out; the order in which they will be completed; and the resources you will use. You should carry out your plan within the agreed timescale.

In your report you should:

■ describe and explain the objectives of the business and judge how successfully the business is meeting them

■ identify how the business is owned and explain the benefits and constraints of this type of ownership

■ describe the business's structure, management style and culture and explain how they affect the business and help it to meet its objectives

■ describe the functional areas of the business and explain how they interact with one another to help the business meet its objectives

■ analyse how information and communications technology (ICT) has impacted on the internal and external communications of the business

■ describe the production process and quality assurance system used by the business and consider the effects of an alternative approach to quality control.

Your plan should be presented in a suitable format, using oral, written or computer-based methods as appropriate.

Section 1 *Business objectives*

What you need to learn

In this section you will learn about:

● why businesses set themselves targets and objectives

● the objectives they may set and why they differ from business to business

● how a business may judge whether or not it has reached a target

● how to identify and describe different business cultures.

Business objectives

If you make a journey, you are aiming to get from where you are to somewhere else. You have a starting point and an end point. The end point is your objective. A business is also aiming to get from where it is to somewhere else. Its end point is an objective or set of objectives. You can compare the journey a business makes with a journey that you might make.

Imagine that you are biking to school or college. You will know where you are starting from; the best route to get there; and when you've arrived. This is when you've achieved your objective. You have a number of choices that you can make: do you go by the most direct route; or the scenic route; or the least polluted route? How do you make your journey? Do you ride slowly, sedately, with a great deal of regard for fellow road users; or furiously, seeking to get there as quickly as possible regardless of others; or with a great concern for the environment? You might even hitch a ride by hanging on to a passing lorry!

Now, think about your journey in business terms:

● The way that you ride is the equivalent to the 'culture' of the business. You will have a particular method or way of riding – carefully, quickly, taking risks, avoiding problems. A business will have a particular way of achieving its objectives. Some businesses have a culture which involves aggressive sales tactics or a desire to maximise profits at any cost. Some businesses seek to maximise customer satisfaction, or to operate in as environmentally friendly a way as possible.

● You may have intermediate targets on your journey, such as to crest a particular hill in a faster time than before, or to cut out as much main road as possible. A business will also have intermediate targets which show it how far it has travelled towards achieving its ultimate objective.

● Your journey takes place within a context – a set of rules and regulations and the activities of other road users, for example. The context in which a business operates is laid down by national and international legislation and agreements as to what is fair and above board. You may break the rules (riding on the pavement in order to avoid that red light), and so may businesses.

● You will have a particular method for the completion of your journey in mind – the fact that you are on a bike means that you have adopted a strategy. Business strategy is the way in which businesses decide how they will achieve their targets.

Think about your bike ride. You are able to define the purpose of your journey, the strategy you will use to complete it, and the culture and values within which your journey will take place.

Think about a business. It will have objectives, and strategies for reaching these objectives. It will have intermediate targets. It will have a culture within which it operates. A business may define some of these in terms of its mission statement and objectives.

Mission statement

The mission statement of a business outlines its general aims and the context in which it operates.

It provides the framework for the activities of the business. Look at some examples:

● First Direct, the telephone banking subsidiary of HSBC, states its mission as being 'to create harmony between the services it provides and the way people live their lives with simple, straightforward products'.

● Kodak includes the statement 'to build a world class, results oriented culture' and aims for 'the fundamental objective of total customer satisfaction'.

● The Body Shop has a Charter which states, among other things, that it will 'dedicate the business to the pursuit of social and environmental change; courageously ensure that our business is ecologically sustainable: meeting the needs of the present without compromising the future; meaningfully contribute to the local, national and international communities in which we trade; passionately campaign for the protection of the environment, human and civil rights and against animal testing'.

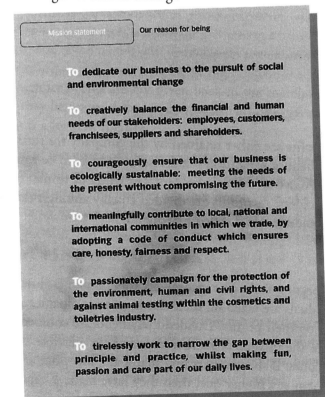

FIGURE 1.1 *The Body Shop Charter outlines its ethical character*

ASSESSMENT *activity* ❶

See if your chosen business has a 'mission statement'. This will be a short phrase that will give you a good idea of the aims of the business and the way in which it operates. You may find it in a company report or in promotional literature. You could compare it with some other mission statements to see in what ways it is similar or different.

Objectives

Objectives are the goals or targets the business is seeking to achieve. Sometimes these are open-ended, for example: 'to achieve maximum sales potential' or 'to reach maximum profits'. For example:

● Coca Cola wants to become the 'beverage of choice' and states on the front of its company report 'This year, even as we sell 1 billion servings of our products daily, the world will still consume 47 billion servings of other beverages every day. We're just getting started.' Its objective is unlimited growth: 'This is a business in its infancy, a true growth company with true, incomparable growth opportunities all over this world', states its Chief Executive Officer.

● A G Barr plc, the makers of Irn Bru – a small fish in the world of soft drinks when compared to Coca Cola – aim to 'continue to invest in production, sales and distribution facilities and the promotional activity that puts quality products on retailers' shelves and into the hands of our customers'.

Targets or objectives may be short-term, medium-term or long-term. Short-term targets are sometimes called 'intermediate' targets and are seen as milestones on the way to achieving the long-term objective. Often intermediate targets are specific and quantifiable. ICI's aim, developed after the demerger with Zeneca, is 'to achieve an average return on net assets of 20 per cent'.

Categorising business objectives

Business objectives can, broadly speaking, be put into three categories: maximising, satisficing and minimising objectives.

Maximising objectives

These are where a business wants to reach the maximum – the most – of something.

It is often assumed that organisations are in business primarily as profit maximisers. However, there are several other areas that organisations might prefer to maximise. Management writer Peter Drucker suggests that there are eight possible areas in which businesses may have objectives – including the obvious one of profit. These are:

1. **Profit.** This is also called 'surplus'. It is the difference between the costs that a business has to pay out and the revenues that it receives. Profit is often seen as the primary motive for a business to be in business and for it to stay in business.

2. **Marketing objectives.** This could mean increasing the business's share of the market, increasing market penetration or seeking market domination. For example Sky, when introducing satellite television into the UK, was willing to make losses in order to establish itself in a dominant market position.

3. **Social responsibility.** A business may wish to be recognised as one which has concern for the environment or for the local community. Under this heading might come activities such as sponsoring a local school or college or providing prizes for competitions. A number of supermarket chains have run promotions whereby they have provided equipment or technology for schools. While there is a cost to the business, schemes such as these have the added benefit of advertising the business name and improving its reputation.

4. **Productivity.** A business may wish to maximise the returns from its workers and machines in terms of productivity. There can be really large gaps between the productivity of one plant and another, or one business and another, which can have a major effect on the business's performance.

5. **Innovation.** This may be a separate target but could be linked to productivity. Some businesses will want to introduce new technology whenever it is available in an attempt to increase efficiency. Some will want to innovate in other areas such as the introduction of new products or product ranges.

6. **Manpower.** A business may want to maximise the quality of its workforce by ensuring that it employs the best workers. It will go for the best educated, the best trained or the most experienced workers. For example, some businesses will only recruit graduates.

7. **Resources.** Businesses may wish to ensure that they have the most reliable sources for raw materials, component parts etc. so that, even if other businesses in the industry suffer from a lack of supply, they will still be able to operate.

8. **Management.** Businesses may want the best management available. This could be in terms of efficiency, training and knowledge; or focus more on the loyalty of a manager to the business organisation.

ACTIVITY **1**

Despite the fact that Drucker implies that there are objectives apart from profit maximisation, it is quite possible that achieving any or all of these aims may contribute to profit.

■ Apart from profit maximisation, which of the objectives listed do you think are likely to lead to higher profits? Why do you think these will lead to higher profits?

■ Compare your reasoning with a partner. Are there any objectives which you have both included or both left out?

Satisficing objectives

These are objectives where a business or organisation is able to say 'I am satisfied'. It may be that the organisation has reached a pre-set target or decided that it has 'done enough'. These objectives are often very important to small firms. Satisficing objectives may include:

● **Survival.** This is particularly important for a small business that is just starting out. It may be the only objective possible for the first few months or years of operation. Further objectives may only be possible when this one has been reached.

● **Breaking even.** This means reaching the point where revenues are equal to costs. As this will include the wages or 'drawings' of the owner in a small business, it means that a 'living' is being made. This may be all that the owner wants.

● **Reaching a certain level of income, profitability or return on investment.** ICI has set a satisficing target of a 20 per cent return on investment and will be satisfied if this minimum level is achieved. (Of course, it won't stop it from striving for higher levels.)

Minimising objectives

These are objectives where a business wants to make the least, rather than the most, of something. For example, a business might want

FIGURE 1.2 *Activity: fold like this*

to minimise labour turnover; or limit the damage to reputation caused by the building of a new plant; or minimise interest repayments on loans. Many older or more bureaucratic organisations want to limit risk. These so-called 'risk averse' businesses are slow to respond to change and reluctant to innovate.

 **ACTIVITY** **2**

Take a piece of A4 paper and fold it into three sections as shown in Figure 1.2.

■ In the first section, write down a list of 10 businesses that you can think of.

■ Next to each business, write down what you think might be its major objective.

■ Fold over the third section of your paper so that the names of the businesses can be seen but not the objectives, and exchange it with a partner.

■ Using your partner's list of businesses, fill in what you think is the main objective for each.

■ Now compare your notes. How many times did you agree on an objective? What is the most frequently occurring objective? What conclusions can you draw from this information?

■ **Look at the conclusions that you reached. How many times did you and your partner assume that profit maximisation was the main objective of an organisation? What does this tell you about objectives?**

Non-profit-making organisations

Some organisations don't have the specific aim of making a profit. These fall into the categories of:

● public sector businesses – owned or controlled by national or local government

● charities – set up to collect money and act on behalf of a deserving cause

● voluntary organisations – usually providing a service using volunteer labour.

Public sector organisations

These are under the control of national government, local government or QUANGOs. Their main aim is to provide services to the public, spending money raised through local or national taxation and National Insurance contributions. Types of public sector organisation include:

● QUANGOs. This stands for 'Quasi Autonomous Non-Government Organisations'. These are organisations that are set up and funded by government. Most of them are accountable to government, and have a public duty to provide a particular service. Examples include the National Rivers Authority, the National Parks, the Forestry Commission and the Sports Council.

● Public services. Many services traditionally supplied by government-owned bodies, such as water, gas, and electricity, are now provided in the private sector. The government still runs some essential services. Some services, such as defence, could not be put into private hands without endangering the country's security. Others, such as the Post Office and the Stationery Office, are kept in government hands because the government considers it is

unlikely that a business could provide a commercially viable and totally reliable service.

● The National Health Service is a special type of business. Its was established with the main objective of providing health care for everyone, regardless of ability to pay. However, each health authority is expected to manage its own budget and to be as 'efficient' as it possibly can.

● Local government, in the form of councils and local authorities. These provide services such as education, social services, leisure and recreation. They maintain highways, provide environmental health services and carry out refuse collection and disposal. They also build housing and are involved in planning and economic development.

Top Tips

Local councils are usually able to supply a great deal of information about the areas under their control. Much of this can be useful when looking at the context within which a particular business operates. Even better, the information is generally free.

ACTIVITY   ❸

What services are provided by your local authority? You will be able to obtain a leaflet from your local authority which explains where its income comes from and what it is spent on, as well as listing the services, or you could look in the telephone directory.

1. **Look at your information and say what you think are the main objectives of each local authority.**

2. **Compare your conclusions with a partner. Do you agree?**

3. **Prepare an oral presentation which describes the main objectives of your local authority.**

                                   Key Skills C3.1b

Private sector organisations

Non-profit-making organisations in the private sector include both charity and voluntary organisations. They do aim to make a surplus of income over costs, but will use this to further their charitable aims. They are still likely to be run with business notions of efficiency, value for money and a number of satisficing targets.

The objectives of non-profit-making organisations will be closely linked to their activities.

- Some are single issue organisations, for example LYNX which fights the fur trade. It will have achieved its objective when that one issue is resolved. Anti-fox-hunting protesters will have no issue if fox hunting is made illegal.

- Some organisations exist to raise awareness of something. An objective like this is never likely to be achieved. For example, when would Greenpeace or Friends of the Earth claim that all environmental issues had been resolved? This does not, of course, prevent them from working towards such an unattainable objective.

- Some charities and voluntary organisations have the objective of providing a service. The Royal National Lifeboat Institution is a good example of this. Organisations such as these will be achieving their aims constantly.

Business Culture

All businesses have a set of values, attitudes and beliefs. These make up what is called the business or corporate culture. This describes the way in which an organisation works ('the way they do things') and is the commonly held beliefs and accepted patterns of working within the organisation.

The corporate culture will determine the way in which the business operates and how it interacts with both its employees and other businesses with which it deals. Culture will affect business objectives and structure. It may help or hinder the business's success. Management theorists have classified organisational cultures into the different types discussed below.

Role culture

In the role culture, the jobs that people do – their roles – are more important than the people themselves. Managers have power and influence due to their status within the organisation and not because of personal influence or expertise. Internal operations are controlled by the existence of set procedures and rules. Individuals are not encouraged or expected to step outside the fixed boundaries set by these rules.

The structure of the organisation tends to be hierarchical. A small group of senior management will control the business, there will be several layers of management and the lines of command will be clear. Objectives may be modest as managers do not want to risk their position by failing to meet them. Managers may be unwilling to take risks which might endanger their position and, as a consequence, the business may not grow or succeed as it should.

This sort of organisation tends to be slow to react to change and finds it difficult to adapt to new conditions. Role cultures can only be successful where the environment in which the business is operating remains stable. Where a business faces rapid change, the role culture is likely to collapse. Very large organisations, which can be difficult to control, often have a role culture. The Civil Service is one example.

 Top Tips

You may also come across the term 'bureaucracy'. Bureaucracy is a type of role culture where the management structure and control of operations have become very formalised and inflexible.

Power culture

Power cultures are those that are dominated by one influential individual. Control over the business is achieved by the appointment of a few key individuals who can be trusted by the leader. They tend to be results-focused and don't worry too much about how results are achieved. This can lead to the business being seen as aggressive and tough.

The structure of such an organisation is centred on the leader. Around the leader are key individuals, each with their own area of control. The organisation can be very competitive, especially in the middle layers of management where people are competing to please the leader and reach the top. Important objectives will be those that gain the attention of the leader by achieving the right results. Other objectives and issues may be overlooked.

This culture often exists in smaller businesses where the business owner will be the central figure. The advantage of this culture is that it can respond very quickly to change, because it is controlled by the leader and the chosen few.

Task culture

The task culture focuses on getting the job done. Groups or teams within this culture are not fixed but are made up of individuals brought together to achieve a specific task. Individuals are chosen for their expert knowledge and teams are left alone to complete their task. These organisations depend on putting the right resources and people together to achieve each project, aim or objective. This might be, for example, a marketing objective, a production objective or a development objective. This sort of approach tends to make the organisation much more dynamic and focused on objectives. The structure of such an organisation is likely to have few levels of management, with each manager having a wide span of control. Some consultancy firms have this sort of culture.

Person culture

The person culture is unusual in that the emphasis is on the individual rather than the organisation and its objectives. It is more a group of individuals than an organisation. The individuals group together in order to have a better chance of achieving their individual aims. The group could be compared to a family, where the individuals are all equally important and have their own aims and ambitions, but look to one another for support and encouragement and share some resources. It is rarely seen in practice. Perhaps the closest we can come to an example is a barrister's chambers, or some other groups of professionals.

In reality, most businesses will display a mix of cultures. Different parts of a business organisation may have different cultures. For example, a large accountancy firm may have a task culture among its professional staff whilst the business functions, such as the personnel and marketing departments, may be more role-oriented. You may find this mix of cultures in the business you choose to investigate for your assessment.

ASSESSMENT activity ②

Look at the types of culture detailed in this section.

1. Which of these types of culture does your chosen business fit into?

2. Do you think that it is the most appropriate culture for your business?

3. Explain your reasoning.

Key Skills C3.2

The culture of a business organisation tends to evolve over time. There are many different influences on businesses that help to shape their culture. Some of the main ones are:

● **The economic environment.** Different cultures respond to different economic

the story

Delicious fair trade Divine milk chocolate, made by The Day Chocolate Company, was launched last autumn with enthusiastic support from The Body Shop, Christian Aid and Comic Relief. The Department for International Development pulled out all the stops to guarantee our business loan, and NatWest offered sympathetic banking facilities....

Here's how it all happened . . . .

GETTING IT TOGETHER
Cocoa growers in Ghana, West Africa, pooled resources to set up Kuapa Kokoo, a farmers' co-op which would trade its own cocoa to get a better price on the market. The farmers were supported by Twin Trading, the fair trade company that puts the coffee into Cafédirect.

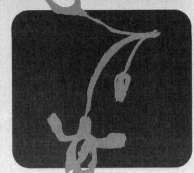

BIGGER AND BETTER
Kuapa Kokoo – which means 'good cocoa growers' in Twi – now has a membership of 30,000 cocoa farmers. Its premium quality cocoa beans are now sold to chocolate companies from around the world.

A CHOC OF ONES OWN
Already getting a fair trade price from some international customers, the farmers decided to invest in a chocolate bar of their own, and helped to establish The Day Chocolate Company last autumn.

A FIRST FOR FAIR TRADE
The farmers shareholding in the company is unique in the fair trade world, and means that Kuapa Kokoo has a meaningful input into how Divine is produced and sold and a share of the profits.

**PA PA PAAA –
THE BEST OF THE BEST**
Made from the best of the best beans, every melting mouthful of delicious fair trade Divine milk chocolate means that more cocoa farmers get a secure price for their crop.

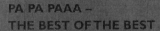

WHERE TO GET YOUR HANDS ON DIVINE
Divine is now stocked in Sainsbury's, Iceland, Co-op, NUS shops and in independent wholef... fair trade stores.

Fairtrade

FIGURE 1.3 *The Body Shop underlined its ethical principles by being one of the supporters of 'Divine' – a chocolate produced with the help of Fair Trade*

situations. In times where the economy is stable, role cultures can be very successful. They are also prevalent where a business organisation has a large amount of control over its own environment. This is usually where it is the only business in a particular market (a monopoly). Where the economic environment is unstable, a power culture will be able to respond much more quickly to the changes. In situations where one business merges with another, it is often a battle of powerful personalities at the centre of each business. A business that has a very diverse market, supplying lots of different products to lots of different customers, will operate better with a task culture. As the economic environment changes, the business culture will change. If it fails to change, the business may not be able to survive.

- **Social environment.** There is some evidence that different social cultures will affect the culture and structure of business organisations. So different national cultures or strong religious cultures may affect the business culture. It is suggested by theorists that Anglo-Saxon countries have a tendency to more individualistic, or power-based, cultures. The Japanese business culture tends to be more collective and team-centred, but at the same time authoritarian and quite materialistic. This can be a very successful combination for businesses but it may not work in all social environments.

- **Technological environment.** Technology has a tendency to influence the culture and structure of business organisations. This is because where a business relies heavily on technology, work tends to be organised around that technology. Factory production lines, where work tends to be routine and organisations tend to be large, encourage the growth of role cultures. In industries where the technology changes rapidly, task cultures or power cultures will operate more efficiently.

- **Ethical influences.** Business ethics are really the moral stance of the business. Just as you decide on the right way to behave, businesses can also be influenced by what they see as right and wrong. This might be in relation to environmental issues, or the rights of workers, for example. Many businesses today take some sort of ethical stance, and this will affect their culture as well as how they operate. There are some businesses that are built around their business ethic. The Body Shop is built around environmental issues, providing cosmetics that don't damage the environment. The culture of the organisation is built around the ethics of its founder and chairperson, Anita Roddick. Employees pull together as a team because of their belief in a leader and a purpose. Organisations such as Fairtrade operate on the principle that the worker should not be exploited, and should be given a fair deal. This gives rise to a democratic culture, where workers make decisions as a collective.

 ACTIVITY

Research Machines, or RM, developed its first micro-computer in 1977. This, the RML 380Z, was one of the first to be sold to local authorities for use in schools. At that time there was some reluctance on the part of local authorities to invest in what was seen as very new and untried technology but RM was successful in forming a relationship with a number of local authorities. Its objectives were market-based. It could see a new market developing and wanted to penetrate that market. Its employees worked in groups, developing software and systems, while other groups sought marketing opportunities.

RM was already developing its own versions of hardware and software specifically for the education market and was ready with products when education went over to the PC-based technology which had become the industry

standard. RM's teams aimed at the educational market and it has become the leading supplier of software, hardware and ICT support services to schools. Its objective is to become the leading player in each sector (primary, secondary and higher education) by having the largest market share, and it is already well on its way to this target.

RM's teams analysed the primary school market in detail, looking at the hardware and software that was available. They realised that the systems that were appropriate for office and industrial environments were not particularly useful or user-friendly for young, primary-age children.

As a result RM developed the RM Window Box which provides user-friendly access for young people to primary software. This, and the earlier partnerships and relationships, have meant that it has achieved at least one of its objectives and is the leading supplier in the primary educational market.

It could not have achieved this target without a flexible and renewable structure. The business needed to be dynamic to match the dynamic market in which it operated.

1. Describe the culture in which RM operates.
2. What are the main objectives of the business? What do you think are its subsidiary objectives?
3. Explain how RM's culture helps it to meet its objectives.

Key Skills C3.2

Section 2 *Types of businesses*

What you need to learn

In this section you will learn about:

● businesses in the voluntary, private and public sectors

● the characteristics of the different types of business organisation and when they are appropriate

● the implications of different types of ownership

● changes in types of ownership and how and why they occur.

 ## ACTIVITY ❺

Write down the names of 10 businesses that you know. How many different ways can you think of to classify them? Exchange your ideas with a partner to see if you have come up with the same ideas. Which do you think is the classification used by business? See if other members of your class or group agree.

Classification of businesses

Businesses are classified as being in either the private sector or the public sector. They are also classified by whether they are directly or indirectly owned.

Private sector businesses are those which are owned by 'private' individuals, either through

● wholly owning the business (a sole trader)

● owning in partnership with another or others (partnerships, co-operatives)

● owning a share in the business (joint stock companies).

FIGURE 1.4 *A typical high street*   *Source: Life File/A. J. Slaughter*

Public sector business are those which are owned and/or controlled by central or local government *on behalf of* the public.

Businesses are then classified as being directly or indirectly owned.

- In the private sector, there are three types of direct ownership: the sole trader, the partnership and the co-operative.
- In the private sector, indirectly owned business organisations are limited liability companies.
- Under public sector are those organisations directly or indirectly owned by the government.

 **Top Tips**

Confusions often arise between the public and private sectors of industry and public and private limited companies. You could devise your own diagram to help you remember the differences. Figure 1.5 is an example.

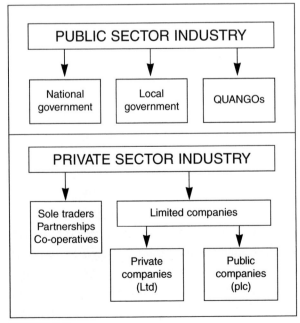

FIGURE 1.5

Characteristics and comparisons of types of business organisation

You can compare and contrast business organisations by looking at a number of key characteristics. These include:

- the nature of the business
- how the business is owned and controlled
- the liability of the business – this means who is liable to pay its debts
- the sources of finance to which the business has access
- how it uses or distributes any profit or surplus that it makes
- its legal obligations in relation to the type of ownership.

Sole traders

'Sole trader', 'sole owner' and 'sole proprietor' are interchangeable terms all used to mean that there is just one owner of the business. In some cases this may be the only person that works for the business. In other cases they may employ a number of staff. For example, the owner of a small supermarket or a building firm would have employees. The sole trader is the most common form of business ownership, making up around 65 per cent of all businesses in the UK economy. Many sole traders are service providers such as plumbers, electricians, hairdressers or driving instructors. Many operate in the retail sector, with small shops and market traders forming a large proportion of the total.

The business is controlled by the owner; who makes all the decisions and carries all the responsibility for those decisions. While they can take advice from others, the final decision always rests with the owner. The sole trader can be personally sued or prosecuted for actions taken in the course of business operations. In the case of the sole trader there is only one recipient for the profits of the business and that is the owner. The owner does not have to share the profit with anyone. Many sole traders will re-invest a major part of profit in the business. Sole traders will be liable to pay income tax on the business profits.

A sole trader will also be responsible for providing the initial finance to set up the business and for paying the business debts. Finance is provided directly from personal funds of the owner, or indirectly though loans. Sole traders have unlimited liability. This means that they are liable for the business debts to the extent of their personal wealth. If the business fails and there are insufficient funds to pay business debts, the owner has to pay these debts from their personal wealth. The owner may even have to sell personal assets, such as the family home and car, to meet business debts.

An individual does not have to officially set themselves up as a sole trader, nor register with anyone other than the Inland Revenue and Department of Social Security. The moment that they start trading they automatically become a sole trader. This means it is cheap and easy to set up. Many new small businesses will choose this structure.

ACTIVITY 6

List the advantages and disadvantages of operating as a sole trader. Compare your lists with others in your group to see if they have identified different issues.

Key Skills C3.1a

Partnerships

A partnership is where two or more people agree to own or operate a business jointly. Many partnerships are formed as a way of expanding a business or gaining expertise. Partnerships are common in the service sector of the economy, among professionals such as accountants and solicitors. A business of solicitors, for example, may have one partner who specialises in criminal law, one in house purchase, one in family cases, one in company law and so on. This sort of

partnership will be able to provide a range of services to its clients. Partnerships will also be found in trades where different skills may be combined to create a service, for example a painter with a decorator. In general, partnerships cannot have more than 20 partners. Exceptions to this rule are professional accountancy and legal firms. There is no limit on the number of partners they can have. Some are international businesses with hundreds of partners.

The nature of partnerships is governed by the Partnership Act 1890. This states that everything is shared equally by the partners unless there is a partnership agreement that varies these terms. Most partnerships choose to draw up a partnership agreement through a solicitor in order to define the relationship between the partners.

Ownership and control are shared equally among partners unless the partners have agreed otherwise. However, any decision made by one partner is actually made on behalf of the partnership and is therefore binding on all the partners. This applies whether or not all partners are involved in the decision-making. Additionally, any partner can be sued or prosecuted for the actions of another partner in the course of the business, whether or not they were aware of these actions.

The profits of a partnership will be distributed either in equal proportion to all the partners or in the proportion agreed in the partnership agreement. Partners are liable to income tax on the profits from the business. The financing of a partnership is similar to that of a sole trader. Initial finance will be provided directly by the partners or indirectly from loans obtained by them. They may have access to larger funds than a sole trader because there are two or more of them. Lenders may see a partnership as more stable and a 'better bet' than a sole trader and therefore be more likely to lend money to them.

Like the sole trader, the partnership has unlimited liability. Each partner is liable for the business debts to the extent of their personal wealth. Partners are said to be 'jointly and severally' liable for debt. If one partner was unable to pay their share of the business debts, the other(s) would have to cover the debt. In effect, the wealthiest partner actually carries a greater risk in terms of liability. The liability of some partners can be limited. A 'sleeping partner', for example, may decide that they wish to invest in a partnership and share in its profits, but have nothing to do with the day-to-day decision-making or control. The law allows such partners to limit their liability in the business to the extent of their investment. However, at least one partner must have unlimited liability.

Partnerships come into existence whenever two or more people start to run a business together. There is no need to draw up any formal agreement or register the partnership.

ACTIVITY 7

List the advantages and disadvantages of setting up business in partnership. Think about why it is important that you trust anyone with whom you are starting a business venture. Compare your lists with others in your group to see if they have identified different issues.

Key Skills 3.1a

Limited companies

Limited companies differ from sole traders and partnerships in a number of ways. Ownership of a limited company is indirect. A limited company is owned by its shareholders. Shareholders are investors who own shares in the business. Ownership of the company may be separated from control. The shareholders of the company are not necessarily the managers. The company is run by a board of directors who may appoint managers to take day-to-day control. The shareholders have ultimate control because they vote directors on to the board.

The process of becoming a limited company is known as incorporation. To become incorporated, a business needs to register with the Registrar of Companies. It needs to prepare two documents which regulate the company's business operations, and lodge them with the Registrar:

- the Memorandum of Association regulates the external affairs of the business (its dealings with the outside world). The Memorandum should set out the company name, which must include the word 'Limited'. It will also set out the objects of the business. This is what the business intends to do. Often it is left fairly vague so that the owners have some flexibility. The Memorandum then sets out details of the company's initial share capital

- the Articles of Association regulate the internal affairs of the business. They will set out the rights of shareholders, the role of directors and the powers of the company to transfer shares and borrow money. They also state how shareholders' meetings should be arranged and how often.

Most businesses will employ a solicitor or specialist consultant to set up the company for them. There is a charge for registering the company. Once incorporated, a business has to comply with certain conditions. These include making annual returns to the Registrar, providing financial and other information about the company. All but the smallest companies have to lodge full accounts with the Registrar, which then become available to the general public. The financial accounts of a company must be audited by an independent firm of auditors who will charge the company fees for their services. Limited companies have to hold annual general meetings for their shareholders.

Incorporation is a legal process that creates a separate legal identity for the business. This means that, unlike sole traders and partnerships, for the limited company the business has a separate existence from its owners. In law this means that the company can be sued and prosecuted in its own name, and can take legal action in its own name, without the owners being held personally responsible. There are some cases where the directors could be held personally responsible for actions taken in the course of the business. For example, under some health and safety law directors can be held personally responsible. In some cases where directors of a company have behaved fraudulently in the course of the business, they will be held personally liable. The shareholders, who are the owners of the company, would never be held liable.

The company is 'limited' because its owners (or shareholders) have limited liability. The shareholders buy shares in the company and their liability for company debts is limited to the amount they used to buy the shares. If the company is unable to pay its debts, all assets will be sold to pay the creditors. If there is not enough money to pay all the creditors, then they will not be paid.

A limited company is financed by the sale of its shares. It may also borrow money for which the company is liable for repayments. The shareholders receive a share of profits in the form of dividends on the shares they own. The directors will decide how much to pay out in profits and how much should be retained in the company to re-invest in the business. The company will pay corporation tax on its profits. Shareholders will pay income tax on the dividends they receive.

There are two types of limited companies which have different rules and characteristics.

Private limited companies

The name of a private limited company must include the word 'Limited' or the abbreviation 'Ltd'. A private limited company may not advertise its shares for sale to the general public. The shares can only be sold privately to, for example, friends, relatives and interested investors with whom the promoters of the company have come into contact.

Private limited companies vary greatly in size. They can operate with just one shareholder and one director. In reality, this means that the company can be similar in size to a sole trader. Alternatively, they can be global business organisations. Many private limited companies are family businesses and they can be quite small. The directors, shareholders and day-to-day managers might be the same people (or person), so the separation between ownership and control of the company does not exist. These small companies can find that when they borrow money, lenders require personal guarantees from the directors. This, in effect, can 'unlimit' their liability.

Public limited companies

Public limited companies must include the words 'public limited company' in their name, or the abbreviation 'plc'. A plc must have a minimum of £50,000 in initial share capital. The initial share capital is raised by the company issuing a prospectus detailing the company's aims and objectives and containing its accounts and details of its main personnel. Effectively it is an advertisement brochure 'selling' the company. Once the 'offer for sale' is taken up, the price of the shares will be determined by the demand for them. Thus a successful company, with a good future, will attract a lot of buyers, pushing the price of the shares up.

The shares of a plc can be traded on the Stock Exchange. Listings in newspapers such as the *Financial Times* show the current prices of shares for plcs. The cost of floating on the stock market can be high. Control of the company may be spread across large numbers of shareholders. This means that a shareholder with as little as 5 per cent of the shares may have quite a lot of influence over the company.

Potential lenders and investors will tend to have more confidence in a plc, so such a company will find it much easier to obtain finance and credit facilities. In addition, the detailed accounts of plcs are published and freely available, so potential investors and lenders can check out business performance before making their decision.

ACTIVITY 8

List the advantages and disadvantages of limited companies. Compare your list with those of others in your group to see if they have identified different issues.

Identify and list the differences between private and public limited companies.

Key Skills C3.1a

Mutual societies

Mutual societies were originally set up as non-profit-making organisations to benefit the members. Today, they do declare profits which may be re-invested in the business or used to improve the benefits of members. The two main groups of mutual societies are insurance companies and building societies. Insurance companies work on the principle that everyone pays a fee – a premium – into a central fund and anyone who suffers a misfortune is compensated from these funds. Building societies were originally set up so that people could co-operate in the building of houses and, when every member in a group had a house, the society would be closed. Today, they have a continual existence, but one of their major activities is still mortgage lending.

Co-operatives

A co-operative exists where a group of people have decided to band together for the shared benefit of the group. Perhaps the most famous UK co-operative is the retail Co-op. In some Scandinavian countries, the co-operative is a common form of business organisation and has been called the 'third way' between the extremes of Capitalism and Communism. The main groups of co-operatives are:

- Consumer co-operatives – groups of consumers who have come together because their combined purchasing power means they get better deals than if they operated as individuals. The retail Co-op is one of these.

- Worker co-operatives – groups of workers sharing their labour. In the case of some small manufacturing businesses, workers have bought out the business and operate it as a co-operative. The most famous UK example of this is probably the BSA motorcycle plant, which now operates as a worker co-operative.

- Producer co-operatives – groups of producers working together for greater efficiency, sales etc. An example would be the South American coffee growers who banded together so that they would get a fairer deal for their produce.

Control of a co-operative is shared equally between the members. While this might be quite easy in a small co-operative, once membership has grown above a certain level, it will be impossible to make decisions by asking for everyone's opinion. In this case, appointed managers or delegates representing groups of workers may make the decisions. Co-operatives may set up as partnerships or, more usually, as limited liability companies.

In a consumer co-operative, dividends are paid in proportion to what members buy. Co-operative

---

GETTING IT TOGETHER

Cocoa growers in Ghana, West Africa, pooled resources to set up Kuapa Kokoo, a farmers' co-op which would trade its own cocoa to get a better price on the market. The farmers were supported by Twin Trading, the fair trade company that puts the coffee into Cafédirect.

FIGURE 1.6 *Cocoa farmers in Ghana formed a producers' Co-op to produce their own chocolate*

Source: Divine leaflet

dividends used to be issued in the form of stamps, with every purchase made. In the case of worker and producer co-operatives, the workers or producers will decide on how much is to be re-invested and then the rest will be distributed equally.

The original source of finance for a co-operative will have come from its members. Members of producer co-operatives might need a new machine or factory, for example. The cost will be divided equally among the members. In the case of the original consumer co-operative, members all paid in a certain amount to buy goods that were then sold at fair prices.

ASSESSMENT
activity 3

Look at the different types of business ownership. Consider the business that you have chosen to study.

1. **Classify the business according to its type of ownership. Try to find out if it has always had this form of ownership or if it has developed from something else. Try to find out if the owner(s) want(s) it to become something else.**
2. **Explain the benefits and constraints of this type of ownership.**

Key Skills C3.2, C3.3

Non-profit-making groups

Some bodies are run very much on business lines, but their primary objective is not profit-making. These are public sector organisations and voluntary and charity groups.

Public corporations

These are quasi-governmental organisations. They were established by Acts of Parliament, and are owned and financed by the state. Day-to-day control is placed in the hands of a board of management, whose chairperson will be directly responsible to a government Minister. Examples include the Post Office and the BBC.

Central government enterprises

Government departments are responsible for a variety of public services such as defence, the National Health Service and the Benefits Agency. In each case a government Minister is responsible, but the day-to-day running is carried out by civil servants. Many of these services, including the NHS and the Benefits Agency, are now run along similar lines to private sector organisations in the belief that this will make them more efficient. These organisations are funded by taxes and government borrowing.

Local authority enterprises

Local authorities must, by law, provide certain services. These include education, refuse collection, fire and police services and the taking of responsibility for most roads. Some authorities also provide other services such as libraries and recreational facilities, car parks and local transport services.

Local authority enterprises are financed by:

● income from the services – for example, charges will be made for the use of leisure facilities or for the operation of planning consents

● revenue support grant – this is an amount of money which is given to a local council by the central government

● local taxes – which currently include rates payable on business premises and council tax charged to householders.

Charities

Charitable bodies will be linked to a specific issue or set of issues. Most of us will recognise major charities such as Oxfam, Guide Dogs for the Blind or the Royal National Lifeboat Institution. Charities have three major functions:

● collecting and distributing resources – raising money through voluntary donations and then using that money to support their cause. Supplying personnel, advice, expertise, services or materials where needed

● raising awareness of a particular problem or issue

● providing a service (such as education). The charity charges fees but does not seek to make a profit.

Voluntary organisations

Volunteers may offer their services free to voluntary organisations. Some of the organisations which accept volunteers are also charities. For example, both the Scouts and the Salvation Army are voluntary bodies. The Salvation Army is a charity whereas the Scouts are not. Some organisations exist to provide volunteers where they are needed. These include the Red Cross and VSO (Voluntary Service Overseas).

Franchise

The franchise has been left until last in this section due to its odd nature. It is not really a separate form of business ownership or organisation. It is a way of getting into business by trading on the success of an established operation. The franchiser owns a successful product, idea or business. The franchisee buys the right to trade using this successful formula. Either body may be organised as any of the types of private business organisation. There are many examples of franchise operations that are well known nationally, including the Body Shop, Kwik Fit, McDonalds, Burger King and the British School of Motoring.

Sometimes the franchiser will exercise very tight control over the franchisee. They will limit their scope for selling other products, or for using their own pricing structure. In return the franchiser provides point-of-sale material, national advertising and successful products and services. The day-to-day running of the business is the responsibility of the franchisee.

For the franchiser the main source of finance will be the sale of franchises and the royalties that accrue from their successful operations. Franchisers charge an initial fee for a franchise and the franchise agreement will include provision of a royalty. This is usually a percentage of turnover and is paid as a sort of annual 'rent'.

For the franchisee – the person who has bought the franchise – income will come from the provision and sale of goods and services.

ACTIVITY ⑨

The history of Dave's Dodgems has been one of almost continuous growth. Dave started out as a repairer of fairground dodgems in the 1970s. Initially, he only operated at the Goose Fair in Nottingham. He chose this fair because it was the biggest in the country and marked the end of the fairground 'season'. After it had finished, he had the three months in which the ride operators 'rested' to sort out the mechanical problems of the dodgem cars. For the rest of the year he travelled to wherever he was needed, mending all types of ride.

As business grew, Dave joined up with two other repairers so that they could provide a more complete service. Changes in technology meant that the business had to learn electronics as well as mechanics. It also meant investment in specialised machinery. The three operators decided that the outlay needed was so high, it was time they protected themselves from bankruptcy before negotiating a loan. This achieved, the success of the business meant that the operators were able to take on more experts as technology advanced.

By the 1990s, the services provided had expanded way beyond fairgrounds, incorporating repairs to anything mechanical, electronic or computer-based. The chance to provide systems for the Millennium Dome and the London Eye meant that more capital was needed. The owners decided to float the company and this took place successfully in 1999.

1. Describe the changes in ownership that Dave's Dodgems has passed through.

2. Outline the likely changes in name that have taken place.

3. Give reasons why each type of ownership was appropriate at each point in the history of the business.

Key Skills C3.2

Section 3 *Organisational functions*

What you need to learn

In this section you will learn about:

● the factors needed for production to take place
● the functional areas that exist in a business
● the importance of these functions
● how these areas help the business to meet its objectives
● the interdependence of these areas.

Top Tips

A product does not have to be a good (a physical product). It can also be a service. 'Product' is used to refer to both goods and services.

Factors of production

Before any product – good or service – can be produced it is necessary to have certain essentials. Economists call these essentials the factors of production. These are:

● land – a site or place from which to trade
● labour – the energies of the business owner, mental or physical, or employees
● capital – materials, machinery, tools and/or equipment
● enterprise – the planning and risk taking in order to manage these factors in the most efficient way. The person involved in the business is generally referred to as the entrepreneur.

Top Tips

Do not fall into the trap of thinking that money is one of the factors of production; it isn't. Money is, however, used to buy the actual factors that are needed.

 ACTIVITY

Think of 10 different businesses which produce a range of goods and services, and list them. For each business, write down the factors of production that are used.

1. Under 'land' you should identify the location and size of the premises. Remember, some businesses may be run from home or be Web-based. Their 'land' needs will be quite small, but they must still be operated from somewhere.
2. Under 'labour', give an indication of how many people are employed by the business and the sort of labour. Is it qualified? Experienced? Specially trained?
3. Under 'capital' identify what machinery or tools you think are used and what raw materials or components may have to be bought.
4. Under 'enterprise' say who you think is the entrepreneur or organiser behind the business.
5. What factors of production are used by the business that you are studying?

Without a combination of all four factors, production is not possible. The factors are combined by the carrying out of a number of functions within the business. These may all be carried out by the same person where the business is a sole trader, for example. In a larger business they may be carried out in separate departments. The functions that are necessary are finance, production, human resources, marketing, administration, and research and development.

Each function carries out particular activities, and has different responsibilities and characteristics. In studying your business you will need to say how well each function is carried out and how this helps the organisation to meet its objectives. You also need to be able to recognise the connections between functions.

Finance and accounting

The finance function is responsible for all flows of money into and out of the business. It is also responsible for keeping financial records of such flows and providing financial information to managers in the business. The finance and accounting staff may be involved in the following tasks:

- Financial planning – businesses need to plan their finances to ensure that they can meet all their commitments and continue in business. The finance staff will identify the short-, medium- and long-term finance for the business.

- Advising management on raising finance – from the planning carried out, staff will be able to identify any shortfalls in cash flow. They may also advise management on how to raise finance to cover the shortfall.

- Financial control – businesses need to control their cash flow and costs. Finance staff may help to monitor cash flow and cost levels by checking actual flows against planned flows. Alternatively, they may provide information to other department managers so that they can carry out this task. Budgets are forecasts of business revenues and expenses which are used to help plan and monitor cash flows.

- Costing – finance staff may be involved in estimating the cost of new products, processes or equipment. They will be able to tell management whether any new venture is worthwhile.

- Record-keeping – businesses are required by law to keep financial records for tax purposes. It makes sense for a business to keep records, anyway. These will help in planning and control of finances and also inform any business decisions.

- Preparing financial statements and reports – the finance function will generally be responsible for preparing financial documents for shareholders, managers and outside parties such as the VAT office or the Inland Revenue. These include the annual accounts of the business. They will also provide reports and information to management on issues such as levels of cost, and profitability of products. These help in day-to-day decision-making.

- Payroll – finance may be responsible for paying employees of the business and providing them with payslips. Note that there are specialist businesses who will run the payroll for the business. Many firms use these rather than operate their payroll in-house.

Most businesses now use computers in their finance function for keeping records, monitoring cash flow and preparing plans and reports. The finance function is important as it supports all the other functions and activities within a business. You will learn more about the finance function in Chapter 5.

Production

Production is responsible for organising, planning and monitoring the output of the business. In some larger concerns there will be a separate purchasing department to buy materials and equipment at the right price to enable production to take place at the right cost levels. This department may also decide on transport, delivery and storage arrangements.

The process of production involves three distinct stages:

- input – raw materials, components etc.
- processes – the use of factors
- output – the finished product.

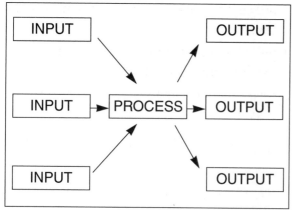

FIGURE 1.7

Organising production means deciding what to produce, how many to produce, how to produce and where to produce. Production involves the process of transformation – turning one set of materials and inputs into a set of outputs. At each stage of the transformation process, value is added to the product.

In a manufacturing business, the production department is generally seen as the centre of the business. Without it, no production will take

Value is added at each stage of production:

A live pig	worth, for example, £150
A dead pig	once slaughtered, worth £200
Pork joints	butchered into joints adds further value, now £300
A pile of bacon	sorted, graded and cured, now worth £400
Packaged bacon	packaging adds further value, £450
A supermarket shelf with bacon on it	finally sold for a value of £500

FIGURE 1.8

place and therefore there will be no sales and no sales revenue. However, it is also dependent on all the other departments. In the case of businesses providing a service, the production function may be minimal – take, for example, a driving school. The input is the expertise of the driving instructor, the output is a pupil who passes the test; production undoubtedly takes place for this to happen, but it is difficult to quantify.

ASSESSMENT activity

4

Look at Figure 1.8. Now choose five different types of product or service and draw a similar chain for each of them to show how value is added.

Draw the chain that would apply to your chosen business.

Key Skills C3.2, C3.3

Human resources management

Human resources management (HRM) plans the manpower needs of the business and recruits and selects the best people to meet the needs of the organisation. The function is also responsible for training of employees, industrial relations, keeping staff records and managing staff welfare. Part of its function may also be to keep staff motivated.

'Human resources' are not just the people in the organisation but is the term used to refer to the wider idea of their qualifications, talents and abilities. Many businesses have a personnel department that deals with the people in the organisation. Forward-looking businesses have expanded the function to include all aspects of employees' welfare and to try to have a workforce that is as fulfilled and as motivated as possible.

The human resources function is important because it manages one of the business's most important, and most expensive, resources. Businesses need to employ and retain the right people for the smooth running of the organisation.

Marketing

Marketing is the part of a business that is concerned with both informing the customer that a product is on sale and persuading them to buy the product. Customer service is a part of the marketing function although, in some large businesses, it will be considered important enough to have a department of its own.

The marketing function involves the collection of information relating to a market or potential market. The marketing department will analyse this information, make predictions about the market and create and place advertising. It will be responsible for seeking new clients. It may also involve customer service. This means ensuring that customers get what they want, when they want it and in the quantities that they require. It also means ensuring that customers receive good after sales care and service.

Marketing and advertising can take up a large part of a business's budget, but good advertising will pay for itself many times over. A single effective campaign may be enough to secure a market share and allow the other functions to continue to take place. Without some form of marketing, it is unlikely that any product will be sold.

Administration

Administration and administration systems support all the other functions of an organisation. In a small business, the administrative functions may be carried out by a single person. As a business grows larger, its administrative requirements and systems will also grow. Almost all administrative services can be bought from outside agencies and, in small businesses, this will often be the case.

All administrative functions follow the same basic routine:

- input – this could be internal or external information. It could be in any one of numerous different forms – spoken, written, electronic
- process – the way in which the information is handled, modified or used
- output – what response is produced to the original input.

A simple example of an administrative task might be:

- a letter being received (input)
- it being read and a reply decided on (process)
- the reply being written and forwarded (output).

The administrative function involves communicating, monitoring and record-keeping. Some record-keeping is a legal requirement. Although the process of administration may seem fairly mundane, the workings of this department are essential to all the other departments. Finance may be able to set budgets, but it is administration that will publish them. Marketing may be able to devise a brilliant mail shot, but it is administration that will carry out the mail merge. In some respects, administration can have a large effect on the public view of a company and on its reputation. The first person most people deal with in a company is the receptionist or telephonist; if the reception area seems inefficiently run, or the telephonist untrained, then the client will form a poor impression of the company. On the other hand, if such functions are carried out well, then a good impression can be created.

Research and development

The decision on what to produce may involve existing products but, if a business is to stay competitive, it also needs to develop new products. Research and development (R&D) involves the investigation of the potential for new products, and for new and more efficient methods of producing them. Much research and development takes place away from business and industry. In particular, a great deal of research takes place in academic institutions such as universities. Businesses may buy in such research rather than having their own research facilities. Specialist testing facilities are also available which businesses buy in from outside sources.

The R&D function will be related to three main areas:

1. **product design** – here there should be an emphasis on style, innovation and customer satisfaction.
2. **researching new processes** – the emphasis will be on efficiency and cost reduction, perhaps by using new technology.
3. **R&D** should have close liaison with the marketing department, studying market research findings and directing development accordingly.

Sometimes it may look as if the research and development part of a business is taking up a large proportion of finance for very small reward. This may be true in industries at the 'cutting edge' of new developments, such as telecommunications and microchip technology. However, the rewards of a successful innovation may well affect the entire future of a business and impact heavily on all other functions. Some businesses are completely led by innovation. For instance the invention of the 'bagless' vacuum cleaner by James Dyson has led to a large international business. Sometimes the R&D function works very closely with marketing and production. This is called simultaneous engineering and is designed to manage innovation.

ACTIVITY 11

List the main responsibilities of each of the main business functions. This will help you to analyse the functions in your chosen business.

Interdependence

None of the functional areas can exist in isolation. Each function is dependent on the others. It is worth remembering that in a small organisation – a sole trader, for example – all of these functions may be carried out by a single person. By contrast, in really large businesses, some of the functions may be spread over two or more departments. Sometimes one function is more or less important to a particular business. Their relative importance depends on the scale of the operation, the market in which the business is operating, the structure of the business and the product that is being offered for sale.

ACTIVITY 12

Look at the following scenarios and note, in each case, which functions will be involved in dealing with the matter:

- **purchase of, and payment for, raw materials to make the product**
- **receiving and replying to a customer complaint about a product**
- **the request of a sales catalogue by a customer, and the placing of an order to be paid for with a credit card**
- **the design and implementation of a new production process involving new technology.**

You should have seen that a number of different functions are involved in each case.

Key Skills C3.2

Functions and objectives

The objectives of a business are likely to fall into one or more of the following eight categories (see Section 1). Each functional area will have a particular importance to play in reaching specific ones of these objectives.

- **Maximisation of profit.** It is likely that all functions will operate to contribute towards this objective.

- **Marketing objectives.** A business which aims to become the dominant business in a market, or to enter new markets, will be market-driven, giving importance to the marketing function.

- Seeking a good reputation for **social responsibility.** A business wanting to enhance its reputation will find that human resources may be its most important function. If it is seen as a good employer and draws its employees from the local community, then it may also be in a position to play a social role in that community.

- **Productivity.** If a business is aiming to maximise the returns from its workers and machines in terms of productivity, then there is a central role for both human resources and production. In terms of human resources, greater motivation will lead to better productivity. In terms of the production function, better machinery, properly maintained, will be an important element. A combination of both these factors will be even more effective.

- **Innovation.** In this case it will be the research and development function that is the driving force behind the business. In some industries, good R&D will be essential if the business is to keep up with rapidly changing developments.

- **Manpower.** Businesses which want to maximise the quality of their manpower will have a human resources department which is central to the business.

- **Resources.** Ensuring reliable and quality resources for an organisation may not be a job for production, but could be carried out by administration. Whilst it will not be involved in checking quality, it can search databases and other sources of information and gather data on prices, availability and so on.

- **Management.** Businesses may want to maximise the quality of their management. Again, the human resources department will play a vital role in recruiting and selecting the best candidates available.

 ACTIVITY

Christmas 1999, and the mobile phone has become the 'present of choice' for thousands of buyers. Older teenagers, busy fathers and mothers and remote grannies have all been touched with the bug that first affected only city types. Many special promotional offers have meant that it has become worth buying the phones for specific uses. One offer meant that if a customer bought two phones, the calls from one to the other were free, which was ideal for a busy couple who just wanted to stay in touch with each other. Another offered cheap rate international calls. Yet another offered free airtime and Internet access. The explosion in sales means that in 10 years, ownership of mobile phones has increased 25-fold, heading for 25 million people.

BT Cellnet has reacted to the increase in ownership by opening a huge new customer care 'call centre' at Bury in Lancashire. The Office of Fair Trading has responded by giving complaints about mobile phones a code of its own. 'Customer care has just not kept up with the phenomenal growth in sales', said a spokesman, although BT Cellnet would, of course, disagree. Advice for trading standards officers has been posted on the Office of Fair Trading website. 'Complaints include incorrect bills, bills for services either not wanted or not taken, changes in terms and conditions, poor reception and a low standard of aftercare', said the spokesman. The number of complaints means that mobile

phones are now in the Top 10 list of complaints, along with home improvements, double glazing and second-hand cars. 'Our new customer care centre is exclusively for pre-pay mobile phone users', said BT Cellnet, 'that doesn't suggest a company that isn't dedicated to customer care'.

1. Explain how the functional departments of a mobile phone supplier would have to work together to meet the increase in demand. Think about marketing, production and finance in particular.

2. Explain the importance of the customer care function to a firm like BT Cellnet.

3. How is customer care dealt with in the business that you are studying? Could you suggest any improvements?

Key Skills C3.2

FIGURE 1.9 *Source: PA Photos*

Section 4 *Organisational structures*

What you need to learn

In this section you will learn about:

- the ways in which organisations are structured
- the different types of structure – tall, flat and matrix
- the different ways in which the structures operate – hierarchical, centralised, decentralised
- how businesses decide on the most appropriate structure
- the different management styles that operate
- how organisational structure and the culture of a business are interlinked

 ACTIVITY **14**

Think of an orchestra and the way in which it must be organised in order to produce harmony. The organisation extends to the places where each instrument is put, the time signature, and the beat provided by the conductor.

FIGURE 1.10   *Source: © Shelley Gazin/CORBIS*

1. **List as many other organisations that you can think of that have a formal structure.**
2. **Compare your list with that of a partner; what sort of different organisational structures can you find?**
3. **Explain how important organisational structure is to the smooth functioning of an organisation.**

Structures

Businesses are structured in different ways according to how they operate and in line with their culture. Section 1, on business objectives and business culture, should have given you some insight into this already. Structures may be formal or informal.

- **Formal structures** have planned relationships, limited communication channels and authority with limits and powers formally recognised. Formal structures tend to be quite rigid and operate within strict hierarchies. The police force is a good example of a formal organisational structure.

- **Informal structures** cannot be shown on an organisation chart. They are the relationships and communication channels which exist within and between informal groups of workers in a business. Because these are based on friendships, working groups or shared interests, communication within groups tends to be highly efficient. This communication within such organisations is often referred to as the 'grapevine'. Such groups can therefore be more effective and have more influence than formal ones.

Different businesses have different organisational structures. The way in which the business is organised will be affected by its:

- size
- type of products

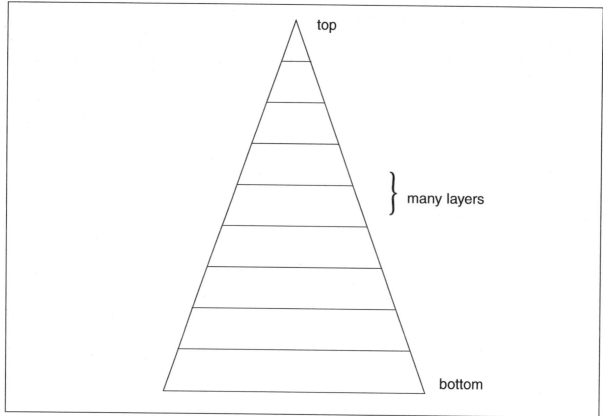

FIGURE 1.11 *Tall organisational structure*

- objectives
- culture
- market.

The way in which a business is structured will affect all aspects of its performance, its contact with other businesses and its treatment of its own stakeholders. Organisational structures are needed in business so that efficiency of planning, communication and control can be maintained. Organisation charts are the conventional way to show a business's organisational structure as these give an 'at a glance' overview. Such charts also link closely to the descriptions of organisational structures. A structure is 'tall' or 'flat' because the general shape of the chart or diagram showing the structure appears as tall or flat.

Tall structures

Tall organisational structures have many layers of command. Each layer will have a narrow span of control – that is, the number of people directly

under its authority. Authority is defined as the legitimate power that a manager or person with power in an organisation actually has. Anyone under a manager's authority is called a subordinate. A senior manager may have authority over subordinate junior managers; a junior manager may have authority over subordinate workers. With more layers, each layer has only a narrow span of control. In such an organisation, there are many chances of promotion, making for better motivation. A typical tall structure can be shown by the armed forces.

The chain of command is the way in which orders or instructions are passed from layer to layer down the organisation. The longer the chain of command, the less efficient it is likely to be.

The tall structure is likely to suffer from a rigid bureaucracy. This is the rule book or set of rules within which decisions have to be taken. This tends to mean there is little room for initiative or regard for new ideas. Communication of orders or decisions tends to be very good. Communication within the organisation – particularly between people at a similar level of responsibility in the organisation – tends to be poor.

Flat structures

Flat structures have fewer levels of command and control but more people at each level. Each level therefore has a wider span of control. The structure of the Catholic Church is a good example of a flat structure. There are not many 'ranks' between priests and popes but each level (apart from the Pope himself) has a large number of members. The Pope is drawn from a college of cardinals, for example. Promotion in such a wide, flat organisation tends to be difficult, but each level has greater authority than it would have in a tall, thin structure.

Flat organisations may suffer from lack of motivation connected with the limited chances for promotion. The efficient operation of the organisation may suffer from rules and levels of

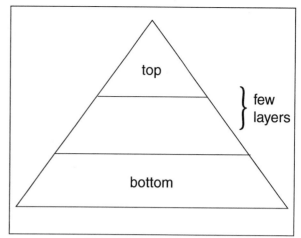

FIGURE 1.12 *Flat organisational structure*

authority not being clear enough. The main advantage is that there will be less bureaucracy and more involvement for people lower down the organisation. There is also likely to be good communication both between levels and at the same level in the organisation.

Matrix structures

Matrix charts show the two-way relationships between the various parts of a team. In many organisations it has been discovered that teamwork is a more efficient way of working.

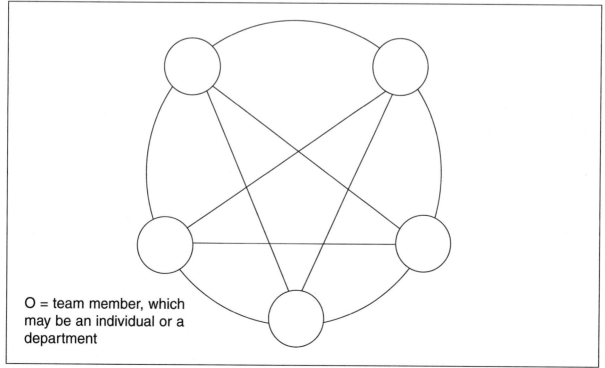

O = team member, which may be an individual or a department

FIGURE 1.13 *Matrix organisational structure*

Nissan, for example, uses this approach. Teams may be formed according to workers' and managers' expertise. The team or project leader may be the person best fitted to the role in that particular situation or for that particular project. In this case a shop floor worker may be in a better position to lead a team than a senior manager. The senior manager may be needed for his or her particular skills, experience or expertise. This type of organisation is extremely successful at bringing together different skills from different parts of the organisation. It may suffer problems due to the blurring of levels of authority. A senior manager, for example, may feel uncomfortable having to act as the subordinate to a shop floor worker, even though the shop floor worker is the best person to lead the team.

ASSESSMENT activity **5**

1. **Analyse the structure of your chosen business. Does it have a tall, flat or matrix structure?**

2. **Can you see any problems with the structure?**

3. **Can you suggest any improvements?**

Key Skills C3.2

Top Tips

Most charts show the 'hierarchy' within a business. A hierarchy is an organisation with grades ranked one above the other. Look at the ranks in the army, for instance.

Operations

These three types of organisation – tall, flat and matrix – show the general shape of an organisation. They do not, however, show how that organisation is operated. Is it a strict hierarchy? Is it centralised, with all power lying with a single person or department? Is power shared around the organisation? To get the complete picture, the operation of the structure must also be known.

● Most organisations have different levels of responsibility, resulting in different layers being shown on their organisation chart. At each layer people will have a certain amount of responsibility and a certain amount of authority. They will have a number of subordinates – their span of control. The higher up the organisation, the more responsibility and the more authority. This is called a hierarchy. Each level has more power and responsibility than the level below it. Organisations such as this narrow as a person moves up the organisation because there are less people in senior positions than in junior ones. The shape of chart formed by this is triangular or a pyramid. It is called a hierarchical pyramid. In a hierarchy, instructions and orders are passed down the organisation, from one level to the next: in a strict hierarchy a level may interact with only the levels directly above it and directly below it.

● A typical hierarchical structure for a company will have directors at the top of the pyramid, then senior managers, junior managers and employees. The larger the organisation, the more layers of management there are likely to be. The reason for this type of structure is that the people at the top are deemed to have more expertise and experience (possibly through promotion or length of service) and should therefore be the ones to take decisions. They must also have the power and authority to carry out those decisions.

● A centralised organisation has all of the power and decision-making lying with a single, central body or person. This has the effect that generally decisions are made much more quickly and effectively. The organisational centre keeps good control over the rest of the organisation. Providing that the centre is able to keep a good overview of the whole organisation, there should be a clear set of targets and a unified strategy for reaching them. The weakness of this system is in the amount of authority that is held by a single person or body.

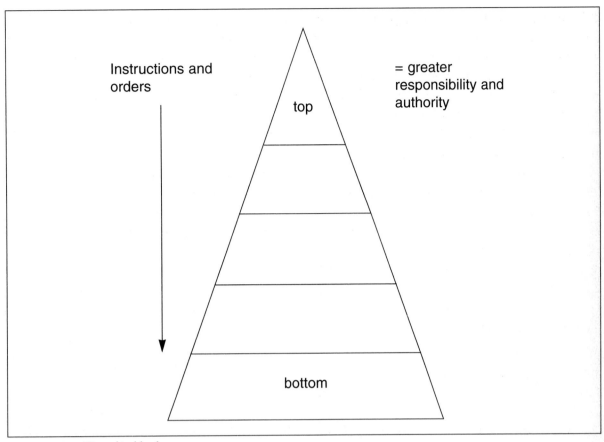

Instructions and orders

= greater responsibility and authority

top

bottom

FIGURE 1.14 *Hierarchical levels*

There is no guarantee that the central power will make the correct decision. There is no guarantee of any continuity should the central power leave or decline in some other way.

● A de-centralised organisation delegates decision-making to subordinates lower down the organisation. Allowing subordinates to take responsibility for decisions increases both their status and their motivation. The disadvantage is that disagreements might occur between different decision-makers in the organisation. It is also a problem if communication is not efficient enough to ensure that everyone knows what decisions are being made by others. Managers can lose control of parts of an organisation if too much power is delegated by them.

De-layering

In some modern markets, the ability to respond to change may be the major factor which keeps a business successful. Changes in organisation structure may be used to sharpen that ability to respond. Sometimes businesses decide that they could be more efficient with fewer layers of hierarchy.

'De-layering' means cutting out some levels of management. The structure of the business becomes flatter, meaning that managers have an increased span of control and more responsibility. The downside is that these increased levels may lead to over-stretched managers who may then make the wrong decisions.

De-layering does not mean just shedding staff in order to make a business more efficient. It means cutting out layers of a structure. It is often, wrongly, used as a term to try to make redundancies sound better.

Culture and organisation structure – their effect on each other

The organisation structure is linked to the culture of the organisation. The culture is the way in which an organisation operates and is perceived by other organisations. Certain types of business will operate as a particular culture. A legal business, for example, will want a culture of stability and established good practice and reputation. A mobile phone company, on the other hand, will encourage a culture of enterprise and innovation. A business with a person-centred culture, for example a doctors' practice, would find it difficult to operate as a strict hierarchy. It is likely to be much more efficient if it adopts a team approach and a matrix type of organisation.

Equally, the organisation structure may have a strong influence on business culture. A strict hierarchical pyramid would discourage a culture of innovation and change. Such an organisational structure would lead to stability. A matrix structure, however, can help to establish an innovative, problem-solving culture.

ACTIVITY ⑮

The main types of culture were outlined in Section 1.

1. Look at these again and then at the types of organisational structures.

2. Draw up a table which matches type of culture to the most appropriate type of organisation.

3. Give examples of businesses that might be found in each section.

Charts

Different organisations find that different structures suit them. The usual way to show organisational structures is on an organisational chart or diagram. The three diagrams above show the general shape of a structure. Detailed charts will show who is where in the organisation. They show who is in charge of whom, who people's superiors or managers are and where the power bases in the organisation lie. The main types of chart are:

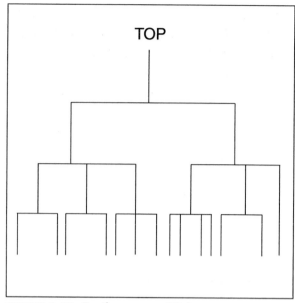

FIGURE 1.15 *Family tree-type or 'T' chart*

- **family tree-type** or **'T' charts** (each junction forms the letter 'T'). These are particularly useful for showing the complexity of an organisation, especially one that is divided by function or division. They are not very good at showing positions in organisations where people may have multi-functional roles

- **sideways 'T's**. These charts may show the same organisational structure as normal 'T' charts but are used so that the organisation

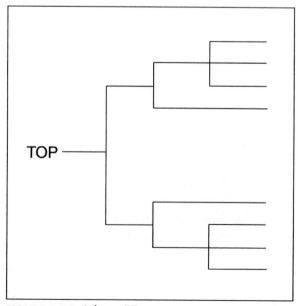

FIGURE 1.16 *Sideways 'T's*

appears less hierarchical. This may not seem particularly important but it can be very advantageous psychologically to have subordinates see the organisation in this way

● **pyramid charts.** These are used to show hierarchies and become more accurate if small 'sub-pyramids' are added to show the detail of the organisation

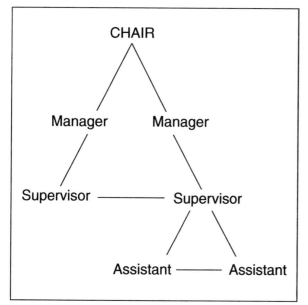

FIGURE 1.17 *Pyramid chart*

● **circles.** These are a way of trying to show an organisational structure without emphasising the hierarchy. People within the same circle are

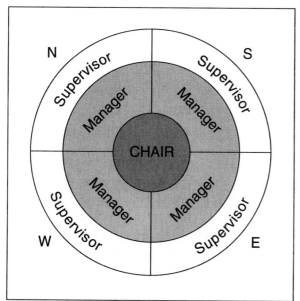

FIGURE 1.18 *Circular chart. Such charts could be divided according to region, like this one.*

at the same level. The organisation will probably still be a hierarchical one, with the greater authority nearer the centre of the circle, but will not appear to be as rigidly hierarchical as a pyramid

● **matrices.** These show the relationships between individuals or parts of the organisation in a non-hierarchical manner; matrix organisation is used for project management (see Figure 1.13)

● **Venn diagrams.** These are useful for demonstrating overlapping functions where people may be involved in more than one responsibility in an organisation. A school or college provides a good example of this type of organisation.

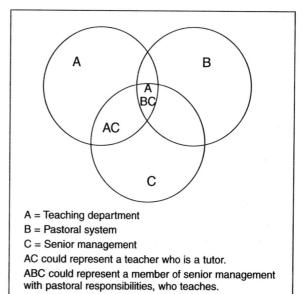

A = Teaching department
B = Pastoral system
C = Senior management
AC could represent a teacher who is a tutor.
ABC could represent a member of senior management with pastoral responsibilities, who teaches.

FIGURE 1.19 *Venn diagram*

ACTIVITY **16**

Use your school or college to practise making a Venn diagram. Divide the functions into three sections, for example administration, pastoral and academic.

1. Draw three overlapping circles to represent these areas.

2. Which members of staff go in the central area (have functions in all three areas)?

3. Which members of staff could be placed in two areas? (Administrative and academic, academic and pastoral, for example.)

4. Which members of staff will only appear in a single area?

5. Draw a Venn diagram for your chosen business. Identify staff who have single functions and those with multiple functions. Explain why you think it is that some have single functions and some multiple functions. This may help you with your analysis for your assessment.

Key Skills C3.2, C3.3

 Top Tips

Many businesses already have their organisational structure set out in chart form – you could use this as the basis for your own commentary on their organisational structure.

Leadership

Think of the different types of leadership in a military organisation. What would make you follow a leader? Sometimes recruits follow leaders because they are frightened of them or have been threatened. Sometimes it is because they respect and admire them. Sometimes it is because they have a confidence in their leaders' ability to do a job. Sometimes its merely a question of 'not letting the side down' and maintaining a team spirit. This is the same in all forms of leadership including management. Different managers will have different leadership styles. The main ones are autocratic, democratic and consultative.

- **Autocratic** management means that decision making is centred on a single person or group. Decisions are made without the help or advice of other parts of the business. Tasks and goals are likely to be clearly defined. However, the motivation of subordinates is likely to be low. A centralised organisational structure is likely to reflect an autocratic management style.

- **Democratic** management involves subordinates in decision-making. It means listening to and taking note of subordinates' ideas and suggestions and allowing them to make decisions. This is likely to lead to greater motivation among junior managers and employees. Power and decision-making are decentralised. In many cases, democratic management is linked to a team-based, matrix structure.

- In **consultative** management, subordinates' ideas and suggestions are heard, but the decision-making power remains with the senior manager or group. It is a cross between autocratic and democratic management. Decisions are taken at the top of the hierarchy, but subordinates can feel that they are part of the decision-making process. Managers working in flat structures may find that they can consult all layers of the organisation before making a decision. However, power is still centralised.

Which style?

The best managers will not operate a single style of management, but will change their method of management according to the various factors associated with a task or objective and the variations in those factors.

An authoritarian style might be appropriate, for example, if the task needs to be precisely defined; the timescale is short or likely to prove difficult; and personnel and materials need to be organised quickly and efficiently. Most importantly, the personnel need to respect the authority of the manager. If a rush order, made to precise specifications, needs to be processed as soon as possible, central direction and authoritative management will be the way to ensure success.

For other tasks, a different approach will be more suitable. For example, if a business was seeking new innovations or new methods of doing things, then a consultative approach would be more beneficial.

The factors that are likely to determine appropriate management style are:

- the nature of the job to be done – whether it is more or less complex, or important

- the timescale involved – whether this is a job that needs doing immediately or can be postponed, whether it is a job that will take a long time or can be accomplished quickly

- the staff or personnel available – including both the amount of staff and the levels of qualifications and experience needed

- the materials needed and their availability

- the personnel's opinion of the manager. If the manager has proved him – or herself to be competent, successful and a motivating force, then the personnel will take this confidence in managerial ability into the task. A good opinion is therefore a major asset to the manager.

Appropriateness of structure

An appropriate organisational structure will deliver many benefits to the business. The appropriateness of the structure will be linked to the scale and type of operations in which the business is engaged.

- If the structure is the right one, then costs can be kept down as the business will be running with greater efficiency.

- A structure which invites workers to participate in decision-making and encourages them to give feedback will motivate the workforce.

- An appropriate structure may mean that faster and more accurate decisions will be made, giving the business a commercial edge.

The market in which a business operates may have a big influence on the combination of structures and styles that it adopts. A traditional business operating in a stable and little-changing business environment will have a different structure and approach to a business operating in a new, dynamic or fast-changing market. The key factor for a business is to ensure that its organisation structure is the most appropriate one – the one that best suits the size and objectives of the business and the market in which it operates.

Organisations may have grown in a particular direction and see no need to alter what they perceive as a successful structure. In some cases, an unwillingness to adapt to change may be seen by some customers an advantage if a 'traditional approach' is wanted. A butcher's shop, for example, might prosper by offering traditional cuts and services which supermarkets are unable to match. In many cases, however, an inability to change will prove crippling to the organisation.

 **ACTIVITY** **17**

Fireflies Limited

Fireflies Ltd is a business that manufactures garden and other outdoor lighting. It has plants in Wales, Yorkshire and the South. The business is run by the chairman, the managing director and three regional directors, one in charge of each of South England, Yorkshire and Scotland. Each regional director has been chosen because of a particular quality that they have. The Yorkshire director is an innovator and designer, the Scottish director is a financial expert, the South England director an expert in customer relations. Each director controls five managers, responsible for production, marketing, administration, sales and customer services respectively. The managing director has an overview and also looks after finances. Each manager has five staff: two senior and three junior operatives.

1. **Draw an organisation chart for Fireflies using two different methods (a 'T' chart and a circular chart).**

2. **Which chart best shows the structure of this business?**

3. **Two junior operatives from Scotland have presented a plan for a new range to their manager. Suggest a matrix structure for developing this project that might make best use of the expertise within the business.**

7. **What other information would you need to know before being sure that your matrix was the most efficient?**

Key Skills C3.2, C3.3

Section 5 *Communication and ICT*

What you need to learn

In this section you will learn about:

● the reasons why businesses need good communications

● the ways in which businesses communicate internally and externally

● why different types and direction of communication are important

● how good communication links with business objectives

● where ICT has changed methods of communication within and between businesses

● what strengths and weaknesses such changes have brought.

FIGURE 1.20 *NASA satellite in space*

Source: © Bettmann/CORBIS

  ACTIVITY **18**

Satellites and space age technology have meant that communications have become more and more sophisticated.

1. List all the communications devices, or ways of communicating, that you can think of which exist today.

2. Use a coloured highlighter to cross out all those devices or methods that didn't exist 10 years ago.

3. In another colour, cross out all those that didn't exist 20 years ago.

4. In another colour, cross out all those that didn't exist 50 years ago.

5. In another colour, cross out all those that didn't exist 100 years ago.

6. In your group, discuss what you think is the single most important invention in the communications field.

Communication

Communication takes place both within and outside all business organisations. In the smallest businesses most communication will be with outside agencies such as suppliers, the tax authorities and customers. As the organisation grows larger, communication becomes more complex and the need for more internal and more external communication grows. The channel of communication is the way in which messages are passed from sender to receiver. These may be formal or informal channels.

All communication consists of a five-part structure.

Think of the communication that is taking place during your studies:

● **sender:** for you this might be an examination board or the government which lays down the guidelines as to what examination boards should examine

KEY SKILLS UNIT

Communication

What is this unit about?

This unit is about applying your communication skills to deal with complex subjects and extended written material.

You will show you can:

■ contribute to discussions;
■ make a presentation;
■ read and synthesise information;
■ write different types of documents.

How do I use the information in this unit?

There are three parts to the unit: what you need to know, what you must do and guidance.

Part **A** WHAT YOU NEED TO KNOW	Part **B** WHAT YOU MUST DO	Part **C** GUIDANCE
This part of the unit tells you what you need to learn and practise to feel confident about applying communication skills in your studies, work or other aspects of your life.	This part of the unit describes the skills you must show. All your work for this section will be assessed. You must have evidence that you can do all the things listed in the bullet points.	This part describes some activities you might like to use to develop and show your communication skills. It also contains examples of the sort of evidence you could produce to prove you have the skills required.

LEVEL 3

FIGURE 1.21 *QCA Key Skills Unit*

Source: © Qualificatons and Curriculum Authority

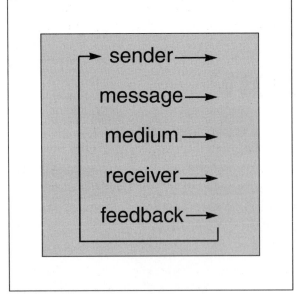

FIGURE 1.22

- **message:** this is information on what you need to learn, how best to learn it, why you are learning it, when you need to have learned it by. It could be written in the form of a subject specification

- **medium:** the way in which the message is passed to you. There will be some oral teaching, so speaking and listening are involved. There will be some written work, some exercises and assignments

- **receiver:** this is yourself! There are various ways in which you can receive the information – spoken, written, reading, etc.

- **feedback:** your examination or assignment results will let you know how well you have done – whether the message has been passed on effectively or not!

Top Tips

It is always important to choose the correct medium for the message. Choose the wrong medium and the message will never reach the receiver. Imagine advertising motorbike leathers in a gardening magazine!

Why is good communication important?

Within this structure you can discover some of the other important functions of communication. You need, for example, to keep receiving feedback on how you are progressing. This will be given in terms of your marks and how they were gained; grades to show achievement and improvements that you can make. Feedback can help improve motivation by letting you know how well you are progressing, how well you are doing a job.

Communication is used for setting targets and providing support. You are at a particular level and need to do certain things to reach a higher level. So it is with business communication. Business communication should be conveying:

- what the organisation is trying to do – its aims and objectives

- what the particular role of the manager or employee is in reaching these objectives

- what tasks you need to complete, both short- and long-term

- how you will know how well you have completed tasks.

Communication provides effective links between different parts of an organisation and between organisations. It may be looked on as the oil or lubricant that helps make the cogs of the business run smoothly.

ASSESSMENT
activity   **6**

1. **Look at the communications structure of the business that you are studying.**
2. **Write a short report which highlights the strengths of the system.**
3. **Explain where you think the weaknesses lie and how you would improve them.**

Key Skills C3.3

Media

The particular medium used to carry a message should be chosen because of its ease of use, its suitability, its speed, its cost and its effectiveness. The media which are available include the following:

- **face-to-face:** Used in conversation or to make presentations. Used to make suggestions and requests and to carry out briefings. Users need to adopt the correct tone and be familiar with the content of the message. They must use the correct delivery (this may mean knowing how to address people formally), be sure in their knowledge and demonstrate confidence. Businesses may call press conferences to announce particular policies, appointments or successes.

- **telephone:** In some situations an easier way to use voice than face-to-face communication, as body language and expressions cannot be read by the receiver. There is a particular skill to dealing with electronic answering systems and in leaving voicemail messages. Some business and banking conversations may be recorded so that an official record is kept.

- **fax:** Operators need to ensure that the document is legible and suitable for faxing. Faxes do not cope well with photographs, colour, small writing or columns of figures, for example. Faxes are rapidly being replaced by e-mail.

- **e-mail:** Electronic mail can be sent to anyone with an e-mail address, which is now over half of the UK population. Many people have e-mail addresses at work and separate ones at home and can swap information between them. E-mails have the benefit of being almost instantaneous communication. They are sent immediately and can be received whenever the recipient decides to open their electronic mail box. Attachments of photographs, video clips, scans of documents etc. can all be forwarded. Signatures sent by e-mail will soon become legally binding. E-mail tends towards the informal because of the nature of the medium but is rapidly becoming the single most important method of business communication. Its one drawback is that security is not always as tight as it might be and it may be possible for other users to read unprotected e-mail.

- **letter:** This can be formal or informal. A short handwritten note of thanks may, for instance, be more genuine and therefore more important to a client or supplier than a formal letter. Formal letters are necessary in particular situations, for example resignation letters.

- **published information:** This could be in the form of leaflets, catalogues, price lists and other publicity material aimed at particular stakeholders. Material aimed at consumers could be direct mail shots, advertisements and promotional literature. Internally, this could be newsletters or company magazines.

- **broadcast:** In some cases, this is the most effective medium but it is also the most expensive. Businesses may call press conferences and include the broadcast media or pay for 'airtime' – usually meaning advertisements.

- **video:** Increasingly, businesses are producing video cassettes so that they can either demonstrate or instruct. This is a relatively inexpensive way of getting the benefits of broadcast media at a fraction of the expense and to reach a specific target audience.

A business will need to communicate with – and receive feedback from – all the stakeholders in its organisation. Internally this will include managers, workers and owners. Externally, it will include suppliers, the government and regulatory bodies, the community in which the business operates, the general public, financial stakeholders (such as investors and financial institutions) and, perhaps most importantly, its customers.

External communication

- Legally, some documentation and publications must be prepared by all businesses. For example, any business employing anyone must draw up a statement of employment and a contract of employment. This applies to sole traders and partnerships as well as companies.

- Some publications have to be produced by companies but not sole traders or partnerships. These include the Memorandum and Articles of Association and, in the case of a company going public, the offer for sale and prospectus. The main formal external document which must be made available is the company report and accounts. It is on the basis of this that shareholders will make the decision to endorse or reject directors and their proposals. A public limited company must make these details public.

- Businesses need to have information about different possible suppliers so that they can make choices based on quality of materials and service, reliability of supply and cost considerations. The use of a website may be another way in which suppliers can show what they have on offer, price structures and delivery dates; this is an area where e-commerce is becoming increasingly important.

FIGURE 1.23 *Company reports*

- Financial stakeholders include anyone who has lent the business money or otherwise invested in it. Information for lenders, investors and financial institutions such as banks and building societies will, of necessity, be more detailed than that provided for public consumption.

- It is important to the interests of most businesses to maintain a good and positive relationship with the local community in which they operate. It is this community that is likely both to gain the benefits from the business being where it is – such as increased employment opportunities or increased local demand – and suffer the costs – pollution, for example. To keep its reputation with the community a good one, a business may be involved in community projects or partnerships (links with a local school or college, for example, to show its concern for local young people) and will want to have its good relationships publicised.

- The main way in which organisations communicate with customers is through advertising and promotions. Advertising is used to inform customers of the availability and qualities of new products and to try to persuade them to buy. Without some form of advertising, however primitive, it is unlikely that customers would ever know what was on offer for sale from various businesses.

- Businesses also receive feedback from customers. They seek this through their own formal channels – conducting customer surveys, for example, or monitoring customer satisfaction – how many times do customers return, does their average spend increase or decrease? They may also monitor statistics such as the number of goods returned or the number of complaints handled by customer services.

 **ACTIVITY** **19**

1. **Monitor the information in your local paper over a period of time and record examples of business partnerships or business sponsorship of non-commercial organisations such as schools, bands or charities.**
2. **What do businesses hope to gain by spending money in this way and ensuring that they get publicity for such activities?**

Internal communication

The system of internal communication within a business may be shown diagramatically by the use of communications nets. The most usual presentations are as a circle, a wheel or a web.

● The **circle** (Figure 1.23) shows that the business is organised on a team basis, with good horizontal communication between people or teams at the same level within an organisation. It shows a team or 'corporate' approach to decision-making.

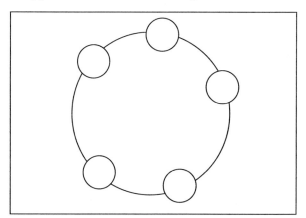

FIGURE 1.24 *Circle*

● The **wheel** (Figure 1.24) shows that power and authority lie with the person at the hub, with communication tending to take place between the centre and each of the 'spokes'. These do not have to be individuals, but could be different parts of the organisation. This is a less coherent approach to communication than the circle but means that the centre retains control of what information each part of the organisation is allowed to receive.

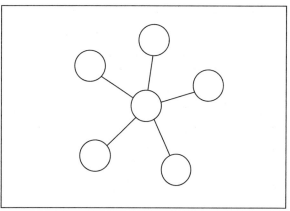

FIGURE 1.25 *Wheel*

● The **matrix** or **web** shows that two-way communication occurs both with a central, controlling 'hub' and also between the various parts of the organisation. In some organisations it would appear as at Figure 1.27 where there is no centre, just a good network of communication channels.

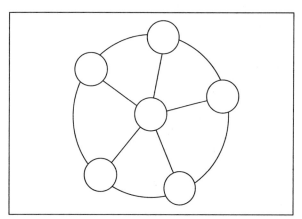

FIGURE 1.26 *Matrix/web*

Formal and informal channels

● Formal channels of communication will take place within a framework that has already been laid down. Communication through such channels will be restricted to taking place only according to the rules and only in the directions that the channels will allow. Such communication will also include the keeping of a formal record of whatever discussion has taken place and of whatever has been agreed.

● Informal channels allow communication to take place at any time and almost anywhere.

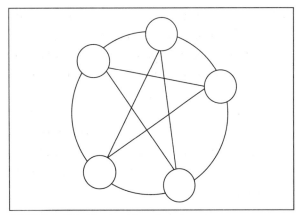

FIGURE 1.27 *Matrix with no 'centre'*

They are not recorded nor are they limited by any sort of framework. Informal channels can include conversations, notes, telephone messages and so on.

Some oral exchanges are not informal but carried out according to a set procedure.

Formal oral channels

- For many employees the first contact with a business is a formal job interview. Sometimes this will be carried out by a panel of interviewers, sometimes by an individual. For some jobs part of the interview may be deliberately made informal – to try to get a better idea of the strengths of the candidates – or interviewees may have to carry out part of the job to show that they are capable of doing it.

- Once employed, there are certain other procedures that will be carried out both formally and orally. An important one of these is the formal verbal warning – the first part of a disciplinary process.

- Information may be communicated to teams or to customers or potential customers in the form of a verbal presentation. This will include such things as a team briefing, formal lecture or speech. Team briefings now form an important part of the communications systems of many organisations. They can be the single most used and most effective method of communication and feedback. Team briefings usually allow for a period of discussion and exchange of ideas after the briefing which helps both to improve the decision-making and to motivate the staff by encouraging participation.

- Formal presentations may be made to customers or to large teams, for example to the representatives of an entire region. They may include the use of slides, handouts, figures, graphs and charts. They have the benefit to the presenter of being able to address a number of people at the same time, and to use various display methods to keep their attention.

- Formal business meetings are usually held according to a set pattern. This pattern makes sure that certain important actions take place. First, the structure ensures that an accurate record is kept of who attended particular meetings, who was unable to attend and why, who spoke and what – in essence – they said. Second, it ensures that the decisions which are made are recorded, and details whose responsibility it is to carry out each decision and report back to the next meeting. The business of the meeting will be spoken but the record will be written.

Remember that sometimes messages are passed on without the person conveying them noticing – through body language. In a situation like an interview you should make sure that your body language shows interest and enthusiasm.

Formal written channels

- **Letters.** These may be letters of enquiry; responses to enquiries; letters of invitation to, for example, a meeting, conference, presentation or exhibition; letters of acceptance, for example, to an interview. First contact with another organisation will usually be made by letter in a formal way.

- **Reports** may have to be written according to a certain style or set of 'in-house' rules. In general, a report should contain an introduction outlining the purpose of the report; a brief summary of the report; the main body laid out in paragraphs and using sub-headings; and a conclusion.

- **Memoranda** (the plural of memorandum). When internal communication needs to be formalised, such as in a summons to a meeting, it may be done using a formal memorandum. Such memoranda may also be used to pass on formal and official messages to the whole staff in a business.

- **Documentation.** Some documentation is, of necessity, formal. This includes all documentation concerning employment, such as contract of employment, pay and conditions, itemised pay slips and pension arrangements; and documents relating to health and safety and employee rights.

- **References.** Employers intending to employ someone may well want to know how they got on in their last employment and may ask for a formal reference from the previous employer.

Informal oral channels

This means the spoken word. This may be an instruction, the passing of information or even a reprimand. Much informal communication is in the form of conversation, but this can be more powerful than many formal methods. Information may spread within an organisation through the 'grapevine' faster than any formal channel. Often misinformation and rumour are passed in this way. Managers may also use the 'grapevine' to float ideas or possible changes so that they can gauge the reaction of employees or team members before any formal proposal is made.

Informal written channels

- **Notes** taken at a meeting or presentation. There are a number of ways of doing this and systems, such as shorthand, have been developed to make it easier.

- Internal information may be passed on through company **newsletters** or **in-house magazines**. Many organisations run their own internal newsletter which carries news of the business – especially developments and successes – and may also be a forum for the views of staff. Such newsletters are used to let people know what is happening in other parts of an organisation and to advertise social functions and competitions.

- Formal memos may be typed on the company memorandum paper and sent through the internal mail. Informal memos and messages may be **scribbled** on a **pad** or put on **sticky backed notes**. It is important that such messages are brief and to the point.

- **Notice boards** are used for messages which need to be read by a large number of people. Sometimes the notice is not considered important enough to be circulated, sometimes it needs to be available quickly, sometimes it is the number of people who need to have access to it that is important. Social announcements – such as a staff party – would also use notice boards.

ACTIVITY ㉒

This activity is designed for you to compare different forms of information. You will therefore need at least two different information sources. ICT sources might include websites and CD-ROM information. None-ICT sources could include interviews, printed company reports and documents and your own observations.

1. Collect information on your chosen business. This might include videos, publications or ICT-based material.

2. Use a search engine on the Internet to visit the company's website if it has one.

3. List the information provided by the company under different categories, for example financial information, product information and information regarding objectives.

4. Compare this information with that collected by a partner. Whose business has the most information? Which is better presented? What improvements would you suggest?

Key Skills IT3.1

Direction of communication

The direction of communication within an organisation is important. Messages need to be passed up the organisation, from subordinate to superior; down the organisation, from those in authority to subordinates; and across the organisation, between peers and colleagues. The first is important so that the decision-makers in an organisation are aware of what is going on at 'grass roots' level. They need to know how decisions are being implemented, how successful changes or innovations are and how well policies are working. Downward communication is important for passing decisions to subordinates. Horizontal communication is important for people and functions to work efficiently together.

Upward communication will include feedback in the form of official and unofficial comment and complaint. Comments may be encouraged anonymously via a 'suggestion box' or people may be encouraged to write to the newsletter or in-house magazine. There may also be more formal official reporting channels.

Downward communication will consist mainly of information and instructions. Once a policy decision has been made at the highest level in the organisation, the information and instructions for carrying out that policy will be passed to the next management level.

Horizontal communication takes place at the same level within an organisation, for example, senior manager to senior manager, director to director. It is easier if an organisation is flatter and 'leaner'. One of the reasons usually given for de-layering is to improve communications – horizontal communication is poorer in a taller organisational structure than it is in a flatter one.

Restricted channels

Some communications will be sensitive in one way or another. It may be that they contain information of a personal nature such as a person's work history or disciplinary record. It may be that they contain information which is sensitive in terms of the company, for example regarding a new process, customer or advertising campaign.

Sensitive information may be restricted to a certain level of staff or to certain departments. Human relations may, for instance, have legitimate access to an employee's personal records but production will not.

Company information may be restricted to certain people or levels and stamped as 'not for all eyes', 'secret' or 'confidential'. Financial information may be particularly important to competitors and, other than that which must be published by law, such information is likely to be heavily restricted.

Open channels

Open information channels include newsletters, notice boards and the published minutes of meetings. In many companies mail is opened before being distributed to recipients and unwanted mail, junk mail etc. is filtered out. Personal assistants may answer low-level enquiries on behalf of managers. For example, requests for application forms do not have to be handled by the human resources manager personally. Some companies have open computer systems, where anyone can access the information. Usually a part of the system will be open, such as the internal e-mail system, while other parts will be restricted.

 **ACTIVITY** 21

Discuss with a partner what you think would be the most effective form of communication in each of the following scenarios. Note in each case

whether the communication is formal or informal, internal or external, open or restricted, and the direction of the communication. Note the reasons for your choice in each case. Compare your answers with those of others in your group.

- **A reply to a customer's letter of complaint.**
- **A telephone enquiry from a customer about a product.**
- **Passing of information to a number of colleagues about a change in company procedures.**
- **Exchanging of information with colleagues about the success of a new product.**
- **Your resignation from your job.**
- **Booking time off for your holidays.**
- **Establishing whether there is any truth in the rumour about redundancies.**
- **Reprimanding a subordinate.**
- **Arranging the department Christmas party.**
- **Checking whether your manager has received the information you sent.**

Information and communications technology

Information and communications technology (ICT) has become increasingly important in business and office environments. It makes communication quicker, cheaper and more effective. It has allowed for the growth of a whole new area of business called e-commerce and it is still expanding at a phenomenal rate, with new applications coming onstream all the time.

The amazing thing about ICT is not just its rapid growth but the fact that, because a mass market for the applications developed so quickly, it has continued to fall in price. This has made even the most sophisticated hardware and software available to the smallest business. In many areas of business, ICT has revolutionised the way that the business is handled or run.

The UK government has recognised the importance of ICT knowledge and understanding by building training and education in ICT into both the National Curriculum for students at all ages. It has set levels of achievement and expertise for each age group. It has also introduced ICT into the training undertaken by all trainee teachers, who must reach a certain level of competence in ICT before being awarded qualified teacher status.

Business uses

ICT has made a number of processes easier, faster and more efficient. In business its main uses are:

- communicating – fax, telephone conferencing, video conferencing and e-mail are the most common

- recording information – records no longer have to be kept on paper and extensive and complicated filing systems are not needed; records are easy to store, protect and access

- checking – systems can be used to measure and check accuracy, to verify documents and to check, for example, publications for grammatical and spelling errors

- editing – documents can be altered and adapted for particular audiences; sections of text or images can be cut and pasted elsewhere; font styles and sizes can be altered to enhance presentation for particular target audiences. For moving pictures, businesses can edit their own videos, add titles, voice-overs, music etc. to a professional standard

- personalising – documents can be 'mass produced' but appear personal. Mail merge can be used internally, for example for meeting members, or externally, for example for personalised direct mail

- storage and retrieval, sorting and classifying – databases can be used to sort and classify information so that it is easier to find and easier to handle; searches through thousands of records take milliseconds rather than hours

- calculating – spreadsheets have become invaluable to many parts of a business; calculators and calculating tills have become commonplace

- projections and modelling – computer programs can make predictions of future sales, for example, based on the figures of current sales and other variables that they may be fed

- reproducing – scanners, digital cameras, digital versatile disk (DVD) drives and writeable CDs all make the reproduction of text, still and moving images and sound extremely easy

- stock control – bar code technology can trace stock movements and ensure stock rotation and replenishment as necessary

- presentations – slide shows and overhead projector slides can be prepared for meetings or briefings

- designing – computer-assisted design systems are used in many businesses. They make designing both easier and more accurate

- replacement of manual labour – robots and automated manufacturing systems are used for a variety of purposes. They are sophisticated pieces of machinery which are capable of carrying out either complicated tasks (some robots can be used in surgery); repetitive tasks (such as on a production line); or dangerous tasks (such as robot mine-clearing equipment).

Software

The main computer software used by businesses are:

- word processing – documents can be standardised according to particular layouts or 'templates'. They can be personalised, edited and corrected on screen, and stored for later use or re-use.

- Desktop publishing – these are more sophisticated than word-processing packages, allowing users to produce professional-style documents ranging from promotional leaflets to book layouts

- Databases – these carry a store of information and are able to search and sort it extremely quickly. Businesses often keep details of customers, clients or employees on a database and can use this to great effect

- Spreadsheets – these are set up to carry out calculations. Spreadsheets can accept numbers, letters or formulae. The use of formulae makes them powerful tools for dealing with routine or complex calculations, and for modelling or predicting future sales patterns

- Graphics – there is various drawing, painting and image manipulation software which can be used to produce logos, enhance presentation, or as a tool for design

- Specialised programs for specific tasks – these could be Computer Assisted Design (CAD) packages, Computer Assisted Manufacture (CAM) packages, accounting packages, or packages to cover any of a range of routine or specialist jobs that a computer can carry out more accurately than the human hand and eye. In some industries the computer has almost completely replaced traditional manual skills. In engineering, for example, the computer has almost totally replaced traditional technical drawing skills.

ASSESSMENT
activity

One part of your report could look at the ICT used by the business that you are studying.

1. **If it uses a lot of ICT, look at the benefits and problems that this has brought in comparison to the previous non-ICT systems.**
2. **If the business has yet to move into ICT systems, you could discuss the benefits and problems that such a move might bring.**

The Internet

The Internet has grown as computer technology has grown. The term 'Internet' refers to the vast global network of computers. It has a number of applications, the main ones being:

- communications: e-mail, chat rooms and IRC (Internet Relayed Chat) use the Internet

- file transfer (ftp or file transfer protocols): this enables files such as software files to be transferred across the Internet

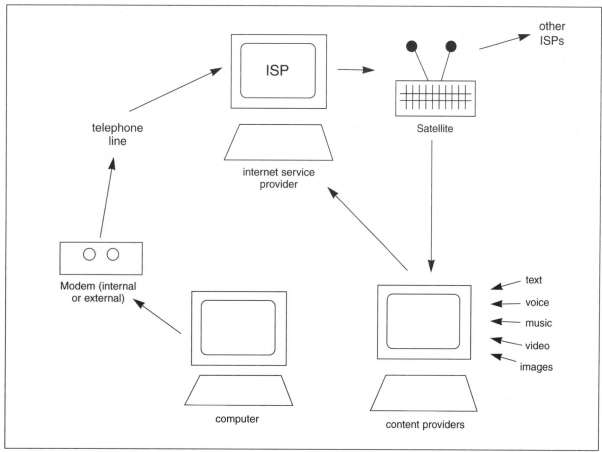

FIGURE 1.28 *Accessing the World Wide Web*

● the World Wide Web (WWW): this is a series of interlinked information pages

● WAP (wireless application protocol): a relatively new use of the Internet. This is a series of information pages specifically designed for access by hand-held computers and mobile phones – a sort of mini World Wide Web.

The applications that most people use are communications and the World Wide Web. Anyone with a computer, access to a telephone line, a modem, Internet browser software and a subscription to an Internet service provider can access the Internet. Browsers include Microsoft Internet Explorer and Netscape Navigator. There is now a wide range of Internet Service Providers (ISPs), including Microsoft, AOL and many communications companies and High Street organisations.

The World Wide Web holds a huge amount of information on a vast range of subjects. Information is put on to the Web by individuals or organisations to serve their interests. They control the content of their own pages. No one has overall authority over content on the Web. It is self-policing and self-regulating. Businesses and individuals need to handle Web-based information with care. It is important to check the integrity of the information and source before relying on it for important decisions.

The Web has become an enormous positive resource used by government, schools, universities and individuals for recreation, education and business. It is, in effect, a giant database but one that is not sorted or indexed. It is almost like a huge library, containing every book and magazine that you could ever want. The difficulty lies in being able to find the information. Search engines allow you to locate information on the Web but questions need to be asked in the right way to locate the information that you actually want. There is a vast number of different search engines. You may have heard of some, such as Yahoo, Alta Vista and Northern Lights. Search engines are becoming more sophisticated. They can be given a number of variables and carry out more complex searches.

Businesses, on the whole, currently use PCs to access the Internet. Hand-held computers and the new generation of mobile telephones now have Internet access. They can use this to communicate via e-mail and access WAP pages. Mobile communications technology is developing and changing rapidly, and it is difficult to predict the future of Internet access.

Businesses often attempt to control employee access to the Web, restricting access by physical means or by the use of 'fire walls'. These are software controls that restrict information coming into an organisation. Businesses do this to prevent access to and downloading of inappropriate information.

Intranets

Many businesses build their own intranet which adds to or replaces information available on the Web. This consists of linked websites of information that have been created in-house or downloaded from the Internet. They provide all the information which the business wishes to be available to its employees. As this is an internal system, the systems manager has complete control over the content and access to it.

ACTIVITY 21

Bryant Homes is an example of a business that has made great use of new technology. It is a large house-building organisation with developments spread over the length and breadth of Britain. There are over 120 housing developments and 13 regional offices. The company has recognised that communication, both external and internal, is vital to it.

Bryant has developed an information technology-based communications system which links all its operations. This handles external communications, with features for customers, suppliers and specialists such as solicitors. It also handles internal communications between sites and offices.

Computer technology means that customers can 'virtually' visit each site where they can see the outside of houses and take a virtual walk round the inside. Customer details can be entered when purchasing decisions are made and the system is linked to solicitors to provide a complete house-buying service.

In addition, Bryant also has a Web presence with a system called Homefinder. This allows potential customers to enter their needs and have them matched with Bryant house types and locations. Photographs and floor plans are updated every day, with all information held on a central database. The system accepts 'leads' (customer enquiries). Because potential customers have already outlined what they want, sales staff can follow these up in a very focused manner.

1. How does the use of such systems increase the business's efficiency?

2. How does the use of such systems increase customer satisfaction?

3. How could Bryant monitor the effectiveness of its website?

4. What recommendations could you make to the business that you are studying, in the light of Bryant's experience?

Section 6 *Production and quality*

What you need to learn

In this section you will learn about:

- how businesses change inputs into outputs
- the production process
- how value is added
- how businesses meet customer requirements
- how businesses control and assure quality.

 ACTIVITY

1. **List 10 different businesses that you know. Make sure that they are producing different goods and services. For each one state:**
   - **what inputs go into production**
   - **how transformation takes place**
   - **what outputs are produced.**

2. **Manchester United plc is a business. What do you think its inputs and outputs are?**

3. **What are the inputs and outputs of the business that you are studying?**

Production

Production is the process of taking a set of inputs and turning them into outputs. The process transforms the inputs into something else. The something else – whether a good or a service – is called a product. The inputs are the factors of production. The transformation takes place in between. The idea of this process is that the product will yield greater value than the sum of the individual inputs. This is known as added value. Organising production involves deciding:

- **what** to produce – based on market research data and information
- **what** mix of inputs to use in production

FIGURE 1.29 *The usual place where transformation happens – but not the only place*

- **where** to produce – location decisions based on considerations such as raw materials, infrastructure and the cost of a base or site
- **how** to produce – choosing the most efficient or appropriate production methods
- **how many** to produce – linked to scale economies and diseconomies, the size of the market and the productive capacity of the business.

Adding value

There are three main ways in which production adds value. Inputs may be combined to:

- produce a physical change
- create a service
- meet the requirements of customers.

In each case, the value of the product will be greater than the combined value of the original inputs.

Producing a physical change

Production inputs are also known as the factors of production. These are the four factors without which production is impossible and have already been discussed in Section 3. They are:

- land – this could be a place to site the production, or a base from which to operate
- labour – human action of either hand or brain
- capital – machinery, tools, equipment, buildings, transport
- enterprise – risk-taking and innovation, provided by the entrepreneur.

These can be broken down further by looking at an example of a product – an output – and tracing it back through the processes and factors that have been used as inputs in its manufacture.

Take something simple like a jacket and look at the materials and processes that have been used in its manufacture. In the case of the jacket shown in Figure 1.30 the raw materials are:

FIGURE 1.30 *A typical jacket*

- cotton material for thread (grown, for example, in the United States of America)
- artificial material for the main part of the jacket (much of this is chemically produced as by-products of oil)
- metal for press studs and zips
- dyes for the various colours
- material for padding and quilting.

The production process will proceed from raw materials through manufacture (or transformation) to the production of a good.

- Raw materials or part-finished component parts (the zip, for example, is likely to be produced elsewhere) are delivered to the manufacturer. Already a certain amount of value has been added to the product through the extraction and processing of the raw materials.

- The next stage is that of manufacture – further inputs of machinery, power, labour and expertise are added to the raw materials and components in order to produce the finished item. Each input adds more value.

- The product is then packaged and distributed to retailers for sale.

All four factors of production have had to be used and combined in certain proportions. The machinery, factory, tools, transport and raw materials are all capital, the site is land, the human resources used are labour and it is the entrepreneur who has raised the initial money for the venture and then decided on the different combinations of inputs.

FIGURE 1.31 *Creating a service*

Source: © Bob Rowan; Progressive Image/CORBIS

ASSESSMENT *activity* ⑧

Consider the business that you are studying.

1. Does it produce a good, a service or a variety of outputs?

2. Explain how the business adds value to its products.

3. In your business, which is the most important part of the process, i.e. which do you think adds most value? Explain your reasoning.

Creating a service

A service is still a product, even if it is not a concrete or tangible one. So what happens in the case of a service? Take the example of a simple service which is called just that – the servicing of a car engine. The inputs used are:

● labour – of the mechanic, who needs to have a certain level of expertise and experience

● capital – in terms of the tools and parts which need to be used

● land – in terms of the site for the service to take place

● enterprise – the mechanic has advertised his services for sale at a particular price.

The amount of value that is added will be linked to the service that is being offered, the precision and expense of the tools and the amount of training needed. Look at the difference between the cost of the service of window cleaning and that of heart surgery. The inputs that are required for the heart surgeon are much more expensive than those for the window cleaner. Both services add value, but the monetary value of this is different in each case.

Meeting the requirements of customers

The aspects of a product that are most important to the customer are:

● the product identity – this is often equated with the brand name of a product; if Rolls Royce produced pedal cycles people would expect them to be up-market and expensive, the 'Rolls-Royce' of the pedal cycle world. Often businesses will have to go to great lengths to throw off a particular product image. (Could Woolworth's ever manage to sell up-market products?)

● product performance and reliability – does the product operate or act according to the performance standards expected by the consumer; is it reliable; if it needs attention (after sales service) how easily may this be obtained, how expensive will it be?

● aesthetic appeal – what does the product look like, is it appealing to the eye?

● price – does the product fall within a price range that is reasonable?

● extras – what additional tangible and intangible extras does the product bring? These could include prestige or status as well as features such as warranties and guarantees.

Consider the products which your chosen business makes.

1. Which of the aspects outlined above are most important to its customers?

2. Which do you think are least important?

3. Give reasons for your answers.

What is a product worth?

Products may be worth different things to different people. A lively pitch produced by a cricket groundsman may be of great benefit and value to a fast bowler and of no use whatsoever to the batsman. What the customer actually wants is a major factor in the value of any product – however, it is not one that can necessarily be measured because different customers wanting different features.

One way of measuring what a product is worth is the concept of 'value added'. At each stage of production a product is worth a particular amount; value is added by manufacturing, processing or other production processes.

Consider a lamb chop. The product starts life as a lamb; the inputs that lead to its growth include food, shelter and medical treatment against disease. The lamb is then slaughtered, with value added by this process. It is then butchered, i.e. the various joints are taken off and trimmed. It will then be packaged and distributed. At each stage value has been added by the addition of a particular input or set of inputs.

The concept of added value is to see the value of a product in terms of all the production processes and inputs which add value and have gone into its manufacture. (See Figure 1.8.)

Value analysis

This looks at an entire production process, from initial raw materials through to the finished product. It evaluates the contribution of each input that has been used in the production of a good or service. It looks at the cost of each input and the amount of value that it can be said to have added and then decides whether that particular input is paying for itself.

Value analysis can be applied to see which aspects of production could be cost-reduced without affecting the value as perceived by the customer. An expensive component or process may be replaceable with one which does not cost as much. The idea is that if small savings can be made on a number of processes – without affecting the quality of the product – then these will add up to a substantial overall saving. The important point is that any changes must not affect the perceived value of the product. It's no use having a cheaper version of something at the same price if the consumer just sees it as being cheaper.

Each input will be looked at individually and in detail to see if a saving can be made.

● For **land**, is there an alternative, cheaper, site which provides the same or better facilities? Land is often a major factor because of governments wanting industry to site in particular areas for economic, social or political reasons. Governments can therefore make certain sites more attractive through improved infrastructure or cheaper costs.

● For **labour**, can a source be found which is as well-trained and experienced but which costs less? One consideration might be for the organisation to decide to lower costs in this area by training its own labour. Labour considerations would also extend to management and human resources – are all layers of management needed? Do we need to pay as much as this for management expertise.

● For **capital**, is there more efficient machinery or are better tools available, can tasks be performed to the same standard with less expensive capital inputs? Can raw materials be sourced from elsewhere or delivered more cheaply? All factors will be considered: power, transport, distribution systems, the costs of borrowing money etc.

● In the case of the **product** itself, consideration will be given to what features can be altered, adapted or reduced without affecting the quality of the product.

ACTIVITY 23

Companies like Nissan turn raw materials – like the rolls of metal for the bodies of its cars – into finished products in a period of only 18 hours. Much of this time is taken up in turning the sheet metal into a pressed car body. From then it takes just three hours to produce a family car. Nissan's Sunderland plant has been singled out twice as Europe's most productive plant (1997, 1998) by the Economist Intelligence Unit.

1. **What are the factor inputs used by Nissan in making a car?**

2. **How do you think that Nissan has improved each input?**

3. **What further improvements could you recommend for Nissan's Sunderland plant to maintain its top position?**

4. **What lessons do you think that the firm you are studying could learn from Nissan?**

Why seek improvements?

Improvements in productivity and efficiency will be linked to the objectives and culture of the business organisation. A competitive, innovative culture will mean that the business is constantly seeking ways to improve its products and the services which it delivers. Businesses can compete through the provision of quality – in terms of what the customer wants rather than any arbitrary measure – and will do so by raising standards of production and after-sales service. Even businesses without the competitive culture will still seek improvements to efficiency because of the cost benefits that are involved. If costs can be reduced while revenue levels are kept the same, then it should be inevitable that profits increase.

Quality defined

Quality can be defined by the customer or by the business.

● To the customer, a quality product is one which exactly meets his or her needs, one where no substitute product could have done the job better.

● To a business, it means producing a product that will sell at the price being asked for it.

Products will only sell if they reach a certain minimum quality. This involves doing the job that they are meant to do, or fulfilling customer requirements. Should the customer want a certain car to do a certain amount of miles per gallon, in a certain colour, at a certain price – and the manufacturer can provide the product within these specifications – then the car is a quality product. Customers will accept a higher price for a job done better, or quicker, or more efficiently.

● There is no absolute measure of quality. What may be a 'quality' item to one person may not seem so to another. Because any definition of quality involves a value judgement, it is impossible to quantify quality.

● An American business writer, P. Crosby, defines quality as being 'conformance to customer requirements'. 'Quality has to be caused', he wrote, 'not controlled', so that any quality system should be based on prevention and zero defects. In other words, mistakes should not happen in the first place and the standard output should be one where there are no faults.

- Quality should be measured in terms of what it costs if quality standards are not reached. This Crosby called the 'price of non-conformance'. Ultimately, if quality – in terms of fitting with what the customer wants – is not delivered, then the customer will go elsewhere to have their wants fulfilled

- Quality management is the set of techniques which a business uses to try to make sure that it is providing the goods or services which meet the needs and wants of its customers in the most efficient and cost-effective manner.

Inspection

Historically, quality control involved a check or series of checks at or towards the end of the production process. It was carried out by a quality controller who was the sole interpreter of whether a product had reached a particular quality standard or not. If any faults were detected, the good would be rejected. This was an expensive method as it meant that:

- finished goods were rejected due to faults occurring earlier in the process and which could have been put right

- some components or materials could not be recovered as they had already been used in the production process (for example, paint or dye could not be re-used)

- the whole manufacturing time was wasted by waiting until the product was 'finished' before checking (and accepting or rejecting) it.

Self-checking

Businesses realised that, in all cases, quality control should make sure that quality problems have been solved before the product reaches the customer. The traditional method of achieving this was through inspectors checking finished products before they left the production line. This was then extended to self-checking. This meant that the quality of each worker's contribution was checked by that worker, spreading the responsibility for quality throughout the business. More and more businesses have recognised that quality issues are everyone's business, not just that of the quality inspector.

Contemporary quality management systems emphasise continuous quality control at all stages of the production process. This means that faults and defects should be detected as early as possible and anyone who detects them should have the power to report them and/or rectify them. Major quality control and assurance systems are TQM (Total Quality Management), quality circles, ISO 9000 and benchmarking. Training and development can also be used to ensure quality.

ACTIVITY 24

The improvement to Gradeways Farm Foods has been dramatic since it sacked its quality inspectors. Instead of quality suffering, it has actually increased. Gradeways made everybody in the company into a quality inspector. Staff inspected the materials which they received, to make sure that there were no faults, and checked their own work before passing it on. This meant that every part of the production process was checked at least twice.

As an incentive to even better standards, Gradeways promised to pay a bonus out of the savings that were made. The first of these were paid out and savings have continued to grow.

1. **Describe the main factors involved in Gradeways' quality management strategy.**

2. **Explain why such a quality strategy might prove successful.**

3. **If your chosen business has adopted such strategies, explain how this has benefited it. If it hasn't, explain what benefits it might gain if it did.**

TQM (Total Quality Management)

Total Quality Management is usually referred to as TQM. The major idea of TQM is that quality is the responsibility of everybody who has anything to do with the production of a good or service. The system is efficient in terms of time and materials and cuts down waste. Should any faults or defects occur at any part of the production process, they should be detected and rectified as soon as possible before the production moves on to the next stage. Quality is everyone's responsibility and each person is empowered to act as a 'quality inspector', spotting and putting right problems as they happen. If what everyone produces is fault-free then the entire product should be perfect. Experience of this concept should mean that, because everyone is checking that faults do not happen, they don't actually occur.

J. Edward Deming, an American business writer, is considered to be the 'father' of TQM. Deming admired Japanese production management methods and recommended that these be adopted wherever possible. His own theories regarding production were applied first in Japan and the Far East. This meant that the Japanese were the first to recognise the benefits of 'lean production' and were able to flood Western markets with well-made but cheaply priced consumer goods.

Deming wrote a 14-point plan for senior management which covered aspects of human resource management, production and operations management. He advocated a system of statistical process control (see below) where a straightforward numerical calculation could show whether an operation or process was efficient. Deming included the customer in the chain of production and said that the customer was the most important part of the chain, so that all organisations should be customer-focused.

Quality is defined by the customer (in terms of the product's 'fitness for purpose') and everyone,

FIGURE 1.32 *The British Standards Institution 'kitemark'*

in a TQM system, is treated as a customer. This includes suppliers, sub-contractors and service providers. A business should seek to only interact with businesses that practise TQM themselves. In this way they ensure quality at all levels and in all aspects of production. The only people not treated as customers are employees, but these should (according to Deming) be handled according to a quality system of human relations management. The main parts of TQM are:

- quality is everyone's responsibility
- there should be no defects
- all employees are empowered to take action to maintain quality
- teamwork and training are encouraged so that skills and experience are shared
- procedures are as important as production and must be monitored constantly.

Quality circles

These are where groups of workers get together on a voluntary basis to discuss problems and possible solutions. They can form an integral part of TQM and were originally a Japanese idea meant to involve workers more in decision-making. The items for discussion were known quality problems, such as faulty goods or poorly performing machinery. Quality circles benefited from the fact that the members are knowledgeable in their own field of production or process. Quality circle members were encouraged to report findings to management for possible action. They were adopted by a number of UK companies in the 1980s. It was found that such circles were more efficient if employees were paid for the time that they spent in meetings so this was the model adopted in Japan.

ISO 9000

External bodies will set quality standards. This means that there is a recognised and independent level of quality which can be seen by any customers or other businesses wanting to work with a particular business. The achievement and maintenance of certain quality standards shows other companies that a business is taking a serious approach to quality and quality management issues. One of the most important UK and international standards is BS5750 or ISO 9000.

The British Standards Institute (BSI) established the BS5750 standard and the International Standards Organisation (ISO) has agreed on this standard which it has called ISO 9000. It is an internationally recognised standard and symbol of good quality management. Businesses who reach the standard are allowed to display the BSI 'kitemark' to show that its systems and controls have reached this level.

To do this, the business must:

- allow all of its quality control and quality assurance procedures to be checked by outside inspectors
- publish a detailed document (a quality 'manual') which gives descriptions of its quality procedures and quality management systems
- show the methods by which it ensures quality from the beginning of the production process to the end.

All quality systems have to be included to reach the overall ISO 9000 standard, meaning that businesses have to have systems in place for all processes, management and human relations.

- Every person and process in the business must be covered by the ISO 9000 manual. Everyone in the organisation must be fully conversant with the requirements and willing and able to carry them out.
- The award of the standard is independently checked by an external assessor who will return at regular intervals to ensure that the business continues to comply with the standard.

There are various benefits which may be gained from reaching the ISO 9000 standard, not least the fact that many businesses will choose an organisation awarded it ahead of the competition. This means that such businesses have an increased competitive edge which will probably lead to greater sales and better profits.

Other benefits may be linked to the fact that quality is treated as an overall concept – staff are better motivated because of human resources quality systems and there will be less staff turnover. Greater quality in processes will mean that there are cost savings, less waste and improved efficiency and productivity. Management quality systems should lead to better communication and understanding which, in turn, will again lead to increased efficiency.

By having a strict 'set of rules' that must be adhered to, organisations can ensure that everyone is focused on quality – this is probably the major benefit of ISO 9000.

Benchmarking

In the late 1970s and early 1980s traditional Western markets were penetrated by Japanese companies who produced good quality but lower-priced products. Much of this was due to Japanese management techniques and new approaches to process and operations control.

Western companies lagged behind their Japanese counterparts and wanted to benefit from their advances.

One way to do this is through 'benchmarking'.

Companies measure their own performance against that of a competitor and see where they might improve. The best practices in other companies are studied and applied to their own business.

The process of benchmarking involves:

● identifying the best competitor – this means finding a suitable benchmark partner making similar products for similar markets and at a similar stage of development

● measuring performance in a number of key areas such as material wastage, labour and capital productivity, lead-in times and supplier reliance, measuring your performance against that of the benchmarking partner

● comparing and evaluating performance in all of these areas

● improving those areas where your competitor is doing better by adopting your competitor's approaches, systems or processes

● re-measuring your performance against your competitor to see if you have reached the same standard

● finally, starting the process all over again so that further improvements can be made – the idea is that you keep going until you are the benchmark company, i.e. the best in your field.

The main drawback of benchmarking is that companies don't develop their own systems – which might be better than those being copied. The main advantage is that the systems they do adopt have been trialled successfully. Companies can improve bench marking by 'piggy backing' – adopting the successful process or system and then adapting it to suit their own requirements.

In the UK, the importance of benchmarking has been recognised by the government and the Department of Trade and Industry has published a small business's guide to benchmarking. The Confederation of British Industry has also accepted its significance and has set up a computer database called PROBE which will help companies to find suitable benchmarking partners.

Problems occur with benchmarking when:

● measurement of a system or process is not possible

● a chosen benchmarking partner does not wish to co-operate by disclosing its systems

● to implement such changes as are necessary would be either too costly or too impractical.

ASSESSMENT **10**
activity **1**

Consider the size of your chosen firm, its structure and its type of production. Which business or businesses would you recommend as suitable benchmarking partners? What do you think that each 'partner' business would gain from the exercise?

Training and development

Part of the total quality approach must include the training and development of staff. All staff from management downwards must believe in the philosophy which the company has embraced, and may need training in that philosophy. In particular, changing a culture or style of management can be difficult.

When Nissan first established operations in the UK, for example, it was up against traditional levels of manning, trade union concerns and a completely different culture to the one that it had developed in Japan. This was gradually changed and, as it changed, the productivity of the Nissan plant grew to rival that of its Japanese parents.

Traditionally, the UK has been poor in the area of training, devoting less than a twentieth of 1 per cent of turnover to training. This compares with European competitors such as Germany and France and overseas competitors such as Japan who invest up to 2 per cent (over 10 times more). Similarly, the UK has less of its workforce in training than its industrialised competitors. The

UK produces fewer technologists, fewer engineers and fewer scientists than its major competitors.

This imbalance has been addressed in recent years by government in trying to encourage more training to take place. It has also subsidised certain education and training for engineering, science and technology. Businesses have been encouraged to introduce such measures as Investors in People (IIP) to demonstrate that they value all of their staff and recognise their training needs.

Business organisations need to recognise that it is in the area of human resources, not capital resources, that the greatest benefits can be gained from improvements. In the case of human resources these improvements can only come about through training and education.

Quality assurance (QA)

Quality assurance means that a business has quality systems in place to ensure that quality standards are met. Some businesses set their own strict quality standards. Marks and Spencer, for example, ensures that any product which carries the company's label is perfect. It will reject entire batches of products, particularly clothes, if it spots even one defect in the batch. Other examples of QA include businesses introducing systems of continuous quality checking of processes as well as products. Like TQM, QA is an organisation-wide approach to quality management issues. This must be achieved from the point of view of:

- product perfection – all products must be inspected and checked for quality
- process quality – all parts of the production process should be checked to ensure that they are working at their most efficient (this will include statistical process control)
- systems quality – all of the systems that are used to check quality should themselves be

checked constantly to ensure that they are up to standard

- human resource quality – all employees (including managers) should be trained to be aware of quality issues and work towards quality improvements
- environmental quality – can the product be produced to the same quality but using either less or cheaper inputs?
- quality of inputs – if the cost of the inputs is reduced, this must not lead to a fall in the quality of the product
- consumer satisfaction – the organisation should be attempting to respond as quickly and efficiently as possible to the wants and demands of the consumer; this means that there must be built-in flexibility

Businesses can apply for QA status and have their quality management systems checked by an external assessor. The use of the QA symbol shows that the business takes a serious and thorough approach to quality.

The 'moment of truth'

This is when a business finds out if its quality systems really work. If they do, the customer makes a purchase; if they don't, the customer buys a competitor's product.

- For organisations producing goods, the 'moment of truth' is when the customer actually buys the good. They have chosen it ahead of its competitors and therefore must believe that this is the quality item.
- For other businesses which provide services, the 'moment of truth' is defined as any point of contact between the service provider and customer. All points of contact should leave the customer feeling that they have been treated as important and significant.
- Sometimes there is only one 'moment of truth' – for example, in visiting a shop to make a purchase, the way that you are dealt with by

the sales staff defines what they think you are worth (and what you think of them).

Imagine booking a table for a restaurant. Here there are several 'moments of truth':

● the way the receptionist answers your telephone enquiry

● the impression you get of the restaurant on arrival

● the ancillary services, such as car parking availability

● the way the restaurant deals with any special requests.

All of these have happened before the food has even arrived! There is little point in chefs creating wonderful food for you to eat if you have already formed a poor opinion of the restaurant due to the way that you have been treated at an earlier 'moment of truth'.

For businesses practising a 'total quality' approach it is essential that any contact with the customer is a positive one – and it is here that the benefits of training may be most pronounced. A slip by any member of staff at any point of contact can ruin the work of the rest of the organisation, however good it is.

Appropriateness

In different circumstances, different methods of ensuring quality might be appropriate.

● TQM (Total Quality Management) is most appropriate in a business operating a production line. If a product is being passed from worker to worker, and through various processes, it is essential that quality is everyone's responsibility.

● In a business seeking continuous improvement, quality circles will be appropriate. The idea that any improvement, however small, is worth implementing is part of the philosophy behind quality circles. This means that a

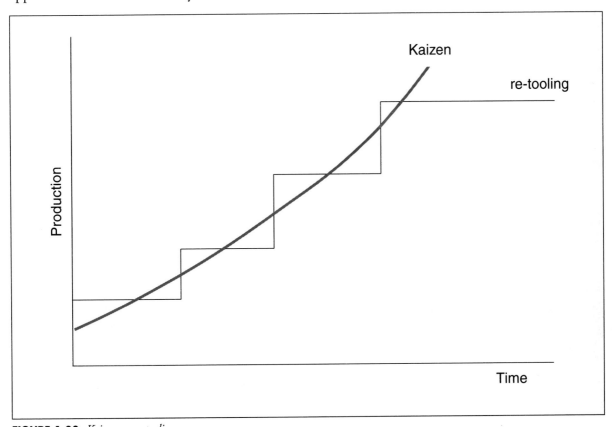

FIGURE 1.33 *Kaizen vs. re-tooling*

business does not have to improve through big 'shocks', for instance, changing a whole production line, but can reach the same levels by gradual improvement. This is the basis for the Japanese idea of Kaizen – continuous improvement. Quality circles will also be important to smaller businesses, especially to those where working in teams is usual.

- ISO 9000 is a standard worth having, especially to join the 'club' of ISO 9000 businesses. Many businesses with the standard will only deal with other businesses who take a similar approach to quality. A business without ISO 9000 could find that it cannot get the best suppliers or ancillary services, and so on. The award is a signal to the outside that the business takes a serious approach to quality.

- For benchmarking to operate, the business needs a suitable partner, needs to know that it is a good match and needs their co-operation. This will not always be possible. Sometimes, if the business is already the one with best practice, it will be unwilling to share this expertise. Even if a business can find a suitable partner (through the use of the government's PROBE service, for example) then there could still be problems. Remember, if the two businesses are operating in the same market, they are likely to be competitors.

Small businesses

What about the small business how does it measure quality?

Generally, it can judge quality through levels of repeat business, expressed customer satisfaction and the lack of returns. Quality systems such as benchmarking and ISO 9000 are not appropriate to such businesses but good training certainly is. For some small businesses, quality circles may be an approach which 'brings the staff together'. The effect on the motivation of staff who are given a role in decision-making can be very good. Certainly in small firms, and particularly in service industries, a philosophy of quality must be encouraged.

2

The Competitive Business Environment

What this chapter is about

Businesses exist in order to supply goods and services to satisfy consumer wants and needs.

They do this is in competition with other businesses who are trying to achieve the same or similar ends. It is this competitive environment within which business takes place that is studied in this chapter.

Businesses need to track the moves of their competitors both in the UK and overseas. They must anticipate how governments will react to changes in price, employment and output. They must make sure that they are looking after the interests of all of their stakeholders.

All businesses operate in markets. You will learn what is meant by a market and find out why governments and businesses try to intervene to control the market mechanism. ■

What you need to produce

The Unit covered by this chapter is assessed through an externally set assessment which is graded by the examination board. It may be helpful to study the Unit at the same time as studying Chapter 1, due to the strong links between the two Units. The information on which assessment is based will contain both numerical and written data which relate to businesses operating in a global competitive context. You will be tested on your ability to:

■ identify the market and sector in which a business operates

■ recognise and describe the characteristics of a market

■ identify what conditions affect businesses in a market

■ explain how and why businesses try to influence these conditions

■ evaluate the good and bad points of operating in particular markets

■ analyse and explain how competition affects stakeholders

■ analyse how and why governments intervene in markets

■ explain how businesses operate in and are affected by the international dimension.

| Section 1 *How competition in the market affects business* |

What you need to learn

In this section you will learn about:

- the different types of market in which businesses operate
- the factors that influence how markets operate
- how businesses seek to shape their markets
- how factors combine to affect market conditions
- the changing pattern of industry.

Market forces

There is a story of a famous American stamp collector. This collector knew that there were only three copies of a particular stamp in existence. One was in a museum, one was in his private collection and one was in another collection. When the other collector put his stamp up for sale, the American bought it for several million dollars. He then publicly burnt the stamp that he had just bought. With a partner discuss:

1. Why he would do this.
2. What you think happened to the value of the remaining stamps?
3. Why? What forces were at work?

Look at Figure 2.1.

Discuss these questions with a partner:

1. What is it that makes some of these things expensive and others cheap?
2. If another three or four genuine versions of the Mona Lisa were found, would this make the value of the first painting go up or down?

FIGURE 2.1

3. **Under what circumstances would FA Cup Final tickets be cheap?**
4. **Why is moon rock considered so valuable?**
5. **What makes diamonds expensive? (Remember, it's no more expensive to mine them than it is to mine coal!)**
6. **What happens at a second-hand car auction? What makes prices high or low?**

Your answers to these questions should lead you to some of the following conclusions about market forces.

- If a lot of people want a product, then the price is likely to rise (Cup Final tickets, auction).
- If there are very few of the product, prices are likely to be high (diamonds, moon rock).
- If more of a product is introduced, this is likely to bring prices down (more Mona Lisas).
- If very few people want the product, price will be low (wood shavings).

Any combination of these factors will have an even greater effect on price. So, if not many people want a product yet there is a lot of it (wood shavings), price may be very low. It may even be nothing. However, if a lot of people want a product and there is not much of it, prices will rise. The stamp collector knew what he was doing. His remaining stamp had far greater value due to its increased rarity.

Market prices are set by a combination of factors: how much people want a product and how much of a product is on offer. The first is called demand, the second supply. These are called market forces. It is the interaction of demand and supply that decides what the price will be. This interaction takes place in a market.

What is a market?

A market is anywhere where buyers and sellers come together to agree on a transaction. Markets do not have to have a physical existence – indeed, many markets exist only over telephone lines or between computer or other telecommunication links.

Traditionally, markets took place at cross-roads, fairs or other temporary sites where sellers would set up their stalls and buyers would come to buy. The prices of products would not be pre-determined but arrived at by negotiation between buyer and seller. In many markets of the world this process still takes place dynamically. The seller starts with a high price and the buyer counter-bids with a lower one; offer and bid are adjusted by buyer and seller until an agreed price is reached (this is called haggling).

A similar process takes place in auction rooms, where successively higher bids are made for what is usually a product that is in limited supply, until only one bidder remains for the one product. Price has therefore been agreed at this level.

Different market conditions are defined by:

- the product that is on sale
- the number of buyers in the market
- the number of sellers in the market
- what related products are available
- national, international and government influences.

Markets defined by product

Markets may be defined by the type of product that is traded in the market. These fall into the following groups:

- end products
- commodities
- capital goods
- industrial goods
- services
- financial
- labour.

End products

These are those goods that are most often bought by you, the consumer. They are the result of a manufacturing or making process. The consumer market is usually divided into:

● consumer durable products – Durables means lasting; these goods are those which may be used again and again without being immediately 'used up'. The group includes household goods, furniture and 'white' goods such as refrigerators, freezers and washing machines.

● non-durable or consumer goods – These are sometimes referred to as 'single use' goods because these goods are 'used up' immediately. Food and fuel are the main goods in this group. Other items which are used up quickly and therefore considered as consumables, such as batteries, are also included.

Commodities

These are metals or crops that are capable of being graded and stored. The largest commodity trade is in oil, the second largest in coffee. Commodities are defined as either 'soft' or 'hard':

● hard commodities are metals such as tin, zinc, silver and gold

● soft commodities include wheat, tea and coffee.

Commodity markets are often seen as being the closest thing to a 'perfect' market, with market forces setting price on a daily basis. Commodities are not bought only by producers for use or sale. There are three main reasons to trade in, for example, coffee:

1. You are a coffee manufacturer.

2. You are buying at today's price as a hedge against future price rises.

3. You are buying at today's price with the intention of selling to make a profit in the future.

Commodity futures are one of the main reasons why commodities are traded. Many futures traders do not need the commodity at all, but trade in it in order to make money from the price difference between today's price and that in the future. Major commodity markets exist in London, Tokyo and Chicago.

Capital goods

These are those goods which are used to make other goods or services. To the window cleaner, the bucket and wash leather are capital goods. To a car manufacturer, capital goods are the machines and robot production facilities. They include tools, machinery and commercial vehicles which are used as a part of the production process.

The capital market will obviously overlap with the consumer market in certain areas (for example, vehicles) but is defined by the good being used in production. If a consumer buys a van in order to pack his camping gear for a holiday, it is a consumer good. If he or she buys it to carry tools for a plumbing service, it is a capital good.

Industrial goods

These may be used in large-scale projects but are not traded or obtainable in commodity markets. Effectively, industrial goods are those which allow industry to continue in production but which are not specifically consumer, commodity or capital goods. They are goods which are, of necessity, bought on a large scale, involving international trade. Usually, they are 'one-off' orders, such as the material for the covering of the Millennium Dome or the concrete for the building of the Channel Tunnel. (This may have been a one-off order, but it was one which lasted for several years!)

Orders for industrial goods tend to be very large, meaning that those businesses ordering can not only take advantage of scale economies but can also negotiate. Their demand for a product may be so high that they can have suppliers bidding to fill their order rather than having to seek out suppliers themselves.

FIGURE 2.2 *The special material covering the Dome was a 'one-off' industrial goods order*   *Source: Life File/Andrew Ward*

Sometimes, in order to obtain industrial goods in the quantities desired, companies will have to negotiate joint supply agreements. This means that companies that might otherwise have been in competition are forced to work in partnership. The important thing about industrial markets is that the company which is demanding the product is demanding in such quantities that it is in a good position to negotiate price.

Sometimes the industrial market overlaps with the commodity market – if a company should, for example, need a large amount of a precious metal for a particular project, this would affect both markets.

Services

These are provided either to the consumer or to the producer.

● The market for consumer services includes everything a consumer might need from personal services – such as hairdressing, tourism and retailing – to those services which are also provided to business and industry, such as banking and insurance.

● Producer services include banking, insurance, transport and communications – all huge service industries in their own right. The service sector is the tertiary, or third, sector of the economy and forms the last link in the chain of production. Producer services also include industrial services.

● Industrial services enable production to take place. These could include items such as machine maintenance or parts of transport and distribution. Industrial service providers also serve what might be thought of as non-industrial markets, such as local and national government.

Financial markets

These are specialised markets dealing in finance for businesses. They include money markets and capital markets. They are the market for long-term loan capital for:

- companies, usually in the form of stocks, shares, bonds and similar securities. New capital for companies is raised through loans or share issues
- governments, in the form of bills and bonds; governments sell short-term bills (usually 90-day bills) or long-term bonds.

Labour markets

These are markets for workers and jobs.

Businesses want a ready supply of labour:

- at the right price
- of the right quality
- in the right place.

Workers want to be able to get a job when they want need one. They would like:

- good working conditions
- a fair wage
- job security.

If the demand for workers is less than the supply, then prices will be pushed up. This can be seen by looking at certain jobs:

- There may be a very high demand for the skills of a top surgeon but few doctors with the skills. This leads to a high price for the labour.
- There may be very high demand for unskilled labour such as hospital porters but plenty who can do the job. This leads to a low price for the labour.
- There may be a high demand for teachers and a good supply. Wages are neither particularly high nor particularly low.

Because levels of unemployment are important to governments, labour markets tend to be governed by certain laws. These include trade union legislation, minimum wage legislation, health and safety legislation and employment rights. Longer-term labour market problems might revolve around the quality of labour and mean extra training or qualifications.

Internal markets

The idea is to introduce market forces of demand and supply into areas where these did not previously operate, for example in local councils. Departments within corporations and councils have to compete with each other to provide the best service at the lowest rate. Thus the council-employed dustbin collectors may have to set themselves up as a private concern in order to bid for the council's contract for this service. A school meals service may have to bid to provide school meals of a certain quality but within a certain budget.

In some cases, the forces of demand and supply cannot be left to govern the market but it must be regulated in some other way. In the case of the National Health Service, for example, everyone pays through their National Insurance contributions but the market is actually regulated according to need – those judged to have the greatest need of care should receive it ahead of others.

ACTIVITY ②

In which type of market would you place the following?

1. A car manufacturer.
2. A components manufacturer for a car manufacturer.
3. An advertising agency employed by a car manufacturer.
4. A rubber planter who provides raw materials to tyre makers.
5. A steel manufacturer who provides steel for car bodies.
6. A business producing car transporter vehicles.
7. The business which provided the loan to set up the car manufacturer.
8. The consumer buying the car.
9. The petrol for the car.
10. The oil that was refined to make the petrol.

Some may fit into more than one category.

How price is determined

Markets have two sides: demand and supply. Demand is the number of people wanting a product. Supply is the number of people willing to sell the product. Market price is decided by the interaction of demand and supply. There are many factors which act on demand and supply to change them.

On the **demand** side they include:

● the size, structure and distribution of the population
● the amount and distribution of the income and wealth of the market
● seasonal variations
● changes in taste and fashion
● the availability of substitutes and complements.

On the **supply** side they include:

● price
● costs
● levels and availability of technology
● physical or environmental conditions
● taxation and subsidies.

Demand

Demand factors are:

Population

This includes development, size, structure and distribution.

● **Development.** For example, populations that are agricultural will have different patterns of demand to populations that are more developed, or industrialised.
● **Size.** The bigger the population, the bigger the potential level of demand.
● **Age structure.** Markets will alter and adapt to changing population structures. In the 1960s there was a greater proportion of the population under 25 than there is now. In the UK, the growth markets were fashion clothes and pop music. In 2000 over a quarter of the

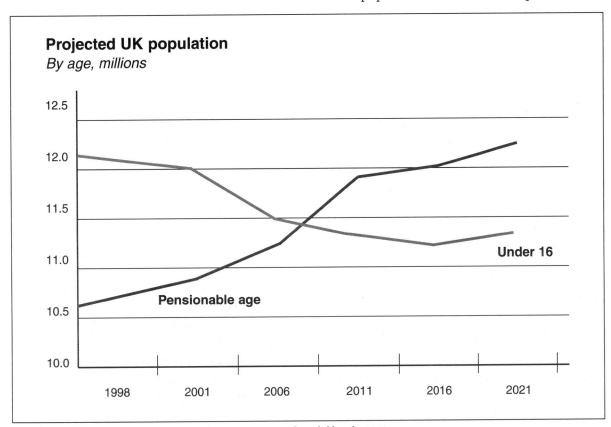

Projected UK population
By age, millions

FIGURE 2.3 *It is predicted that there will be more pensioners than children by 2008*

population (16 million) is over 65 and only a fifth (11 million) is under 25. This means that the market has swung towards providing more products for the older end of the scale.

● **Distribution.** In some countries (like France) there is an uneven distribution of population. A large proportion of the French population lives in and around Paris. Much of the rest of the country is very thinly populated. This means that, for example, it is expensive to provide essential services because of low levels of demand.

Income and wealth

● At lower levels of income more basics are likely to be demanded, such as staple foods (cereal, potatoes, rice) and basic clothing.

● At higher levels of income these basic needs may be satisfied and demand turns towards more luxury-type goods.

● In the UK wealth is unevenly distributed, with a small percentage of wealthy people owning a large percentage of the wealth.

Seasonal variations

Some goods and services will have their demand affected by changes in the seasons.

● Weather-related products such as umbrellas, deck-chairs, suntan lotion and wellington boots, will have peaks and troughs, with demand throughout the year. As suppliers anticipate increases in demand, supply is increased to match it – thus, for example, shops will stock more suntan lotion in the summer months.

● Fluctuations may also be due to different festivals or customs – the demand for fireworks, for example, or Easter eggs.

● Seasonal fluctuations can be followed by logging when particular types of television advertisement first start to appear, for example holiday advertisements just after the January sales; Christmas-type advertisements from September onwards.

Taste and fashion

These might be better thought of as 'preference'. Advertising and promotion are used to make buyers preferences change. Products are presented as being of better quality, or greater value, than competitors'. If businesses can increase taste or preference then they can:

● sell more of the product at the existing price

● sell the same amount of the product at a higher price, or

● a combination of the two.

Substitutes and complements

Many products have links with other products, either as alternative purchases (substitutes) or as products that are bought at the same time (complements). In both cases, changes in the price of the linked product will affect demand.

FIGURE 2.4 *Car and bike = substitutes. Car and petrol = complements*

 **Top Tips**

Don't mix up complements (products bought together) and compliments (you look nice)! Complements has two 'e's. Think of them as having been bought together.

● If the price of a substitute to a product falls, more of the substitute will be demanded and therefore less of the product.

● If the price of a substitute rises, less of the substitute will be demanded and therefore more of the product.

The strength of the switch in demand will be governed by the closeness of the substitution. If, for example, blue cars – identical in all other respects – were charged at a higher price than red cars, then demand would be greater for the red ones (ignoring, for the moment, the fact that people might prefer the blue ones because they are more 'fashionable'). These are very close substitutes so any change in the price of one would have a big change on the demand for another. Where goods are not close substitutes, the effect will be less – a change in the price of motorbikes, for example, will have only a small effect on the demand for cars.

● If the price of a complement falls, more of it will be demanded and therefore more of the product.

● If the price of a complement rises, less of it will be demanded and therefore less of the product.

Some things in joint demand are such close complements that one will not be of any use without the other – CDs are of no use without a CD player; CD players are of no use without CDs. There is therefore a close complementary relationship between them.

Demand diagrams

If a business was able to plot the amount of product demanded at each price level charged, it would be able to draw a demand curve. This would be similar to the one at Figure 2.5. A normal demand curve shows that as price falls, more of a product will be demanded. As price rises, less of a product will be demanded. The slope of the curve shows how responsive demand is to a change in price. This is important information to a business. It needs to know whether a decrease in price, for example, will increase or decrease its total revenue.

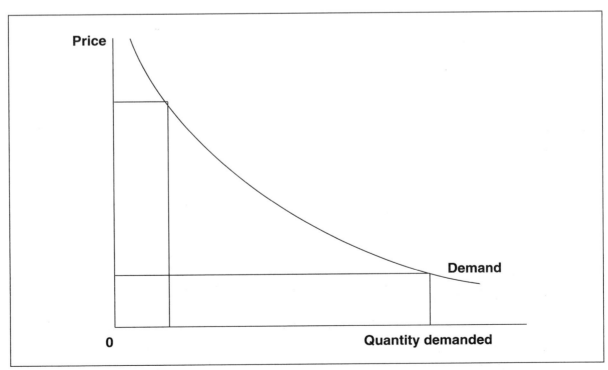

FIGURE 2.5 *A normal demand curve*

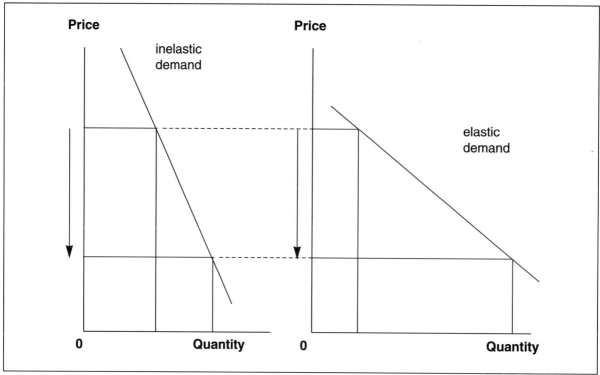

FIGURE 2.6

A word on elasticity

Price elasticity of demand is the responsiveness of demand to a change in price. It is important for a business to know whether a change in price will have a large effect on demand (price elastic) or a small effect (price inelastic). Usually, if there are many substitutes, and they are close substitutes, demand will be very responsive (elastic). If there are few substitutes, demand will be inelastic.

If a large change in demand is caused by a proportionately smaller change in price then the product is said to be price elastic. This will be the case if the product is not a necessity or has many and close substitutes. If only a small change in demand results from a proportionately large change in price then the product is price inelastic. This will be the case for products which consumers have to buy – necessities such as salt, water, refuse collection services – or for products which have few or no substitutes – petrol, for example. Price elasticity is measured as

$$\frac{\text{\% change in quantity demanded}}{\text{\% change in price}}$$

With price elastic demand, a fall in price leads to an increase in revenue; with price inelastic demand, the same fall leads to a decrease in revenue. You can see on Figure 2.6 how the same fall in price will have a different effect depending on the slope of the demand curve.

Demand elasticity and taxation

Elasticity is particularly important when the government imposes a tax. This is because it affects who pays the tax, the consumer or the producer.

Supply

On the whole, suppliers are willing to supply more of a product the higher the price is; this is because, as they produce more, it generally costs less to produce each extra or 'marginal' item as economies of scale are gained. It also relates to the number of businesses in the market – if, as price rises, a greater number of businesses are able to sell and produce the product at a profit, then market supply will continue to increase. The shape of the supply curve therefore shows this

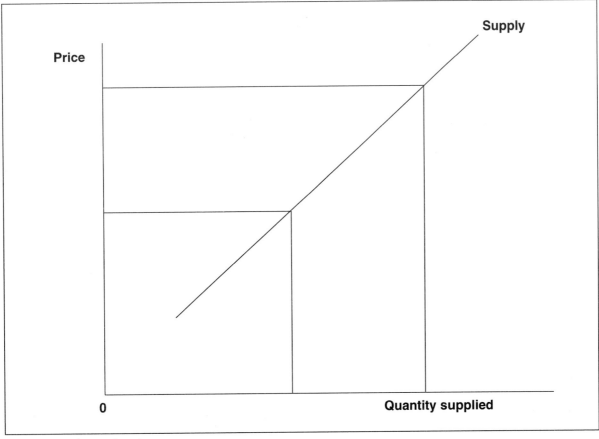

FIGURE 2.7 *A normal supply curve*

relationship (Figure 2.7). At higher prices, the business is willing to supply more.

Factors influencing supply are:

● **Price**. Most businesses are not powerful enough to be able to influence price, so must accept the market price. There is an obvious link between this price and the costs to produce a product. Businesses, on the whole, will only supply a product if they consider that they can at least cover their costs and, preferably, make a profit. The higher the price that the business can ask for its products, the more likely it is to be able to cover costs. Lower prices may lead to businesses being forced to leave that particular market.

● **Factor price changes**. Changes in the prices of any of the factors used in production – land, labour or capital – will lead to changes in the level of product which a supplier is willing to supply.

– An increase in wage rates, for example, would mean an increase in the cost of labour and therefore an increase in the production costs of the product. Each change in factor price will have an effect that is larger or smaller as the importance of the factor input is larger or smaller. If the production of the product is highly labour-intensive then an increase in wage rates will have a large effect. If, however, it is capital-intensive then the increase in labour rates may have little effect.

– Costs may be increased by factors completely outside the control of the supplier. An example could be an overseas government imposing a tariff on the export of a raw material, or the UK government agreeing a policy such as a minimum wage.

● **Changes in technology**. It may be possible to produce higher quantities of product and/or a better quality product by using better technology. An improvement in technology may mean that:

– less factors have to be employed. A new machine or computerised system may need less labour than the previous version

– more efficient use can be made of current factors. A change in technology is almost always considered to be 'for the better' as the introduction of new technology should lead to lower prices.

● **Taxation and subsidies.** Governments may subsidise particular businesses in order to achieve objectives. For example, they may want businesses to locate in areas of high unemployment. They may also subsidise businesses so that they can compete better in international markets. Taxation may be used to discourage the supply of certain products. For example, tobacco products carry high levels of taxation. Taxation may also be used to try to make people use resources more efficiently. This is one of the reasons for tax on petrol.

● **Physical and environmental conditions.** Some lines of supply are only possible because of particular environmental conditions, or because deposits of a material may be found. The supply of gold, or oil, or tropical fruits, is affected by factors such as climate, physical conditions and environment.

FIGURE 2.8 *Oil can only be extracted where it has been geologically created*

ACTIVITY   3

Oil companies were aware that there was oil in Alaska and in the North Sea long before they bothered to explore for the actual deposits and extract them. Worldwide geological services had let them know where the most likely places for oil deposits were but they did not go out and extract the oil. Only after the two oil price shocks of the seventies – as Middle Eastern producers twice doubled the price of petrol – did companies move into Anchorage, Alaska and Aberdeen, Scotland to begin the serious business of extracting the oil. Other countries also found that they were suddenly on the guest list of the major oil giants as deposits in South America and Africa also became of interest.

Use CD- or Internet-based resources to research the background to this statement, then:

1. Explain what market changes took place that made it worthwhile to start extracting oil from Alaska and the North Sea.
2. Explain how the Middle Eastern producers could have kept control of the market so that further exploration would not have been worthwhile.

Key Skills IT3.1

Factors which vary competitiveness of markets

Supply and demand will interact to bring about market price. This is called the equilibrium price by economists and is the price at which there are no market forces pushing price in either direction. The point at which this price settles will depend on the strength of demand and the willingness of businesses to supply at particular prices. The equilibrium point is shown as the point where demand and supply intersect (Figure 2.9)

A major influence on the price will be the type of market in which the product is traded. Some markets are very competitive, with a lot of small

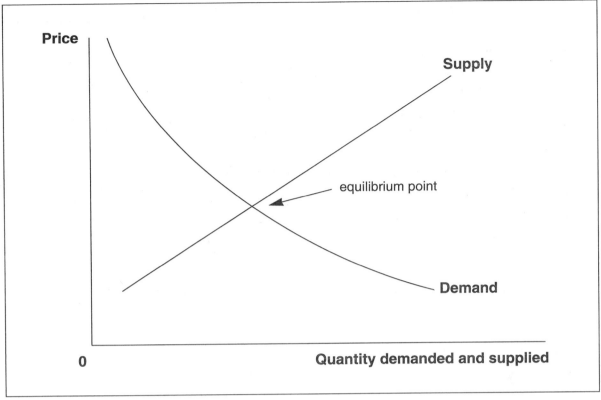

FIGURE 2.9 *Equilibrium*

businesses all competing against one another. Some are highly uncompetitive, dominated by a single or a few producers.

- The power of the **consumer** is greatest in those markets where there is a lot of competition and therefore a lot of choice of suppliers. This is even more true where there are a lot of alternative or substitute products.

- The power of the **supplier** is highest in those markets with a few suppliers and where the product has few or no substitutes. It is highest where there is only one supplier and the product has no substitutes.

Markets exist at both extremes of this scale and the influence which any particular business may have varies considerably with the market organisation that it is in. Some businesses can dictate the price in their market – these are price **makers**. Some must accept the price that is made. These are price **takers**.

Figure 2.10 shows the range of different types of market. The further towards pure monopoly, the less competitive is the market. The further towards perfect competition, the more competitive. Businesses need to know what sort of market structure they are in to be able to predict what competitors will do.

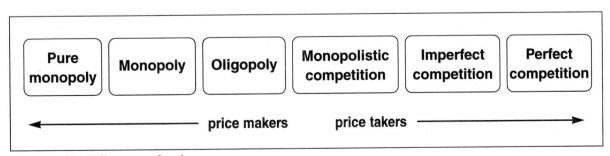

FIGURE 2.10 *Different types of market*

ACTIVITY ④

Imagine that you have gone into business for yourself. The product you are selling is a new invention, an alternative to petrol. You need to charge a minimum of 10p a litre to cover your costs. Petrol is priced at £1 a litre. Decide what price you would charge if:

■ you are the only business selling the product

■ you are one of just three businesses selling the product

■ you are one of over a hundred businesses selling the product.

Give reasons for your choice of price in each case.

What action could you take to protect your market in each case?

FIGURE 2.11 *Waddington's Monopoly is won when one player has control of the board – so, in a market, if one player has control, a monopoly is created* *Source: CORBIS*

Markets defined by market power

Your answers to the activity should give you some insight into the characteristics of certain markets. Market types are:

Monopoly

The most uncompetitive market is that dominated by a single producer. An ordinary monopoly is defined as a single producer having control over 25 per cent of the market for a good or service. In fact, much less than this is necessary to control a market if all the other businesses in it each have only a small percentage of the market share. The monopoly position can be defended by raising barriers to stop other businesses entering the market. These include:

● patents protecting specific inventions

● sole access to a particular form of technology or source of raw materials

● lower costs due to producing in large amounts

● excess profits which can then be devoted to research and development.

In the case of a pure monopoly there is only one business in the industry. In effect, the business is the industry. The idea of pure monopoly is used as a yardstick against which to measure the extent of monopoly power that a business actually has. True pure monopolies are extremely rare.

Oligopoly

In this case the market is dominated by a few businesses each of which has a large share of the market. Some of the features of oligopoly are:

● the major companies compete with each other, but not always on the basis of price

● price wars might happen if businesses lower prices in competition with each other so oligopolies have a tendency towards price stability because of this interdependence

● although in the UK the practice is illegal, businesses in an oligopoly will often collude with each other to agree, privately, to fix prices or supply at particular levels.

Supermarket chains in the UK are a good example of this sort of market. There are a few major players – such as Tesco, Asda, Sainsbury, Morrison and Safeway – which dominate the market.

Monopolistic competition

There are many businesses in the market, each selling differentiated products. Generally, competition is on the basis of one brand versus another. There is free entry and exit into the market although companies will try to erect barriers through, for example, advertising and brand loyalty.

Imperfect competition

This is the most usual type of market. There are a large number of different businesses and a lot of consumer choice. Consumers seldom, however, have information as to exactly what prices are being charged and where, and will take other – non-price – factors into account, such as convenience and service.

Perfect competition

The theoretical opposite of pure monopoly and, again, extremely rare. It is a market extreme that is used as a yardstick in the same way as a pure monopoly. In perfect competition:

- these are a large number of sellers and buyers in the market
- no business has control over the market
- products are exactly the same (called homogenous products)
- consumers have perfect information regarding price and availability.

The fact that perfect markets do not exist is due to businesses deliberately making their products different to try to make them sell better. They may not be able to compete on price or quality but may offer 'friendly service' or 'convenience' to differentiate their products.

FIGURE 2.12 *How would you decide which one to buy? In perfect competition, the products are identical*

Becoming more competitive

Look back at the last activity. How did you decide to price your product? What factors affected your decision? What would you have liked to change? It is likely that, with no competition, you charged a high price. Did you think of coming to an agreement with the other two suppliers in the second case so that you could keep price high? Did you decide to try to make your product different from the competition in the final case? Could you brand it? Offer premium service? Businesses are always looking for ways to improve their position in the market. They will become more competitive by:

- making changes to products
- making changes to prices
- taking more power in the market.

Changing products

- **Adding value.** Businesses will try to add value to their product. Sometimes this will be in the short term, through promotions or special offers. 'Three for two', '10 per cent extra', 'buy one, get one free' are examples. Sometimes this will be a long-term policy. For example, the business may be able to obtain better or purer raw materials. Other ways of adding value may be to increase the performance of a product or to provide additional extras. 'Now cleans even better' or 'stereo and sunroof included' could be examples of this.

- **Improving quality.** By quality the business means 'fitness for purpose'. A quality product is one that exactly fits customer requirements. If changes can be made that bring the product closer to what the customer wants, this is an improvement in quality. Long-term techniques for adding value may also improve the quality of a product.

- **Product differentiation.** The idea is to make a product or service distinctive from its competitors. This may be achieved through advertising, packaging or branding. A strong brand will achieve differentiation. Product differentiation allows businesses to take a greater market share by providing different products for different parts of the market. For example, Unilever produces fabric cleaning products under the brand names of Persil, Surf and Radion.

The strongest brands become generic terms – Biro and Hoover started out as brand names for ballpoint pens and vacuum cleaners respectively. Some manufacturers ensure that it is the company name or logo design which gives them their strong brand image. Examples include particular colour schemes such as that used by McDonald's, logos such as the Adidas three stripes and the distinctive font in which businesses like Cadbury's and Coca Cola write their names. Other companies have strongly branded products (Whiskas, the cat food, is made by Pedigree Foods).

- **Advertising.** Advertising and promotion are used to try to make the individual want a particular product. Advertising is designed to change tastes or to make a product more 'fashionable'. Products are made to appeal to different segments of the market or to different tastes. Advertising can be closely linked to both promotion and product differentiation. Good advertising is essential to establish and maintain a brand name and image.

Changing prices

Particular pricing policies may be used by businesses to give products a 'boost'. They may be used to provide a short-term increase in sales or to maintain sales in the longer term. They may even be used in an attempt to drive competitors out of business. These include:

- **Promotional pricing.** A special price is charged for (usually) a short period of time.
- **Loss leaders.** An even more specialised form of promotional pricing where the product is sold at less than it cost to produce it. This is used to attract buyers into a particular market. For example, supermarkets often run loss leaders on staples such as bread, to entice buyers into a store.

- **Destruction pricing.** This is where prices are driven down really low in an attempt to force a competitor out of business.
- **Penetration pricing.** This is charging a special low price in order to gain market share. It is usually used by a new entrant to a market.
- **Skimming.** This is charging an initially high price on a new product. Typical examples have been video cameras and mobile telephones. Some people are willing to pay the high price to be 'first' with the new product. As the market grows, prices fall.

Taking power in the market

Businesses will decide to grow for a number of different reasons, including:

- to take over competition
- to protect themselves from competitors in the market
- to be able to gain scale economies.

 **Top Tips**

A *take-over* is where a dominant business takes over a smaller or weaker business. A take-over implies that the rival did not wish to be taken over but this is not always the case. A *merger* is where two businesses agree to merge for their mutual benefit.

Taking over competition

A take-over happens when a business bids for enough of its rival's shares for it to be able to take control. By taking over a business, the predator firm may gain a larger part of the market. It may gain enough of a market to become a price maker or even to have monopoly powers.

Protection from competitors

Two businesses may decide to merge in order to present a better challenge to competitors or to protect themselves from competitors' pricing policies or attempts to gain market share.

The gains from such mergers when the partners have a good 'fit' in terms of operations and management can be immense. For example, take the first major merger of the new millennium, between America On Line (AOL), the Internet service provider (ISP) and Time Warner. The two businesses bring together all aspects of the new technologies:

● AOL's Internet service provision is linked to Warner's entertainment provision

● AOL's 20 million on-line customers who use the ISP will provide an audience for Time Warner's television, film and magazine interests. These include *Time* magazine, the news channel CNN and the Warner Brothers film company

● Time Warner's existing customers will use the AOL ISP.

In order to compete with such giants, it is likely that other mergers will take place. BSkyB, the satellite broadcast company, has been in talks with the French Canal Plus television company. Businesses like Freeserve, the free Internet Service Provider, has thousands of customers but little revenue and would be a perfect partner for a content or entertainment provider.

Scale economies

These are gained through producing a large amount of a product. Businesses can often gain by being able to, for example:

● streamline production processes

● use specialist processes and labour

● buy large amounts of raw materials.

 **ACTIVITY** **5**

1. **Look in current newspapers for a take-over or merger that has just happened or is about to happen. Find evidence that covers the story over several days or weeks and includes both facts and figures. You will find that major** mergers are covered in both news and financial sections while minor ones are only covered in the financial pages.

2. **Having chosen your merger, decide, on the basis of the evidence that you have collected, what benefits the new company will bring, and to whom.**

3. **On the basis of your answer to the last question, explain whether the merger should or should not be allowed to go ahead.**

Key Skills C3.2

 **Top Tips**

Synergy is an important concept for businesses wishing to join together. Synergy means that putting two parts together actually produces a better third part. Put simply, it means that one plus one equals more than two. For example, a bank merging with a building society could produce a much better business.

Stakeholders and competition

The use of any or all of these tactics – changing products, prices or the structure of the market – will also affect the stakeholders in the market. These include owners, shareholders, employees, the community in which the business operates, consumers and suppliers.

Different groups of stakeholders will have different opinions on the type of market which is most beneficial to them.

● **Owners** may seek satisficing targets or maximising targets such as market share or profits.

● **Shareholders** may prefer to see the best return possible on their investment.

● **Employees** may prefer to work for a large business and one that has some power in the market in the hope that this will bring them job security and chances of internal promotion. A small business may be able to offer a lot of less tangible benefits, such as a friendly working atmosphere, but it is likely to be the bigger business that provides better facilities, promotion routes and pension arrangements.

- The **community** will have a range of views. Take the example of a new supermarket development proposed to take place in a rural village. This will provide employment, convenience, variety and low prices. On the other hand, there will be increases in traffic and local suppliers and shopkeepers may well be put out of business. Part of the community will benefit from the development but a part will suffer costs.

- **Consumers** will be interested in maintaining the market structure that will give them the most choice, best prices and best value for money. Sometimes competitive markets will provide this. Sometimes, however, what the consumer wants can only be provided by monopolies using excess profits to develop new products and processes. Such research and development does not tend to take place in competitive markets. Consumers may also prefer differentiated and branded products, believing them to provide greater choice and a guarantee of quality and consistency.

- **Suppliers** will want regular orders and prompt payments. These may be more likely to come from larger firms in the market.

The changing pattern of industry

Markets are very dynamic, always changing. This means that the pattern of industry is also dynamic. Over a period of time the structure of industry is likely to alter dramatically. Industry consists of three stages, corresponding to stages in the production process:

- primary industry – the extraction or collection of raw materials
- secondary industry – manufacturing, making, building
- tertiary industry – services.

Countries pass through various stages of development, from agricultural to mass consumer markets. They also change the countries with which they trade. This will have an effect on businesses and markets within the country. International and global changes will also have an effect.

Changing UK trade

The UK, as head of the Commonwealth, has traditionally conducted much trade with the countries of the Commonwealth, and received favourable trading terms from them. Trade with New Zealand, Australia and the Indian sub-continent formed the basis for much of the UK's trade well into the 1980s. Much of our trade has also been with the countries of Europe. Since joining the EU, Britain's main trading partners are now within the Union. 53 per cent of UK trade takes place within the single market.

Changing UK industry

In the UK, industrial development relied heavily on the country's own raw materials. This led to large sectors of basic industry such as coal, steel and shipbuilding. As other countries industrialised, and began to compete, these industries declined in the UK. As industrialisation continued, there was a growth of manufacturing industry, such as cars and textiles. Finally, manufacturing has been replaced with service industries. As some industries grow, others decline.

Coal and steel collapsed in the 1980s with wholesale closures and redundancies. There is less demand for coal as other forms of power have taken over, and it is imported more cheaply from abroad.

Following the decline in primary industry came a decline in manufacturing. As other countries across the world began to manufacture and compete in traditional UK strongholds such as textiles, home production declined. Manufacturing, particularly in labour-intensive industries, can be carried out much more inexpensively in countries with a large supply of cheap labour.

At the same time the service sector has become the main employer – this includes travel and tourism, entertainment, insurance and commercial services, transport services, banking, and futures markets. Table 2.1 and Figure 2.13 show some of the changes in employment patterns in the UK in the last century.

	1911	1999
% Jobs in agriculture	8.1%	1.1%
% Jobs in mining and quarrying	9%	1%
% Jobs in manufacturing	34%	17.5%
% Jobs in services	46.5%	75.8%

TABLE 2.1

Changing global industry

Many companies now seek not just national markets but global ones. Improvements in transport and giant advances in information and communications technology have allowed businesses to set their sights on operating in a world context rather than a local or national one. Global markets may be accessed through global sales, global distribution, global production or global services.

● **Global sales.** Some companies produce in one location or country, and sell products around the globe. A typical example is the giant Boeing Corporation, which does not employ any regional or other national production facilities.

● **Global distribution.** This may be through the promotion of a global brand such as Adidas, Nike or Coca Cola or by using franchises on a worldwide basis like McDonald's.

● **Global production.** Having production units in a number of different markets. This is often to take advantage of different labour costs, taxation, or other national legislation. Sometimes it is so that producers can access markets that would otherwise be protected from them. Businesses have to produce within the European Union in order to access the single market without tariff barriers. Examples include the Ford Motor Company and Nissan.

● **Global services.** Some companies promote a particular service or level of service as an international brand. Hotel chains such as the Hilton group have hotels in many parts of the world, all providing service and accommodation to the same standard.

● **Combinations.** The ways in which a global company is global are not always particularly clear-cut. Heinz, for example, has recognised global sales of a global brand name (over 50 affiliated companies producing, marketing or

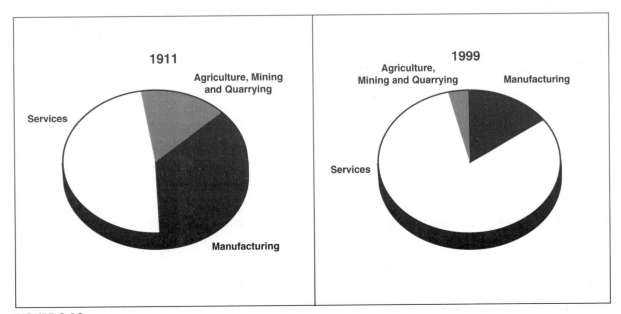

FIGURE 2.13

distributing) and now has not 57 varieties but over 5,000 products. However, it still has its roots and control firmly in America.

 ACTIVITY 6

Coca Cola is to axe around 5,200 jobs in various operations around the world, it was announced recently. 2,500 will go from the Atlanta headquarters of the giant corporation while the other 2,700 will be scattered around the world. The company, which has just over half of the global market in soft drinks, made a loss of $45 million in the three months to the end of 1999. This was mainly due to a contamination scare that affected sales in Belgium and France. The previous chairman has stepped down after criticism from the major shareholder and the new chief is being advised to tone down some of the more aggressive forecasts made by his predecessor. It finally looks like Coca Cola's seemingly unstoppable march to take over the world soft drinks market is slowly coming to a halt.

1. Why do you think that Coca Cola is cutting so many jobs?

2. Who do you think will feel the impact the most, Atlanta, Georgia or worldwide operations?

3. Obtain a copy of Coca Cola's latest company report and visit its website. Does this information back up your view?

4. From the information above and that which you have collected, outline what Coca Cola's current main problems are.

5. Would you recommend anyone to buy shares in Coca Cola? Why?

 *Self-Test Questions*

1 List the different markets in which businesses operate and give an example of one business in each market.

2 Explain how demand side factors affect price in a market.

3 Explain how supply side factors affect price in a market.

4 Outline the factors that affect the amount of competition in markets.

5 Explain how businesses seek to manage the competitiveness of the markets in which they operate.

Section 2 *Business and government policy*

What you need to learn

In this section you will learn about:

- how and why the government intervenes in markets
- the work of the Competition Commission
- how governments protect consumers
- how and why government is involved in environmental, social and ethical issues
- the role of the European Union in social legislation.

producers. It might be said that a number of groups which make up the electorate are stakeholders in the success of the UK.

- Employers and employees, consumers and producers, importers and exporters, business, commerce and industry all have reasons for wanting stable government. They may also have reasons for wanting the government to pass particular resolutions and legislation that will affect them favourably.
- Certain groups within the economy will have greater or less power than other groups. Such

	LOCAL	REGIONAL	NATIONAL	INTERNATIONAL
Myself				
Businesses				

TABLE 2.2

 ACTIVITY

1. Draw up four columns as shown in Table 2.2 and list all the ways in which government has an impact on your life.
2. Now do the same for all the ways in which government has an influence on business.
3. Compare your finished charts with those of a partner to see if you have missed anything out.
4. What do your finished charts tell you about the importance of government to businesses?

Stakeholders

Governments are responsible for the welfare of their citizens both as consumers and as

groups may include single issue pressure groups, opposition political parties and permanent groupings such as the Confederation of British Industry and the Trades Union Congress.

- The government has a commitment to its international trading partners. These include the other members of the Commonwealth and, in particular, the European Union. Indeed, the EU is able to overrule the domestic government on a number of issues through the international court. EU issues are dealt with in Section 3.

As with all stakeholder groups, there will be conflict between objectives and there will always be winners and losers from any government legislation.

ACTIVITY 8

Whatmore Products was a business operating in the UK. It produced agricultural fertiliser in rural Norfolk. The owners employed local labour on a casual basis. They used the River Beck to dispose of unwanted chemicals. Local people objected to this but had no power to stop the business. The business hit the headlines when a man had a hand severed in an accident. The business had no insurance and, as the man paid no tax or National Insurance on his earnings, he was not entitled to any benefits.

1. **With a partner, discuss whether you think that any part of this situation could arise in the UK today.**
2. **Explain what you think that government has done to prevent situations like these.**

The role of government

Government intervenes in business and in the operation of markets for a number of reasons:

● to ensure that business is carried out legally and fairly
● to support and protect businesses
● to manage the effects of market changes on stakeholders such as employees, consumers, suppliers and the community.

Government has a role as controller of the national economy. The policies used for this control will, inevitably, have an impact on businesses.

Government has a role in ensuring that:

● some social and community needs are met
● businesses don't damage the environment
● businesses act ethically.

Government may be local, national or international. In particular, the EU will have an effect on businesses in the UK.

The government aims to strike a balance between the amount of intervention that is necessary for social, political and paternal reasons, and the amount of intervention that it considers is best

FIGURE 2.14 *The High Court in London is one of the main courts where business disputes and problems may be settled*

Source: PA Photos

for economic reasons. It has a duty to legislate on behalf of the public but also does not want to intervene too heavily where market forces are operating effectively. Intervention can become so restrictive that it reduces business innovation and discourages entrepreneurialism.

Legal and fair

Government intervenes in business and in the operation of markets to ensure that business is carried out legally and fairly. It provides a framework for the operation of business which is both legal and social. It encourages businesses:

● to trade fairly

● to be open in their dealings

● to pay their debts.

It provides mechanisms for businesses to recover debt. It provides protection from unfair business advantage. As well as this general framework, there may be specific areas where government intervenes in markets. Each market structure, from monopoly to competition, provides governments with a reason to intervene.

Monopolies have the power to:

● control supply

● fix price

● charge what they will

● make excessive profits and not put them back in terms of research and development

● be very inefficient and wasteful of resources – if there is a lack of competition, there is a lack of any reason to be efficient or innovative.

Duopolies and oligopolies can collude to fix prices or to limit supply. They have to compete on a non-price basis, wasting money and resources on exercises such as advertising and branding that add no value, use or utility to the product. These exercises are ultimately paid for by the consumer or the economy.

Imperfect competition wastes resources on marketing exercises such as product differentiation and branding while not really providing the consumer with any additional choice.

Perfect markets don't exist because it is in the market's interest to make them imperfect – this involves wasteful attempts at product differentiation.

Government intervention

Governments intervene to make markets operate in a manner that is more fair and equitable. They discourage restrictive practices and encourage competition. Monopolies and mergers are investigated to see if the business is against the public interest.

Restrictive practices happen where businesses interfere with the normal working of markets to the disadvantage of the consumer. They include cartels, where there is agreement in a market between two supposed competitors to fix either price or supply or both. They also include practices where suppliers could dictate prices to retailers.

The Competition Act 1980:

● regulates agreements between suppliers, distributors and retailers to ensure that they are in the best interests of the consumer.

● makes anti-competitive practices, such as cartels, illegal and increases the fines for this sort of practice to a massive 10 per cent of turnover.

● prevents suppliers from dictating prices to retailers.

The Restrictive Practices Court (RPC) looks into allegations of unfair practices.

The Competition Commission (CC) used to be the Monopolies and Mergers Commission. It is a body set up by government to investigate proposed mergers. If the merger would result in a monopoly situation it can prevent it. This is if the CC judges the merger to be against the interests of consumers. It also investigates monopolies to make sure that they are not operating against the public interest.

The Office of Fair Trading (OFT) has powers to look into market operations and decide whether actions are being taken in the public interest. It provides the government with advice on monopolies, mergers and restrictive practices. It can recommend which mergers or industries are referred to the Competition Commission for investigation. The OFT also supports the consumer by:

● watching consumer affairs in general

● suggesting and negotiating codes of practice to regulate industries

● acting against those who break current legislation

● dealing with any trading practices which are or appear to be unfair to consumers.

Support and protection

Government intervenes in business and in the operation of markets to support and protect businesses. Parts of government are dedicated to helping businesses. They also set up organisations to support businesses.

● The Department of Trade and Industry (DTI) provides a range of help and advice to small businesses. Its booklet 'A Guide to Help for Small Businesses' may be obtained on application.

● Business Links (called Business Connect in Wales and Business Shop in Scotland) are partnerships between TECs (Training and Enterprise Councils), chambers of commerce, enterprise agencies and local authorities. They help both new and existing small businesses by providing training in business skills, counselling, information and advice. Advice can be gained on a range of problems which confront new businesses, such as finding suitable premises, drawing up a business plan and being aware of and complying with business law. Your local Business Link organisation can be contacted through www.businesslink.co.uk.

Top Tips

Training and Enterprise Councils were set up by government to cover the UK. They are involved in making grants to small businesses, providing training and generally giving help to people who want to establish new businesses. They are gradually being replaced by Learning and Skills Councils (LSCs).

Managing the effects of market changes

Government intervenes in business and in the operation of markets to manage the effects of market changes on stakeholders such as employees, customers, shareholders, suppliers and the community.

Employees

Government has responsibilities towards business and employment. It passes laws to protect employees from dangerous or unhealthy practices and conditions. It gives employees certain rights and responsibilities. It is involved in providing employment opportunities through legislation such as the New Deal. This was introduced in 1998 and is designed to help employers to employ young people. Employers receive a grant of £60 per week for the first six months that they employ an unemployed person between the ages of 18 and 24 who has been unemployed for more than six months. EU legislation also helps to make workers' lives better through legislation such as the Social Chapter. This includes measures such as:

● parental leave when a new child is born

● the Working Time Directive, to limit the length of the working week

● worker representation in business decision-making.

Customers

Customers are protected through consumer protection legislation. The government acts to protect consumers from unfair or illegal practices and from shoddy or unserviceable goods or services. There are various laws to protect consumers:

- The Sale of Goods Act 1979 and the Supply of Goods and Services Act 1982 regulate agreements made between buyers and sellers. Under these Acts:
  - goods and services must be fit for the purpose for which they are sold – a hair-straightening product should straighten hair; a three-minute timer should run for three minutes
  - goods and services must be of satisfactory quality – products must be safe to use (e.g. electrical products correctly wired)
  - goods and services must correspond to their description
  - services must be of a reasonable standard.

- The acts also give the consumer the right to assume that the seller has a right to sell the goods or services.

- The Consumer Credit Act 1974 protects consumers in relation to credit agreements used to buy goods and services.

- The Unsolicited Goods and Services Act 1971 states that recipients need not pay for, or return, unsolicited goods. The sender has to collect them within six months of delivery, or within 30 days of being notified that they require collection. Otherwise, they become the property of the recipient.

- The Trade Descriptions Acts 1968 and 1972 cover descriptions of goods by a seller to a buyer, where the goods are sold in the course of business. (It does not cover private sales between individuals, such as for the sale of a second-hand fridge.) The description on the packaging or given by the seller must not be false.

- The Food Safety Act 1990 governs the sale of food and makes it illegal for businesses to sell food which is unfit for human consumption, is sub-standard, or is incorrectly labelled.

- The Consumer Protection Act 1987 stops businesses giving misleading information

FIGURE. 2.15 *West Yorkshire Trading Standards Service's magazine*

about goods, services, accommodation or facilities. It also makes manufacturers liable for product defects which cause injury or loss.

All consumer protection legislation affects businesses because they have to conform to regulations or face court action. This may increase costs in some industries, for example, because of having to conform to particular safety or hygiene regulations. Some changes are resisted (as when HGV drivers' hours were first monitored by the tachograph and their hours restricted), while others are welcomed.

 **Top Tips**

Your local council or, in some cases, a group of local councils, will provide a trading standards service. This covers inspections, publicity and issues such as safety and consumer complaints. Some have websites and produce magazines (see Figure 2.15). Look in *Yellow Pages* for your local group and contact it for up-to-date information.

Shareholders

It is important to business that shareholders are confident enough to buy shares.

The government's role in this includes creating a stable environment in which business can take place. Good economic management should mean that many of the uncertainties that would prevent people from buying shares have been removed.

It is the government that insists that all dealings of limited companies should be 'transparent' This is so that shareholders are able to obtain company information and accounts before committing any money to that business.

● The government has also encouraged wider share ownership through the sale of public companies into the private sector (privatisation).

Suppliers

Suppliers need stable conditions as much as shareholders do.

● Government legislation is designed to ensure that suppliers can extend credit without fear of not being paid. Without this, business would be impossible.

● Government also intervenes to restrict supply from abroad if such supply is

– heavily subsidised and therefore competing unfairly

– from a country with a poor political record (for example, human rights abuses)

– from a country not following environmental agreements.

The community

Businesses have responsibilities to the communities in which they are established.

Businesses not only provide employment, but, in doing so, become a vital part of the infrastructure of a location. The income directly generated by the business is multiplied as it is spent in the community and entire regions can come to be dependent on single industries.

Government can encourage employment in a region through grants and subsidies.

It can discourage practices likely to harm the community, such as pollution.

Economic control

Government has the role of controller of the national economy. Economic policies will, inevitably, have an impact on businesses. The purpose of economic policy is to try to create a balanced economy, within which business can operate. The four main aims of the UK government (similar to the aims of many 'Western' governments) are usually listed as being:

● full employment – or as near to this ideal as is practicable

● a favourable balance of payments – the balance between income from exports and payments for imports

● stable prices – either low or no inflation

● economic growth – hopefully with a consequent rise in individual income and wealth.

Each of these aims is designed so that business can operate in a climate of certainty rather than uncertainty. Businesses can be devastated by the rising prices of inflation, or by problems with overseas trade. They can suffer if there is a lack of growth in the economy. Unemployment means a lack of demand for products, while too many imports mean that business is going abroad. A beneficial exchange rate can encourage people to spend more on imported goods than on home-produced ones, causing unemployment.

Full employment

Governments aim to ensure that there are jobs for all who want them. If someone is employed they are contributing to the economy through:

- taxation
- production
- expenditure on goods and services (creating more jobs).

If someone is unemployed they are likely to be taking money out of the economy in terms of unemployment benefits or social security payments. Full employment can have an adverse effect on businesses. If there is a shortage of labour, this could mean that labour prices are pushed up, making businesses reluctant to employ. Unemployment means lower levels of demand.

The government has tackled some forms of unemployment by creating schemes to help small businesses to set up. It also guarantees bank loans through the Loan Guarantee Scheme. The operation of this scheme is that the government will pay banks back 80 per cent of a loan if a new venture fails. The cost is a loan interest premium paid by the borrower. The government have also introduced the New Deal scheme for young unemployed people.

Government has a role to play in ensuring the quality of labour. Businesses need well-trained and well-educated recruits if they are to compete effectively. The education system can play a large part in this process. Recent UK governments have changed the emphasis of the National Curriculum so that subjects such as science and technology have a higher profile and extra funds are available for people wanting to train to teach certain subjects, such as information technology.

Balance of payments

This is the balance between money earned from abroad by exports and money spent on imports. It is usually presented in a standard two-part format. The first part is the balance on current account and the second the capital account. The current account shows the balance of trade (goods imported and exported) and the invisibles balance (services imported and exported). The capital balance show inflows and outflows of currency for capital investment. For example, Nissan building a plant in Wales is a capital inflow; ICI building a plant in Holland a capital outflow. The totals show whether the UK is earning more from abroad than it is paying out abroad. A balance of payments deficit occurs when more is spent on imports than is earned from a exports; a surplus when more is earned from exporting than is spent on imports.

The balance of payments is closely linked to the exchange rate. A floating exchange rate, such as the pound sterling, will provide an automatic adjustment to balance of payments imbalances. A deficit would see the exchange rate pushed downwards, leading to an automatic 'correction' (look at the effect in Activity 12); a surplus would see the exchange rate alter to make exports more expensive and imports cheaper.

Stable prices

A period of continuously rising prices is known as inflation. Because of the damaging effects that inflation can have on businesses, government has often sought to make control of inflation its main priority. Rising prices lead to:

- business uncertainty – businesses will find it hard to plan and predict
- increased price sensitivity – consumers will be more likely to seek cheaper substitutes as prices rise

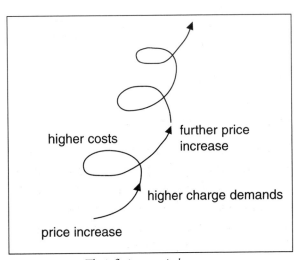

FIGURE 2.16 *The inflationary spiral*

- wage inflation – workers will seek pay rises to cover the increased cost of living
- less international trade – UK products become more expensive in international markets.

At its worst, inflation forms a 'spiral' of increasing prices (see Figure 2.16).

Economic growth

This is measured as the increase in total output of products in a year. It is used as an indicator of increasing efficiency and increasing wealth. Generally, the higher the levels of economic growth, the 'better off' the population of the country will be. The business cycle in the UK (see Figure 2.17) shows how growth tends to fluctuate from 'booms' to 'slumps'. Government will try to iron out these fluctuations and keep the trend of growth upwards.

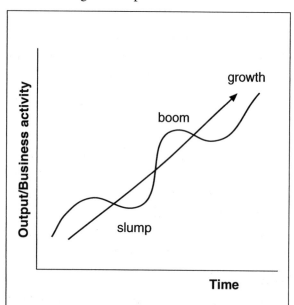

FIGURE 2.17

1. **Look at the four aims of government; now decide which is the most important and why, and which is the least important and why.**
2. **Collect information to support your points of view, including graphs and charts where applicable.**

3. **Make a presentation to your class or group which outlines your positions and your reasons for them.**

Key Skills C3.1b, C3.2

Types of government policy

Government economic policies are carried out using:

- fiscal policy – those which involve variations in government spending and in levels and types of taxation
- monetary policy – regulating the supply of money in the economy
- interest rates – now regulated by the Bank of England
- regional policy
- exchange rate policy – changes to the value of the currency in international terms.

Some policies may also be seen as more politically motivated. Many of these will still have economic effects and effects on businesses.

Fiscal policy

This consists of the government's 'tax and spend' plans. The amount of money to be raised in

FIGURE 2.18 *The Chancellor on Budget Day* *Source: PA Photos*

taxation, and where it is to be spent, is outlined in the Chancellor's annual Budget. The effect on business is felt through changes in:

- taxation
- government expenditure.

Direct taxes are on individual or company income. These are income tax and corporation tax. The statements below assume an increase in tax. A decrease would have the opposite effect. Businesses will be affected by:

- increases in personal direct taxation (people having less to spend)
- increases in corporation tax (businesses keeping less of their profits).

Indirect taxes are levied on products such as VAT on purchases or duty on tobacco and alcohol. Businesses will be affected by specific increases (such as a cigarette manufacturer) or by a general increase (for example in VAT).

Taxation increases may be absorbed by businesses or passed on to the consumer. This will depend on the elasticity of demand or supply for the product. Generally, monopoly and oligopoly suppliers are able to pass tax increases on to the consumer while in more competitive markets the increase has to be absorbed by the business which will reduce profits.

ACTIVITY ⑩

Find out all you can about the latest Budget measures. You will need to identify the information that you require and then find suitable IT sources for the information – these could include on-line newspapers, the government's website (the Treasury site is www.hm-treasury.gov.uk) and comments from interested parties.

- **Carry out a number of searches to obtain the information that you need.**
- **Select the information that you need and**

present it in two ways; first so that it highlights all the 'good' points of the Budget to businesses, i.e. supports the government; secondly so that it highlights all the 'bad' points, i.e. is opposed to the government.

- **You could develop the two versions into presentations to reach Communications Key Skills levels.**

Monetary policy

Monetary policy involves regulating the supply of money in the economy and controlling credit and interest rates. If the money supply is reduced or 'squeezed', this means less money in the economy and therefore a brake on spending. This has an obvious effect on businesses because demand for products is reduced.

Alterations in monetary policy that will affect businesses include:

- changes in interest rates (now under the control of the Bank of England)
- changes in credit regulations, leading to credit being easier or harder to obtain
- other direct policies to change money supply.

Interest rates

One of the first actions of the Chancellor in the newly elected Labour government of May 1997 was to take the control of interest rates out of government hands and to give it to the Bank of England. This was so that interest rates should only be changed for economic reasons, not for political ones.

A nine-person-strong committee of the Bank of England meets on a monthly basis to review the state of the economy and the levels and directions of current economic indicators. It then makes a decision as to whether the economy needs to be 'speeded up', 'slowed down' or left alone, and changes interest rates accordingly.

By increasing interest rates, the Bank is making money more 'expensive'. This means that people and businesses will find borrowing more expensive. Business decisions to borrow (for example, for

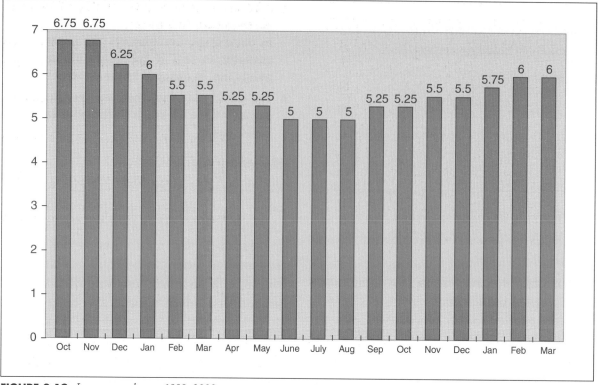

FIGURE 2.19 *Interest rate changes 1999–2000*

expansion) may be postponed or cancelled. Consumer decisions to purchase may be similarly affected. On the other hand, saving will be a more attractive proposition if interest rates are higher.

A reduction in interest rates will have the opposite set of effects. It is likely to bring borrowing decisions forward and encourage spending. Lower interest rates are seen as being better for businesses than high ones, enabling them to borrow easily and cheaply.

The rate of interest can be used to 'fine tune' the economy and has, since 1997, tended to be moved in half- or quarter-point 'jumps' only (see Figure 2.19).

ACTIVITY ⑪

Three S Robots has a factory in Hull. It manufactures industrial robot parts for use in the car industry. Half of its production is sold to plants in the UK. The rest is sold in Europe and North America. Explain what effect each of the following would be likely to have on the business. Think about the business itself, its industrial customers and the final consumer.

1. Increase in rates of interest.

2. Increase in the value of the pound.

3. Increase in taxation on spending.

4. Increase in taxation on income.

5. Increase in imported robot parts.

Regional policy

Government may make certain areas more attractive for the location of businesses. It may do this through tax incentives or through grants. Usually such payments are linked to areas of high unemployment or industrial decline and are designed to attract jobs to the area.

The European Union also operates a regional policy to help depressed areas of the Union.

Exchange rate policy

The exchange rate refers to the worth of a currency in terms of other currencies. In the UK the exchange rate is not altered directly; the

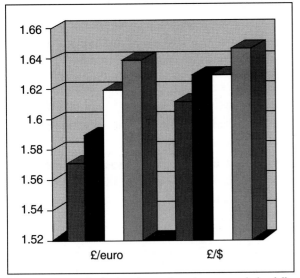

FIGURE 2.20 *Sterling's value against the euro and the dollar (January to April 2000)*

currency is allowed to find its own level as a reflection of the strength of the economy and the level of interest rates. Currencies which tend to fluctuate a lot can cause a great deal of uncertainty for businesses. and, as can be seen from Figure 2.20, sterling has not remained particularly stable.

Governments can intervene directly in currency markets to affect the price of a currency by buying or selling it. Speculators will also buy and sell currency for profit on international money markets. Fluctuations in a currency's value can be caused if speculators lose confidence in a particular currency and start selling it.

ACTIVITY 12

Work out the differences to the following transactions if the exchange rate is:

- **£1 = $2**
- **£1 = $2.5 (a stronger pound)**
- **£1 = $1.5 (a weaker pound).**

In each case, state what the implications of the change in exchange rate are for the importer and the exporter.

1. A UK exporter intends to sell £100,000 worth of machinery to America.

   The exporter will only accept sterling, not dollars (as these would have to be converted to sterling anyway).

   The US importer pays in sterling, bought with dollars.

2. A UK importer wishes to buy $100,000 worth of American machinery.

   The American exporter will only accept dollars.

   The UK importer pays in dollars, bought with sterling.

Politically motivated policies

Government may intervene in a belief that it can introduce the benefits of competition to a market. Usually such decisions are motivated more by politics than economic or business reasons. Competition was seen as having greater benefits than state ownership so a programme of privatisation took place.

Privatisation

This is where the government moves an asset from the public sector into the private sector by:

- privatisation – the sale of shares in a previously state-owned industry by offer to members of the public; this was also politically motivated
- competitive tendering – making local services (such as school catering or the local council's refuse collection service) subject to bidding from private groups; this is also part of the strategy of allowing services to be 'contracted out'. Often the groups of employees who were already providing the service have had to join the bidding for the contract – usually awarded on the basis of the lowest price tendered
- sale of assets owned by local or national government – for example the sale of council houses at reduced rates to the tenants who lived in them

- deregulation – removing artificial restrictions on competition, for example, in the area of transport, bus routes were deregulated to allow for competing operators to offer services, giving passengers the choice of which operator to use.

Private Finance Initiative

This scheme involves the government virtually going into partnership with a private business to provide major new capital projects. The government signs what amounts to a 'hire purchase' agreement with private companies. The business pays for a piece of major investment which could be roads, bridges, hospitals, museums or computerisation programmes. PFI projects include the Royal Armouries Museum in Leeds, the computerisation of the Passport Office, the building of 13 new hospitals at a cost of over £1billion and the building of the M1 – A1 link road in Yorkshire. The government pays the business back over an extended time period. In the meantime, the business operates and maintains the investment that it has built, hoping to make a profit out of it. Sometimes these payments are taken from the public directly in the form of fees or tolls.

Environmental, social and ethical legislation

The government also has a role to play in the protection of the environment; in social legislation that should improve the lot of those who are worse off; and in ethical legislation – ensuring that businesses act in a morally acceptable manner.

ACTIVITY **13**

In an effort to bring down the power bills of households and businesses, the government proposes to make the electricity companies lower bills by 10 per cent. According to the Royal Society for the Protection of Birds, this will **mean that people will be discouraged from energy saving and encouraged to use more energy, with the consequences being a greater strain on the environment.**

1. **Explain why you think the government is taking action to lower electricity prices.**
2. **Explain who might be in support of such measures.**
3. **Explain why the RSPB opposes the measure. What other groups do you think you will find in opposition?**

Environmental issues

The environmental issues which most affect businesses are those regarding pollution and those regarding the use of materials that cannot be replaced. In 1992 the Earth Summit in Rio de Janeiro brought together dozens of world leaders from both the developed and the developing worlds. The final statement of this conference became known as Agenda 21. This detailed the various targets for what is known as 'sustainable development'.

- Sustainable development means that the environment is not harmed by production. Throughout the production process steps are taken to ensure that the environment is protected.
- The use of raw materials should be limited, wherever possible, to renewable resources;
- Energy should be produced in a non-polluting manner. More renewable energy sources, such as wind, wave and solar power, should be developed, rather than relying on the burning of carbon fuels. The carbon fuels, like coal and oil, are not renewable.
- Harmful emissions should be reduced and, where possible, cut out completely.

Many of these targets will be reflected in government measures. For example, the government introduced the widespread sale of unleaded petrol; then in January 2000, leaded petrol (4 star) was withdrawn from sale within the EU.

Legislation which is designed to control pollution and 'make the polluter pay' has been passed to try to make sure that businesses are paying all of their costs – not avoiding the social costs of their business or industrial activities. If a company causes pollution while producing a product, then the cost of that pollution should be met by the business.

Policies to encourage one section of industry may, however, harm others. Policies designed to cut down the amount of traffic on the roads, particularly heavy goods traffic, should be of benefit to the rail freight industry. However, such policies, which include increases in road tax and fuel excise duty, may have a detrimental effect on the road haulage industry. If regulations are different in other EU countries, this might cause problems. Many road haulage contractors have threatened to register vehicles in EU countries where vehicle excise duty is a tenth of the levels in the UK. The existence of the Single European Market allows them to do this.

ACTIVITY 14

Consider the following newspaper cutting:

'The government today announced the abolition of road tax. It said that such a tax – collected in the road fund licence – had always been unfair as it penalised those road users who did not make much use of their vehicles. The shortfall in government income would be made up by increasing the taxation on all forms of fuel. "In this way", said a government spokesman, "those who use the roads the most will pay the most for their upkeep while the casual user will pay little." Environmental groups also welcomed the move as it would lead to manufacturers developing more fuel-efficient vehicles. The Road Haulage Association claimed that the move could cost thousands of jobs and lead to higher prices for everyone.'

1. Outline the effect that the new legislation will have on:

■ **low-mileage private car users**

■ **high-mileage private car users**
■ **business car users**
■ **the road haulage industry.**

2. Why does the RHA think that jobs will be lost and prices rise? Do you agree with it?

Social issues

Social reasons for intervening in the market include the production of social and public goods and services. The main features of public goods are that they are available to everyone and that the use by one person does not prevent another from benefiting from the service at the same time. For example, because a fire service is already tackling one blaze should not prevent another part of that service from being available to you if you have a fire emergency.

● Social goods are those which the market would not produce because there is no real way of charging for them.

● This includes include public goods and services like streetlights and road maintenance.

● Other public goods include the police force and the fire service.

● Merit goods like education and health care, which the government believes should be available to everyone, are provided by local or national government and paid for by local or national taxation.

There are also private alternatives to government provision in the form of private health care and fee-paying schools but the government provides a universal service for those who cannot afford the private sector.

Ethical issues

Taking the ethical option means doing the right or moral thing. Some of the ethical decisions which a business will have to take are linked to its social responsibilities. In other cases, a business may wish to act ethically but such a policy may conflict with the objectives of its stakeholders.

The Co-operative Bank, for example, is keen to advertise its credentials as a bank that is ethically sound, refusing to invest in companies or countries that deal in arms, under-pay labour or have otherwise unethical policies. This ethical investment policy may not, however, suit stakeholders if what they want is the best return for their money.

If a company found that it could make more profit by employing cheap labour in a developing country, does it have an ethical or moral duty not to do so? Or a duty to its stakeholders to take the 'least cost' option?

You can see from this how various groups of stakeholders may find their objectives in conflict with other groups. In the case of the Co-operative Bank, the policy has actually attracted many wealthy customers who want to be ethical in their investments and the bank enjoyed large rises in profits in the late 1990s.

The UK government has an ethical foreign policy which states that it will not sell arms or armaments to countries with a repressive government or poor human rights record. Decisions made on who or who not to sell to may be morally correct but could cause businesses to struggle at home and cause unemployment.

Businesses like to be seen as being ethical as it enhances their image. A non-ethical decision could not only tarnish their image but actually cause real damage in the market. Some examples include:

- Barclays Bank suffered over a number of years from a high-profile boycotting campaign due to its involvement in the apartheid regime of South Africa
- petrol companies were affected by various disasters such as the collapse of the Piper Alpha oil drilling platform and the proposal to dispose of the Brent Spar platform by sinking it into the North Sea. In a number of these cases, pressure groups such as Friends of the Earth or Greenpeace become involved in generating publicity

- a recent series of controversies highlighted by such groups has been the gradual introduction of genetically modified (GM) foods by the giant Monsanto Corporation. Some of Monsanto's decisions have been shown to be ethically flawed – providing a particular GM seed that was disease-resistant also meant that it was sterile and farmers would have to buy new stock (from Monsanto) every year. Trials of GM crops were not perceived to be properly conducted and, bowing to public opinion, many major retailers (including the UK's largest supermarket chain, Tesco) have refused to stock GM produce. The business damage to Monsanto has been enormous.

The wood in this product comes from well managed forests, independently certified in accordance with the rules of the Forest Stewardship Council.

CERTIFIED BY SGS QUALIFOR . SGS - 0755/6236/0099

FSC *Trademark* © 1996 *Forest Stewardship Council* A.C.

FIGURE 2.21 *Companies like to advertise their ethical and environmental credentials*

ACTIVITY 15

Figure 2.21 shows the logo and trademark of the Forest Stewardship Council.

1. **Look on product packaging for products that you have in your household to see what other environmental organisations or claims you can find.**

2. **Which of these do you think are voluntary; which are government controlled?**

3. **Which type of regulation do you think is most-effective? Why?**

Codes of practice

Many companies have seen fit to adopt ethical codes of practice and to publish them; some people would say that this is just a marketing ploy and others that business is genuinely trying to 'clean up its act'. The growth in such policies has been rapid; in 1990 just 20 per cent of companies had them; by 2000 this had risen to 55 per cent of major businesses.

European Union role in social policy

The 12 members of the European Economic Community (as it then was) signed the Social Chapter as part of the Maastricht Treaty of 1992. The Maastricht Treaty was designed to bring the Single European Market into existence – removing trade barriers between all member countries.

The intention of the Social Chapter is to bring the same working conditions into being for all workers within the Union. This means that EU standards would apply to:

● health and safety
● working conditions
● the right to belong to a trade union
● the right to strike
● the right for workers to have a say in the plans of the companies for which they work.

Because it includes ideas that may be costly to implement or seen as disadvantageous to employers or employees, the Social Chapter became something of a political football. The Conservative government decided, in 1993, to exercise the UK's right to opt out of the Social Chapter. The 1997 Labour government thought it right to be opted in.

The Social Chapter agrees and imposes directives on member countries to change practices to fall into line with the rest of Europe. The three directives so far are:

● for multi-national companies to set up works councils involving employees so that workers are consulted and participate in decision-making
● for both parents to be entitled to a period of extended leave after the birth of a child
● for the length of the working week to be limited (the Working Time Directive) except in specific exceptional circumstances.

The drawbacks of the Social Chapter include:

● the raising of labour costs to businesses if they have to reduce working hours and/or increase wage rates
● the problems of participation in management of people who are not trained in it
● the fact that some businesses will incur much greater costs than others in implementing the directives.

The government has recognised some of these problems and is trying to ensure that not all changes are implemented at once or immediately. However, as the directives are part of the social legislation of the EU, there is no right of veto – that is, no individual country can prevent the legislation from passing – and member states will be expected to implement the measures as soon as possible.

Apart from the laws affecting employment and workers' rights, there are other laws where the EU is working, thanks to Single Market legislation, towards harmonising taxes and duties. One effect of the Single Market has been the death of the duty-free trade for travel within Europe; another is an attempt to ensure that the rate of VAT is the same in all member countries. Excise duties have also been brought into line so that the same proportion of duty is levied on tobacco and alcohol products to make competition within Union states more fair.

Self-Test Questions

1   Outline the four aims of government.

2   Outline the main areas for government expenditure.

3   Explain the difference between fiscal policy and monetary policy.

4   Explain how exchange rate policy would affect an export business.

5   Outline the arguments for and against privatisation.

6   Explain why governments might intervene in markets under the headings of:

■ social issues

■ environmental issues

■ ethical issues.

7   Outline the main features of the EU Social Chapter. Which bodies are likely to welcome them and which likely to oppose them?

Section 3 *How businesses are affected by international competition*

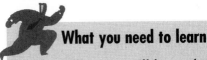

What you need to learn

In this section you will learn about:

- the meaning of international competitiveness
- the developing global economy
- how multi-nationals and trans-nationals compete
- the European Union and the Single Market
- European Monetary Union.

International competitiveness

Many businesses have an international dimension to their operations. In some cases this will be a major part of their operations; in other cases it will be very small. The international dimension will be either in the buying of raw materials, components etc., or in marketing and selling products abroad.

- Businesses may buy raw materials from abroad. Some types of raw material may only be produced in bulk abroad because they need to be grown, or mined, or quarried in a particular place. For example, any firm which uses paper in large quantities, such as a newspaper publisher, is likely to buy it from abroad.

- Businesses may also sell some of their production abroad. Some businesses will have a very small level of exports, perhaps selling just a small part of production to one or two other countries. Others may rely heavily on overseas markets for sales.

Globalisation

International competition has seen a period of rapid growth towards the end of the twentieth century. There are a number of factors behind this.

- Established businesses have sought expanded markets. Often these are only to be found outside their own country.

- Transport has become relatively cheaper. Air freight, in particular, now costs a fraction of what it did in the past.

- Communication has improved. It is now faster, cheaper and more efficient than ever before.

- Political situations have changed. This has opened up vast new markets such as the former USSR and China.

- On the whole, trade has become less restricted. However, there are still problems with this. (See section on the World Trade Organisation (WTO) below.)

When businesses grow sufficiently to operate on a worldwide basis they become known as global concerns. This process of globalisation means that many businesses will source raw materials, capital and labour inputs in those countries where they are cheapest. They will sell products in worldwide markets.

Top Tips

Remember: goods can be seen, services can't. Goods are visible exports and imports; services are invisibles. If you can't work out whether it's an import or an export, see which way the money went; the good or service must have gone in the opposite direction. If an American tourist buys a taxi ride in London, the money has gone from America to the UK. The service can therefore be said to have gone from the UK to America – an invisible export. (What about if a British tourist buys a taxi ride in New York?)

 # ACTIVITY **16**

Look at the following types of business:

- firework manufacturer
- book publisher
- cosmetics manufacturer
- car manufacturer
- jeweller.

1. **List the raw materials that each might use.**
2. **List the countries that these materials might come from.**
3. **What does this tell you about the importance of international trade?**

International competition brings its own problems. Some of these are obvious, such as language, culture and currency problems. The names of products, for example, have to be checked carefully to ensure that they are not offensive in the language of the country to which they are being exported. Rolls-Royce had a problem selling the Silver Mist car in Germany, for example. You could look up 'mist' in German to see why. The government, through the Department of Trade and Industry and the Foreign Office, provides help and advice to businesses competing internationally.

 # ACTIVITY **17**

Speak to someone at your school or college, or in your circle of family and friends, who has lived in another country. Ask them what cultural problems there could be from exporting to the country that they lived in. This will give you an idea of the genuine problems that face businesses.

What problems do you think that you would experience if you went to work and live in another 'non-English-speaking' country

Why compete internationally?

Businesses will wish to compete internationally for a number of reasons.

- Operating in different countries allows companies to take advantage of local markets for their products and services. Domestic markets may be saturated, so that the business can only find opportunities elsewhere. A product considered unsophisticated in a European market may find a take-up in (for example) an African one. The Bayliss clockwork radio is a case in point. In many parts of Africa there is no access to cheap electricity, unlike in Europe. There was therefore a ready market for a radio that ran off clockwork. This market did not exist in Europe and America.

- Businesses can ensure that they have sources of supply. For some companies, it is vital that they secure their supplies of raw material – a company such as Nestlé, for example, based in Switzerland, could not produce chocolate and coffee without a guaranteed supply of cocoa and coffee from countries such as South America. This relationship can be a disadvantage to the host country. Many sources of raw materials are in developing nations and large companies may extract materials with little regard for the local environment or the long-term damage caused. Particular controversy, for example, is to be found over the felling of virgin rainforest for timber or for paper manufacture.

- Businesses may be attracted by government incentives. In the UK, for example, policies such as lower taxes, low business rates or rent-free premises have attracted investors. Microsoft is one such investor. It has a £306m facility near London and a further £49m base in Cambridge. Other examples include Honda, which has a £700m plant in Swindon, and IBM, which has established an £11m call centre in western Scotland. France attracted

Toyota to Valenciennes in 1998 by offering subsidies and incentives in return for the £350m investment.

● Businesses may be attracted by the availability of facilities and labour in the host country. The UK, for example, has a flexible and well-educated labour market and strong trading links with Europe. It also has a leading edge in certain areas of research, particularly in pharmaceuticals and in Britain's own version of the American 'Silicon Valley'. This is in Cambridge and is involved in developing computer and micro-processor technology.

● Businesses which operate in more than one country can practise transfer pricing to take account of differentials in tax rates. This means that, by deciding on where value has been added, they can claim high profits in low-tax areas and only declare low profits in areas where levels of taxation are higher.

● Businesses can take advantage of lower labour costs in the countries in which they operate. This is often seen as exploitation of labour but is a practice which most large corporations carry out as a way of cutting their costs.

Benefits of free trade

The economies of countries gain from trade between businesses. The reasons why countries trade with each other underline the benefits of free trade to all countries concerned. Trade takes place because:

● we can't produce the product here – in some cases natural resources determine what can be produced

● we can't produce the product economically here – this is more likely; most products can be produced in most places. Given the right artificial conditions, bananas could be grown in Kent, but they would be very expensively produced bananas

● we can specialise in what we do best – the benefits of specialisation mean that in some things we may be better than anyone else; if we specialise in these products, we can trade with the rest of the world for the other products that we need

● even if we're not better than everyone else, we can specialise in what we're least bad at – countries should produce those goods and services at which they are relatively better; this allows other countries to import these and frees resources for them to concentrate on what they are better at producing. Even though we could grow bananas in Kent, other countries can produce them much more cheaply. Therefore, we should concentrate on what we can produce more cheaply: say, hops or apples.

There are also certain problems or drawbacks associated with international trade. The problems of free trade include:

● specialisation means re-training and may mean temporary unemployment problems (unfortunately, temporary can be quite a long time)

● a transition between jobs may mean workers having to move geographically; this is not always easy

● production of non-geographically related products (a car plant, for example) can be moved easily to where the prevailing conditions are best (cheap labour, low taxation)

● allowing international markets access to cheap labour puts them in competition with skilled labour in industrialised countries.

Protecting trade from competition

Some countries protect domestic businesses from competition by erecting barriers to international trade. Barriers include tariffs, quotas, embargoes, technical barriers and barriers connected to foreign currency exchange. Such measures may be used for a number of reasons including infant industries, domestic job protection, the maintenance of a particular sector of industry, control of strategically important resources and in retaliation to barriers set up by other countries.

The most commonly used protectionist measures are:

- **Tariff barriers** – duties or additional charges levied on imports, thus making them more expensive to buy. Tariffs may be:
  - *'ad valorem'* tariffs – a fixed percentage of the value of the product is added to its price. In the case of a £100 import an *ad valorem* duty of 10 per cent would yield a price of £110; for a £200 import this would be £220
  - specific duties, levied on products as a fixed sum. In the case of a £100 import a specific duty of £10 would yield a price of £110; for a £200 import this would be £210.
- How effective the tariff is depends on the price elasticity of demand for the imported good; if demand is price inelastic, tariffs will have little effect and the use of a quota would be a more effective measure.
- **Quotas** – the government can restrict the volume of a particular import to a maximum level, i.e. it says that only a certain number of cars of a certain type may be imported.
- **Embargoes** – complete restrictions on trade in certain items or types of product, by government directive. A trade embargo may cover particular goods – such as armaments – that would not be allowed to be exported to a hostile power, or may be used for political reasons. When used for political reasons such restrictions are often called 'sanctions'. There was a long-term set of sanctions against South Africa while it pursued its apartheid policies and also against Libya while it refused to release the suspected Lockerbie bombers. Sanctions, containing embargoes on certain products or services, may still exist against countries that have been hostile – in the case of the UK, at the time of writing, there are still sanctions against the regime in Iran.
- **Technical or legal barriers** – governments can place these so that only countries with a certain level of technology will be allowed to export some goods to them. The USA, for example, has, in the past, raised the requirements for fuel emission levels and certain safety aspects, making imported cars with these additional extras more expensive than home-produced ones. This type of barrier can be defended by a country if its home-produced goods are subject to the same restrictions. In practice, it is often a lot cheaper for home-produced products to make the necessary modifications.
- **Foreign exchange controls** – for example, an exporter in the UK will only accept payment in pounds sterling; an exporter in the USA will only accept payment in US dollars. These are the home currencies into which payment must be converted. If there are restrictions on the amount of foreign exchange that can be bought and sold, this can affect a business's ability to export or import.

ACTIVITY 18

For many years Western countries have been making their car manufacturers produce 'better' cars. Exhaust emission levels have been reduced, the use of leaded petrol is banned throughout the EU and safety features such as seat belts and airbags have become or are becoming compulsory. Cars are also judged on their fuel efficiency. Since only major manufacturers can hope to meet all these specifications, the new rules effectively prevent small businesses from entering global markets.

Tariff and quota systems have been designed to protect small domestic manufacturers. This has failed as rival manufacturers have simply moved their operations to inside the restricted zone.

1. **Explain the difference between a tariff and a quota system.**
2. **Explain how a manufacturer would benefit from moving production to inside a restricted zone.**
3. **Explain why only major manufacturers can cope with the changes given.**

The main reasons given for using protection are:

- the **infant industry argument** is that domestic industry may need protecting for a period if it is just starting up. The idea is that once the industry has 'found its feet' it will no longer need protecting against international competition. The decision as to what is an 'infant industry' and the point at which it ceases to need to be protected make this particular argument tend to be more of a political argument than an economic or business one. Barriers to trade may be legitimised by countries claiming that industries are in their infancy and such barriers may well remain long after the industry has any need for them. If other countries perceive this to be the case they may well retaliate with barriers of their own.

- **job protection.** This may be a priority of government which overrides the free trade argument. Although it may make business sense to buy cheaper goods from abroad, this could lead to job losses and the problems related to job losses at home. For example, government and industry found alternative sources of coal and alternative sources of power in the 1990s leading to the destruction of the coal mining industry in the UK and to massive job losses. Had the coal industry been protected from foreign competition this either may not have happened, or could have been managed so that it happened much more slowly.

- the **control of strategically important resources** and industries may mean that governments are reluctant to buy, for example, nuclear fuel or defence equipment from abroad. Some industries may be strategically important because of national security, because of the research that is carried out, or because governments do not wish to trust to supplies that may not be guaranteed. They may also be strategically important for social and ethical reasons.

- the **maintenance of a particular sector of industry** may also be important for social or ethical reasons. In France, for example, the wine industry is heavily subsidised as part of a government policy of support. Should the industry be allowed to fail, then there are no alternative practical uses for the land. France and Germany also have a history of small farmers and make sure that they are supported through the European Community. In some cases (as in the south of Ireland) it would not be appropriate for any industry other than farming to be established. In parts of England and Wales this may also be true of fishing.

- **retaliation.** Barriers are often set up in retaliation to barriers erected by another country. This situation reduces trade (and the benefits from trade) to both countries and may result in a trade war. A trade war may consist of two countries continuously building higher and higher tariff barriers against each other or imposing lower and lower quotas. Either way, it inevitably results in a loss of benefit to both countries and to the international trading community.

- **export drives.** It is also possible for a country to be protectionist internally by boosting exports through various measures rather than by limiting imports.

ACTIVITY ⓲

There are five main reasons given above for the use of protectionist policies.

1. For each reason, explain whether you think the UK government would be justified in its use. Suggest examples to support your arguments.

2. What conclusion would you draw from the reasons that you have given?

How do businesses compete internationally?

Businesses can compete internationally in the same ways that they compete in national

FIGURE 2.22 *International non-price competition through advertising – in this case, sponsorship*   *Source: CORBIS*

markets. They will compete through:

- charging lower prices than competitors
- using non-price competition (advertising and promotion, for example)
- improvements in productivity and efficiency
- creating new demand for existing products
- expanding demand by moving into new product areas.

In a domestic market, businesses are likely to be controlled and regulated by government. They will also have their profits taxed by government. In an international market, the international institutions to regulate and control business may not be present or effective. Businesses could, for example, therefore:

- undercut domestic businesses and drive them out of business
- have enormous resources for advertising and promotional activities, far outweighing domestic businesses

- be able to 'improve' efficiency by, for example, paying lower wage rates than they would have to 'at home'
- introduce products that are inappropriate for developing economies.

Multi-nationals

Multi-nationals or trans-nationals are businesses which operate on a global basis. The reasons for this are to gain the advantages of operating in more than one country. Multi-nationals are able to establish operations in certain countries for reasons of low tax, or low labour costs or other factors. This does not just apply to developing countries. For example, multi-nationals are keen to establish in the 'Eurozone' – the countries of the EU operating the euro – to gain the advantages of the single currency. The advantages of operating in many countries may include:

- low local labour costs – businesses can shift production facilities to those countries where labour is cheapest or labour regulations easier

- low taxation – multi-nationals can declare high profits where taxation levels are low

- being close to local markets – this cuts down on distribution costs and also links in to employing local labour

- government incentives – it is often in the interests of government to attract businesses if they are bringing employment to a country

Multi-nationals would also claim that they are bringing benefits to the countries in which they operate. Businesses provide:

- jobs, expertise and technology which may well help the host nation to develop its own industries

- investment in infrastructure systems such as transport and communications

- foreign currency – in many cases considered to be 'hard' currency – dollars, sterling, yen, euros – which can be spent on international markets, rather than 'soft' local currency.

Current trends are towards ever larger international conglomerates. The biggest multi-nationals have turnovers that are bigger than the gross domestic product of some European states such as Greece and Portugal.

What other factors affect the competitiveness of international markets?

Other important factors affecting the ability of businesses to compete include:

- the developing global economy – new businesses from developing countries are beginning to compete

- the unevenness of the distribution of wealth – the 'rich world' is dependent on the 'poor world' for raw materials, expanded demand and, often, cheap labour. The 'poor world' may be dependent on 'rich world' technology or expertise

- interdependency and dependency – some countries are dependent on certain products; some have enough of a share of world supply to be able to control market price

- the cycle of debt – the developing world's chances of competing are stifled by the burden of debt payments

- the success or failure of international agreements to promote trade – for example GATT and its successor, the World Trade Organisation.

The developing global economy

Wealth is not spread evenly throughout the world. Figure 2.23 gives a good idea of the split between the rich world and the poor world. It is more of a north/south split than east/west, even though usually it is the industrialised, rich 'West' which is referred to. If the 'north' is taken to include North America, Europe and the 'European' part of the Russian Federation, Japan, Australia and New Zealand, then the 'south' is dominated by Africa, Asia, the Indian sub-continent, China and South America.

There are a number of striking differences between the 'north' and the 'south'. Businesses are often accused of exploiting these differences for their own gain. For example:

- the 'south' has three times the population of the 'north'

- the 'north' has four times the income of the 'south'

- life expectancy in the 'south' is three-quarters that of the 'north'

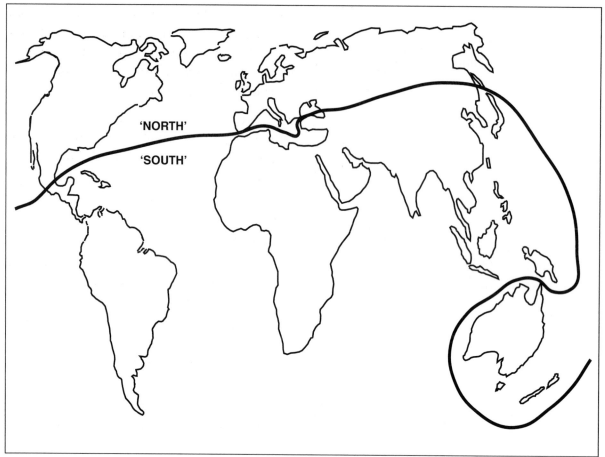

FIGURE 2.23 *The industrialised 'West' is really much of the northern hemsisphere*

- on average there are five times as many students in higher education in the 'north' than the 'south' (in places a great deal more than this)

- 90 per cent of the world's industry is in the 'north'; just 10 per cent in the 'south'.

Dependence and interdependence

The fact that the prosperity of 'north' and 'south' is linked one to the other is usually described by the word 'interdependence'. This means that if one country is to enjoy a better standard of living, higher incomes and economic growth, this will depend on the performance of other countries. Many primary producers are not 'interdependent' but dependent, relying heavily on one particular export item and therefore being highly vulnerable to changes in market conditions for that item. For example, Nigeria relies on crude oil for 94 per cent of its export income; Uganda earns 92 per cent of its export income from coffee.

The cycle of debt

Many developing countries have had to borrow large amounts from the industrialised nations to try to remain competitive. This has led to a debt crisis as increasing interest rates have made it harder and harder for the developing countries to service the debt. In many cases, countries have been unable to pay even the interest, let alone the capital. This means the debt is ever increasing and placing a burden on the people of these countries.

A great deal of the lending has been politically motivated and environmentally unsound. Loans intended to better the lot of the poor, for example, may be spent on arms and armaments in order to destroy or suppress opposition groups or may find their way to only a small proportion

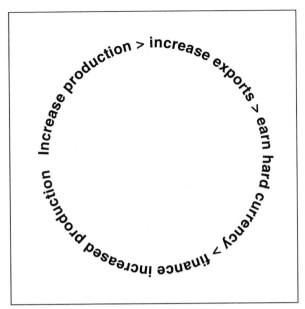

FIGURE 2.24 *The virtuous circle*

of the population. As interest rates rise, the burden of debt becomes ever greater.

The movement to wipe out what is collectively known as 'Third World debt' gathered momentum at the start of 2000. It has received some political support so may yet prove successful.

ACTIVITY ⑳

Bring yourself up to date with some of the current controversies surrounding the political giving of aid and lending of money, for example the problems and controversies which surround awarding the hosting of the Olympic Games and football World Cup to various countries.

Newly Industrialised Countries

New industrialised regions are developing around the world. In particular there has been strong growth around the Pacific Rim – this has included South Korea, Taiwan, Hong Kong, Singapore and the Philippines. These countries have been joined by other Newly Industrialised Countries (NICs) such as Brazil, Mexico and even parts of southern Europe such as Portugal

and Greece. This increased competition has meant that business in the industrialised nations has had to meet or match the improvements or lose market share to the NICs. Some of the reasons for these changes are:

● governments have made a point of encouraging industrial growth by providing areas of low taxation or high subsidy

● initial cheap labour and poor working conditions have been largely replaced as enough local capital has been earned to allow for re-investment

● re-investment often means that the NIC has better and more up-to-date plant and processes than competitors

● beneficial working practices (such as team working and empowerment) can be established without first having to dismantle traditional practices

● trans-nationals may have relocated production to these countries because of cheaper labour or less regulation

● tourism has been encouraged to bring in hard currency.

Increased freedom of trade and the WTO

The General Agreement on Tariffs and Trade (GATT) was the first international body, established just after the Second World War, which sought to reduce tariffs and other barriers to trade to encourage free trade the world over. A gradual reduction in protectionism was meant to bring the benefits of trade to more businesses.

Complex negotiations have taken place – often stretching over a number of years – to try to agree on less trade restrictions. The last 'round' of negotiations was called the Uruguay Round. This finished in 1994. Part of the agreement was that GATT would be replaced by the WTO.

There have been several rounds of talks since then, aimed at the liberalisation of trade but all tend to come up against the same barriers. These tend to be either developing nations not wanting unprotected trade or developed nations objecting to the cheap labour of developing countries. Typically: 'my country is not yet ready for competition', 'your country gives too many subsidies', 'your labour force is unrecognised, exploited and underpaid'.

For example, in 1996, the suggestion that countries with cheap labour should adopt 'Western' employment practices caused a rift. Some countries demanded that there should be a link between free trade and a core package of labour rights, including freedom to join trade unions and negotiate wages collectively. This included opposition to child working and enforced employment. Many developing nations saw these conditions for employment standards as a way of removing their trading advantage of cheap labour costs. Many industrialised nations put a moral gloss on the proposals. As with many parts of trade negotiations, a conclusion was not reached.

The latest round of WTO talks aimed at freeing up more world trade took place in Seattle in 1999. An enormous protest, organised across the Internet, disrupted the trade talks and prevented them from reaching a satisfactory conclusion. The concern of the protesters was more with wiping out Third World debt than with the further liberalisation of trade, although, to many, more trade only meant further disadvantages for those countries already suffering. Some protesters were worried about the effect on labour markets in developing nations, some about opening up their own markets to competition, some about the sustainability of world growth in environmental terms.

The conference was unable to reach conclusions and was suspended (this has happened at such talks before, however, with later agreement being reached) but the Chair gave an upbeat statement which re-stated the aims of the WTO.

ACTIVITY 21

There are many complex issues surrounding the WTO. Read these extracts from the statement made by the WTO Chair at the close of the Seattle talks:

'We all left Seattle last Friday disappointed but not dismayed that it was not possible to finish the job we went there to do. A great deal was achieved in the short time Ministers had for serious negotiation. Gaps were narrowed considerably in a number of important areas. ... I feel particular disappointment because the postponement of our deliberations means the benefits that would have accrued to developing and least-developed countries will now be delayed, while the problems facing these countries will not be allayed. A package of results is within reach. ... Despite the temporary setback in Seattle, our objectives remain unchanged:

■ to continue to negotiate the progressive liberalisation of international trade

■ to put trade to work more effectively for economic development and poverty alleviation.'

1. In theory, what are the advantages of liberalisation (freeing) international trade?

FIGURE 2.25 *EU membership*

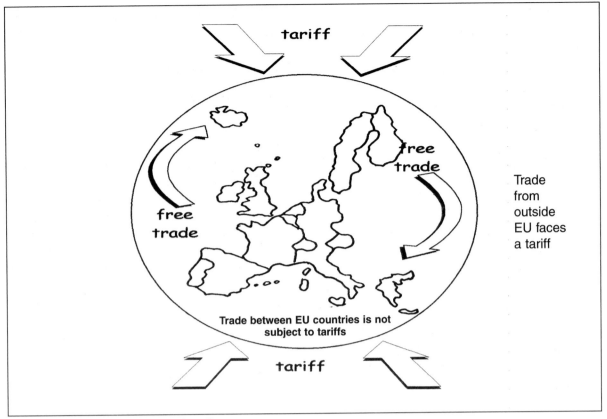

FIGURE 2.26 *The Common External Tariff*

2. **What advantages would an agreement have brought to 'developing and least-developed' countries?**

3. **Explain how trade could work more effectively for:**
   ■ **economic development**
   ■ **poverty alleviation.**

The European Union (EU)

The origins of the European Union lie in attempts to free up trade in Europe. Its aims include:

● free trade between member states
● social and economic progress to raise standards of living
● common standards of justice
● common citizenship as shown by EU passports
● economic and monetary union.

There are now 15 member states. This is likely to be increased further in 2000 or 2001.

The European Union started life as an agreement in coal and steel trading and then became the European Economic Community. In 1991 the member states signed the Maastricht Treaty which created the European Union. This had aims of not only economic and monetary union but also, eventually, possible political union.

The first step towards this was the establishment of a free trade area with no restrictions, tariffs or (except in the UK) border posts. This was finalised with the Single Market (1992) within which there is complete freedom of movement for goods, people and capital. Countries outside the Union pay a tariff to trade with countries inside it.

The benefits of the Union

The customs union which is still the basis for the EU imposes a common external tariff; that is, while trade is free and unrestricted within the Union, businesses trading from outside it must pay a tariff as their goods cross the border. This has encouraged businesses to establish inside the

Union in order to gain the benefits of free trade. Nissan, Toyota, Microsoft and IBM are just a few examples of such businesses.

Further harmonisation has taken place, with many EU laws becoming part of UK law, such as the Social Charter which guarantees certain workers' rights, the advent of the single European currency and the possibility of monetary union.

The Single Market

The Single Market was a massive undertaking because much legislation and harmonisation had to be agreed before it could take place. Harmonisation is the bringing into line of various different national laws and regulations.

- Harmonisation of taxation within the Union is a process that is still continuing. This is necessary so that different countries do not give tax advantages to businesses over other countries.

- Common technical and quality standards have been established so that products may be sold in all member countries (the adoption of ISO 9000, see Chapter 1) has had some effect).

- The free movement of labour, capital and products has been established; businesses are now seeking to extend this to investment funds and pension funds within the Union so that financial instruments can also benefit from free movement.

There is still a long way to go. National traditions and habits will mean that certain industries are supported and that there are tax differentials. For example, in the area of transport, the French have traditionally subsidised rail transport and charge users to travel on their main motorways. In the UK, rail transport is not subsidised, motorway travel is free, but duties on vehicles are much higher. It would be an advantage, given the current situation, for a haulage contractor to move his registrations to Belgium but continue to operate in the UK. It is an advantage to French lorry drivers to be able to travel on UK motorways without payment.

Criticisms of the Union

Not everyone has always been in favour of the Union. Some businesses have suffered because of EU changes and policies. Agricultural and fishing businesses, in particular, have often lost out. Criticism of the Union has often centred on:

- the Common Agricultural Policy: this was designed to protect small farmers from price fluctuations. It has been criticised for keeping farm prices artificially high through subsidies, the major part of the Union's expenditure. Supplies of foods where there has been excess production have been kept from the market. Sometimes these were destroyed, sometimes given away, sometimes sold outside the market. This led to much consumer dissatisfaction as EU surpluses were destroyed just to keep farm prices high. Food prices in the EU were higher than in many other industrialised countries. The subsidies given to farmers were the major source of EU expenditure. However, due to the political strength of the agricultural lobby, it has proved difficult to wind down the CAP.

- EU directives: these are instructions from the EU to alter or change something so that it is harmonised. Often this may be to the detriment of some member countries. Many EU directives have been held up to ridicule as bureaucrats have attempted, for example, to define products without taking national tastes or traditions into account.

European Monetary Union

The amount of trade within the EU has grown since the Single Market was established. The removal of border controls and the free movement of goods and labour have meant that businesses have been more inclined to trade across international borders than at any time in the past. This has made it essential that the minimum of currency transactions should take place.

Historically, as a product crossed an international border, its value had to be expressed in the terms of the country that it was currently in. While customs seals actually made it unnecessary to do anything about currency calculations until the cargo arrived at its country of destination, it was still a necessity for the seller to be paid in the currency of his own country whilst the buyer would pay in the currency of his. A single currency would:

● cut down the number of currency transactions
● therefore substantially reduce currency risk – businesses are protected from fluctuations in currencies
● also substantially reduce business costs incurred in exchanging currency.

ERM or ECU?

There were two possibilities for the solution of this problem.

● One was to have all of the currencies of Europe so closely linked together that they could become interchangeable – removing the need for currency exchange and exchange rates.
● The other was for a unit to be created so that all transactions could be expressed as a single currency. This second option is called the European Currency Unit or ECU. Eventually, this unit could replace individual currencies.

Black Wednesday

The first of the above options was called the Exchange Rate Mechanism (ERM) – this linked the value of all member state currencies. Within the ERM each member states' currency had a value expressed in 'ECUS' (European Currency Units).

The movement of currencies in terms of their value was restricted to a defined band. This gave them a target value ('parity') and allowed them to move no more than two and a quarter per cent either side of this (3 per cent for the UK and Italy). (See Figure 2.27.)

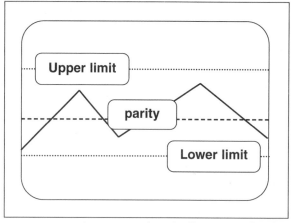

FIGURE 2.27 *A movement either side of 'parity' was allowed*

Member states were to support their own currency by buying it on foreign exchange markets if it looked like it was going to fall outside the limit set. The idea was that currency bands would become narrower and narrower until currencies remained stable at or around parity.

However, the system failed to work because it could not take account of currency speculation and domestic economic problems.

One day in September 1992 (known as 'Black Wednesday') the pound lost value heavily as speculators sold it on foreign exchange markets. To try to get people to re-invest in sterling, the government raised interest rates by a massive 5 per cent during a single day. Even so, selling continued and the pound dropped below its ERM 'floor'. At this point the pound left the

FIGURE 2.28 *EU notes and coins*

ERM. It is partly this experience that has led to economic caution about adopting the single currency.

ERM

The ERM was replaced by the euro on 1st January 1999 when member countries' exchange rates were locked together. The euro will replace member states' domestic currencies in 2002.

Britain has not yet adopted the single currency because the government does not believe that the good points outweigh the bad ones. At the time of writing, the pound is strong. This has had a detrimental effect on UK exporters. It has also led to threats by some inward investors (such as Toyota) to abandon plant in the UK in favour of countries operating the new currency.

The decision of whether or not – and, if so, when – to adopt the single currency will be a complicated political and economic decision. The economic indicators seem to show that the euro will be a success and that the benefits to UK trade will outweigh the disadvantages. The political decision is more difficult to predict.

To join or not to join?

The benefits of adopting the single currency are:

- there are no exchange rate costs to businesses trading across international borders. This is estimated to save businesses between a half and one per cent of their costs

- there are no fluctuations between currencies to plan for and take into account. This means that companies can operate in an atmosphere of certainty rather than uncertainty – they will know what materials or products will cost and be able to forecast their own income and expenditure accurately

- companies and consumers will find that comparisons of prices are easier – instead of having to make a calculation to see how much something is in French francs, or Italian pesetas or German marks, the prices will all be expressed in the same currency

- harmonisation of interest rates would mean that there would be no need for financial institutions and large corporations to move capital in order to seek different interest rates; this would add to business certainty

- investment from outside the Union (inward investment) is likely to increase as a result of the size of the single market (360 million people).

The disadvantages of adopting could be:

- the loss of control over domesic currencies means that a large slice of economic policy would no longer be in the hands of national governments. Alterations that might be beneficial to particular industries, or to particular sections of the economy, could not be made

- there is a feeling that, with the loss of a national currency, there is a loss of sovereignty; a feeling that the country is no longer in charge of its own affairs but that power has, instead, moved to Brussels

- the costs of transition may be particularly high. The UK has already gone through the transition to European weights and measures and this involved a period of dual pricing (weights and prices given per pound and per kilogram, for example). The cost of converting to a new currency has been estimated by some businesses to be as large as 2 per cent of turnover, wiping out any gains made. However, conversion would be a 'one-off' cost while the gains would continue to be made over a number of years

- around half of Britain's international trade is with countries outside the EU. This proportion is constantly changing – recent figures show that British exports to the EU are at over 60 per cent – but traditional markets are still more important to many UK businesses than is the case in other EU countries. Those businesses which trade outside the EU will bear the costs of transition but gain no benefits from it

● There could be a regional imbalance within the Union. Some regions, particularly those with weaker currencies, will benefit more than others; some may not benefit from the changes at all but could in fact lose out.

ACTIVITY 22

Read the section on the benefits and costs of European Monetary Union and answer the following questions.

1. Why was it necessary for a system of monetary union to be devised?

2. What were the two possible alternatives for a solution?

3. Why did the ERM break down?

4. Balance the positive benefits of a single currency against its drawbacks. Comment on whether the currency is a good or bad thing for:

   ■ businesses in the UK

   ■ businesses in the EU

   ■ businesses outside the EU.

5. Give reasons for your opinions.

ACTIVITY 23

Strong pound leads to less investment?

Inward investment in the UK has been an important source of jobs. Many businesses have decided to locate here due to the flexible labour market and to government help to attract businesses. This has included tax relief and grants. Now, however, because the UK is not a part of the European Monetary System, businesses are beginning to think twice about establishing here – even, in some cases, beginning to think of leaving. Their exports are being hard hit by the strong pound, which continues to rise against the Euro, and preventing them from being competitive in Europe.

However, it may soon become cheaper to abandon plants in the UK – even when £2b and £3b investments – as with Toyota and Microsoft – have been made – and to move to other parts of Europe. The new applicants Eastern Europe and Turkey, once they are admitted, would prove much more attractive than the UK.

The Eurozone is the area of Europe within the Euro system and new investors are likely to think that establishing within the zone is more important than establishing in the UK, whatever other benefits are on offer.

1. Look at the map in Figure 2.29. Explain which of these businesses would be happy to establish elsewhere in Europe and which would be less likely to move. Give reasons for your answer.

2. Explain what effects a pound which is strong against the Euro will have on:

   ■ inward investors

   ■ UK importers

   ■ UK exporters.

3. Outline why the new applicants to the EU might prove more attractive to inward investors.

4. Outline why established members of the EU might prove more attractive to inward investors.

5. If you were a car manufacturer, about to build a £1b plant in Europe, what factors would be most important in making your decision on where to locate?

Key Skills C3.2

Pulling in the money

A sample of recent inward investment

1 Honda, Swindon: £700m

----

2 Motorola, Swindon: £49m

----

3 Toyota, Burnaston (phase 2), Derbyshire: £202m

----

4 Microsoft, Thames valley: £306m plus Cambridge: £49m

----

5 Oracle, Solihull: £20m

----

6 IBM, Greenock call
centre: £11m

MCI-Worldcom,
UK network: £393m

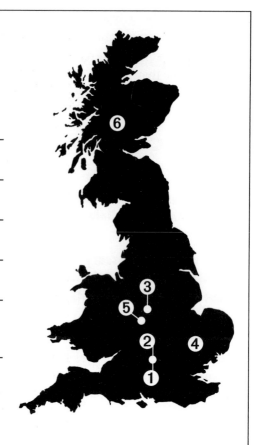

FIGURE 2.29 *Location of some recent major investors*

Source: Adapted from The Guardian; 18 January 2000

Self-Test Questions

1 Explain what is meant by 'globalisation'.

2 What factors have contributed to further globalisation?

3 What are the advantages of free trade?

4 What disadvantages might there be to free trade?

5 Explain the purpose of the WTO.

6 What advantages might Newly Industrialised Countries have over traditional producers?

7 Outline the reasons for a country to erect barriers to trade.

8 What are the main barriers to trade that a country could use?

9 Explain the factors that make businesses compete internationally rather than nationally.

10 Explain the importance of the Eurozone to multi-nationals.

Marketing

What this chapter is about

Businesses exist in order to supply goods and services to satisfy consumer wants and needs. Marketing allows businesses to inform customers of products that are on offer and to persuade customers to buy those products.

Marketing is based on developing an understanding of the customer and of what they may want or need, and working out ways in which customers may be persuaded to buy. In this chapter you will learn about the process of marketing, from the initial stages of market analysis and market research to studying how strategies are constructed and how you may judge whether or not a strategy has been a success. You will learn about the principles of marketing and how marketing activities contribute to the turnover and profits of a business.

You need to study this chapter alongside Chapters 1 and 2 as they cover the business environment within which marketing takes place. It also provides knowledge and understanding that can be used for the assessment of work covered by Chapter 6. ∎

What you need to produce

You will need to produce a marketing strategy for a new or existing product. You should be able to draw on information and knowledge learned in other areas of your course. It is important that you learn how to link the various parts of your course together and do not treat each part in isolation from the other parts. You may be able to link your marketing strategy to your assessment for the work covered by Chapter 6.

You will need to draw up a plan of action to say what tasks will be carried out and in what order and what resources you will utilise in order to complete your strategy. You should choose different and appropriate ways to present information and may use whatever medium is appropriate — ICT, oral and written methods. You must make an oral presentation as part of your assessment. Your strategy should show that you have:

- based your work on the principles of marketing

- identified, collected and used relevant primary and secondary data, having checked its validity

- analysed the impact of the external environment on your marketing decisions

- analysed the marketing context before deciding on a strategy

- developed a mix of strategies for different consumer needs and profiles

- used effective presentation skills to explain an aspect of your strategy and demonstrate how your strategy will be effective.

Section 1 *The principles of marketing*

What you need to learn

In this section you will learn about:

- how marketing can help businesses meet the needs of actual and potential customers
- how marketing can help businesses anticipate competitive actions and reactions
- how functions are co-ordinated to achieve a successful marketing strategy
- constraints on marketing activities.

Ever filled in a guarantee card? Or the information asked for on a 'money-off' coupon before redeeming it? Have you ever answered questions on a telephone survey? Ever wondered why the bread counter is furthest from the door in a supermarket? If so, then you have encountered some of the more visible aspects of marketing. Marketing is about knowing, understanding and influencing the customer.

The management guru Peter Drucker said that: 'The aim of marketing is to make selling superfluous. The aim is to know and understand the customer so well that the product or service fits him/her and sells itself.' This emphasises the basic requirement of marketing, which is to understand the needs of the customer. The aspects of marketing we see around us every day in advertising and promotions and brands are the end results of a process that begins by researching what the customer wants.

There are three main elements to planning a marketing strategy:

1. finding out about the customer – their needs and anticipated needs
2. finding out about the market – analysing the competition

3. finding ways of satisfying customers – communicating with customers and co-ordinating business functions to meet their needs.

The planning cycle involves:

- analysing the market position
- setting marketing objectives
- deciding on the marketing strategy
- implementing the strategy
- monitoring and evaluating the effects.

The cycle is a continuous one because markets are dynamic. They constantly change in response to a variety of factors. This means that businesses need constantly to analyse the market, identify changes and adapt products and promotions to meet changing customer needs.

FIGURE 3.1 *The planning cycle*

Marketing objectives

The starting point for any business planning is the corporate goals of a business. Marketing objectives will be decided in the context of the business's other objectives and a marketing

The largest independant Health Club Operator in the UK with over 50 clubs & 110,000 plus members nationwide with no need for Annual Contracts!

Facilities to be found in your club

- 14.000 Sq. Ft of Luxurious Facilities
- Two Air conditioned State of the Art Gymnasium
- The very latest in Cardiovascular & Resistance equipment
- Personal Exercise Programmes - for everyone
- Comprehensive weight management programme
- Fully supervised gymnasium for safe healthy exercise
- Spacious Air Conditioned Fitness Studio - (Fully sprung hardwood floor)
- Over 40 classes per week with probably the best instructors in town
- Special Programming for the mature member
- Spa, Sauna & Steam Room
- Beautiful Changing rooms with Oak Lockers
- COMPLIMENTARY Toiletries
- Beauty Room, Sunbeds
- Creche
- Juice Bar with COMPLIMENTARY Tea, Coffee & Soft Drinks
- Fitness First quarterly Magazine (£2.50 to non-members)
- Members only COMPLIMENTARY Video Library over 600 titles
- Full Social Calendar - Meet new friends!
- Reciprocal use of all Fitness First Health Clubs Nationwide

Pictures illustrated represent the quality & standard of Fitness First Health Clubs Nationwide

FIGURE 3.2 *Health club facilities*

Source: Fitness First Health Club

strategy or strategies will be determined alongside the corporate strategy.

Marketing objectives be different depending on whether the product is:

● new
● established
● a market leader
● a smaller player in the market.

They will also depend on whether the business has satisficing or maximising targets.

Typical objectives might include targets regarding sales revenue, sales volume, profit levels, market penetration, market share, growth or acquisition.

 **Top Tips**

Sales revenue and sales volume are different. Sales revenue is number of sales of a product times its price. Sales volume is just the number of sales.

Revenue should not be confused with profit. Revenue is the amounts received. Profit is the surplus after costs have been deducted from sales revenue.

Consumer demand

Marketing involves anticipating and manipulating consumer demand. The elements of demand, as detailed in Chapter 2, Section 1, each provide an area for marketing to target. These include specific factors such as price, the price of substitutes and complements, income, taste or preference. They also include general factors like population and seasonal changes in demand.

Remember that changes are not likely to happen in isolation. Often many changes to demand happen at the same time. It is the job of the marketing department either to anticipate what changes are likely to take place, or to manipulate the market in such a way that more of the business's product is demanded.

Remember, also, that demand and supply interact. If a business has control over supply, this can be used to manipulate demand. A business could deliberately engineer a shortage of a product, for example, in order to make prices rise. This recently happened in the international market for silver as one particular buyer stocked up. This was in order to make prices rise. He then released the metal to the market in only small amounts, in order to keep price at a high level.

 **ACTIVITY** **1**

Look at Figure 3.2 which details the facilities on offer at a health club. The company is obviously targeting the change in attitude towards a healthy lifestyle. This has led to an increase in demand.

1. **What other trends you think that the company has noticed?**
2. **What trends should it be taking into account for the future?**
3. **What strategy do you think it should be following to maintain and increase market share?**

Customer expectations

What do customers expect of a particular good or service? This is a vital question in marketing. Marketing departments need to discover customer expectations and then satisfy them. They need to be able to communicate effectively with customers. To do this, they first need to understand customer expectations.

Expectations tend to centre on being able to buy the right product – the one that is most suitable for the purpose or the job to be done.

- It needs to be in the right size, shape, colour or variety.
- It needs to be at the right price.
- It needs to be available at a time and in a quantity which matches when and where the customer wishes to buy it.

Customers expect good levels of service and advice. They expect after-sales attention where this is appropriate. Above all, perhaps, they expect value for money.

Customers want information about the product. This needs to be accurate and honest. It must be presented understandably but not patronisingly. Marketing needs both to inform and to persuade customers. Information needs to be properly 'packaged' and presented and the 'hard sell' is not always acceptable or desirable.

Business reputation and customer expectations

Many businesses trade on expectations by building themselves a reputation. Effectively, they communicate with customers by establishing their type of customer. The customer knows that they will obtain a certain level of quality or of customer service by using a specific business. Compare, for example, the corporate identity of businesses such as Aldi and Netto in the UK against businesses such as Sainsbury's or Marks and Spencer. The appeal of the first two retailers is the low prices of their products. The second two retailers, on the other hand, promote an image of luxury and customer service. Each business is successful. They have just targeted a different type of customer.

- Netto and Aldi promote low prices as value for money. They could not promote an ethos of 'people only shop here because they can't afford to shop elsewhere'. Instead they promote the image that 'sensible, caring

people shop here, rather than waste money on unnecessary frills'.
- At Sainsbury's and Marks and Spencer customers are happy to pay premium prices because of the quality that they believe they are buying. In both cases customers believe that they are gaining value for money.

Market orientation

A market-oriented business will try to put the customer first. It will develop products and variations of products to meet customer expectations. This may increase its costs but in the longer term, increased sales generated should also increase its profits. The days of 'you can have any colour you like as long as it is black', by which Henry Ford introduced the notion of mass production to the world, have long gone. Customers expect to be able to buy the exact variety of product which they want – successful businesses must therefore be geared up to supply it.

Competitive reactions

Businesses need to judge the possible ways in which a rival business will react to a new product. They may be able to judge this from historical information – how a business has reacted in the past – or may have to try to analyse the reaction from the point of view of what it would do if faced with the same situation. The health club literature shown in Figure 3.3 has been produced as either an attempt by this group to increase its membership, or as a reaction to a development. In fact, the area has seen several new health clubs established which will have taken some of the market share from this business. This is its attempt to win back customers and attract new ones. Businesses will always react to threats to their market, whether they centre on price, promotions, advertising, or changes to the product itself.

FIGURE 3.3 *Health club literature*

Source: Fitness First Health Club

Internal and external constraints

There are various limitations – known as constraints – on the marketing activities of businesses.

- **Internal** constraints are those that arise from inside the organisation and are within the control of the business. The main internal constraints involve the product itself, the personnel available and sources and types of finance.
- **External** constraints arise from factors outside the business and which are outside its control. The main external constraints are caused by the competition in the market, government legislation, moral and ethical factors and macro-economic factors.

Internal constraints

- **Product**. If the right product is not available, then this is a constraint. The business needs to make a choice between a low-cost, mass-market product, or a high-cost, differentiated product. For example, a manufacturer might decide to produce a 'cheap and cheerful' family shampoo, or to produce a range of shampoos for different types of hair, men and women etc. Businesses may also decide to concentrate on small, specialist 'niche' markets. The choice which the business makes will build in a constraint. Most businesses cannot compete on all fronts!
- **Personnel**. The type and calibre of staff available will be important to a business. Again, if the right type and amount of staff are not available, this will be a constraint on the business. A business may not have the staff with the requisite skills, training or expertise to cope with new products or new markets. The alternative is to train existing staff to the right standards or to take on new staff from outside the organisation.

- **Finance**. Any innovation or change in marketing will have to be financed. Financial constraints may include:
  - not enough finance available
  - opposition to the use of finance in risky ventures
  - other calls on the finance that is available.

In large organisations, marketing will have to compete with production, human resources and other departments.

External constraints

The main external constraints are caused by the competition in the market, government legislation, moral and ethical factors and macro-economic factors – all factors outside the control of the business.

Marketing operations may be constrained by:

- **The levels of existing competition**. The business is likely to be doing one of two things:
  - opening up a new market – in which case other businesses may be attracted to it, if it proves successful. If the business can erect barriers to entry, it may be able to limit competition. These may include high initial costs (such as research costs) and heavy expenditure on advertising. Legal barriers such as patents and copyrights may also be used
  - trying to enter an existing market – in which case competitors will react to the new entrant. Marketing objectives will need to take the direction and scale of such reactions into account.
- **Government legislation**. This can restrict or encourage the sale of certain products. Marketing for some products that are controlled, licensed or forbidden by law is illegal. Obvious examples include dangerous

weapons, drugs and pornography. In other cases, for example where age restrictions are placed on the purchase of goods such as cigarettes and tobacco, alcohol and fireworks, there will be restrictions on how and where marketing may take place. For example, the manufacturers of alcoholic fizzy drinks ('alcopops') had to change their marketing when the government decided that marketing campaigns for these drinks were being aimed at under-age drinkers.

- **The need to act ethically.** Acting ethically means doing what is 'right' or moral. With certain products there are moral objections to marketing. These may lead to restrictions on the types of marketing that may be aimed at vulnerable groups, such as children. A typical ethical problem in business might involve the use of animals for testing. Consider the possible arguments and that a point of view may depend on the nature of the testing which is undertaken:

  - testing is ethically wrong, as the animals are made to suffer unnecessarily
  - animal testing for cosmetics causes unnecessary suffering for an unnecessary product
  - testing is ethically right, as it may lead to great advantages for humans
  - animal testing for drugs which may be developed as life-saving drugs is essential.

- Pressure groups may also become involved in the interpretation of what is ethical or moral. Pressure groups are groups of people who will join together in order to try to influence opinion and policy. Marketing needs to ensure that it does not offend powerful pressure groups through its activities.

- **Macro-economic factors.** The state of the economy, changes in population growth or structure and changes in fashion and taste may destroy, diminish or create markets. Take, for example, one of the trends already noted, that of a more health-conscious population.

This will have effects on:

- the dairy industry, as people find substitutes for butter, cream and full fat milk
- the market for sports clothes and trainers
- the market for outdoor leisure activities
- the Health Service, if rates of heart disease drop
- sales of unhealthy products such as alcohol and tobacco.
- The key to good marketing is to spot what these trends are likely to bring before they happen and to make sure that products are available to fill any new demand. One market which has expanded massively in the past 10 years, for instance, is the market for mountain bikes. Government has responded by providing funding for cycle routes.

Co-ordinating functions to achieve marketing aims

The various functional departments within an organisation will need to be co-ordinated in order for it to meet its marketing objectives. New products, processes or markets mean change and the successful management of this change is vital to a business. Management has a responsibility to ensure that all departments are able to contribute to an overall marketing strategy.

- The marketing department itself will carry out an analysis of product position which will determine which brands or products will receive the most promotion, the highest levels of production and the heaviest budget.

- Research and development will have been responsible for the initial product idea and will work with marketing on product trialling and testing. Prototypes will need to be tested or pilot marketing and field testing carried out. No one really knows how good that new super duster is until it has been field tested – perhaps by providing it free to a business of contract cleaners in return for their opinions.

- The finance department will be involved in the setting of an appropriate budget. The most common ways of setting marketing budgets are as follows. Each method has its drawbacks.

  - Competitor parity – seeing what the competition is spending on marketing and matching it. This relies on it being possible to measure accurately what competitors are spending – not generally possible – and could also lead to 'war spending'. As competitors see expenditure matched, they increase their expenditure. If the original company then responds, a spiral has been established.

  - Sales-related budgeting – increasing the budget as sales increase. This relies on sales being able to increase without the extra marketing expenditure and then 'rewards' the product by increasing expenditure when it may no longer be necessary.

  - Incremental or marginal budgeting – adding an additional increment or margin to what was spent in a previous period. Budgets should be flexible enough to allow for switches in expenditure as circumstances dictate. Incremental budgeting lacks this flexibility.

- Human resources will be responsible for ensuring that the right amount and quality of labour is available – a good sales force may be essential, or a good training programme for anyone who is going to deal with other stakeholders in the organisation like customers or suppliers.

- The entire process of managing change is a managerial problem and thus involves the managerial cycle in Figure 3.4.

In marketing terms this means producing the strategy, 'selling' the strategy to the organisation and then co-ordinating functions to manage the changes needed to implement the strategy.

ACTIVITY 2

Competitive reaction

Polo (the popular 'mint with the hole') has been a leading product for Nestlé and a central plank in its marketing strategy for a number of years. It had a good market base and provided a steady flow of income and had long held the market leader's position in the market for mints.

It lost its market leadership position in 1992 to Trebor Extra Strong Mints after a major advertising campaign succeeded in establishing them as market leaders. The marketing objective of Trebor was to take sufficient market share from Polo for it to become the market leader, and this was achieved. However, it had not taken into account the possible reaction of Nestlé, who decided that they would fight to re-gain its market leader's position. The response from Nestlé was to launch a counter-offensive designed to re-establish Polo and to re-position the sweet so that it appealed to a wider market segment. This meant both diversification and product re-positioning at the same time, a risky strategy. It produced and marketed a diversified range of Polo products in order to target wider market segments, including extra strong (aimed at men), spearmint flavour (aimed at capturing the younger end of the market) and sugar-free (aimed at the health conscious). At the same

FIGURE 3.4 *Managing change*

time it re-launched its core product, re-branding it as Original Polo.

By 1994, two years after Trebor's successful campaign, Polo had regained its market leadership of the sugar confectionery market with 19.6 per cent of the market and had grown its market share through the diversification. By 1998 this had grown to 23.9 per cent (by value). Trebor held third place with its Softmints brand at 19.3 per cent and fourth place with its Extra Strong Mint at 18.4 per cent.

1. Explain what internal and external constraints you think that Nestlé and Trebor were operating under.

2. Find out what is meant by 'diversification' and 'product re-positioning' and explain the terms.

3. Suggest what different products (within this market) Trebor could have produced had it decided to fight Nestlé's marketing campaign.

4. Look in your local sweet shop or supermarket to see what diversified products both Nestlé and Trebor have produced. See if you can find out who is currently the market leader.

Section 2 *Establishing customer needs*

What you need to learn

In this section you will learn about:

- how a business needs to explore the market in which it is operating before deciding on an appropriate marketing strategy
- the types of primary research
- the types of secondary research
- how such research may be interpreted and evaluated
- the different research methods appropriate to different products.

You need to be able to use types of research and interpret the information collected.

ACTIVITY

NBA sports bottle

With a partner, look at the application form shown in Figure 3.5.

1. **Decide how many specific pieces of information it asks for, and list them. Compare your answer with another pair to see if you agree.**

2. **Which information could be said to be 'demographic'?**

3. **How is each piece of information important to the manufacturer?**

4. **How could the manufacturer make use of parts of the geographical information, such as 'county' and 'postcode'?**

Market research

This is the collection of information from existing and potential customers. A business has to find out:

- the needs of its customers
- the activities of its competitors

before effective marketing strategies can be developed.

The accuracy of research is of paramount importance to a business. To ensure accuracy, data need to be validated. Different methods of collecting information are used and one type of information can be used to validate another. For example, data from statistical analysis can be compared with existing knowledge of the market. Devices like the application form on a packet of Frosties (in Figure 3.6) are used, for example, to update customer profiles. They help the business describe the group which is the typical buyer of the product.

Market research can never be completely accurate as businesses will never be in a position to ask all of their customers the same questions. Nor are customers obliged either to respond at all or, if they do respond, to answer truthfully questions put to them. Businesses rely on sampling a section of their customer base.

Research will be either primary or secondary research.

- **Primary** research involves collecting information that has not been collected before. It is 'primary' because it is the first time the information has been collected. Most primary research is conducted as field research. This is research that takes place in the market.

- **Secondary** research is using information that is already published and available in one format or another. It may be thought of as 'second-hand' research. Secondary research is collected away from the market, at a desk, and is sometimes called desk research.

Quantitative or qualitative?

Researchers need to structure primary research carefully in an attempt to get the most accurate

APPLICATION FORM

UK applicants post to: Frosties/NBA Sports Bottle, P.O. Box 121, Blackburn, Lancs. BB0 1GR

ROI applicants post to: Frosties/NBA Sports Bottle, P.O Box 1156, Crumlin, Dublin 12

Please send me _____ NBA Sports Bottle(s). I enclose six tokens, plus 20p towards postage for each bottle required. Please affix 20p coin(s) to back of form.

PLEASE DO NOT SEND STAMPS. PLEASE PRINT IN BLOCK LETTERS IN BLACK OR BLUE BALLPOINT.

Name (Mr, Mrs, Miss, Ms) _____

Address _____

_____

County _____ Postcode _____

We may wish to use your name and address for marketing purposes. If you do not wish to receive any further communication from Kellogg's please tick here. ☐

To help us at Kellogg's produce the very best products for your family, we would be grateful if you could answer the following questions (please note that the information you provide will remain confidential to us and will not be handed to any other third party).

1. How many packets of cereal do you buy on average each month?
   ☐ 1-4   ☐ 5-6   ☐ 7-9   ☐ 10 or more.

2. Do you have any children under 16, what age group do they fall into?
   (Please tick all relevant boxes.)
   ☐ 0-4   ☐ 5-9   ☐ 10-15   ☐ no children.

3. Please write in the name of the store where you do most of your grocery shopping.
   _____

4. Which age group do you fit into?
   ☐ Under 18   ☐ 18-24   ☐ 25-34   ☐ 35-44
   ☐ 45-54   ☐ 55-64   ☐ 65+

FIGURE 3.5 *Kelloggs offer application form*

Source: Kelloggs

information possible. Primary research is costly and time-consuming to carry out so it is essential that researchers are asking the right questions of the right people. In terms of dividing or segmenting a market, primary research is generally used to find out which market segments exist.

The first decision to take is on what balance of quantitative and qualitative information will be sought.

- **Quantitative** research is designed to be analysed using statistical tools. It will produce figures and percentages of the nature of '90 per cent bought product X because ...'. Sophisticated statistical techniques can make quantitative research very useful but there is always the danger that it may end up being superficial. Quantitative questions need to be carefully designed to ensure that they aren't 'leading' the respondent. For example, 'Would you like to see your pub turned into a pub with an Indian restaurant upstairs or knocked down for a car park?' could have results presented as '90 per cent said they preferred a restaurant' when really 90 per cent didn't want a car park! It is also important that the sample is large enough to make any survey valid.

- **Qualitative** research seeks in-depth answers and is usually conducted through focus groups – a small cross-section of a business's market divided into groups of five or six – or lengthy telephone or face-to-face interviews with customers. Qualitative research will produce not statistics but opinions. People who conduct qualitative research are often highly trained so that they understand the psychology behind both questions and answers. In this way they are able not just to record responses but also to interpret them.

The cherry cake

The cherry cake problem illustrates why both quantitative and qualitative data should be used. However carefully a survey is designed and conducted, there can still be amounts of bias in the results. However carefully a cherry cake is mixed and baked, there will often be many more cherries in one slice that there is in another. Market research should always include qualitative data as well as quantitative in order to try to iron out anomalies or bias of this nature.

ACTIVITY 4

Application form

1. **Using the application form in Figure 3.5 as a guide, devise a mini-questionnaire to be used in your class or group. The results should show both demographic and geographic information. Because you already have a target segment – targeted by age and an interest in Business Studies – you will need to re-write some of the questions.**

2. **Present your completed questionnaire to your group and explain:**
   - **how each question will work**
   - **what use a researcher could make of the information.**

Key Skills C3.1b

ACTIVITY 5

The Millennium Dome

Consider this description of a product:

'Millennium Dome – big enough to fit St Paul's Cathedral in on its side, room for 28 football matches to take place at the same time, trapeze equipment installed, waterproof, central heating, centrally situated, excellent transport links, now empty and ready for immediate use, offers in the region of £5 million.'

Below are five of the questions asked of potential buyers.

- **Why do you want to buy the Dome?**
- **Would purchase be for commercial gain or to help the community?**

- **Would you use the Dome for:**
  - **(i) sport**
  - **(ii) exhibitions**
  - **(iii) entertainment**
  - **(iv) religious services**
  - **(v) other?**
- **Which groups of people would you expect to visit the Dome?**
- **What benefits would you gain from owning the Dome?**

1. Explain which of these questions is qualitative and which quantitative.

2. Explain which question you think might be the most useful and why.

3. Explain which question you think might be the least useful and why.

4. Outline what other information the government should be seeking.

Structuring primary research

Primary researchers have to set out the structure of their research before they are able to carry it out. The structure can be outlined through deciding:

- **who** to ask
- **how** many to ask
- **what** to ask
- **how** to ask
- **how** to present the information.

The information obtained should provide the researchers with a customer profile for the product. Once this has been established, advertising and promotion can be used to target that particular profile. The profile will tell the researchers:

- who will **potentially** buy the product. This may be by factors such as age group, gender, single or married, home-owning or not.

- who will **actually** buy. Boxed chocolates are mostly bought by men for women, baby clothes are targeted at adult purchasers – for obvious reasons!

- how the buyer found out about the product. Was it through a print advertisement? If so, in which publication? Was it through a broadcast advertisement? if so, on which channel? When? Was it through recommendation or word of mouth?

- how often they will buy it. Will it be daily, weekly, monthly, twice a year?

- the retail outlet at which they would normally buy the product. Is it a corner shop, catalogue or supermarket, a High Street store or the Internet?

- why they would buy it. Is it the taste, smell, shape or colour? Is it for its use, quality or convenience?

It will also seek to establish:

- what the buyers think of as the main competitor or competitors to the product. Are the competitors good or close substitutes?

- what types of product are bought at the same time. Are there marketing opportunities to be gained by linking with complementary products?

Setting questionnaires – types of question

The types of questions which can be asked are important. In some cases quantitative responses will be sought, in other cases it will be qualitative information. Remember that quantitative results may be statistically presented and validated whereas qualitative results are likely to give further depth to research by finding out opinions. The most common types of question are:

- closed questions – such as the ones in the Kellogg's promotion, where a limited number of answers is possible. Some closed questions may have only a single answer, for example the question on how many packets would be bought. Some have more than one possible answer, such as the one regarding children. Parents may have children in more than one of the age ranges given. The most specialised form of closed question is the Boolean question (Boole was the mathematician who invented the logic gate which can only be 'open' or 'closed'). In this form of specialised closed question, if one answer is correct, the other must be incorrect (yes/no or male/female are the most common).

● open questions are used for qualitative answers. They generally ask for a statement or opinion which the researcher then has to record. This makes the use of open questions a much more time-consuming – and therefore more expensive – method of collecting information. Such questions are important to give depth to the research being undertaken. Researchers may be trained to interpret the way that such questions are answered as well as the answers themselves.

● psychologically based questions. Such questions are asked of individuals or focus groups to try to get at the 'feeling' behind purchases. What is it that makes someone purchase on impulse? What is it that makes a particular brand popular? What characteristics of a product or even a product name are important to the customer? In this way companies can find out if they ought to be emphasising (or improving) their community spirit, their efficiency, their environmental credentials, the size of their product range or their after-sales service. Qualitative questions may be asked such as 'What makes you buy Kellogg's Frosties?' or 'How do your children react when you buy Kellogg's Frosties?' or 'What values do you think of when you think of Kellogg's?' You can see from the nature of these questions that the answers may well need interpreting.

> *Please mark where you would place your satisfaction with the product: 10 being the highest, 0 the lowest.*
>
> | 0 | 1 | 2 | 3 | 4 | 5 | 6 | 7 | 8 | 9 | 10 |

FIGURE 3.6 *Scale of responses*

● specific questions. Some questions are designed for specific responses – they may ask for a mark out of 10 for a product, or for a respondent to mark a position on a scale or graph to indicate their opinion. They may use scales such as that shown at Figure 3.6.

Setting questionnaires – question bias

The types of question researchers ask may affect the answers given. Questions can be 'loaded' or biased towards a particular answer. Questionnaire setters need to be careful that they do not build such bias into a question.

An example from political history will illustrate this point. When Britain first entered the EEC, there was no referendum on membership. Had the electorate been asked 'Do you want to join?' or 'Do you want to stay out?', it is likely that they would have opted for the existing situation and voted to stay out. When the referendum was held, two years later, the angle of the question had changed subtly, so that it now asked 'Do you want to stay in?' or 'Do you want to come out?'. The electorate duly voted in favour of staying in.

The type of research and types of questions asked will also depend on the type of market involved. Patterns of demand for consumer goods which are purchased by thousands of people can be established by questionnaire surveys and other devices. In industrial markets, the approach might need to be different – there may be very few buyers, so that statistical information of this nature is of little use.

ACTIVITY 6

Look at Figure 3.5 again.

1. **Explain why you think that Kellogg's have chosen to ask these questions.**

2. **If you had room to add another four questions to the promotion, what four would you add? Explain why.**

3. **Explain the marketing link between Kellogg's Frosties, the NBA (National Basketball Association of America) and ITV Sport.**

4. **What is the main weakness of primary research of this nature?**

5. **What is its major strength?**

ASSESSMENT activity 1

1. **Look through the list for the sort of questions to which a customer profiling exercise would be expected to find answers.**

2. **Now design a questionnaire of your own that covers all of these questions.**

5. **Test the questionnaire on a small group of people.**

4. **What changes would you make before using the questionnaire to find out about the customer base for your own marketing strategy?**

Setting questionnaires – sampling

When deciding who to ask, a business can target its existing customers in various ways. It may use devices such as questionnaires in guarantees, competitions and promotions like the one for Kellogg's shown. It can target potential customers through a variety of sampling techniques.

Sampling attempts to ask a number of respondents who will stand as a representation of the whole market. If you are in a group of 20, you could ask five people their views and call this a representative sample. While 25 per cent is a much larger sample than any commercial manufacturer would ever manage, you can see the problem that is caused by using low numbers.

If you asked 50 people out of 200, the views would be much more representative. This is because statistically each respondent is balanced by 49 others, so that extremes of opinion will be disregarded because such anomalies are ironed out by the majority. In small samples, extremes can skew results. Such skewing is called 'bias'. Statisticians use the '19 out of 20' rule for accuracy. Decisions are only recommended if there is a 95 per cent chance that the information is correct (19 times out of 20). This will depend on the size and composition of the sample and the type of questions asked.

Top Tips

If you try to think of samples in percentage terms, you will avoid the problem of results being skewed. For example, each respondent in the sample of five represents 20 per cent of the sample and 5 per cent of the whole group. In the 50, each respondent represents 2 per cent of the sample and 0.5 per cent of the group – you can see that the likelihood of results being skewed by a small number of respondents is thus diminished.

Sampling

A business will recognise that, except in limited cases such as some industrial markets, it cannot question the whole of its market and will therefore try to question a cross-section that will accurately reflect the make-up of the market. Different types of sample can be taken, the main types being probability samples and non-probability samples.

Probability samples

● **Random sampling** means that each member of a population has an equal chance of being sampled. Usually it involves taking numerically large samples. This makes it difficult, slow and expensive but can be accurate if the sample is large enough. Some telephone surveys tend to be of this nature, with operators choosing, for example, a name from each page of the telephone book. This can be refined by making it more systematic – for example, every 50th name in the phone book might be chosen.

- A **stratified** random sample asks only those in a particular stratum or level of a population. They may be identified by characteristics such as age, race, parents, shared interests, married or single. This means that information must first be collected to establish who is a member of the particular stratum. As long as everyone in the stratum fulfils the requirement (everyone is the parent of a child under the age of 16, for example) then a random sample can be taken. The information requested by Kellogg's could produce information of the type that '25 per cent of respondents have children between the ages of 10 and 15'. They could use this information to make sure that a survey sought responses from a similar segment.

These are called probability samples because researchers can estimate the statistical probability of who will be asked. In the case of the phone survey, above, choosing one in 50 will give a sample of 2 per cent of the total. Each person in the total therefore has a one in 50 probability of being asked. Accuracy of such statistics can be maintained by moving down a name if a contact declines to respond.

Non-probability samples

In non-probability samples, estimates of this nature cannot be made. Such samples tend to be easier to conduct and less costly than probability samples but, of course, the results will not be as accurate. The main types are:

- **quota** sample. In this the population is defined by segments and the sample taken would reflect the size of each segment. If half of the population was female, then half of the quota sample should be female. Researchers would have a particular quota to fulfil – for example, in a 1,000-person survey they would be expected to ask 500 men and 500 women.

- **targeted** sample – sometimes called a cluster sample – generally means that research is targeted at a particular group or area, usually one that can be defined fairly easily. Samples may be targeted using postcodes, the circulation areas of regional or local publications or commercial TV franchise areas. The group within the cluster will be taken at random. Sometimes it is not the size or structure of a sample that is important, but the information which it may hold. For example, research carried out among retailers of a particular product may be much more revealing than research carried out among customers. This particular target sample may be able to spot patterns of expenditure and type of customer because of the overview that they have.

How is research conducted?

The situation in which questions are asked will affect the likelihood of accurate and honest answers. Researchers who approach people in town centres on rainy days are likely to get either no responses or the quickest ones that people can give! Some researchers go to the trouble of providing prizes or rewards as incentives for people to complete survey information.

Response rates measure the number of people who actually answer or return a questionnaire, compared with the number asked to do so. A good response rate can make a piece of research much more efficient. If a researcher knows that a 20 per cent response rate is likely then they know that to reach a quota of 1,000 respondents they must actually ask 5,000 people. If the response rate can be increased, then the cost of collecting the information can be reduced. Response rates to face-to-face 'street' surveys are highest as it is often made difficult for people to refuse to answer questions without seeming bad-mannered.

Response rates to postal surveys tend to be much lower unless some form of reward is attached to the completion of the survey. Other methods include:

- **Fill in yourself** – delivering a form and either collecting it or encouraging the respondent to return it, perhaps with special offers or competition entries. This may be more successful as it combines the personal touch with giving the respondent time to complete the questionnaire at leisure.

- **Telephone questionnaires** are increasingly popular. They can be conducted relatively cheaply and reach a segment of the target market without the need for travel. Responses can be either recorded or entered into a computer as they are made. What is termed 'cold calling' – approaching a telephone respondent without having first established that they are willing to participate – tends to have low response rates. Seeking permission to call at a convenient time and offering rewards for participation are likely to make response rates much higher.

- **Focus groups** were developed in America and have become a reliable source of customer information. A focus group will be carefully put together to represent a particular market segment or segments and will then be questions about actions and reactions. The group may be a 'one-off' group that reports on a specific part of a marketing strategy. For example, the group members may be asked how many times they noticed a particular advertisement or promotion, what the features were that made them notice it and whether or not it induced them to change their spending patterns. More permanent focus groups might be used over a period of time. Established groups may be used by various researchers for various different questions, products or promotions.

- **Panels of customers** will sometimes be put together to provide a stream of information, but not necessarily to provide opinions. Such

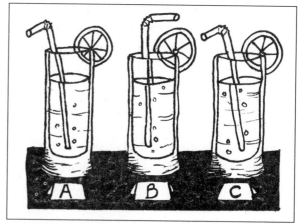

FIGURE 3.7 *Blind tasting*

groups include the panels that report to television companies on what channels they were watching, from which information viewing figures (very important to advertisers) are calculated.

Tasting and testing

Sometimes customers' opinions are sought by letting them actually taste or test a product.

- In the case of **tasting**, this could take place as a consumer panel or focus group or might be conducted as a street survey. People will be asked to comment on particular taste characteristics which the company is trying to promote. For example, is the product too sweet, too acid, too sickly, too dry? Blind tastings may also be conducted so that researchers can check the performance of one product against another. In a blind tasting, respondents are not told the brands that they are tasting and are then asked for opinions. Researchers then know that the responses they are getting are genuine taste responses, not influenced by branding or packaging. Results can, of course, therefore be used to gauge the effect that a brand name or a particular style of packaging has on customer responses.

- **Testing** of a product sometimes takes place over a wide area. A new soap powder or shampoo, for instance, may be delivered to all the houses in a particular area and then followed up with a survey. Surveys may be attached to the product in the hope of increasing response rates. If people are receiving a free gift, they may be more inclined to reply.

Pilots and field trials

Pilots and field trials may also be included under the heading of testing. A pilot launch will be limited to a particular area. The results of such a launch can be used either to make modifications to the product or to confirm its success. In some cases, the pilot may reveal flaws or problems which the business had not considered. This could result in the product having to be withdrawn and either dropped or re-modelled completely. This 'back to the drawing board' scenario may be disastrous to a business and is usually the result of poor or inadequate market research. It is not, however, as disastrous as if the product had been rolled out nationally.

Pilots can easily take place in defined areas. A postcode might provide a particular area or, for larger pilots, the circulation of a local or regional newspaper or the broadcast area of a regional commercial television company. Trials or pilots may also be run concurrently in different parts of the country to gauge whether a national reaction to a product is likely. The reaction of a Londoner to a particular product or concept may be entirely different to that of a Yorkshireman or Cornishman. Results may show that rather than a national product, regional differences and variations would be more successful.

Field trials of a product – letting the customer try it in the situation that it is designed for – will also help to iron out difficulties or to show up possible flaws.

ACTIVITY 7

All Bar One

All Bar One is a new concept in the brewing business that came from discussions within Bass in 1994. Research revealed that, for a large number of younger people, the traditional pub no longer held any attraction. People liked eating out but were not happy at paying excessive amounts for drinks in restaurants. What appeared to be needed was a new concept – a meeting, eating and drinking place that could not be described as a pub or a restaurant and that would not be categorised as a down-market café or bar.

The target market was business professionals (AB social class) in the 25–40 age group. The pilot of the concept – a non-traditional, up-market place serving drink and good food – was opened in December 1994. Some early problems with the concept were exposed and put right. The brand was then 'rolled out' nationally, with more than 30 outlets now open.

1. Describe the process behind the pilot launch of All Bar One.

2. Explain what advantages Bass would gain by going for a pilot launch before the national roll-out.

3. Collect some information regarding the concept and its marketing from the company (Bass can be found at www.bass.com) and use this to help you with your own marketing strategy.

Key Skills IT3.1

Observation

Not all techniques of primary research involve questionnaires or surveys. Effective techniques also include observation, providing it is done in a scientific way.

Observing how many people pass a particular point in a given period of time (a footfall count) could, for example, show:

- which time of the week is busiest
- the age and gender structure of passers-by
- how many of them stop to look in the window
- how many of them then enter the premises.

Marketing research studies much consumer behaviour through observations of this nature. For example, researchers have observed people's behaviour in shops and can alter the shop layout to take maximum advantage of this. Did you know that most people turn right on entering a shop? That there are certain 'hot' zones in shops where people are more likely to buy? That customers often head to the back of a shop first?

Supermarkets have built a whole science of shop lay-out, music played, displays, directions and 'hot spots' up on such observations. Product links, where two products are placed close together because it has been observed that one is usually bought with the other, are established. The detail of such observations is fine enough that the very height at which goods are displayed is important.

Observations have the advantage that no interaction with the subject is actually needed. They are therefore much less costly than other methods and there is little chance of bias.

Personal feedback

This is particularly important in the sale of capital or industrial goods. This may be disguised as something totally informal, like a business lunch, but actually be carefully constructed so that a representative of the supplier can find out whether the customer is happy with the service or not and what changes he or she would like to see. With products of this nature, the personal touch is essential.

Purpose

The final purpose of the information must inform the way in which a researcher decides to structure it. The information may be required in a particular format – able to be entered into a computer for analysis, for example, or cross-referenced to different market segments. Researchers need to ensure that they study the research brief carefully so that all relevant information is being collected and can be presented in a the way that the client wishes.

Interpretation of data

Once researchers have collected and presented data, it will still be part of a manager's job to interpret it. There are a number of factors which must be taken into account when doing this. When looking at research commissioned for their own business they need to check in particular:

● what the purpose of the research was and whether it has fulfilled it

● whether it has been conducted according to their specifications

● whether the results can be validated

● whether there are any circumstances that might have skewed the research.

When interpreting research data that has been commissioned by others they need to consider:

● who is doing/has done the research, and how reliable they are likely to be. What questions are they likely to be addressing?

● the size and composition of any samples used

● the questions in a questionnaire. Are they fair? Do they show bias?

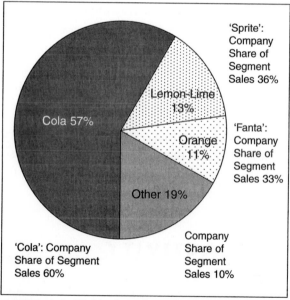

FIGURE 3.8 *Worldwide carbonated soft drink industry by flavour segment*

Source: Adapted from The Times 100

In all cases it is important that interpretation:

● looks for trends or patterns

● spots which figures are predictions or forecasts, and judges whether they will be accurate

● is wary of absolutes and percentages and is aware of which is which

● is aware of statistical accuracy – the 19/20 rule – and can see if it can be applied

● always compares like with like.

Interpretation should include validation where this is possible. Managers should look for one piece of research data validating another. If there isn't one, then the manager should do some secondary research to see if he or she can find one. For example, in Activity 8, the growth of e-cards is likely to be linked to the growth of e-mail, which in turn will be linked to growth of Internet use. Information on this growth may be available in a secondary source.

Sometimes interpretations are incorrect because something obvious has been missed: a date, for example, or the way that a particular figure is expressed. Look at the share figures for the soft drinks market in Figure 3.8. Fanta had 33 per cent of an 11 per cent share, representing 3.6 per cent of the global market. Easy to misinterpret or misrepresent!

Top Tips

When looking at research findings, it is always a good idea to make sure that you know who has funded the findings. Research funded by the Society of Motor Traders is unlikely to show that rail is a better form of transport than road! Research findings may be deliberately skewed or biased to present 'opportunities' to particular industries.

Interpretation of research

Wishes Cards is a High Street retailer of greetings cards, wrapping paper, stationery and small novelty goods. The core of its business is in printing and selling greetings cards for all occasions. It has been worried by a fall in sales over recent years. Newspaper reports have suggested that e-cards, electronic greetings sent across the Internet, have been increasing in recent years. The following information is available.

Key Skills N3.1

1999				2000				2001	
Q1	Q2	Q3	Q4	Q1	Q2	Q3	Q4	Q1	Q2
4.1	3.8	3.7	8.2	3.6	2.9	3.0	7.5	3.0	2.4

TABLE 3.1 *Sales by quarter (£m)*

1999		2000		2001	
FIRST	SECOND	FIRST	SECOND	FIRST	SECOND
1.7	2.3	1.5	2.0	1.1	1.5

TABLE 3.2 *Profits by half-year (£m)*

Information was collected from shops and from a questionnaire which produced these results:

1999		2000	
MEN	WOMEN	MEN	WOMEN
5.7	10.2	4.8	9.9

TABLE 3.3 *Cards purchased by gender (millions)*

1999

MEN				
Birthday	Anniversary	Leaving	Christmas	Other
53	24	2	12	9

WOMEN				
Birthday	Anniversary	Leaving	Christmas	Other
29	4	6	60	1

2000

MEN				
Birthday	Anniversary	Leaving	Christmas	Other
54	27	2	14	3

WOMEN				
Birthday	Anniversary	Leaving	Christmas	Other
28	4	6	61	1

TABLE 3.4 *Cards purchased by gender and type (%)*

A sample of 1,000 men and 1,000 women were asked if and when they had ever sent an e-card. The 'yes' responses were:

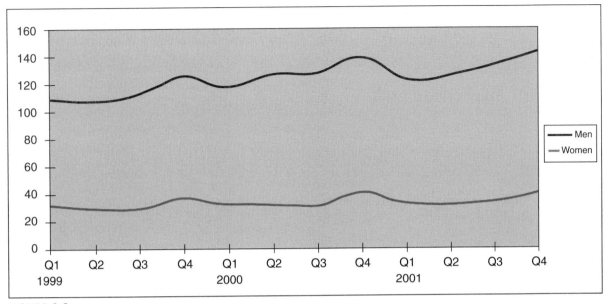

FIGURE 3.9

To the question 'Have you ever sent an e-card?', the following percentages replied 'Yes':

MALE	11–16	17–24	25–35	36–44	45–55	56 plus
	70	80	54	32	10	2
FEMALE	11–16	17–24	25–35	36–44	45–55	56 plus
	31	38	31	23	4	1

TABLE 3.5

1. How would you explain the sales patterns by quarter?

2. How would you explain the sales patterns by gender?

3. How would you explain the sales patterns by type of card bought?

4. What does the market research data tell you about the future of greetings cards?

5. How could you validate these data?

6. What would you suggest as a possible marketing strategy for this business?

Key Skills N3.1

Advantages and disadvantages of primary research

Primary research:

- can be targeted
- will be up to date
- can ask the precise questions to elicit the precise information that is needed
- can be given greater depth and worth by looking at factors such as psychological reasons behind purchases.

Its disadvantages are that:

● it is costly

● it can produce skewed or biased results

● it may need to be validated by cross-referencing it with other, historical, data.

Secondary market research

Secondary research is research that has been previously published or made available. It may be based on either internal or external information.

● **Internal** information includes the business's own records and internal reports. These will be accurate and up to date and, in general, will not be made available to other businesses.

● **External** information is that information which has been collected or collated by other organisations.

Such information includes all published resources – whether in print, on CD-ROM or on the Internet. Any information that is available that has been collected by another body, or for another purpose, is classed as secondary information. You could almost call it 'second-hand' information as it carries some of the drawbacks of second-hand clothes and goods. It may not quite fit, it may not quite be right, it may have been developed for a different job altogether. Some information (and the biggest single source is now the Internet) will be free while other information may be either very expensive or very difficult to obtain. Commercial bodies collect and publish information as a profitable business in itself.

Commercial publications

Market intelligence reports are extremely useful but extremely expensive. They range from publications like BRAD (*British Rate and Data*) which contains details of all publications along with their circulation and advertising rates, to major business trends reporters such as Mintel and Keynotes. These publications, usually produced monthly, show the latest figures on market share and segmentation, who is advertising what and where, and what distribution networks are in place.

Other organisations that publish research include:

● ABC (The Audit Bureau of Circulation) which checks and ratifies newspaper circulation figures

● Gallup and MORI, which produce opinion polls

● JICTAR (the Joint Industrial Committee on Television Audience Research) which produces the weekly viewing figures for each television channel.

Published resources may also be available through the trade press for a particular industry. *The Grocer*, for example, is a magazine with a national circulation. There will also be publications from trade associations, umbrella bodies who represent a particular trade or industry. Often parts or digests of this information are published in newspapers and magazines – the *Financial Times*, the *Guardian* and the *Daily Telegraph* all produce reports based on such statistics and all have Internet sites from which further information can be gained. (Just put the name of the relevant newspaper into a search engine. You may have to register to gain access, but this is usually free.)

National information

Some information is collected on a national basis by government and published at regular intervals. There are Treasury quarterly reports, *Economic Trends*, the *Annual Abstract of Statistics*, the Family Expenditure Survey and *Social Trends* detailing levels and types of expenditure by social and income group. Such publications can show trends that might be useful to a new entrant to a market. For example they could show that the consumption of a particular product is rising or falling in a particular age or gender group. Such initial information may lead an entrepreneur to decide to initiate further research in that area.

Census

The biggest exercise in the collection of national statistical information is the National Census. This takes place once every 10 years in the year ending in '01'. The last census was in 1991; the next will be in 2001. The Census questions every household in Great Britain and produces so much information that it is often years before it is published in any sort of usable form.

The 2001 Census will be the first one that has taken place in the 'computer age' and it will be interesting to see whether this makes the publication of results any faster. Information is collected on household size, incomes, spending patterns, migrations, number of children, education, income, social status, car ownership and many more categories. The information is then processed and provided by the Office of National Statistics (ONS).

Number crunching

With improvements and the lower costs involved with information technology, many market researchers now rely on technology rather than the face-to-face approach. This will not give the depth of response or psychological information that focus groups or interviews would but can provide a mass of information which has the advantage of being able to be 'crunched' very easily. 'Number crunching' is the term given to the turning of raw data into understandable and usable statistics.

Marketing databases

Businesses can very quickly build up huge amounts of quantitative information in giant databases – many of which will be sold on for use by other businesses. The database 'search and sort' facility can be used to identify almost instantly clusters or groups of customers to target.

The 'and/or' and 'and/not' question facilities mean that identification of particular groups is easy. For example all people with dogs **and** who drive cars could be targeted for an appropriate product. Getting people on the database can also be easy – if you or your family have ever had a Christmas card or piece of direct mail from a retailer this shows that your name is on its database. The computer will also hold details of what you tend to spend, when you tend to spend it and what you tend to spend it on. If, for example, you are a regular buyer of 40 cans of dog food a month then this information could be very important for a pet food manufacturer who may target you for other products.

Further information will be collected as you fill in guarantee cards, enter competitions or subscribe to magazines or journals. Such database information may be sold on to other retailers – there is a box to tick to prevent this happening but it is generally rather small! Manufacturers can use this information to regionalise product launches or to provide product variations. If a database reveals that cider is the drink of choice in certain parts of the country, lager in others and bitter in others then it makes sense to divide marketing expenditure accordingly and direct it where it will be most effective.

 **Top Tips**

You can gain the benefits of some professional publications by going to a local library, where they may be found in the reference section. You will also be able to obtain government data from the library, or may be able to reach this source through the Internet at http://www. open.gov.uk/. *Economic Trends*, the *Annual Abstract of Statistics* and *Social Trends* are all available from the Stationery Office.

ACTIVITY 9

Targeting the ultimate niche

The ultimate niche market is the wants and needs of a single customer. The new century sees ever more sophisticated computer technology – mobile phones which access the Internet, on-line shopping and the facility for massive databases (the British Telecom database for telephone numbers, for example, has over 100 million entries. It can be accessed accurately in seconds (try ringing Directory Enquiries!). Interactive cable television, palmtop and laptop computers and video phones are all developments that are or will be onstream shortly.

1. **How do you think that market research techniques will develop in the new millennium?**
2. **'The ultimate niche.' What is it and what combinations of technology could be used to find out this information?**
3. **How could the marketing strategy of a business alter if it had access to the ultimate niche market?**

Advantages and disadvantages of secondary research

Secondary research may not:

- be as up to date as primary – the mere time that it takes to publish the research may make it out of date
- cover exactly the ground that a researcher wants to cover
- ask exactly the questions that a primary researcher might be able to ask
- be accurate or complete or in the right format for the business's needs – it may be presented as pie and bar charts, for example, and have to be re-written to find out the raw figures before an organisation can make use of it
- be any cheaper than primary research but not be as accurate (especially true of good secondary research as provided by market intelligence reports, for example).

On the plus side, secondary research is likely to be:

- much more far-ranging than primary, giving a good overview of a market or market segment
- very accurate at the point of collection because such large samples are taken or because it is based on actual figures such as the number of sales in a particular period in some cases, obtainable very cheaply.

Suitability of research

Different market research techniques will be suitable for different products and different businesses. This may be related to the cost of obtaining the data and their accessibility, reliability and validity.

Managers will need to answer a set of questions before proceeding with research. These will include:

- What do we want to know? What question or questions should we be asking?
- What are we willing to pay? If large-scale research is necessary, then this will be costly.
- Should the research be 'in-house' or outsourced to an agency?
- How confidential do we need to keep the data?
- What data collection methods will we use?
- What will be the scale of the research?
- What's the value of the information?

There are other factors which must be taken into account. Research must be accessible and easy to interpret. Results must be reliable. It should be easy to understand and analyse. Managers should be able to draw clear conclusions from it.

Some markets will suit particular types of research.

- **Consumer** markets are where a lot of mass-market research may be appropriate. Large numbers are needed to give the statistical 95 per cent certainty on which recommended action will be taken. Consumer research is thus expensive but tends to be accurate. Consumer markets and tastes can change very quickly and it is therfore essential that businesses involved in this market keep up to date with market changes. A single comment can change the direction of an industry. (The MP Edwina Currie announcing that all UK eggs had salmonella did little for the egg industry!) Businesses must therefore be prepared to act rapidly on good market information.

● **Financial and capital** markets tend to follow longer-term trends and patterns. Research in such markets will consist of studying economic trends, published figures, such as those provided by the ONS, and results, such as company reports and statements. Market movements around the world will be important so information will have to be collected on a global scale. Spotting the underlying direction behind the trend can make or lose fortunes. Businesses of analysts are employed to make forecasts – they are often groups or sub-groups of city businesses of accountants and bankers. Primary research is often of little use to such groups who rely on good sources of secondary information.

● **Commodity** markets will also be studied in depth by specialist businesses looking at the future state of the industry or possible future demand patterns and market trends. If, for example, an artificial substitute for rubber, that didn't wear out as rubber tyres do, was being developed, rubber suppliers and importers would want to be able to judge what effect this would have on their industry.

● **Industrial** markets involve businesses selling not to the final consumer, but to other businesses. In this case brand and image tend to be much less important. Personal contact will give businesses a lot of market information, as will reading the trade press for that particular industry or visiting trade exhibitions and fairs. The National Motor Show, the Ideal Homes Exhibition and the Boat Show are all examples where the exhibition is aimed at the trade, and only indirectly at the final consumer. Some trade fairs and shows may not open to the general public at all, but only be open to businesses within the industry.

Research and the product life cycle

Research needs to be linked to the stage on the product life cycle that the product has reached. If the research carried out is not appropriate, then it is not likely to be of any use.

The position of a product on this cycle will determine how important marketing expenditure is, how much expenditure should take place and may even decide whether a product will be allowed to live or die. The early part of the cycle, through research and development to national 'roll-out', is where marketing research may be most important. Both qualitative and quantitative research should be used. The standard six phases of the product life cycle are:

1. **Product development**. The business is receiving no revenue from the product but is spending on research and development. It will be seeking opinions on what products might sell. This is likely to be qualitative research through interviews and focus groups. Later stages may include 'tasting and testing' where prototype products are introduced to selected markets.

2. **Introduction or launch**. This may be a pilot launch in a small area, preceding a national launch. Marketing data could be gathered through questionnaires, surveys or focus groups. There will also be feedback on sales from sellers.

3. **Growth**. The business experiences growing volumes of sales.

4. **Maturity**. Competitors will have entered the market and the original product will find that it is having to compete on price and quality. Advertising can be used to reinforce a brand or message. Focus groups can be used to search for improvements.

5. **Saturation**. By this stage there are so many competing products on the market that it may be said to be saturated.

6. **Decline** and **death**. The product has reached the end of its useful life cycle and no one now is interested in buying it. It has been replaced by better products. Is there still a market for black and white televisions, for example? For gramophone record players? Market research information is no longer needed.

Table 3.6 shows how market research techniques relate to parts of the product life cycle.

When a product is about to go into decline it can be 'rescued' by a product extension strategy. This

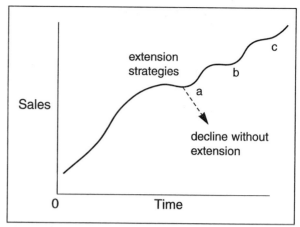

FIGURE 3.10

means extra marketing expenditure (at a, b, c in Figure 3.10) to extend the life of the product. For example, the market for televisions may be said to be saturated. Hasn't every household got one? Product extension strategies such as remote control, wide screen, stereo and surround sound have all been used to ensure that people are still 'updating' their television.

STAGE		
EARLY R&D	Seeking opinions on what new products might sell	Interviews
EARLY R&D	Testing the water' – with new concepts, packaging ideas or brand names	Opinion surveys
R&D	Trialling product ideas	Focus groups Consumer panels
R&D	Product tasting and testing	Focus groups Consumer panels
RESTRICTED LAUNCH	Product launched in a region. 'flagship' service (e.g. new concept shop)	Interviews and customer feedback Sales figures
LAUNCH/ROLL-OUT	National product launch Advertising campaign	Focus groups, psychological questioning
MATURITY	Reinforcement advertising	Focus groups, psychological questioning
INJECTING NEW LIFE	Product modifications and improvements	Interviews Focus groups Consumer panels

TABLE 3.6

 **ACTIVITY** **10**

1. Make a list of 10 products you can think of that have come on to the market in:
 ■ the last 10 years
 ■ the last 25 years
 ■ the last 50 years
 ■ the last 100 years.
2. For each product, say where you think it now is on the product life cycle.
3. Choose one product that you think is in decline and suggest ways of halting this decline.
4. Put these ways into a presentation that you could give to the manufacturer of this product – use a range of techniques and images to make your points clear.

Accuracy

Market research can be wildly inaccurate. Politicians relying on large-scale popularity polls to tell them when would be a good time for an election have been caught out on many occasions. Sometimes (and political polls are a case in point) people are reluctant to let their true views or opinions be known and this therefore biases the results. People may give what they perceive to be the 'right' answer to a question. A survey asking people how much they gave to charity would be likely to return a much larger figure than was actually given because people inflate their donations to stop them seeming mean to the surveyor!

ACTIVITY **11**

Jaguar has been a leading player in the luxury car market for a number of years. In 1999 the business launched the Jaguar S-type at the Birmingham International Motor Show. The car is a mid-sized Jaguar, aimed at a younger and less wealthy market segment than its 'big brother', the E-type Jaguar. However, it still carries the prestige and brand loyalty that goes with the Jaguar marque. The original version of the Jaguar S-type was launched in 1963 and it was decided to revive the name as the car shared many characteristics with the original – small, powerful and racy looking.

The market research carried out by Jaguar (now owned by Ford) showed that customers wanted a car that was stylish, safe and secure but also fun to drive, high performance and technologically advanced. The price of the car would mean that customers would need to be in the professional and executive class of occupation.

1. Describe the various types of market research that Jaguar is likely to have carried out during the research and development phase of the project.
2. Explain how Jaguar would validate such research before embarking on such an expensive project.

Section 3 *Methods of analysing marketing opportunities*

What you need to learn

In this section you will learn about:

- using market information to analyse competitiveness
- the importance of understanding the environment within which the business is operating
- using models such as PEST and SWOT to give information on the business environment
- analysing the internal and external constraints on marketing activities
- how businesses develop different marketing strategies.

You will need to be able to use market information to analyse the competitiveness of your chosen product. You should be able to analyse the market to see the nature of the environment that the business is in.

FIGURE 3.11

 ACTIVITY 🔟

Complexity

Look at Figure 3.11. Goods and services are provided for different types of market.

1. **List the goods and services which you think have been involved in the scene shown.**
2. **Categorise them into consumer goods, capital goods, industrial goods or services.**
3. **What does the length of your list tell you about the complexity of markets and therefore the need to analyse them?**

Types

Remember, there are three main types of market:

- consumer goods – divided into consumer durables and consumer goods (consumer non-durables)
- services – these are intangibles such as insurance, transport, banking and tourism
- capital goods – also called industrial marketing (goods which will be used to make other goods and services such as machinery, equipment and tools).

Marketing in each type of market will be very different. Industrial marketing, for example, relies heavily on the personal approach and may be linked to the availability of finance. Businesses try to see which markets can be broken up into smaller sections or segments so that marketing activities can be targeted accurately. This is the process of market segmentation.

Market segmentation

Market segmentation describes the division of a market into separate groups which can be expected to respond differently to promotions, communications and advertising. Each group or segment can be targeted by a different marketing mix as each is designed to be separate from the other.

Market segmentation has taken over from product differentiation as the major way in which businesses try to compete and expand sales. In the 1990s the concept has developed to the extent that many marketing strategies are based on offering products that are as customised as possible to a consumer's wants.

The ultimate market segment and smallest niche market is one person; in services the product can usually be tailored to this person – to individual requirements (for example, holidays, pension schemes, haircuts); in goods markets such levels of segmentation are more difficult to achieve.

One market that is highly segmented is the entertainment market. Figure 3.12 shows one way in which this might be broken down. This diagram is only a start! Each sub-section could be broken down further. 'Theatre' could include opera, ballet, plays and musicals. Music, books and video obviously have many sub-divisions.

Market differences

Segmentation can only be used if there are recognisable differences in a market. It is also important that the differences in the market can be measured by primary and secondary research methods. Usually there are obvious large segments in all markets – male/female; young/old; rich/poor, for example. Possibilities for segmentation depend on:

- costs. The cost of segmenting a market must be outweighed by revenues derived from the success of the segmentation

- size of market. Small markets are usually not suitable for segmentation; generally, the bigger the market, the more opportunities there are for segmentation. The entertainment market is huge

- approachability. Each segment must be able to be targeted. The use of particular media should be linked to particular markets. Look at the magazine market, for example. There is a magazine called *Babycare and Pregnancy* on pregnancy, birth and baby care and another called *Motorgliding International* for glider enthusiasts, both established in the 1990s.

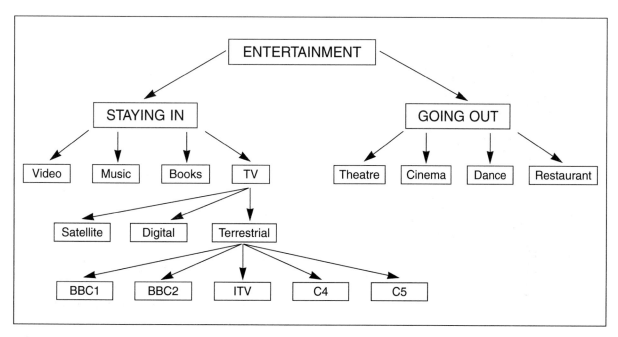

FIGURE 3.12

These have been created because these particular market segments exist. The entertainment market has also seen the growth of dance clubs and rave music

● different wants. Members of different segments should gain utility from a product in different ways. An item of clothing could be sold because it keeps you warm, because it is fashionable or because it is cheap or expensive. Different people must want to buy it for different reasons for segmentation to work.

Why segment?

The main reasons for segmenting markets are:

● it is easier for marketing strategies to target groups which share the same characteristics

● niche markets can be found or created. If products match niches exactly, then sales are assured

● focus. Segmentation allows organisations to make more efficient use of resources by focusing only on those segments that are targeted. A 'scattergun' approach of targeting many segments will lead to wasted resources

There are two ways in which segmentation can take place.

● instinctively. This involves the use of secondary market data and the manager's 'feel' for how the market may be divided. Examples may include gender, age groups, geography (north versus south), usage (high, low, average mileage), wealth and race.

● research-based. Primary research takes place across a whole market and segments are defined according to a statistical analysis of the research. Research-based segments will be much narrower than the 'instinctive' ones. Variables will include:

  – **demographic** variables – age, gender, income, race, marital status, education and occupation. The size, structure and trends in population will affect tastes and wants. Consider the market segment for live theatre compared to that for dance clubs

  – **ethnographic** variables – tastes and wants will differ among different racial and religious groups

  – **geographic** variables – country, region, county, town urban or rural; in the UK this can be segmented easily by using postcodes. Tastes and wants will differ in different parts or regions of a country, or internationally. How popular is live theatre in one part of the country compared to bingo in another?

  – **behaviour** variables – where do you shop, are you a light or heavy user of the product, how do you respond to advertising? Why would someone buy a product? Is it because it is functional, glamorous, colourful, cheap, expensive? Will they buy it again? If so, why? If not, why not?

● **socio-economic** variables – this is usually done by household and based on the occupation of the head of the household (see Table 3.7). The most important segments in terms of

CLASS	GROUP	TYPICALLY
1	A	professionals, e.g. doctors, judges
2	B	managers, technical and executive, e.g. directors, accountants
3	C1	supervisory and clerical (non-manual), e.g. secretaries, salespeople
3	C2	skilled manual, e.g. electrician, plumber
4	D	semi-skilled manual, e.g. packers, assembly line workers
5	E	unskilled manual and low-income groups, e.g. labourers, pensioners, students

TABLE 3.7

approximate size are C1 at 20 per cent, C2 at 33 per cent and D at 20 per cent of the population. The segments which have the majority of the spending power, however, are A and B – although B is approximately 12 per cent of the population and A a mere 3 per cent, between them they represent the market for luxury goods and services.

- **psycho-graphic** variables – those to do with behaviour and habits, such as lifestyle, hobbies, entertainment enjoyed, attitudes, personality.

C1, C2 and D make up almost three-quarters of the population and so are the most heavily targeted sector.

Top Tips

You will need to use up-to-date statistics to make your marketing strategy effective. These can best be obtained from the Internet although you will also find them published in newspapers. Many statistics were published for the end of the old millennium. For example, half the population aged 16 and over is married, there are 1.6 million cohabiting couples; the earth is getting warmer (the hottest 12 years ever have all occurred since 1980). Which of these might a business see as marketing opportunities? Which as threats to their market?

ACTIVITY ⑬

You will need a current TV guide.

1. **Look at a typical day's entertainment on a commercial TV channel.**
2. **Study the descriptions of the programmes and decide which market segments they are targeting. Some examples might be mothers with children, young children, older children, teenagers, women, men, students.**

3. **Draw up a pie chart which shows how the segments are divided according to the time of day.**
4. **Watch the advertisements at certain times of day to check if your segments are the same as the advertisers'.**
5. **Explain why you think that the daily TV market is segmented in this way.**

How do businesses develop marketing strategies?

Marketing strategies will be based on the different circumstances of different businesses. The marketing strategy for a business will follow a planning cycle which is similar to the one used to decide on its overall objectives.

- First, the business decides what its long-term aims and objectives are – maximisation of turnover, of profit, of market penetration or market share or some other less ambitious aim.

- Then it must decide on the intermediate targets that are the 'stepping stones' on the way to achieving ultimate goals. The strategy will depend on the information which the business is able to collect. This includes internal information about its own operations, strengths and weaknesses and externally about its position in the market. It also includes the positions, strengths and weaknesses of its competitors.

- There are various different methods of collecting and analysing such information and the business needs to choose that method or those methods to which its organisation and market are best suited.

- The business then, in the light of these analyses, develops appropriate marketing strategies and implements them.

- Finally, the business needs to measure and evaluate outcomes to see how close they have come to achieving targets and then to start the whole process again by setting new aims and objectives.

Gap analysis

One way for a business to study whether or not it is 'on track' is to use gap analysis. This involves the business looking at the objective that it had set for a particular time period and at what the gap between that objective and actual performance is. The size of the gap will be important, as will the reasons for the gap to be there – for objectives and expectations to have been greater than actual performance. For example, a business might have aimed to reach 15 per cent of a market but managed only 12 per cent. Managers would seek the reasons for the gap and devise strategies to try to close it. If such strategies could not be devised, the business might be forced into revising its objectives.

 **ACTIVITY** 14

Mars launched its 'Celebrations' miniature chocolates in 1996; by November 1998 it had gained a 12.6 per cent share of the £3.3b count line confectionery market, securing 14th position, sandwiched between Nestlé's Polo and Mars' Bounty. (Count lines are 'counter-based' confectionery such as chocolate bars, tubes and 'fun' boxes.) The entire confectionery market is worth over £5 billion. The product was aimed at the market dominated by Cadbury's Roses and Nestlé's Quality Street. The product hardly made a dent in sales of Quality Street, its market share falling by a tiny 0.2 per cent from 20.5 per cent to 20.3 per cent. The Roses brand saw its market share fall from 27.7 per cent to 25.7 per cent (in an expanding market, this meant a fall in actual sales value of just 2.9 per cent). Cadbury's responded, in time for Christmas 1999, with its 'Miniature Heroes' range – tiny versions of its own favourite brands – and immediately secured a market position.

1. What use might gap analysis be to the business if Mars had the objective of gaining 15 per cent of the confectionery market?

2. What tactics might Mars have used to try to close the gap?

3. What effect might the launch of Cadbury's 'Miniature Heroes' have on the market position of Mars 'Celebrations'? What would you predict Mars' targets for 2000 to be?

 **Top Tips**

Different marketing objectives and how they are reached can be studied by following stories as they appear in newspapers. The rise of Asda and its aggressive marketing since its take-over by the American supermarket chain Wal-Mart has been well reported in the press. Battles such as this are reported in financial pages. You could collect clippings which demonstrate market changes of this nature and mount them as a cuttings file.

The overview

Before embarking on a particular strategy, a business needs to know 'where it stands' in the market. How does a business learn what its current market position, strengths and weaknesses are in order to form the factual basis for its marketing plans? Several models are suggested – the business needs to choose the most appropriate model or range of models for its own market and objectives. Different models will suit different businesses or products at different stages of development.

- **External analyses** are those that look at market position and the position of competitors.
- **Internal analyses** look at the business's own strengths and weaknesses.

Businesses may use SWOT or PEST analyses for a general overview or specific marketing analysis tools such as the Boston matrix, Ansoff's matrix, product portfolio or perceptual analysis. These will be used to answer specific marketing questions or make specific marketing decisions.

Not all of these may be available or useful to all businesses. A small business may have little choice but to budget, not on the basis of what would be most effective, but on the basis of what it can actually afford.

Marketing strategies will also depend on whether or not a business wants to be recognised as an innovator. New markets can be created out of innovations. Creative marketing can also play a part. Cars are sold as lifestyle choices, not as a means to get from A to B. Strategies may also depend on a marketing manager's or entrepreneur's insight into a market. Rupert Murdoch has led News International into new markets where he has seen growth potential. In many cases, the business has made a loss over a number of years before the market has expanded sufficiently to become profitable. This insight is a major factor in making News International such a successful business.

SWOT analysis

This looks at the factors that might affect the success or failure of a marketing strategy. SWOT is an acronym for Strengths, Weaknesses, Opportunities and Threats and is a technique which requires the business to look at its internal strengths and weaknesses and its external opportunities and threats. If the factor is outside the control of the business it is an external factor. If it is within its control, it is an internal factor.

- Internal strengths may not be confined to a product but include things such as a skilled workforce, current market position or penetration and profitability. They could also include items such as the business's reputation, or product, or product range.

- Internal weaknesses may be old plant or machinery, over-staffing or organisational problems, poor employee relations, high staff turnover or product problems.

- Internal strengths and weaknesses can be found out by a business doing an internal audit in order to recognise – and build on – its strengths and to recognise – and remove or minimise – its weaknesses.

- External opportunities are provided by the market, or by changes in demand. They can include new methods of production or distribution, new materials, new methods of communication or information technology over which the business has no control.

- External threats can come from competitors, demand factors or outside bodies such as the government. This could include local, national or international governments or bodies – new laws, regulations or levels of taxation, for example. Competitive threats may come from new entrants to the market, new products or from factors which have affected consumer demand.

In some cases it is difficult to determine whether a particular change is a threat or an opportunity. Some changes may be threats to some businesses but opportunities for others. A scare over the amount of fat in butter may pose threats for the dairy industry but be an opportunity for the margarine and edible oil industry; a fuel shortage or extra tax on petrol may pose a threat to motor car sales but be an opportunity for bicycle manufacturers.

SWOT analysis will suit most businesses. It is especially good at focusing attention on competitors' actions and on other external challenges that the business must face. Managers may meet to brainstorm SWOT analyses. SWOT can be used easily before any major decision is made and will often form a good starting point for discussion.

A SWOT analysis is usually presented as a grid (see Table 3.8).

	Strengths	Weaknesses
INTERNAL		
	Opportunities	Threats
EXTERNAL		

TABLE 3.8 *SWOT analysis*

ACTIVITY 15

SWOT analyses can be used in areas other than marketing.

1. **Practise doing SWOT analysis by doing one on your local football club. It could look like this.**

	Strengths	Weaknesses
INTERNAL	New number 11	Old goalie
	Good captain	Poor coach
	Youth team	
	Opportunities	Threats
EXTERNAL	New competitions	Other teams
	Lottery grants	Ground developers

TABLE 3.9

2. **Practise doing a SWOT analysis on the following:**
   - **a new supermarket development**
   - **a new television comedy by a successful writer**
   - **an existing car model**
   - **a favourite magazine.**
3. **Do a SWOT analysis on your marketing strategy.**
4. **Explain what steps you will take to remove the weaknesses.**

PEST analysis

A PEST analysis is a way of further looking at the external factors that will affect an industry. The acronym stands for Political, Economic, Social and Technological factors. These are all generally considered to be outside the control of the business (although many businesses will go to great lengths to try to control them).

- **Political factors.** Government at local, national and international levels provides rules, regulations, conventions and constraints on industry. These range from devices such as the issue of licences at a local level to export licences, restrictions and encouragements or subsidies at a national level. Internationally, legislation may be designed to prevent or curtail the movement of particular goods or could form part of protectionist policies (see Section 2 of Chapter 2). Other legislation will affect labour markets, monopolies and anti-competitive practices as well as regulating types of marketing.

- **Economic factors.** The main economic factor is concerned with changes in consumer demand. These can occur gradually, over a period of time or very rapidly. Some levels of demand are constant. For example Nestlé's Kit Kat chocolate finger bar has been the market leader, with a stable level of demand of around 5 per cent of the confectionery market, since its launch in 1937. Its nearest rival is the Mars Bar, which in 1998 had 3.9 per cent of the market. Other brands may have explosive or seasonal demand patterns. Cadbury's Creme Eggs, for instance, have a seasonal pattern. Others may flop completely. Tobacco companies have tried launching several substitutes for tobacco – including, at one point, dried green vegetable matter. All have failed to find a hold in the market. Companies need to be able to monitor and predict demand so that they can react to it or – better still – be proactive in turning demand changes to their own advantage. For example, if you are a chocolate manufacturer and you see increase in demand for healthy lifestyles, you produce fruit- and nut-based bars which will take advantage of this change in demand.

  Other economic factors include:

  - the level of interest rates – this will affect the cost of finance to a business and thus profits

  - taxation will have a general effect on demand and may have a specific effect on certain products

  - the value of the currency – an important factor for any business involved in importing or exporting. A strong currency will be good for importers – an opportunity – but bad for exporters – a threat

  - changes brought about by the economic or business cycle – these may be predicted and will affect most businesses. Again, the same up- or down-turn in the cycle may present opportunities to some businesses while being a threat to others.

- **Social factors.** These also involve mainly changes in consumer demand. This time they are changes that have been brought about by changes in attitudes or in society in general. Some are small and gradual changes. For example the fact that more people now live together rather than getting married will have slightly affected numerous markets such as flowers, photography and dressmaking. Large changes may take place in a short space of time. The move away from GM foods happened over a period of approximately 12 months – a very quick change in demand terms. Changes such as demographic or psycho-graphic ones may happen over a longer period . Typical of such changes is the changing structure of the population. This will present opportunities for some businesses as they produce more products aimed at the growth area of the population. It will pose a threat to others if their target market is dwindling. Changes in fashion may also be classed as social changes – outdoor eating used to mean picnics, now it means barbecues. The sale of picnic baskets, thermos flasks etc. is therefore replaced by barbecue charcoal and cooking implements.

- **Technological factors.** Changes in technology may be either threats or opportunities. New techniques of production or new materials may be adopted to make production more efficient or the product more attractive. Or a competitor might adopt the new technology first, thus creating a threat. Entirely new markets, where there is no competition (such as that into which the Sony Walkman was originally launched) are called 'blue sky' markets. Sometimes products and processes become obsolete and, if a business fails to move on, this could spell its failure. Electric bar fires and oil paraffin heaters, for example, have mostly been replaced by newer and more efficient heating appliances. Businesses who made these products will have been forced to alter production or go out of business.

Later versions of PEST have been developed to include legal issues, making SLEPT – although these could legitimately be included under Political reasons – and to include environmental or green issues – making PEEST or G-PEST which could legitimately be included under Social reasons.

- **Legal factors.** Changes in the law which might affect a business. In the UK there is, increasingly, a body of European law which British businesses must follow. Sometimes businesses are not even in a position to lobby as decisions or interpretations may be made by the European Court in The Hague rather than by any domestic legislature.

- **Environmental factors.** Green factors are becoming increasingly important to consumers. They will want to see that a business is recycling or using recycled materials wherever possible and expect businesses to have good environmental credentials. Some companies have used this factor to extend and expand their markets – washing powder and washing products, for instance, make a virtue out of being bleach-free, or biological, or concentrated or available as refills to cut down on packaging waste. All of these ideas also add to the businesses profitability. Perhaps the most successful retailer in terms of environmental image is The Body Shop, with its pledge to use recycled materials and to be as much of a friend to the environment as it can. The environmentally friendly reputation and corporate image of this chain is its main selling point.

 **Top Tips**

Acronyms like PEST, PEEST and SLEPT are designed to help people to remember the factors involved. Although PEST analysis is the standard description of this process, you could easily derive your own acronym or mnemonic for remembering all the factors involved.

 **ASSESSMENT** **2**
a c t i v i t y

Businesses use PEST to analyse the market their product is in. Imagine that a business was about to introduce a low-alcohol alcopop. This would combine two successful products. Alcopops are brightly coloured, sweet, highly alcoholic drinks served in trendy bottles. Low- or no-alcohol products provide an alternative for drivers. The analysis for the combination could include:

- **political/legal.** The business will not be allowed to aim advertising at under-age drinkers
- **economic.** The demand for fashionable drinks is increasing among young people
- **social/environmental.** Society may be moving towards a more responsible attitude to drink driving
- **technological.** It is possible, with new technology, to produce an approximation to the taste without the alcohol?

1. **What other factors could you add into this analysis?**
2. **Do a PEST analysis on your own chosen product.**
3. **How does this help with your marketing strategy?**

Key Skills C3.2, C3.3

Different marketing strategies

Each business wanting to expand will have a choice of marketing strategies. These were arranged in a matrix by business writer Igor Ansoff. The matrix plots how safe or risky various marketing objectives are and can be used by a business to judge the likelihood of success.

- **A1 = market penetration.** This is trying to penetrate a market which already exists. This means competing with those businesses already in the market. The strategy carries the least risk of failure and probably the lowest level of reward. Marketing expenditure does not have to be high so this is a strategy that can suit small businesses seeking new market opportunities.

- **B1 = new product development.** This is developing new products to add to existing markets. For example a new kind of chocolate bar being introduced to the sweet market carries a fairly high risk but also the possibility of high rewards. Marketing expenditure will need to be high to establish the new product. However, it will benefit from carrying an existing brand or reputation. A recent success story involved the Nestlé Kit Kat chocolate bar. A new 'chunky' version was a runaway success and was quickly followed by other versions such as the dark chocolate Kit Kat.

- **A2 = entering new markets.** This is using an existing product to enter a new market, perhaps finding or suggesting a new use for a product, or re-positioning a product, i.e. changing its image or characteristics so that it appeals to a wider market segment. Oxo has recently re-positioned its product to take advantage of an emerging market. This can often be an expensive strategy.

- **B2 = diversification.** This is the introduction of completely new products into new markets. It can be expensive and dangerous. The risk of entering untried markets can be minimised through good market research but cannot be eliminated altogether. The Virgin group has followed a policy of diversification for a number of years, always seeking to invest profits from existing products in new markets. This has taken the business from records to radio stations, trains to mobile phones, aeroplanes to Internet access.

Ansoff matrix

		A	B
	lowest risk	EXISTING PRODUCTS	NEW PRODUCTS
1	EXISTING MARKETS	market penetration	product development
2	NEW MARKETS	market development	diversification
			highest risk

TABLE 3.10

Top Tips

You can spot when a product is being re-positioned by watching advertisements and noting how their targets have changed. Oxo Cubes was repositioned early in 2000. It had always been aimed at the nuclear family and advertised using the 'Oxo family'. A new advertising campaign re-positioned the product to take account of changing lifestyles and depicts it being used in student flats and to make TV dinners rather than the 'traditional' family setting.

Marketing expenditure

Different levels of expenditure will be needed for different product types.

- A new product in a competitive market, at the beginning of its life cycle, will require heavy marketing expenditure in order to launch it and establish a foothold in the market. Examples might include a new type of confectionery.

- A new product – an innovation – in a 'blue sky' market may require very little marketing expenditure if its selling points are obvious. The Sony Walkman, for example, virtually 'sold itself'.

- Mature brands, particularly market leaders, require advertising in order to keep the product in the consumer's mind. Sponsorship, for example, will be used to confirm brand names and values (look at the information regarding Kellogg's and the NBA in Section 1 of this Chapter for an example). They may require extra marketing expenditure if a competitor threatens their share of the market.

- Differentiated products, or products which are the subject of life cycle extension strategies, need a lot of marketing expenditure. The heaviest advertisers are car manufacturers with their many differentiated models. They are constantly trying to persuade people to replace something which has probably not outlived its usefulness with something else. To so this they require heavy marketing expenditure to highlight the new features which differentiate the old model from the new. Clever marketing often makes these extras seem like essentials.

In some markets heavy marketing expenditure is always required. Markets where there are a few dominant businesses engage in non price competition, competing using promotion, competitions and public relations. A good example is the soap powder market in the UK.

The Boston matrix

If a business was looking to make a decision about a marketing strategy it would need to know the current strengths and weaknesses of all its products. The Boston matrix was developed by management consultants in Boston, USA. It is used to plot the percentage of the market enjoyed by each product in a business's portfolio against the type of market that it is in. It allows a business to see:

- which products are achieving their potential
- which products may need to be helped with extra advertising or marketing expenditure
- which may need to be dropped altogether.

	HIGH MARKET SHARE	LOW MARKET SHARE
High market growth	stars	problem children
Low market growth	cash cows	dogs

TABLE 3.11

The four possibilities shown in Table 3.11 are defined as:

- **stars:** These products have a high market share in a fast-growing market. They may have been the first of their kind – an innovation in a blue sky market – in which case they could have been launched with little in the way of marketing expenditure. However, they will need high marketing and advertising expenditure in order to keep them competitive as new entrants, attracted by their success, come into the market. One example is the Psion series palmtop computers, the first really viable palmtops.

- **problem children:** Sometimes also known as question marks. These products have a small market share of a fast-growing market. These could be the competitors that are trying to gain a foothold in a blue sky market dominated by its initial entrant. For example, a star may be created by a new application of technology. The market will then attract competitors who will remain as problem children unless they establish themselves in the market. The market itself is a growing one, and therefore a market to be in, but the business must get the product right.

- **cash cows**: Every established business longs to keep or develop at least one cash cow. These products have a large market share or market leadership of a mature or slow-growing market. Cash cows represent established product lines which need little in the way of marketing expenditure and which produce cash which can be used to support other products. Nestlé's Kit Kat has held its market leadership for 63 years and provided the cash for the launch of many new product lines and innovations.

- **dogs**: These could be problem children who have not made the grade or potential stars in a market that has failed to materialise. They are products with a small share of a slow-growing market and probably cost more in marketing and support to maintain their position than they actually return to the business.

A well-balanced business needs to ensure that it has products in the right categories. Only then can it survive and expand under changing market circumstances. Marketing managers can choose whether to keep or lose each product ('hold' or 'divest') and make decisions on how to use the cash generated by successful products like cash cows. The most usual tactics will be to:

- keep the cash cows, using the cash to support other products (also known as **milking the cows**)

- try to turn the stars into cash cows by using cash cow money (**holding the stars**)

- try to turn the problem children into stars by using cash cow money (**building the problem children**)

- **lose the dogs** – if possible sell these products to another business or, if this is not possible, get rid of them completely by ceasing production (also called 'divesting'). Divesting

the dogs does not have to mean that the product' disappear. Another business may be able to find a niche market for them or be able to support them with sufficient marketing to at least turn them into problem children – from where they can develop star status.

The matrix can be adapted to show the level of turnover being achieved by each product so that the relative importance of each can be seen even more clearly. The size of the box can be used to represent turnover as in Table 3.12.

	HIGH MARKET SHARE	LOW MARKET SHARE
High market growth	stars	problem children
Low market growth	cash cows	dogs

TABLE 3.12

Perceptual mapping

There are other ways in which a business can analyse the range of products that it offers and therefore make decisions about what sort of marketing strategy is needed. A perceptual map of products shows where each is positioned in the market and indicates whether there are gaps in a businesses portfolio which might be filled.

Figure 3.13 shows the way in which the hotel brands owned by Bass Leisure Retail Group might be perceived.

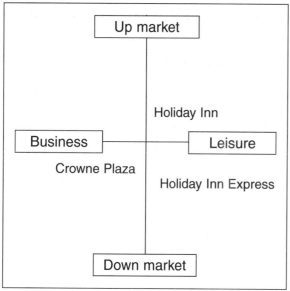

FIGURE 3.13

The leisure side of the business is served by Holiday Inn Express and the more up market Holiday Inn while there was a gap in the business side of the portfolio. Bass bought Inter Continental Hotels and Resorts to fill this gap. This has served to give it a complete portfolio – see Figure 3.14.

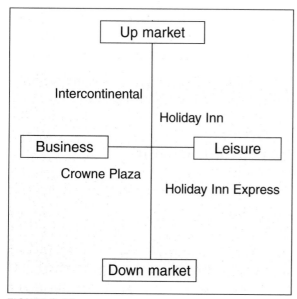

FIGURE 3.14

Any business with a range of products can carry out a perceptual mapping exercise to see where there might be gaps that it can fill.

Choose a market with which you are familiar – clothes shops in your local town centre, for example, or magazines aimed at a certain gender. Carry out a perceptual analysis to see if there are any gaps that need filling.
Key Skills C3.3

Product life cycle

The product life cycle has been detailed on page 139. The life cycle can be used as part of an analysis to see if it is worth spending marketing money on a particular product. If it is experiencing growth, it could be worthwhile to spend on it in order to try to keep competitors out of the market. If it is in decline, and extension strategies are not appropriate, then it may not be worth any marketing expenditure.

Constraints on marketing activities

For details on most of the internal and external constraints look at the part of Section 1 that includes them (page 119). As well as these, there are some specific constraints related to the marketing industry. Constraints are industry-based, based in ethics, or legal constraints imposed by government.

Industry-based constraints
These include:

- **Advertising Standards Authority.** This operates the British Code of Advertising Practice through the Code of Advertising Standards Committee. In short, the Code states that all advertisements should be:

- 'legal, decent, honest and truthful'
- 'prepared with a sense of responsibility to the consumer and society'
- 'in line with the principles of fair competition'.

● Complaints about advertising that falls outside the Code – which may be indecent, immoral, misleading or offensive – will be investigated by the ASA. Advertisers need to be very careful as sometimes only a small number of complaints is needed for the Committee to investigate and take action. The ASA checks a random selection of advertisements and promotions to ensure that they are within the Code. It covers all print and published advertisements. The Independent Television Commission carries out a similar task for commercial TV and the Radio Authority for radio advertising. The parts of the standard mean:

- legal – Businesses may not advertise anything that is illegal (such as drugs) or encourage anyone to break the law or do anything that might be outside the law
- decent – Businesses may not use images such as pornographic ones to promote products; images and words that are likely to cause offence may not be used. This includes things such as racist or sexist comments
- honest – The Code states 'No advertiser should seek to take improper advantage of any characteristic or circumstance which may make consumers vulnerable as, for instance, exploiting their credulity or their lack of experience or knowledge'. Businesses may not make dishonest claims about a product: 'use this product and your hair will grow back', 'this product cleans all stains from all surfaces' are claims unlikely to be true
- truthful – A business must not deliberately mislead customers. If 'in tests, the product worked 9 times out of 10' the advertiser should have evidence to substantiate this.

Obvious untruths, often made for humourous reasons, are not included. People should be able to judge that using a particular deodorant will not make you magnetically attractive to the opposite sex, even if this is what is depicted.

Ethical, environmental and social constraints

● Acting ethically means 'doing what is right' or moral. With certain products there are moral objections to marketing. These fall into a number of categories (some of which may also be controlled by law). Businesses should not promote:

- indecent materials such as pornography or depictions of violence
- addictive products such as drugs (there are also restrictions on the promotion of alcohol and tobacco products)
- products that have involved suffering in their development or production. This category could include products made in less developed countries by under-paid labour, products tested on animals and products where an animal has suffered, such as battery chickens.

● Businesses should also show a concern for the environment. Green issues have become an important part of marketing. Businesses now make a point of emphasising where recycled materials are used, or environmentally friendly

FIGURE 3.15 *Showing ethical concern: John West Dolphin Friendly Tuna Steak*

methods or ingredients. As public opinion has turned towards a greater concern for the environment, so businesses have had to ensure that their environmental credentials are as good as possible. This makes good marketing sense.

- Social constraints may prevent a business from marketing particular products. For example, the public broadcast of certain lyrics from songs could offend some people. Albums containing tracks with such lyrics may be sold, if warning is given, but the track will not be allowed a public airing.

- Business stakeholders, such as shareholders, suppliers, managers and employees, may insist that a business does not step outside social, moral and environmental constraints. They may also have particular objectives or views that have drawn them to a business. The Co-operative Bank, for example, has a policy of ethical investment. Stakeholders in the bank expect it to adhere to that policy. It may be the main reason why they are using that business.

- Pressure groups may also become involved in the interpretation of what is ethical or moral. These are groups of people who have joined together in order to try to influence opinion and policy. Major pressure groups such as Greenpeace and Friends of the Earth have been instrumental in changing the attitudes of both consumers and businesses. They have run major campaigns against, for example, whale hunting, seal killing, nuclear waste discharges and genetically modified food. Often, the fact that they raise public awareness of an issue will be enough to change opinions. Aerosols have become 'ozone friendly', washing powders 'bleach-free' and timber from 'renewable, managed resources' since awareness of environmental problems was raised. As opinions change, so do patterns of demand. Businesses need to be aware of changing patterns and alter marketing to suit them.

Legal constraints

Businesses are governed by a number of laws. In marketing, the most important ones are:

- The **Trade Descriptions Acts 1963, 1968 and 1972**. These state that sellers must be honest about products, giving accurate descriptions on advertisements, packaging and labelling, point-of-sale material and verbally, to consumers. Nottingham Lace must be made in Nottingham, Champagne be made in the Champagne region of France. Labels must show the composition or ingredients in products and the country of origin. Products must perform to the levels or standards claimed by the manufacturer or their representative. All products must be safe to use. Faulty products should be replaced. Businesses giving incorrect or misleading information may be prosecuted.

- The **Broadcasting Act 1990** set up the Radio Authority and the Independent Television Commission. Both issue licences to broadcast franchisees and operate a Code of Practice which includes advertising. The Broadcast Complaints Commission investigates complaints made by viewers and both publishes the results and broadcasts them on television.

- The **Monopolies and Mergers Act 1965**. This set up the Competition Commission which investigates mergers to see if they are in the public interest and ensures that monopoly powers are not abused. Businesses with monopoly powers in the UK are assumed to be against the public interest and be obliged to prove that they are not. The Office of Fair Trading, set up by the Fair Trading Act 1973, brings possible monopolies and mergers to the attention of the Competition Commission for investigation. Businesses may merge if they either prove that the merger will not be against the public interest or sell off parts of the business to ensure that monopoly powers are not created.

Other constraints

Businesses may also be governed by their own codes of practice or by international bodies.

- The European Commission may also block mergers which would create monopolies in the EU. When Grand Metropolitan proposed a merger with Guinness to form the giant Diageo drinks corporation, the European Commission would not allow the merger unless the businesses sold off some of their brands.

- Privatised industries have regulators or regulatory bodies who investigate the profits being made and prices charged. These are often referred to as 'watchdogs'. A number of such industries have been ordered to lower prices to the consumer or even re-pay excess profits made where they have been taking advantage of their monopoly positions.

- Many industries also operate voluntary codes and are said to be 'self-regulating'.

ACTIVITY 17

The following statistics were published on the last day of 1999. Study them carefully and then answer the questions which follow.

- 185 million cups of tea are consumed each day in the UK
- solvent abuse accounts for 2 per cent of all deaths of 15–19 year olds
- 4 million Britons are vegetarians
- alcohol is consumed by 9 out of 10 adults in the UK
- 63 per cent of households in the UK own a CD player
- 25 per cent of households own a computer
- 40 per cent of households own a mobile phone

- 11 million (19 per cent) of the UK population are under the age of 25
- 16 million (28 per cent) of the UK population are over the age of 65 (see Figure 3.16).

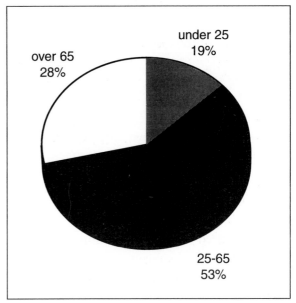

over 65
28%

under 25
19%

25-65
53%

FIGURE 3.16

1. Which of these do you think would be seen as marketing opportunities? Which as creating marketing problems?
2. Describe how these statistics would be of use to:
   - a mobile phone provider
   - an Internet service provider
   - a solvent manufacturer
   - an entertainment provider.
3. Outline the other statistics which each of these organisations would need to collect before writing a marketing strategy.
4. What other businesses might be interested in these statistics?
5. What use can you make of these statistics in your strategy?

Key Skills N3.1

Section 4 *Creating strategies that meet customer needs (the marketing mix)*

In this section you will learn about:

- elements of the marketing mix
- finding the appropriate marketing mix
- price strategies and techniques of pricing
- communications with customers
- image, expectations and ambience
- effective customer service, including trained and motivated staff.

Businesses need to combine a number of factors in order to build a coherent marketing strategy. Each factor may be considered as a strategy in its own right. The different strategies are usually grouped under the heading of the 'marketing mix'. This is the mix or balance of various strategies used to sell a good or service. The parts of the marketing mix include:

- price: price and techniques of pricing
- promotion: the various forms of promotion
- place: which includes both getting products to the right place (distribution) and the places where customers may buy products (retail outlets)
- creating the right conditions for customers
- good and effective customer service

You need to be able to evaluate the marketing strategy for a good or service, using the principles in Section 1 of this chapter. It would be a good idea to remind yourself of these principles before continuing with this section.

Deciding on the price to charge

One of the first decisions that a business has to make is 'What price shall I charge?' The business must understand what level of price customers will pay and communicate this price to them. It must satisfy their expectations in terms of what they expect for that price, i.e. value for money. It must anticipate how competitors might react to that price.

A price which covers the costs of production and provides a profit may look like the most sensible option. However, such a price may have no bearing on the actual price that could be charged. If a business could produce a top-quality training shoe for a cost of £3 then a 100 per cent mark-up would give a price of £6. Is this the price that it should charge? A price of this type is based solely on supply costs.

Cost-based prices

- **Cost-plus** pricing. The business adds up the various costs of making the product and then adds on a percentage of 'mark-up' for profit. Price is the cost of manufacture plus profit.
- **Marginal** pricing. Cost-plus is not as easy as it sounds when many products are involved or, as is usual, many different costs. Marginal or contribution pricing is where a business calculates price so that it will cover the variable costs of production and make a contribution to fixed costs. Once fixed costs (overheads) are covered, the product then makes a contribution to profits. Using marginal pricing, businesses can see how well each product that it produces is doing, and alter strategy accordingly.

The price the business could charge would take into account the demand for the product. Many prices are set according to levels of potential or actual demand rather than just based on cost. Competition- or marketing-based prices are thus more usual than cost-based ones. A business is likely to choose a price that both covers costs and is competitive. The training shoe producer could look at the prices of other shoes

FIGURE 3.17 *In markets like these a business has to accept the market price*

Source: Life File/L. Moss

of similar quality and then charge a slightly lower price.

Competition-based prices

- **Competitor-based**. Where the business chooses to set price, not according to costs, but according to the prices that other businesses are charging. Basically 'what the market will stand'. Often consumers (wrongly) equate price with value so, if one business was selling a good particularly cheaply, consumers would be suspicious of the quality of that good.

- **Market based**. Sometimes the business has no choice but to accept the price set by the other businesses in the market. If price is set by a dominant business, this is called price leadership. If it is set by the market it will be due to the competitive nature of that market. Imagine a competitive market, with many suppliers. If the business prices above market

price, it makes no sales. If priced below market price, its stock is cleared and it leaves the market this way. This is not likely to be a good thing as the low price is unlikely to cover the business's costs.

 ASSESSMENT
a c t i v i t y

Consider the market that your chosen good or service is part of. Look at the structure of the market. Is it dominated by one business? A few businesses? Are there enough small businesses that no single one is able to affect price?

1. **What is the minimum price you need to charge in order to cover your costs?**

2. **What is the market- or competitor-based price that you could charge?**

3. **What price will you charge? Why?**

Top Tips

Attracting buyers to a market

In most cases, a business will want at least to cover its costs. It is likely to also want to make a profit. Having achieved this, it may be able to use certain special prices to give it market advantage. Such prices will be used for new products in new markets or as a reaction to prices charged by competitors.

New products may be introduced with a special low price to encourage purchases or, if the product is a premium one, at special high prices.

● A new product which is seen as a luxury or premium item may be introduced to the market at an initially high price. This is on the assumption that customers will pay to be 'the first' with the product. Innovations such as camcorders, mobile telephones and computers were all initially launched at a high price which later fell as competitors entered the market. This is called 'skimming' or 'creaming' and often applies to products using new technology. Even calculators initially had a high price!

● A business entering a new market may set a price which is **lower** than those of competitors so that it can gain a foothold in the market. A telephone company, for example, may offer discounts and low prices to new customers. Even though these may be short-term, and price advantages may be eroded, customers may stay loyal to the company. Once a business has established a market share through penetration pricing, it is likely to keep it.

● In some cases a business may even be prepared to make a **loss** on a product. This loss may be to attract buyers into its market. It can only do this if it has the resources to be able to stand the losses for the period of time necessary for it to achieve its objectives. Loss leaders are also used by businesses who expect customers to return for other purchases. For example, a computer games manufacturer may sell consoles cheaply, knowing that it will recoup expenditure from profits on the games.

Sometimes prices are set not to gain customers or market share, but to destroy the market share of a rival.

● **'Predatory'** or **'destroyer' pricing** is where a business deliberately undercuts its rival's price with the intention of driving that rival out of business. The success or failure of the strategy depends on which business has the greater depth of financial resources.

FIGURE 3.18 *Promotional and psychological pricing*

Other special types of price include:

● **psychological point pricing** – this is a price tactic whereby businesses try to make goods and services sound like they are cheaper than they are – £99.99 sounds like a lot less than £100. You will notice that many prices finish in .99

● **promotional pricing** – usually short-term pricing strategies to increase sales. Special offers, sales, discounts, '2 for 1', 25 per cent off etc. are all promotional prices. Such prices may often be used as a way of clearing old stock from shelves and warehouses so that new stock can take its place.

Communicating with customers through promotions

Promotion involves communicating the existence, features and benefits of a product to a customer or potential customer. Marketing principles mean that the business must be aware of any legal, moral and ethical constraints. It must also understand what customers want and how competitors might react to a promotion. The intention is to do one of three things:

- increase or create customer awareness of products
- encourage customers to remember a product
- persuade customers to buy the product

Advertising – 'above the line' expenditure

One strategy to achieve these aims is advertising. The AIDA acronym is used to remember the qualities that advertising should possess.

AIDA stands for:

- attention
- interest
- desire
- action.

Effective advertising should attract attention; create interest; develop desire; and lead to action. Advertising is paid-for publicity for a product. Because it is paid for directly it is called 'above-the-line' promotional expenditure. Other methods of promotion are called 'below-the-line' expenditure.

A business does not just embark on advertising. It has to take all the costs into account and estimate the benefits. It is not worth advertising if the benefits do not outweigh the costs. A full-page newspaper advertisement costing £1,000 may be able to sell a £500 second-hand car. This does not make it effective advertising. If a similar-sized advertisement could sell 100 such cars, this would be considered effective.

Businesses need to ensure that advertisements are appealing to the right market segment, otherwise they are wasting valuable marketing expenditure. They need to choose particular media as a part of their marketing strategy. Some advertising can be targeted using particular broadcast times, programmes, magazines and journals. Other advertising, such as posters, will just aim to reach as many people as possible.

Advertising is a way of getting a message from the seller to the buyer and that message therefore needs, as with all communication, a medium to carry it. Advertising media are the channels used to convey advertising messages from the seller to the buyer or potential buyer. Media become more expensive as they become more effective.

The main advertising media are broadcast media, published media and poster and billboards.

- Broadcast media include television, radio and cinema advertisements. Television and cinema advertisements are most effective but also expensive to make and expensive to show, television advertisements being more expensive the wider the audience reached.
- Radio advertisements will reach a mass audience and are reasonably cheap to make and broadcast but are not as effective as television, having the benefit of sound but not movement or visual impact.
- Published media include newspapers, magazines, leaflets and 'flyers'. Advertising costs will depend on the print run or the circulation of a publication.

- Mass-market publications are much more expensive than local ones because they reach a much wider audience; a full-page advertisement in the *Sun* newspaper will cost over £30,000, for example.

- Specialist publications, such as the trade press and magazines covering particular interests, meaning that this type of advertising can gain the benefits of being targeted.

- Poster and billboard advertising includes any print medium that is mounted for display. The largest posters are called '64 sheet' size as this is the number of sheets of paper needed but small posters can be placed almost anywhere. Adshel is a business which sells poster sites at bus stops. Taxis and buses carry posters and many events are advertised with posters mounted in pubs, clubs and shops. National poster campaigns, which must have a strong image and short and to-the-point message, can be very effective but are very expensive. Cigarette advertisers are big users of posters because many other media are denied to them.

- Advertising on the World Wide Web may be thought of as a completely new medium. Effectively, advertising is free – anyone can have a website and can advertise what they want. There may even be no ethical or moral constraints on what is advertised. However, advertising is only effective if people visit a site. This means that commercial advertisers are only likely to place advertisements on popular sites. Many popular Internet sites are supported by their advertisers, who are willing to pay for space because they know that a lot of people will visit them.

Measuring effectiveness

Measuring how effective advertising has been is difficult. If there is an increase in sales, this may or may not be the direct result of the advertising – other factors can also come into play. Further, any increase in sales must produce sufficient revenue to offset the cost of the advertising in

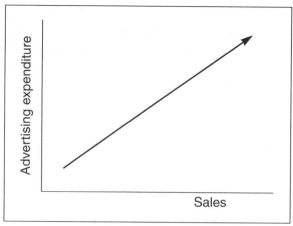

FIGURE 3.19 *But was it all down to the advertising?*

order for a campaign to be considered effective. In judging whether a campaign was a success, a business will look at all the objectives and all the factors involved over a period of time. Statistical techniques will be used to observe whether a positive correlation exists.

Some objectives, such as brand recognition, may be relatively easy to check and quantify. Businesses can use market research techniques such as focus groups or questionnaires to check effectiveness.

ASSESSMENT *activity* 5

You may choose to advertise your chosen good or service as part of your promotional strategy.

1. At which market segment would you aim the advertising?
2. How could you ensure that you reached that segment? Suggest magazine titles or broadcast media times that might reach that segment.
3. Use a copy of *British Rate and Data* to find out the costs of various methods of advertising.

Branding

Branding is the way in which a business develops a name or an image to go with the product that it is producing. Branding is designed to make the customer feel secure – they know that a particular brand means quality, or speed, or level of service, for example. Brands may be established through a number of avenues, the most common of which is the brand name. They will then be further reinforced with special typefaces, colour schemes, logos, slogans or other recognisable features: the Adidas brand's three stripes, for example, or the shape of the Rolls-Royce car's radiator grill. Brands, names and trade marks are protected by registering them – usually shown by the TM symbol after the brand name; this prevents other businesses from copying or imitating the brand.

ACTIVITY 18

1. **Without thinking too carefully, list the first 10 brands that come to mind. You could list them by name, by logo, or by slogan.**

2. **Now compare your list with those made by the rest of your group. Work out which three brands appear the most times and may be thought of as the most recognised.**

3. **What do you think are the qualities of these brands that make them so recognisable?**

FIGURE 3.20 *Inappropriate promotion might put customers off*

Sales promotions – 'below the line' expenditure

Promotional expenditure that is not spent directly on advertising is called 'below the line' expenditure. It may be spent on:

● promotion directly to the trade

● promoting products into the distribution system – to wholesalers or direct to retailers

● promoting products directly to the customer.

Different types of promotion will be effective depending on the circumstances. When promoting a good or service directly to the customer the business needs to make sure that it understands what the customer wants and satisfies their expectations with the promotion as well as the product. Promotion must be an integral part with the other strategies used to market the product. It should therefore link in with advertising, brand values and price and appeal to the target market segment. A marketing strategy for a luxury car should not include a promotional 'give-away' – like a free ballpoint pen – that is out of keeping with this image. A free gold, branded and boxed fountain pen would be more appropriate. This is what is meant by a strategy having coherence. No part of it should seem out of place with the other parts.

At the customer level, promotions include discounts, coupons, competitions, free offers and samples. It includes money-off offers and added value offers such as 'buy one, get one free'; '2 for 1'; '25 per cent extra'. Many businesses now issue customer loyalty cards to encourage repeat purchases. Joint promotions are where one business agrees with another to 'cross-promote' products. Kellogg's might offer a Sega Dreamcast as a prize, for example. This is only effective where businesses share a similar image or market segment. A sports shoe manufacturer would be unlikely to enter into a joint promotion with a classical music distributor, for example.

"Of course, Plato didn't have to mount the school play, schmooze with parents, stay up marking till two in the morning and put up with syllabus changes every fortnight."

So said Stephen Fry, whilst presenting the 1999 Teaching Awards. The point he was making is that the Teaching Awards - the Platos - are a celebration of all that's best about teaching and teachers. And that these awards are a recognition that teachers who do achieve excellence do so in circumstances which are often difficult, pressurised and relentless.

The Teaching Awards 2000 are just around the corner. Indeed the deadline for nominations is 14th February, 2000. So schools who wish to participate in the awards and get some long overdue recognition for their teachers, need to get their skates on.

Schools can put forward up to four nominees, and the judges of the awards are all members of the education community, many of whom are practising teachers themselves. There are hundreds of thousands of pounds in prize money to be won by hundreds of schools. The awards are run by the Teaching Awards Trust, a completely independent organisation with support from right across the education community.

Schools wishing to nominate teachers should call right away for a nomination pack on 020 7907 1500, or email info@teachingawards.com.

FIGURE 3.21 *Sponsorship: Lloyds TSB sponsors the Teaching Awards*

Other types of promotion targeted at the customer include direct mail and public relations.

Direct mail is the delivery of promotional material, offers or sales material directly to a potential customer. It includes direct mail by post and, increasingly, fax and e-mail (known as 'spam'). Direct mail is able to target customers in a way that no other promotion can. Mail can be personalised and, by using information held on customer databases, companies can target market segments that are more likely to respond. They may be people who have bought from the organisation before, have bought similar products from other organisations, or who have expressed a taste or preference at some time and had this recorded on the database.

Public relations is designed to project a positive image of the business, brand or product to the public. It includes:

- sponsorship – a business may wish to be associated with a sport or event that is popular. This also gains extra publicity in places where it would otherwise not be possible, such as the BBC. (The BBC does not carry advertising.) The Worthington Cup, the Allied Dunbar Rugby Union Premiership and the Nationwide League are all examples

- product placement – having the product seen, worn or used on film or television or in photographs. Aston Martin was happy to supply the cars for the early James Bond films because of the enormous publicity it gained as a result. This device has seen further development as businesses and government have used it to put across particular messages. The American government, for example, has spent large sums sponsoring TV hospital soap operas to promote anti-drugs messages

- public endorsement or recommendation by a famous person who the target customer group will see as a role model. Examples are a sportsman endorsing a brand of crisps and an ex-chief constable recommending tyres

- social marketing is a new form of marketing where a business goes into partnership with another organisation in order to show its social or environmental credentials. Cause-related marketing is one part of it, where a product or service is jointly marketed for the benefit of the commercial operator and the cause. Examples include Tesco's 'Computers for Schools', Sainsbury's tokens for school equipment and British Caledonian and the children's hospital appeal. The airline collects unwanted foreign currency from passengers returning to the UK and forwards it to children's hospitals.

FIGURE 3.22 *Social marketing: McVities Jaffa Cakes*

Other promotions are made directly to the 'trade' or are inappropriate for a market:

- businesses will run trade promotions to encourage distributors to stock their products which could take the form of discounts, competitions or any other types of promotional pricing or devices. They will also provide point-of-sale material such as display stands, cards and posters

- industrial and capital markets rely on personal, face-to-face, selling, using sales representatives. The ability of the salesperson to make a sale depends on their own skill and product knowledge and also on the specialist publications, samples and catalogues provided by the business. This form of promotion may also take place through meetings, trade fairs, exhibitions and presentations.

Product presentation

In customer markets part of product presentation is the way in which a product is packaged. Packaging must be functional – in that it must protect the product and allow it to be stacked and stored without it depreciating – but it must also, at the point of sale, be attractive to the final customer. Some colours and styles will reduce sales because they give the wrong image or the wrong message. Certain fonts or typeface styles give a particular image, as do certain colours. Whites, yellows and blues are used for 'clean' in washing powder and soap packaging. Blacks, golds and deep greens are used for 'luxury' in chocolates. The colours and styles chosen will not only represent the product, but also the market segment at which the product is targeted.

Marketing strategies must be designed so that colours, lettering and packaging all appeal to the right market segment and the right image. Would you buy a washing powder packaged in a grey box? Or a luxury product packaged in orange?

ASSESSMENT
a c t i v i t y 6

Consider the good or service that you are marketing and the market segment at which it is aimed.

1. What are the features of your product that make it attractive to that segment?

2. In what ways could you use product presentation to enhance those features. For a product this might be packaging, labelling, point-of-sale material etc. For a service it might still include point-of-sale material but would also include any way in which you can present your product to make it more attractive to that segment.

3. How do your suggestions for product presentation fit in with the price that you have chosen?

Direct selling

Businesses may decide that the best form of communication with their customers is face-to-face – selling the product directly. Direct sales is when the producer sells directly to the customer, for example through mail order catalogue or home delivery. For some businesses it is almost the only way to sell – a business such as a window cleaner's, for example, is likely to get more customers this way than any other.

All direct sales involve the business cutting out all or part of the chain of distribution. They include using a representative or agent and door-to-door and party sales. Businesses such as Avon, Tupperware and Ann Summers have all grown through party sales. Postal direct sales via catalogues, mail order and responses to direct mail shots are also possible. It is the nature of the product and the segment that it is aimed at that make direct sales effective or not. Personal products (such as the Ann Summers range) or industrial products may both be best sold in this way.

FIGURE 3.23 *Just part of distribution*

Source: Life File/Lionel Moss

Factory sales outlets are also increasingly popular, allowing customers to buy products direct from the factory without having to pay the extra added on by wholesalers and retailers for their services. Direct sales may also take place using technology – buying on the Internet is one obvious way in which this takes place. Other forms of such sales, already popular in America, are beginning to take off in the UK. One of these is direct sales via a cable television shopping channel, where a product is shown or demonstrated and people can then ring the channel to order it.

The process of distribution

Distribution refers to two things:

● first, the way in which the product travels from the producer to the customer. This includes the logistics of transport

● second, the outlets to which the product is distributed. This includes anywhere the customer can buy the good or service.

Businesses may have good advertising and promotion and be charging the right price, but none of this will be effective if the product is not on sale where the customer expects it to be. A business must anticipate where customers will expect products to be available. It must anticipate levels of demand so that stocks do not run out. It must satisfy customer expectations as to what will be available, where and when.

The traditional long channel of distribution channel was from manufacturer or producer to wholesaler to retailer to customer. **Short channel distribution** means cutting out a part of the long channel. It may be that the manufacturer distributes to the retailer, or the wholesaler to the customer. The shortest channel is direct supply or direct sales.

Many contemporary businesses no longer use the traditional long chain, preferring to have their own stock and distribution systems. Major retailers such as Tesco and Asda stores are able to act as their own 'wholesaler' for many goods. In this way, they keep control over stock levels and deliveries themselves. Distribution systems are geared up purely for their needs and not for those of a distributor.

Stockless distribution is an adaptation of the 'just-in-time' production strategy. It means that stock is designed to arrive at a store when it is needed and should be rapidly moved on to the shelves. Products are therefore fresher and costs are saved by the need for warehouse space being reduced. A continuous cycle of stocking and selling is needed for this to be effective. It means that the business must have an in-depth knowledge of patterns of customer spending.

Distribution strategies

The main objective of the producer is to get products to the final customer. They can either be pushed out to them using intermediaries such as agents and sales personnel, or rely on customer demand pulling the products from the distribution chain.

● **Push strategy** involves intermediaries receiving benefits and incentives to persuade them to take the items from the producer. This pushes the product down the chain of distribution. Intermediaries such as wholesalers may also use push strategies to get products retailers.

● **Pull strategy** involves special offers, promotions and similar devices to affect customer demand. The focus of marketing activity in a pull strategy is on the customer, to persuade them to demand the product.

Channels are chosen by businesses according to the nature of the product and the nature of the market. Product size, fragility and perishability are factors, as are market size, concentration or diversification. Producers may want the widest possible distribution or only to selected outlets; for example, a producer of luxury goods would not wish to see them on sale in a discount store.

Choices are made about the type of distribution needed by customers, producers and the sales outlets – retailers – themselves. Producers will consider factors such as:

● the possibility of repeat orders,

● opportunities for cross-selling – selling a range

of products into an outlet rather than just a single one

- the type and image of the outlet they wish to use
- which channels are appropriate to the nature of the product.

The various outlets will make decisions on which products or range of products to stock on the basis of which products are likely to have high sales/turnover, which products offer the highest profit margins and for which products they actually have room.

The market position of the product will also be an important factor. A market leader, supported by a strong brand image and extensive advertising and promotion, is more likely to be stocked than a rival brand.

Products that are not widely stocked or widely available will not attract as many purchases as those that are. The efficiency of the distribution network in ensuring that products get to the outlets is thus paramount. A product can be made or broken by the attitude of a major distributor or retailer. If WHSmith the newsagent decides that it is not going to stock your magazine, then not only does this limit distribution but also encourages other retailers to follow suit. A grocery product accepted by Tesco will be widely available: on the other hand, Tesco's decision not to stock genetically modified food made sales of the product no longer viable.

final customer has 'retailed' it. Retail outlets range from local 'corner' and High Street shops to department stores such as Selfridges and Harrods and multiple chains such as the major food retailers – Tesco, Sainsbury, Asda and Safeway. Some multiples specialise (or initially specialised) in a particular line of products, for example, Barratts (shoes), Dewhurst (butchers) and Boots (pharmaceuticals). All multiples are characterised by having branches recognisable by their names, livery and logos. In effect, these stores have created a 'brand image' for the shop – whichever branch you are in, you know what to expect. Retailers may provide services, rather than goods, or a mixture of the two. For example Kwik-Fit provide exhaust, tyre and other fitting services; hairdressers also sell hair care products.

The advent of the supermarket and then the out-of-town hypermarket has meant that much food shopping is done at these outlets. They provide a wide variety and also have a reputation for being less expensive than local shops. The convenience factor is enhanced by car parking arrangements, the existence of ancillary services (such as cafeterias and petrol stations) and the fact that everything is under one roof. UK supermarkets have begun to follow in the footsteps of their American cousins, branching out into non-food items such as electrical goods, clothes, books, pharmaceuticals and even white goods and furniture – truly 'one-stop' shops with convenience and variety as major attractions for customers.

 **Top Tips**

Look for examples of cross-selling in shops. In the chocolate snack market, for example, manufacturers will often try a new line by distributing it with an established one.

Types of retail outlet

Retailers are the final link in the chain of distribution. Anyone who sells a product to a

  ASSESSMENT *a c t i v i t y*

Part of your strategy needs to include the place where your good or service is to be sold and how it will be distributed. Look at the other elements of your marketing strategy before making any decisions. Do you need a specialist outlet? How will your advertising and promotion affect sales? How will you ensure that stock is in place?

1. **What factors do you need to take into account with your particular product? Is it big, small, fragile, perishable, valuable?**

2. **Where are your potential customers going to look to buy your product? This should be related to the type of product and the targeted market segment.**

3. **How are you planning to get your product to the right place?**

How does the business meet customer needs?

Above all else, customers want purchases to be easy and convenient. Products must be available. Buying them must be convenient and comfortable. A customer will buy more fruit if surrounded by variety in a well-lit supermarket than at a rain-soaked roadside stall. To add to the experience the shop can provide customer support, ancillary services and piped music.

Convenience in making payments is also important; most retail outlets accept credit and debit cards as well as cheques and cash. Many even provide banking services – enabling customers to withdraw cash from their accounts – with no charge for the service. The ambience of the retail outlet is also important. This word is used to mean the 'general atmosphere' generated by the shop and its staff. In large stores the ambience may be created by the music played, by the lay-out and decor, by the way in which goods are displayed and staff behave.

- Retail outlets such as supermarkets and hypermarkets will rely on these factors to create an atmosphere in which the customer feels comfortable making purchases.

- A shop such as a clothes or shoe shop, where personal service is required, may make its customers feel welcome (and make it difficult for them to leave without buying something) by being polite and friendly, using formal titles, providing free coffee, and showing respect for the customer.

- Other shops will create a particular ambience or atmosphere to match their custom – young people's clothes or music shops may play loud music or have outrageous decor. Adults are not meant to be attracted. Teenagers are meant to feel that they are in their own environment. Other stores may rely on plush carpeting or soft lighting to attract particular types of customer. There is a whole industry behind shop layout and the various methods of creating the right atmosphere.

- In retail outlets providing a service, such considerations are just as important. A health club, for example, first needs to be well equipped, clean and safe. However, it also needs to be welcoming, well decorated and professional. Staff are likely to be uniformed. Fitness instructors will look fit. Ancillary services – a juice bar, for example – must be well laid out and in keeping with the general image promoted.

It is important that any staff who deal directly with customers are well trained. Customer relations involves dealing directly with customers or potential customers. This will include receptionist and switchboard operators and dealing with complaints. In the first instance, such employees are often the first contact that a customer has with a business and it is therefore important that they present a positive image.

FIGURE 3.24 *Retail outlets must create the right atmosphere*

Source: Life File/Jeremy Hoare

First impressions are important. In the second instance, complaints must be dealt with in a sensitive and professional way if the repeat business of the customer is not to be lost. Staff need to be specially trained for any roles that put them in direct contact with the public – this includes sales.

How does the business create effective customer service?

The appearance and attitude of the staff will also be used to create an image for the outlet. Sometimes staff are uniformed to reflect the fact that they belong to the organisation. The nature of such uniforms is often defined by the corporate culture of the business. For example, a business with a mainly middle-aged, middle-class clientele would be foolish to dress all its staff up in the latest fashions. A business catering to the teenage market might find this essential.

The staff of an outlet are extremely important in both knowing what the corporate culture of the business is and being able to project that culture through their dress, behaviour and product knowledge. This will not usually be achieved without good staff training programmes and staff who are well motivated. Motivation may include specific rewards, perhaps linked to sales levels. More importantly, it will be linked to the general ethos of the business. Staff who are appreciated will be better motivated. Some businesses have recognised this and provide rest rooms and other facilities and even, in some cases, hairdressers and chiropodists (for staff who are on their feet all day). Staff who are well trained, have good product knowledge and are appreciated will be an important asset to a business.

Good product knowledge will be even more important in industrial markets and in markets where professional installation of a product must take place. In this case, not only the installation but the after-sales care and service will also be important.

 **ACTIVITY** **19**

Little Chef

Little Chef is the leading player in the business of providing roadside eating facilities to motorists. It has over 400 outlets in Britain and Northern Ireland. It competes with established brands such as McDonalds, Wimpy and Burger King but has more prime roadside sites than any of these competitors. In trying to cater for a market segment that must include the motorist, it also tries to cater for the motorist's family and friends on whatever journey they happen to be taking. Little Chef thus has to make sure that its appeal is to adults and children, singles, couples and families.

McDonalds, Wimpy and Burger King – plus other similar food outlets attached to licensed premises – are also appealing to the same market; one which includes children – so that Little Chef needed to devise a marketing strategy that would include families with children while not alienating any other part of its market. The direction taken was to try to add value to the 'Little Chef Experience' and make it more attractive to children. Importantly, the promotion also had to appeal to parents, as they are the ones who make the decisions about whether or not to stop and eat and they are the ones who pay. A further intention was to devise a promotion that would encourage customers to return to Little Chef.

1. **Describe the elements of the marketing mix that Little Chef needs to use. How do you think it decides on:**
   - **a price range**
   - **a product range**
2. **Explain what is meant by 'sales promotion'.**
3. **How could Little Chef devise a promotion that would encourage customers to return? What promotional activities would you recommend to it?**

If you want to know what Little Chef did, visit its website at www.little-chef.co.uk.

Producing a marketing strategy

The outline below suggests the possible stages in planning a marketing strategy. You may wish to use this as a guide when completing your assessment.

Stage 1: The intended product

You need to be able to answer some basic questions about the product.

What are the intended **product features**?

- Size? Shape? Colour? Variety? Function?
- How is it different from the competition?
- Where and when will it be available?
- What is its USP (Unique Selling Point)?

Stage 2: The target market

This information can be used to build a **customer profile** to help identify your **target market**. You should collect this information and say how can this information will help you with your marketing strategy.

Information could concern:

- who will potentially buy the product?
- who will actually buy it? Is this the same as the previous group or different?
- how will the buyer find out about the product?
- how often they will buy it?
- which retail outlet will they normally buy the product from?
- why will they buy it?
- what do the buyers think of as the main competitor?
- what do the buyers buy at the same time?

Stage 3: Market research

You will need to use primary and secondary market research. The combination will depend on what it is that you want to find out and how you want to deal with the information.

Initial decisions must concern the balance of primary and secondary information.

For primary information ask yourself:

- what do I want to find out?
- what methods can I use? Examples could be:
  - tasting
  - testing
  - observations
  - interviews
  - surveys
  - panels
  - focus groups
  - questionnaires.
- in framing questionnaires, ask yourself:
  - how do I ensure that the meaning of questions is clear? (test them)
  - how do I avoid bias in the questions? (test them)
  - who do I ask? Should the sample be random or targeted? Why?
  - how many do I ask? What is a decent cross-section? Why? (Remember the 95 per cent rule)
  - where, how and when is research to be conducted?
  - what types of questions do I ask?
- **Closed** questions will provide **quantitative** information. You may be able to present this in graph, table or chart form. You may be able to use ICT for this.

- **Open** questions will provide more detailed, **qualitative**, information. You are unlikely to be able to present this statistically but answers are likely to provide more depth.
- what demographic, geographic, psychographic etc. information do I need? How can I collect it?
- how do I justify the questions I've asked?
- how do I validate the results?

For secondary research ask yourself:
- what is available?
- what are the cost implications?
- how up to date is the information?
- how accurate is the information?
- how specific is the information to my needs?

Stage 4: Mapping

You then need to decide if there is other information that could be useful to you.

- Could you draw a perceptual map for your product?
- Is it appropriate to conduct a SWOT analysis or a PEST analysis? These could show you the impact of the external environment and of other constraints.
- Could you make use of an Ansoff matrix?
- Could you make use of the Boston matrix?

Stage 5: Marketing strategy

You should then be able to be specific about your marketing strategy. You should make decisions about:

- changes to your product to bring it into line with customer requirements
- what price level you will charge; what pricing strategies you will use
- how the product is to be distributed; what channel of distribution will be used; where it will be made available

- what promotion and packaging you will use.

The last of these could be linked to the outline of a possible advertising campaign.

- How will you reach your target market?
- What budget will be appropriate?
- How will you justify the budget?
- What will you spend:
  - above the line?
  - below the line?
- How will you try to ensure that your campaign is effective?
- What will you offer in the way of customer contact and after-sales service?

Stage 6: Presentation

You need to present your strategy, using whatever means are appropriate and effective. These could be:

- oral presentations
- pictures, graphs, charts etc.
- using information technology applications.

Stage 7: Evaluation

Finally, you need to evaluate your strategy. This should take on board comments from other members of your group and from your tutor.

- What features would make it particularly effective?
- What elements could be improved?
- What other methodology could you have used?
- What other information should you have collected?
- How could the presentation have been improved?

4

Human Resources

What this chapter is about

People are an important resource in business. It is important for a business to train and motivate its employees properly. In this chapter you will learn about the factors that affect human resource planning. You will find out about the recruitment and selection process and about how the business can train and manage its staff after recruitment. There are a number of legal and ethical responsibilities related to employment and you will develop an understanding of these. ■

What you need to produce

You will need to produce a report on how one large business manages human resources. Your tutor will help you to select a suitable business to investigate. One with more than 50 employees is more likely to provide the best basis for your investigation.

In your report you should:

■ describe the responsibilities covered by the human resources function of the business and explain the importance of human resources to the business

■ interpret relevant labour market information and explain how it is used to plan human resources within the business

■ evaluate key recruitment documents and describe factors to be considered when planning recruitment and selection

■ identify key aspects of the business's training and development programme and explain its importance to business performance

■ explain the purpose of performance management

■ explain the relationship between the business's training and development programme and its management of performance and explain how the two functions can be influenced by different motivational theories

■ explain the contribution that human resources can make to improving the competitiveness of the business

■ identify potential conflicts between different human resources functions and explain the effects these may have on the business

■ choose one human resources function to explore in depth. Give examples of how the work is carried out. Explain how its contribution to business activities is evaluated.

Evidence for your report may be collected through the use of interviews with representatives of the business, examination of business documents and analysis of statistical information. You should plan your work so that you do not need to visit the business on too many occasions. Some of the Activities in this chapter will help you to prepare for your assessment.

The human resources function

In chapter 1, we looked at the different functions within a business and saw that one of those functions is human resources. Do the following Activity to remind yourself of the responsibilities of the human resources function.

ASSESSMENT
a c t i v i t y   **1**

Write down the responsibilities of the human resources function in a business. Explain why the human resources function is important to the business.

Key Skills C3.3

As part of your assessment you will need to carry out the above Activity in relation to your chosen business. You may find that your answer to this Activity is a useful starting point. Remember that for your assessment you will need to relate your answer specifically to your chosen business.

Section 1 *Human resources planning*

What you need to learn

In this section you will learn about:

- labour market factors and their implications for human resource planning
- the internal factors that affect staffing decisions within a business
- the relationship between internal staffing and external markets
- the statistics you can use to analyse these factors.

The importance of planning

Staff are one of a business's most valuable, but also expensive, assets, so it is vital that a business plans its staffing carefully. It needs to make sure that it employs the right number of appropriate staff to meet its needs.

The starting point for any human resources planning will be the strategic plan of the business. This will give a long-term focus for human resource planning.

To give the business a competitive advantage, human resource planning should consider the future needs of the business as well as current needs.

A successful plan will achieve a suitable mix of employees in terms of age, skills, and experience; and will provide for developing those employees to meet the future business needs.

To plan staffing effectively, a business will need to analyse both its own workforce and the external labour market. Together these can inform the business of short- and longer-term trends that may affect it in terms of future recruitment needs and so help to inform a planning strategy.

External labour market

Whatever the size of a business, it will be affected by national, and probably international, labour costs and trends.

This was shown by the microchip industry. It was confidently predicted that there would be a great demand for these, and 'state of the art' manufacturing plants were built in the North of England, giving hope for recruitment opportunities in their manufacture.

The swamping of the market of these products caused the price to drop. This, in turn, forced the businesses to close down the new factories and to switch manufacture to outside the UK, where employment was cheaper.

	1994 (000s)	1995 (000s)	1996 (000s)	1997 (000s)	1998 (000s)	1999 (000s)
Agriculture, hunting, forestry and fishing	296	270	277	292	298	317
Mining and quarrying	71	67	78	79	76	72
Energy and water supply	262	237	228	227	217	215
Manufacturing	3,923	4,021	4,106	4,162	4,140	3,984
Construction	864	838	882	967	1,095	1,092
Services	16,352	16,658	17,213	17,604	17,938	18,304
Wholesale and retail	3,653	3,707	3,816	3,933	4,025	4,086

TABLE 4.1 *UK employment trends by sector*

Source: Annual abstract of Statistics 2000 (The Stationery Office)

Table 4.1 shows the employment trends in the UK by sector.

You will notice that there has been an increase of employment in the service industries.

If you study Table 4.2, which shows regional employment trends, you will notice that despite the national trend, there are still regional differences. You should be able to pick out the regions that are still dominated by manufacturing and those dominated by services.

ACTIVITY ①

Discuss the following questions with your group:

■ **why do you think similar businesses cluster together in particular areas?**

■ **from the point of view of staffing, what are the advantages and disadvantages for similar types of businesses clustering together in a particular area?**

■ **why do you think there are differences in wages paid for different jobs and in different areas? Discuss the question with your group.**

Key Skills C3.1a

The difference in wage levels is called **wage differential**. There are several factors that contribute to this:

● where there is a shortage of workers with appropriate skills, there will be more competition and wages will be higher

● where there is a high demand for labour, there will be more competition and wages will be higher

● where there is little demand and a surplus of labour, wages will be lower

● dangerous jobs and/or anti-social working hours will require workers to be compensated by higher wages

● jobs that require long training periods and/or higher qualifications will command higher wages.

ASSESSMENT *activity* ②

1. **Using at least three different sources of job adverts for your local or regional area, analyse the types of job advertised in terms of:**

■ **sector (e.g. manufacturing, services, leisure, financial services etc.)**

■ **level of position (e.g. manager, supervisor, operative, junior)**

■ **role: (e.g. the job may be in the manufacturing sector but is the business looking for a shop floor worker or an office**

PERCENTAGES AND THOUSANDS

	AGRICULTURE HUNTING, FORESTRY & FISHING	MINING QUARRYING, (INC OIL & GAS EXTRACTION)	MANUFACTURING	ELECTRICITY, GAS, WATER	CONSTRUCTION	DISTRIBUTION HOTELS & CATERING, REPAIRS
All persons						
United Kingdom	0.4	0.3	18.0	0.6	4.4	22.7
North East	0.2	0.4	21.2	0.6	5.9	20.9
North East	0.2	0.2	20.7	0.7	4.5	23.2
Yorkshire and the Humber	0.2	0.4	21.9	0.6	4.7	22.5
East Midlands	0.4	0.5	25.8	0.6	4.4	21.8
West Midlands	0.2	0.2	26.5	0.7	4.3	21.6
East	0.5	0.2	17.7	0.6	4.5	24.5
London	0.1	0.1	8.2	0.2	3.2	21.9
South East	0.5	0.2	14.0	0.7	4.2	23.9
South West	0.3	0.3	17.3	0.9	4.2	24.2
England	0.3	0.2	18.0	0.6	4.2	22.8
Wales	0.2	0.4	22.2	0.6	4.8	21.7
Scotland	0.6	1.3	16.4	0.8	5.6	22.7
Northern Ireland	2.7	0.3	18.0	0.7	4.7	20.9

PERCENTAGES AND THOUSANDS

	TRANSPORT STORAGE & COMMUNICATION	FINANCIAL & BUSINESS SERVICES	PUBLIC ADMINISTRATION & DEFENCE	EDUCATION, SOCIAL WORK & HEALTH SERVICES	OTHER	WHOLE ECONOMY (=100%) (THOUSANDS)
All persons						
United Kingdom	5.8	18.3	5.8	18.9	4.7	23,136
North East	5.0	12.4	7.0	21.5	5.0	897
North West	5.5	15.5	5.9	19.3	4.3	2,572
Yorkshire and the Humber	5.9	14.9	4.9	19.6	4.4	1,923
East Midlands	5.0	14.2	4.6	18.7	4.0	1,624
West Midlands	4.8	15.1	5.0	17.8	4.0	2,108
East	6.4	19.0	4.6	17.5	4.5	2,015
London	7.8	30.8	6.1	15.0	6.4	3,457
South East	6.3	21.7	5.5	18.7	4.5	3,173
South West	5.0	16.4	6.8	20.3	4.3	1,840
England	6.0	19.3	5.6	18.3	4.7	19,608
Wales	4.4	11.3	7.4	22.0	5.0	962
Scotland	5.3	14.8	6.4	21.2	4.9	1.964
Northern Ireland	4.0	8.4	9.9	25.8	4.6	601

TABLE 4.2 *Regional employment trends by sector*

Source: The Stationery Office

service such as accounts, marketing personnel etc.)

■ pay (e.g. per annum, weekly, per hour). Using local data about average wage levels, assess whether these are high, low or average

■ contracted hours (e.g. full time, part time etc.)

■ skills required (e.g. 'must hold', 'preferred' or 'training given').

Present this information in a suitable format. This might be as tables, graphs or diagrams. You will need to be able to use the data to draw conclusions about local employment.

2. Compare your information with government statistics on local employment trends. State which type of situation is likely to be filled easily and which will be the most difficult. Give reasons for your answers.

3. By studying the adverts again, decide what techniques the employers have used to attract the right type of applicant (e.g. high wages, training, flexible working conditions etc.).

4. What conclusions can you draw about your local/regional employment market?

You should be able to explain how the information you have prepared could be used to create a human resources plan for your chosen business.

Key Skills C3.2, C3.3

 Top Tips

Your analysis should relate to the area in which the business you have chosen to investigate is located.

Government statistical information is available in most reference libraries in the *Annual Abstract of Statistics*. Make sure you use the most recent information available.

Internal staffing

Effective human resources planning also involves looking at labour within the business. Before recruiting externally it is important that a business has access to all the relevant information on its current workforce. It needs to be able to gain an overview of the workforce in the form of statistical analysis in order to form efficient strategic plans for future requirements. For example, if a manufacturing business wants to increase the number of items it produces, it might decide to employ more staff. Before making this decision, it should look at the productivity of the current workforce. If staff are de-motivated or not sufficiently trained, this can lead to low labour productivity. In this case, it would be better to look at why staff were de-motivated, or arrange appropriate training, than to employ more staff.

The following factors will need to be considered in planning human resources:

● The **stability** of the workforce or the **labour turnover**. This is the average length of time that each employee stays with the business. If the turnover is high this may alert the business to motivational problems within the workforce. It could also be linked to external factors such as intense competition for employees, causing other businesses to offer higher wages. The business would need to look at the cause of these problems before planning to recruit new staff. You can use the following formula to calculate labour turnover:

$$\frac{\text{number of staff leaving in a period}}{\substack{\text{average number of staff employed in} \\ \text{that period}}} \times 100$$

Average number of staff employed in the period is:

$$\frac{\text{number of staff at start of period} +}{\text{number of staff at end of period}}$$

2

It would normally be calculated for a one-year period but shorter or longer periods can be used. The resulting figure is a percentage. The higher the percentage, the higher the labour turnover.

Example

A business has 12 staff leave in one year. At the start of the year, it had 260 staff. (At the end of the year it will have 260 – 12 = 248).

$$\text{Average number of staff in the year} =$$

$$\frac{260 + 248}{2} = 254$$

$$\text{Labour turnover} = \frac{12}{254} \times 100 = 4.72\%$$

The figure should not be used in isolation. It can be compared with the turnover rate over a number of years and with average labour turnover figures provided in the *Government Abstract of Statistics*. The 4.72 per cent above doesn't mean much in isolation. If we knew that the figure for previous years was nearer 10 per cent, we could compare the figures. To draw any conclusions from the reduction, we would need further information. A reduction in labour turnover could be due to internal factors such as better staff morale. Alternatively, it could be due to external factors, such as an increase in unemployment, which makes it harder for employees to find alternative jobs.

Note that it may be appropriate to calculate labour turnover for separate departments as well as overall. This would help identify particular problem areas in the business.

A high labour turnover could lead to a lack of continuity in the business operations and can be costly in terms of recruitment and retraining. However, a very low labour turnover could indicate a workforce that is set in its ways and stale. Businesses need to achieve the right balance.

- The **absenteeism rate** and the major **reasons** given. High numbers of employees suffering from stress, injury or sickness should lead the business to ask if the health and safety policy is being properly implemented, or whether there are problems with motivation. Absenteeism will cost the business money in terms of lost production hours. This could lead to other problems such as failing to meet production deadlines. The absenteeism rate for a business can be calculated using the following formula:

$$\frac{\substack{\text{total number of absences for the} \\ \text{period in days}}}{\substack{\text{total number of days that should} \\ \text{have been worked in the period}}} \times 100$$

Note that the total number of days that should have been worked in the period would be:

$$\substack{\text{number of work days} \\ \text{in the period}} \times \substack{\text{number of} \\ \text{employees}}$$

A higher percentage shows a higher level of absenteeism.

Example

A business operates for 50 weeks in the year, five days per week. The number of absences during the year is 476 days. It has 159 employees.

$$\text{Number of days} = 50 \times 5 \times 159 = 39{,}750$$

$$\text{Absentee rate} = \frac{476}{39{,}750} \times 100 = 1.12\%$$

Again, the figure should not be looked at in isolation but compared with other available figures. Calculations for specific departments may be useful as well as those for the whole business.

- The **productivity** of the workforce. If productivity per employee is low, then the business may need to look at the training or motivation of staff rather than simply employing more staff. Labour productivity can be calculated by:

$$\frac{\text{output in a period}}{\text{average number of employees in a period}}$$

How output is measured will depend on the type of business. A garage servicing cars might measure output in chargeable hours (i.e. hours worked on customers' cars). A manufacturer making tyres might measure output as the number of tyres produced. A car valeting service might use the number of cars valeted. The average number of employees is calculated as before: number of employees at the start of the period, plus number of employees at the end of the period, divided by two.

ACTIVITY 2

In each of the following examples, decide what you think would be an appropriate measure of output:

- **a company that makes cricket bats**
- **a firm of solicitors**
- **a window cleaner**
- **a supermarket.**

Examples

A garage has an average of 23 employees in one month. The chargeable hours for the same month are 3,220.

Labour productivity =

$$\frac{3,220}{23} = \begin{array}{l}140 \text{ chargeable hours per} \\ \text{month per employee.}\end{array}$$

This could be compared to other months to see if there has been any change. It could also be compared to the total number of working hours in the month to see what proportion of working hours are actually chargeable to customers. (Note that not all working hours will be chargeable to customers as some time will be spent cleaning up, servicing tools and carrying out administrative tasks.)

A tyre manufacturer produces 33,489 tyres in one year. The average number of employees involved in making the tyres in that year was 27.

Labour productivity =

$$\frac{33,489}{27} = 1,240 \text{ tyres per employee per year.}$$

The figure should be compared with that of other years.

A car valeting business employs four staff and valets 60 cars in one week.

Labour productivity =

$$\frac{60}{4} = 15 \text{ cars per employee per week.}$$

The figure should be compared with those of other weeks.

Other information about absences, or stoppages for any reason, will help to interpret labour productivity figures.

ACTIVITY 3

Look at the following information relating to two mountain bike manufacturers. In each case calculate labour turnover, absenteeism rates and productivity. Comment on your results. Both businesses are thinking about recruiting new staff. Explain what factors should be taken into account in each case.

Apple Mountain Bikes is a specialist manufacturer which hand-builds mountain bikes. The staff consider themselves to be craftsmen and are proud of the product. The business employs 14 staff to make the bikes. In one month it producse 342 bikes. Absences during the month amounted to two days. Only one person has left the company over the past year and he retired due to ill health.

Tiger Mountain Bikes is a small factory which mass-produces mountain bikes. The factory is highly automated. It employs 22 factory floor workers and produces 4,339 bikes in one month. The absentee rate for the same month

was 15 days. Over the last year 12 staff have left and needed replacing. Both businesses work a five day week. There are four weeks in a month.

- The *average age* of the workforce, *skills* and *training*. This will require the business to conduct a skills audit. A skills audit requires collecting information about the skills of all employees. These can then be matched to the skills needs of the business. If there is a good cross-section of skills, age and experience, then the workforce will be renewable from within giving opportunity for promotion.

  A good age range means that as older employees retire, younger employees can take their place. If the workforce is multi-skilled then the business will be in a good position to implement change when necessary. Where the skills do not match those required for the business to operate, there may be a need for training and/or recruitment.

- Businesses need to consider *future needs* as well as current needs when planning human resources. They should carry out some succession planning as part of their human resources strategy. This means looking at whether staff who leave or are promoted within the business can be replaced from within the business. Training can be planned to meet succession needs.

Key Skills N3.2b

Section 2 *Recruitment and selection*

What you need to learn

In this section you will learn about:

- the recruitment and selection process
- the ethical and legal responsibilities related to equal opportunities
- employment contracts and the rights of employees in relation to these
- the importance of recruiting and maintaining a flexible workforce.

Bob Mason owns Mercury Snowboards, a small business that manufactures high-quality snowboards. He started the business from home two years ago and it has become very successful. Bob does everything himself – he is a craftsman and designs and makes the snowboards. He also manages purchases, finance, sales and marketing. He is now finding that it is very difficult to manage the business. He simply doesn't have enough time. Also, he is not very good at dealing with people and keeping financial records. He is happiest when buying materials and making snowboards. Bob decides that it is time to employ someone else in the business.

 ACTIVITY **4**

Why do you think Bob has decided to employ someone else in the business?

Why do businesses recruit staff?

There are a variety of reasons why an organisation may need to recruit staff:

- the growth of the organisation means that there is more work

- the organisation has re-structured, leaving vacancies in some areas
- job roles have changed within the business. This could be as a result of re-structuring; or could be due to the introduction of new technology; or a response to changes in the market in which the business operates
- someone has retired, resigned, been dismissed or suffered serious illness or death. Any of these events will leave a vacancy that the business will need to fill
- the business promotes a staff member, leaving their old job vacant.

In the Activity, Bob had two main reasons for wanting to recruit. First, the business was expanding and there was simply too much work for him to do. Second, the job role was changing and he needed someone with different skills to take over specific parts of the business.

Alternatives to recruitment

Recruitment and selection is an expensive process. Businesses will not take the decision to recruit lightly. They may consider other alternatives before making the decision to recruit. Alternatives include:

- asking remaining staff to work overtime or part-time staff to work extra hours. Many seasonal businesses ask staff to work overtime in the busy season. For example shop workers might be asked to do extra hours at Christmas; hotels may ask staff to work extra hours in the summer months
- re-structuring the work so that other employees can complete it. Sometimes it will be possible to split up the work and allocate it to remaining employees
- retraining existing employees. Where job roles have changed it may be possible to re-train

existing employees to fulfil the new roles. This can often be cheaper than recruiting from outside the organisation

● using computers or machines to automate some of the workload. Businesses can automate many routine tasks. Manufacturing businesses, such as the car industry, often rely more on machines than employees for the routine tasks

● outsourcing the work. This means paying other organisations or sub-contractors to carry it out. For example, there are companies that will take control of and run the payroll systems of businesses. The business will pay them a fee and they will make all the wages calculations each month and print payslips for employees.

In considering the alternatives, the human resources managers will need to ensure that they consider all aspects of the vacant job role.

Human resources managers need to be careful in identifying the need to recruit. Often they depend on other department managers for information. They need to be certain there is a real vacancy and that the recruitment is not 'empire building', or to make up for inefficient staff members. (Empire building is where managers try to obtain more staff or resources simply to make their department bigger and themselves more important.)

Many businesses carry out a job needs analysis to help them decide whether to recruit. The analysis will collect information to help write a job description. Information collected will include:

● tasks the job includes

● which tasks are the most important

● skills needed to complete each task

● how long tasks will take

● responsibilities involved

● likely contact with others – inside and outside the business

● any special circumstances – weekend work, dangerous work etc.

● training that might be offered or required

● reporting lines

● whether the job requires experience

● how the job will develop in the future.

The recruitment process

When a business makes the decision to recruit for a vacancy, it is important that it identifies the right staff to fill the post. It would be a waste of its time, effort and money if it selected the wrong person. This is why businesses need to be very clear about the job role and the kind of person they need.

Job descriptions

The first stage in the recruitment process is to decide what tasks and responsibilities the job involves. The business will need to analyse the job and prepare a job description.

ACTIVITY   5

Look back at the case study on Mercury Snowboards. Which jobs do you think the new person in Bob's business should do?

The job description is a more formal way of setting out details of the vacancy. Figure 4.1 shows a what typical job description might include.

A business will usually write the job description before it fills a vacancy and use it to inform prospective employees about the job. When it has filled the vacancy, it can use the job description to help assess employee performance and salary levels. You should be aware that jobs do change over time. Small organisations, in particular, expect employees to be flexible. Job descriptions will need updating periodically to include new tasks and responsibilities.

Figure 4.3 (see page 185) shows a sample job description for a post as a counter assistant in a building society branch.

Contents of a job description

- job title
- job grade
- location
- reports to
- number of staff
- overall purpose of job
- specific tasks and responsibilities (consider responsibilities in relation to staff, money, equipment, confidential information)
- contacts (internal and external)
- salary and benefits
- working conditions
- career prospects
- training offered

FIGURE 4.1 *Job description contents*

The person specification

The next stage in recruitment is for the business to think about the skills, qualifications and personal qualities required to do the job effectively.

  ACTIVITY **6**

Look back at the Mercury Snowboards case study, and your answer from Activity 5. Write down the skills, qualifications and personal qualities Bob should look for in the person that he employs. What advantages can you see in employing someone with previous, similar experience?

A business will prepare a person specification describing the sort of person it needs to do the job. Figure 4.2 shows the contents of a typical person specification.

Contents of a person specification

For each key task on the job description:

- knowledge and skills
- education and qualifications
- training
- experience
- personal attributes (characteristics and attitudes required)
- physical attributes (e.g. healthy, where job requires physical work)
- other requirements (e.g. ability to drive, prepared to work unusual hours)

Note in each case whether these are:

- essential
- desirable

FIGURE 4.2 *Person specification contents*

The specification will help human resources managers select the best person to fill the vacancy. They will be able to use the person specification to match applicants to the job.

Job description

Job title: Counter assistant

Job grade: Clerical grade 4

Based: Edward's Road Branch

Reports to: Branch manager

Overall purpose of job: To assist with general cashiering and counter duties

---

Specific tasks and responsibilities

- to receive cash from and pay out cash to customers

- to record transactions on customer accounts using computerised till system

- to maintain confidentiality in relation to all customer details and transactions

- to balance till and prepare monies for banking each day

- to take money to bank when required

- to assist manager in general clerical duties as required

- to respond to telephone enquiries from customers

Contacts:	The job involves co-operation with other branch staff and the branch manager. There is a high level of customer contact, over the counter and by telephone.
Salary:	Starting salary £10,500 rising to £12,000 for satisfactory service
Benefits:	A mortgage at beneficial rate will be available to the post holder following the initial six months' probationary period.
Working conditions:	Hours 8:45 a.m. to 5:15 p.m. weekdays. Some Saturday mornings on a rota basis.
Training;	Training for till and telephone systems and general branch procedures
Career prospects:	Promotion to assistant manager and manager available to right person.

FIGURE 4.3 *A typical job description*

Person specification

Job title: Counter assistant

Overall purpose of job: To assist with general cashiering and counter duties

Attributes	Essential	Desirable
Knowledge and skills	Ability to communicate with people in a work variety of situations face-to-face and on the telephone.	Knowledge of general office Some keyboard or typing skills
Education and Qualifications	No specific qualification but must be computer literate and numerate	Vocational A Level Business, Key skills at level 3: Application of Number, Communications, IT.
Training	Willing to undertake training as required	
Experience	No experience required as full training given	Some work experience/work placement in general office environment
Personal attributes	Honest and trustworthy. Able to work in a team	
Other requirements	Must be prepared to work Saturdays where required	

FIGURE 4.4 *A typical person specification*

 **Top Tips**

Job descriptions and person specifications should not break any of the legislation or regulations relating to equal opportunities. (We will cover equal opportunities later in this section.)

The business now has a job description and person specification for the vacancy it wishes to fill. Next it needs to find some applicants.

 **ACTIVITY**

For Mercury Snowboards, consider how Bob might find a suitable person to employ.

As Bob is the only person currently employed in the business, he will need to look outside the business to recruit. Larger businesses have the option of recruiting internally. They may already have staff with the right skills and qualifications for the job, and may decide to give them the opportunity to apply.

The **advantages** of internal recruitment are:

● the opportunity of promotion may motivate staff and attract better external candidates

● internal candidates already know the organisation and so will adapt more quickly to a new job role

● internal recruitment is usually cheaper

● detailed information about the person's past performance will be available in-house

● employees tend to stay with the organisation for longer.

The **disadvantages** of internal recruitment are:

● no new ideas or experience are introduced into the organisation

● the person may be expected to pick up the job very quickly and this may be unreasonable

● the person may have a problem supervising former equals

● there will still be a vacancy to fill.

ACTIVITY 8

Look at the lists of advantages and disadvantages of internal recruitment. Compile a similar list relating to external recruitment.

Where to find applicants

External recruitment can take place from a variety of sources:

● **Job Centres.** These are government-run agencies who collect and advertise vacancies. Each city and major town has a Job Centre so they are suitable for recruiting from the local labour market. Local employers inform the centre of vacancies and the centre advertises them on its premises. The centre will talk to candidates and select those who staff feel are suitable for interview. The business carries out interviews and selection. There is no charge to the business for the service but it is not suitable for highly skilled and professional jobs.

● **Employment agencies.** These operate in a similar way to Job Centres, but are private organisations. As such, they want to make a profit and will charge a business for finding a suitable candidate. Employers will inform them of vacancies, and individuals looking for employment will supply them with details. The agency will find candidates for interview from the individuals on its files or by advertising. They can be useful for finding employees with specific qualifications or skills. Some agencies, such as Accountancy Personnel and Medacs, specialise in recruiting specific types of staff. (Medacs is a specialist recruitment service for secretaries and administrators to the medical profession.)

● **Management and executive recruitment consultants.** For higher-level appointments, there are specialist recruitment consultants. They will charge a fee – often quite a large fee – for finding a suitable candidate. They keep details of individuals on file. They will also approach individuals working in other organisations, who they feel might be suitable candidates, and inform them of the vacancy. This is known as head-hunting. They will filter candidates for interview, and sometimes even be involved in final interviews with the employer. They are useful for finding professional and specialist employees.

● **Professional associations.** Bodies such as the Institute of Chartered Accountants and the Chartered Institute of Environmental Health run employment services for members. Businesses may approach them if they are looking for staff with specific qualifications.

● **Outplacement consultants.** When a major employer makes a large number of staff redundant, it might employ an outplacement consultant. The consultants will try to place the redundant employees in new jobs. The old employer or the employee pays a fee.

● **Schools, colleges and universities.** If the business is looking for a young person to train in the business, it may approach schools, colleges or universities. Many of the larger employers visit colleges and universities each year to tell final-year students about their organisation and the vacancies that they have. Schools might organise something similar on a more local basis.

● **Government training schemes.** Training or re-training programmes created by the government might provide candidates. One example is the Youth Training Programmes. Employers might receive a subsidy to set against wages and training costs. Schemes may require candidates to attend college part-time to gain a relevant qualification. Candidates are likely to be inexperienced.

● **Direct advertising in the press or on the World Wide Web.** Any business can advertise vacancies in the press or on the World Wide Web. Press advertising might include local and national newspapers or specialist publications.

Advertising can be expensive, depending on the publication chosen. (We will consider advertising further below.)

● **Unsolicited applications.** Individuals who are looking for jobs will often write to businesses to see if they have any vacancies. Some businesses will keep these letters on file for when suitable vacancies arise.

ACTIVITY ⑨

Look at the recruitment sources described above. Write a list of advantages and disadvantages for a business using each of the sources.

Advertising

Many businesses advertise job vacancies even where they are using another source of applicants. Advertising can be expensive, so it is important to get it right. Some businesses will employ advertising agencies to help them get it right. The purpose of the advert is to:

● attract the attention of suitable candidates, including those from under-represented minority groups

● encourage those candidates to read the advertisement

● motivate those candidates to reply to the advertisement.

ACTIVITY ⑩

Look at the recruitment pages of a national or local newspaper. Write a list of the type of information that appears in most job adverts. You should find that most of the adverts will contain similar types of information. Write down which advert most attracts your attention and identify why.

Key Skills C3.2

Getting the advertisement right means giving the right information, in the right way and in the right place. Information given in the advertisement should include:

● job title

● key duties and responsibilities of the job

● the type of person required, including any skills, qualifications and experience they will need

● where the job will be based

● a brief description of the business

● how and when to apply.

Many advertisements also include details of pay and conditions of work. This might include hours, pension arrangements, opportunities for overtime, and opportunities for training and promotion. The job description and person specification will provide much of the information for the advertisement.

Details need to be brief. Employers can only include a limited amount of information in an advertisement. The advertisement should encourage candidates to contact the business if they require further details. The business may send applicants the job description and person specification to give them more information.

In the same way that businesses use adverts to sell products, the job advert has to sell the business organisation and the job to potential candidates. The advert should present information clearly and concisely. It should also present the business and the job in the most favourable light. One of the most important principles is to be honest about the job and about the business. If the advert gives candidates an inaccurate picture they will soon find the job does not live up to their expectations and will leave. The business then has to start the whole exercise again, which is a costly. Businesses should see recruitment advertising as a public relations exercise. It is one of the ways that the general public builds up an image of the business organisation.

Where a business advertises a job, will depend upon the type of job. The business will need to consider whether it is likely to find suitable candidates locally or nationally. For jobs that require specialist skills or specific professional qualifications, a trade journal would be suitable. For unskilled or less specialised jobs, the local newspaper is probably ideal. Advertising in the national press or specialist journals can be very expensive, and this may limit the choice for some businesses. Another alternative now available to businesses is advertising on the World Wide Web. There are a growing number of recruitment sites who charge businesses to advertise vacancies. Larger business organisations (such as Microsoft) will advertise vacancies on their websites. The business needs to be certain that the type of candidates it is trying to attract will have access to the Web.

ACTIVITY 11

Look at one or more of the recruitment sites on the Web, and write down the main types of jobs they advertise.

Key Skills IT3.1

Application forms, letters of application and CVs

Job applicants usually apply in writing. Businesses will sort the written applications and decide who they would like to interview. It is unusual for businesses to interview all applicants. Generally, they will receive too many applications. The business tries to match the details provided by applicants to the person specification and job description. This will help it to identify the most suitable applicants. The task is easier where each candidate has provided the same information, in the same format. This is why many businesses provide application forms for job vacancies.

All application forms will ask for basic details, such as name, address and telephone number. Most will ask for date of birth and nationality. Some will ask marital status. The remainder of the form will collect the information needed by the business to decide whether applicants are suitable. This will include details of education, training and past employment. Other sections might ask about skills or qualities that the applicant feels would be useful in the job, or reasons why they are interested in the job. Some forms will ask for details about any criminal convictions, particularly where the job involves working with children or with money. The form may also ask applicants about their hobbies and interests and give them the opportunity to add any relevant details not covered elsewhere. Finally, the form will normally ask for referees and may ask about the applicant's availability for interview.

The design of application forms is very important. A good application form will be clear and easy for applicants to complete. It will request all the information that the business needs to make a decision about whether to interview. This means covering all aspects of the job description and person specification. Most application forms will give the applicant the opportunity to write something in support of their application. They usually achieve this by asking open questions such as 'Why are you interested in this post?' and 'What skills do you have that would make you suitable for the post?'

Top Tips

Closed questions are best to obtain details of the applicant and their experience. They require specific answers, for example asking candidates their name, address and educational details.

Open questions help to gain more of an insight into why the applicant is applying for the job, their attitude and how they might apply the skills that they have. They require the applicant to write something about themselves.

There would be little point in asking closed questions about skills for example. The question 'Do you have skills that make you suitable for the post?' would provoke a 'Yes' from every applicant!

Forms should always give applicants enough space to write their answers. It is good practice to ask applicants to sign and date the form and confirm that the details given are correct.

The business should ensure that they provide clear instructions for completion and return of the form to every candidate. These might include, for example, asking them to complete the form in black ink so that it is easier to photocopy. They will always include a closing date, and name and address for returning the completed application.

ACTIVITY 12

Using a local newspaper, identify three or four job vacancies at different organisations and request application forms and further information. Compare the forms and information you receive and identify which you think are the best and worst. You should consider whether:

- **all relevant information about the vacancy is provided for applicants**
- **the application form requests all the information required by the employer to assess suitability of applicants.**

Write a list of features that you would include on an application form and information to applicants. The list will help you to evaluate recruitment documentation for your assessment. (You may like to carry out this activity as a group and each obtain a different application form.)

Some business organisations prefer candidates to apply in their own words. They will ask for applications in writing. Candidates will normally write a letter of application (see Figure 4.5) and enclose a curriculum vitae (CV). In some cases,

businesses will specifically request a hand-written letter. The letter of application will set out why the candidate is applying for the job and why they think they are suitable. It may give details of qualifications and experience, though this usually set out in an accompanying CV.

A curriculum vitae (CV) is a document that provides details of the applicant, their qualifications, experience and career to date (see Figure 4.6). Applicants should type their CV and include the sort of information that an employer would normally require on an application form. This will include:

- name
- address and telephone number
- date of birth
- marital status
- education, training and details of qualifications
- details of previous employment
- hobbies and interests
- references.

The CV and letter of application give the employer the opportunity to see how well the applicant can present information about themselves. A letter of application that is untidily written, badly organised, grammatically incorrect and misspelled will not give a very good impression. The disadvantage of these documents over application forms is that the applicant chooses what to include. The applicant may leave out information that does not support the application. They are also more difficult to compare as each applicant will use a different layout and include different information.

Employers use the application documents to shortlist candidates for interview. They will match details given by applicants against job descriptions and person specifications in order to identify suitable candidates. All application documents become an important part of the successful applicant's personnel file.

8 Moorefield Way
Benton
North Yorkshire
BD45 4HH
23 June 2001

The Personnel Manager
Benton Building Society
Norton Road
Benton
North Yorkshire
BD28 4JS

Dear Sir/Madam,

I would like to apply for the post of counter assistant recently advertised in the 'Benton Courier'.

I am particularly interested in the advertised post, as I undertook my work experience in your Edward's Road Branch last year which I very much enjoyed. I like working with people and currently have a Saturday job in my local newsagents.

I am in my final year at college and am taking a Vocational A Level Business Studies course. I have GCSEs in Maths, English and Computer Studies. I would like to continue my education when I start work, through further qualifications or training.

I finish my college course on 5th July and will be available for employment from that date.

I enclose my CV and look forward to hearing from you.

Yours sincerely,

Jane Hodgson

(Jane Hodgson)

FIGURE 4.5 *A typical letter of application*

Jane Hodgson – Curriculum Vitae

Full Name: Jane Mary Hodgson

Address: 8 Moorefield Way
Benton
North Yorkshire
BD45 4HH

Telephone: 01777 987000

Date of birth: 5th May 1983

Education   1994 – 1999 Benton High School
1999 – 2001 Benton College of Further Education

Qualifications   GCSE: Maths (B), English (B), Computer Studies (C),
History (C)
Vocational A Level Business (complete in July)
Key Skills: Application of Number, Communications,
IT (All Level 3)

Work experience   1998 – Present: Saturday work in local newsagent.
Responsibilities include serving
customers, cash handling,
stock taking.

May 2000:   Work experience for one month at
Benton Building Society. Experience
included serving customers, cash
handling, general office duties.

Hobbies and interests   Running (have completed three marathons),
amateur dramatics (member of Benton
Players)

References   References may be obtained from:

Mr M Smith   Ms H Dodds
Smiths Newsagents   Vocational A Level Business Course Tutor
7 Hay Street   Benton College of Further Education
Benton   Benton
BD45 7KL   BD32 8FF

FIGURE 4.6 *A sample CV*

Telephone applications

Occasionally, an employer might ask applicants to telephone and talk to someone about the vacancy. This would normally be for jobs where telephone skills are important. The interviewer might ask about the applicants' experience and qualifications, as well as why they think they are suitable for the position. They may then ask suitable applicants to attend face-to-face interview and complete a formal application form.

References

Most prospective employers will ask applicants for details of two or more referees. These are people who are able to give the employer information about the person, their attitudes and abilities. Often employers will specify that one should be a personal reference (from a friend) and the other from a former employer, or school/college tutor. Employers will usually request references after interview, when they have identified the most suitable candidate. Employers might request the following types of reference:

- **Letters of reference** – the employer will request that the referee writes, giving information about the applicant. The referee decides what information might be relevant.

- **Reference forms** – a more structured request for information about the applicant. The form will ask specific questions about the applicant's attitudes, abilities, achievements and experience.

- **Telephone references** – sometimes employers will telephone referees instead of writing. They are able to request more detailed and specific information in a telephone call. The referee's tone of voice and attitude may also give some clues about the applicant.

- **Medical references** – many jobs now require medical references. Often these are simple questionnaires to assess a person's general health. Sometimes specific information will be relevant because of the nature of the vacancy.

For example, where heavy lifting is part of the job, the employer would want to know that the person was physically capable.

Employers need to remember that it is the applicants who choose the referees and they will usually choose people who are going to give a favourable impression. It is important to ask the right questions of referees and identify reasons behind any gaps in information they give.

ACTIVITY 13

Imagine that you are an employer and you need to fill a vacancy. List the information that you would expect to obtain about a candidate from their application form or letter of application and CV. Write down the advantages and disadvantages of application forms, letters of application and CVs. Decide which you would prefer to receive from an applicant and say why.

Shortlisting candidates

Very few employers would want to interview all candidates who apply for a job. It would take too long. Once they have all the application forms, a selection panel can look at the candidate information and choose the most appropriate ones for interview. The selection panel may include a human resources manager and one or two people from the department with the vacancy. Where there are a very high number of candidates, the human resources department may initially sort applications to make the task easier. It will sort and reject any unsuitable applicants. These will be applicants that do not have the attributes detailed in the person specification. The selection panel should consider all candidates properly, including internal candidates who they may know. In some cases, management will have an agreement with staff to interview all internal candidates.

Benton Building Society

Norton Road
Benton
North Yorkshire
BD28 4JS
30th June 2001

8, Moorefield Way
Benton
North Yorkshire
BD45 4HH

Dear Miss Hodgson,

Thank you for your interest in the post of counter assistant at our Edward's Road Branch. I am pleased to inform you that you have been selected for interview. Details are given below:

Date of interview: 17th July 2001

Time: 10 a.m.

Venue: Benton Building Society, Edward Street, Benton.

Interviews are expected to last 45 minutes. Following the interview, you will be asked to take a short test. This is to test the communication and number skills of candidates.

Please confirm that you will attend by telephoning my secretary on 01777 98655, ext.43.

I look forward to meeting with you on the 17th.

Yours sincerely,

Ms K Trowell

Personnel Manager

FIGURE 4.7 *Letter to an applicant inviting them for interview*

Some employers, for example the Civil Service, will set pre-selection tests for all applicants, to help them in selecting candidates for interview. These tests attempt to identify candidates with the right skills or attributes for the job. They might test specific skills or general IQ or assess personality. We will look at tests in more detail later in this section.

Chosen candidates will receive a letter giving a time and place for interview (see Figure 4.7). The letter may also explain what type of interview will take place and whether there will be other activities such as a group discussion session or assessment tests.

Rejected candidates will receive a letter explaining that they have not been selected for interview. Where the selection panel considers that the applicant might be suitable for vacancies that arise in the future, it may keep details on file. It may explain this to candidates in the letter.

Recruitment interviews

The interview is generally the basis for the final selection of a candidate for a job. Tests of various kinds might back up the interview process (see later in this section). Employers still see interviews as the best way to assess a candidate's personality, ability and suitability for a job. Interviews can take different formats:

● **One-to-one** interviews involve the candidate being interviewed by one representative of the business. The advantage of this type of interview is that the candidate feels more comfortable talking to one person. The disadvantage is that only one person sees the candidate and is able to assess their suitability. Employers sometimes use a series of one-to-one interviews so that the candidate talks to human resources and people from the relevant department. However, this can be time-consuming for the business and repetitive for the candidate.

● **Panel** interviews involve a number of interviewers. These might include a representative of the human resources department, a senior manager, and a departmental manager to whom the successful person would report. Panels ideally include three or four people. Some senior positions do use 'board interviews' with larger numbers of interviewers but this is not normally appropriate. The advantages of panel interviews are that there are more people to assess the candidate and that each can ask specific questions, perhaps related to their area of expertise or knowledge. Board interviews can also indicate how the candidate responds to stressful situations. Disadvantages are that the interviewee can be less comfortable, and that the interview needs careful planning so that questions are not repetitive.

● **Telephone** interviews are used occasionally, particularly where the interviewee would have to travel a long distance. This is most often where the vacant post involves working abroad. They are best as a secondary interview, perhaps by the immediate manager, after a local face-to-face interview. Employers use them as an initial interview where the costs of setting up face-to-face interviews are high. They can be one-to-one interviews or, using conference calls, panel interviews.

Sometimes interviewers will talk to groups of candidates initially, before individual interviews. This is usually to give all candidates information about the vacant position. Giving this information to all candidates at the same time ensures that they all receive the same information, and saves time in individual interviews. They can also give candidates the chance to ask any questions about the job role and the business organisation. Employers may also use group exercises to assess candidates. We will discuss group exercises later in this section.

Planning the interview process

The interview process and the interviews will need careful planning to ensure that everything runs smoothly on the day. The first step will be to decide the following:

- what format the interviews will take
- when and where they will take place
- who will be involved and
- whether any additional assessment of candidates, such as testing, will be carried out.

When planning to interview several candidates on the same day, timings should allow each interviewee the same amount of time. Interviewers will need short breaks between interviews to allow them to make notes about the candidates and prepare for the next interview. Details such as who will meet the candidates on arrival, and where they will wait before their interviews, will need resolving. Interviewers and interviewees need to know what will happen on the day of the interviews.

Interviewers will need to decide what it is they are trying to find out at interview. This will include establishing whether the candidate will be able to do the job, and whether they will fit in to the department and the organisation. Interviewers will need to know and understand the person specification and job description. They should compare each application to the job description and person specification to identify any areas for discussion. They should look at each application before the interview and identify any areas that might need further explanation. There might be gaps in the application information which interviewers will need to discuss with the candidate.

A company employed a new cashier. About a year later, a large amount of cash went missing from one of the tills. Management suspected this cashier. They looked back at her application documents. Under 'previous employment' on her CV they saw that there was a two-year period where she was 'living abroad with relatives'. On further investigation, they found out that she had not been abroad, but working for another local company. That company had dismissed her after she was found guilty of taking cash from the tills. What could her new employer have done to avoid this situation?

Interviewers should make notes about each application and devise an appropriate list of questions for each candidate. Questions should generally be open questions that allow candidates to talk about themselves and their experience. All questions should be relevant to the vacancy. They should not be biased or lead the candidate towards a particular answer. Some questions will be specific to individual candidates. These include questions about their experience and qualifications. Other questions will be appropriate for all candidates. These might include questions designed to test the candidates' abilities or technical knowledge. They will also include asking candidates whether they understand the conditions of employment and asking when they would be able to start. Where there is an interview panel, they will need to decide who will ask each question.

Imagine that you are an employer who is interviewing for a new stock control clerk. The job involves receiving deliveries of stock and checking them against orders, issuing stock to departments and keeping records of quantities and stock values. The company keeps its stock records on computer. Write down five areas that you might want to explore in interview with candidates. Write two questions relating to one or more of these areas. The questions should help you to decide whether each applicant has the right skills and abilities for the job.

Key Skills C3.3

The interview

The purpose of job interviews is to find a suitable candidate for the vacancy. Interviewers should aim to find out all relevant information about a candidate and their experience. Interviews are stressful for candidates. Interviewers need to make candidates feel at ease so that they will provide the information required. The candidate should do most of the talking in an interview. The interviewer(s) should listen and observe body language. Body language can give clues about personality, honesty and levels of confidence.

 Top Tips

Listening involves looking interested in what the candidate has to say, to encourage them to talk more about themselves.

The interviewer(s) should not make the decision until all candidates have been interviewed.

The following list identifies some good interview techniques:

- choose a seating arrangement that doesn't put the interviewee at a disadvantage. If they are positioned facing a window, so that the sun is in their eyes, or asked to sit on a chair that is much lower than those of the interviewer(s), they may feel uncomfortable
- welcome the candidate
- introduce the interviewers where there is a panel
- explain the purpose and structure of the interview
- give candidates any background information that is appropriate
- be honest about the job and what it requires
- ask easy questions to begin with, covering familiar areas such as the candidate's

qualifications or experience. Start with their present employment. This will help to put candidates at ease

- use open questions to allow candidates to talk about themselves
- encourage the candidate to talk, and listen properly to their answers, showing interest in what they are saying
- put aside any personal prejudices. Just because the candidate has a nose ring or orange hair doesn't mean they are not suitable for the job
- keep to the time allowed for each interview
- follow the interview plan of which questions to ask and who should ask them
- avoid asking irrelevant questions
- avoid biased questions or leading the candidate in a specific direction with their answers
- try to identify each candidate's strengths and weaknesses
- observe body language but accept that candidates might be nervous
- make sure you get answers to all questions and explore areas further where necessary. For example, where a candidate says that they had responsibility for something, ask specific questions about this
- make sufficient notes to allow you to make your decision. You need to be discreet so as not to make the candidate more nervous
- allow time for the candidates to ask questions
- check that the candidate understands all the terms and conditions of employment
- tell the candidate when they will hear about whether they have been successful
- thank the candidate for attending the interview
- don't make decisions until all candidates have been seen.

 **ACTIVITY**

The previous list gives some ideas on good interview techniques for interviewers. It is also important that interviewees are properly prepared and give a good impression at interview. Make a list of the things you would do if you were to be interviewed for a job. Include things you would do before and during the interview.

After the interview

When all the interviews have taken place, interviewers will need to decide on a suitable candidate. They should consider all the available information and re-consider how each candidate matches the specifications. Where there are two or three candidates who all appear to be suitable, a second interview might be arranged.

 **Top Tips**

Information about applicants should always be treated as confidential. It should never be passed to anyone outside the selection process without the applicant's permission.

Once the interviewers have made their choice they will arrange for letters to be sent to all candidates. The successful candidate will receive an offer of employment which will usually ask them to contact the business to accept the job and discuss terms. Other candidates will receive letters explaining that they have been unsuccessful. Many businesses invite unsuccessful candidates to contact them if they would like any feedback on interview performance. This can be useful to candidates, especially if they are inexperienced at job interviews. Sometimes letters to one or more of the unsuccessful candidates might be delayed until the chosen candidate has actually accepted the job. If the first-choice candidate turns down the offer of employment, the business can then make an offer to one of the other candidates. This should happen only where the other candidates are considered to be suitable but have, for example, slightly less experience.

Occasionally interviewer(s) find that none of the candidates is suitable and that they need to re-advertise the vacancy. This happens when the business has not planned the recruitment and selection process properly. For example, it could be due to one or more of the following:

- the need for the post has been wrongly assessed
- the job description is inaccurate or imprecise
- the person specification is inaccurate or imprecise
- the advertisement gave insufficient or incorrect information
- the application forms did not ask for appropriate information
- the application information was not properly compared to the job description and person specification
- the wrong people have been invited for interview
- the right questions were not asked at the interview.

The recruitment and selection process is an expensive one. It is important that businesses get it right.

Assessment of candidates

Some businesses do not like to rely totally on the interview as a selection method. They like to use additional techniques to assess candidates. These include various types of tests and assessments.

- **Ability tests** usually assess numeracy or written communication. They might be used in jobs where calculation is important, such as working in a shop; or where the candidate needs to write reports, letters or other communications, such as a complaints department. Candidates might be asked to complete a number of calculations or to draft a letter to a customer.

- **Practical tests** assess practical skills such as typing or use of computer software. The candidate would be set a task. Typists, for example, are often set typing speed tests.

- **IQ tests** involve assessment of the applicants' ability to solve problems and analyse information. They are widely used by the civil service. The tests set a series of puzzles and problems for applicants to solve.

- **Psychometric** and **personality tests** try to assess a person's behaviour, attitude to work and personality type. They usually involve candidates saying how they would react in given situations or choosing words that they feel apply to themselves.

- **Medical assessments** are used where there are specific health requirements for a job. For example, pilots in the RAF need to have perfect vision.

- **Group exercises** and **discussions** can be used to assess how candidates perform within a group situation. They may highlight some personality traits and show which candidates are good at team working and those who naturally take a leadership role. Candidates as a group are set a problem to solve or given a discussion topic. Interviewers observe the group during the exercise.

Any tests or assessments used need to be planned and carried out properly. Compiling tests that will be useful is a specialist task and can be expensive and time-consuming. In some areas, standard tests are available for businesses to purchase and use. Businesses will always need to check that tests are suitable and make sure that they interpret the results properly. If tests are used inappropriately, it could result in the wrong choice of candidate.

Equal opportunities

Throughout the recruitment and selection process, and when people are employed, businesses need to ensure that they promote equal opportunities. Some issues are covered by legislation, but others rely on the integrity of the recruitment and selection team. Let's look firstly at the legislation.

The Equal Pay Act 1970 states that employees doing the same or similar jobs should receive the same pay and conditions, regardless of gender. Before the Act was introduced, it was common for women to be paid less than men, even where they were carrying out the same tasks. Now this is illegal. In 1983, a ruling in the European court added the 'equal value amendment' to the Act. This allows women to claim the same pay and conditions as men in jobs of 'equal value'. This means that where two jobs are equal in terms of skill, effort and decision-making, they should be of equal value in terms of pay. In the recruitment process employers need to ensure that men and women are offered the same pay and conditions for similar jobs.

ACTIVITY **17**

A business employs a woman to clean its offices. She is paid £20 a week less than the man who is employed to clean the factory. In addition, her working hours as set out in her contract of employment mean that she works half an hour more each day than the factory cleaner. Discuss the case with a colleague and make notes of your discussion. Can you see any situation where it would be appropriate to pay the male factory cleaner a higher rate? What would the office cleaner need to show to prove she should have equal pay?

The **Sex Discrimination Act 1975** makes it unlawful to discriminate on the grounds of gender or marital status. This means that employers would not be allowed to advertise a job specifying that only women, or only men, should apply. They would also not be able to exclude married women from applying. Employers should also ensure that men and women are given equal treatment at interview and that no questions of a discriminatory nature are asked. Asking a woman about child care arrangements would not be acceptable. The question is discriminatory and implies that a woman would be less reliable because she had the responsibility of caring for a child. Note that although the Act is often used to protect the position of women, it also prevents discrimination against men. The Act does allow some exceptions where employers can show that it is more appropriate to employ a person of one gender. For example, it may be appropriate to employ women warders in a women's prison.

ACTIVITY 18

Tina is employed by a food packaging factory. The management has announced that there will be some redundancies. Tina is not concerned about her job as she has been employed by the company for many years and knows that newer staff are more likely to be made redundant. She tells her supervisor that she is pregnant and will want to take the statutory maternity leave. Two days later she is made redundant. The human resources manager is surprised that she is upset. He says 'We didn't think you'd mind as you are pregnant anyway'. Discuss the case with a colleague and make notes of your discussion. Was the employer justified in making Tina redundant? Why do you think the Sex Discrimination Act applies in this case?

The **Race Relations Act 1976** states that it is unlawful to discriminate on the ground of race. It is unlikely today that such discrimination would be practised directly but employers need to

ensure they do not discriminate indirectly. This would include making all employees using their annual holiday allowance at Christian religious holidays such as Easter and Christmas. This does not allow for the religious holidays of other religions. Employers may not normally specify that applicants belong to a particular racial group. As with the Sex Discrimination Act, there are some exceptions. For example, it is valid for ethnic restaurants to advertise for ethnic staff. A Chinese restaurant would be allowed to advertise for Chinese waiters or waitresses.

ACTIVITY 19

Afsheen, a young Asian woman, has applied for a job as a counter assistant in a bank. All counter staff are required to wear the company uniform. The uniform is a grey skirt and pale blue blouse for women, and a grey suit, with pale blue shirt and navy tie for men. Afsheen explains that she would want to wear trousers as this is part of her cultural and religious beliefs. The bank refuses to employ her because she will not wear the uniform. Discuss the case with a colleague and make notes of your discussion. How has the employer acted unlawfully? What changes do you think the employer should make to the uniform ruling?

The **Disability Discrimination Act 1995** covers discrimination against disabled people at work and in the recruitment process. Employers are not allowed to treat disabled people less favourably than other people. Employers are also required to make reasonable adjustments to the workplace and to job descriptions to accommodate disabled employees. The Act is limited in that it does not apply to businesses with less than 15 employees, and excludes the police, the fire service, the armed forces and the prison service. In addition, employers will not be required to make adjustments in the workplace if it can be shown that the cost is too high for them to bear. Here it would be the employers' responsibility to prove that they had looked into costs and sources of funding and they were not reasonable. The Act says that discrimination may be justifiable in some cases. This would include situations where a disabled person was unable to carry out the main tasks of the job. For example, a blind person could not be employed in a job that required driving as its main task.

ACTIVITY 20

Harry suffers from cerebral palsy. He is a capable young man but people find it very difficult to understand what he is saying, especially on the telephone. He uses a wheelchair. He has applied for a job as a clerk at a large insurance company. The company will not employ him although he has all the right skills and qualifications. It says that the job requires the use of the telephone and that access to the office would be difficult. In fact, clerks rarely use the telephone except for internal calls when they can't be bothered to walk to the other end of the office. Also wheelchair access to the office could be achieved by moving the furniture around. Discuss the case with a colleague and make notes of your discussion. Do you think the employer acted unlawfully? Give reasons for your answer. What would the Act require the employer to do?

The legislation discussed above attempts to make the workplace a fairer place. However, equal opportunity is not just about legislation. Some areas are not covered by legislation but may be just as unfair. Discriminating against someone because they have their tongue pierced, or because they are homosexual, or on the ground of age is unfair but not covered by legislation. Many large organisations have their own equal opportunities policy, such as the BBC, quoted below:

'The BBC is committed to equal opportunities for all, irrespective of race, colour, creed, ethnic or national origins, gender, marital status, sexuality, disability or age.

We are committed to taking positive action to promote such equality of opportunity and our recruitment, training and promotion procedures are based on the requirements of a job.

In this policy the BBC includes all staff whether full-time, part-time or temporary and any person who acts as an agent on behalf of the BBC in employment matters. All staff are made aware of the provisions of this policy.

Anyone who believes they have been denied equality of opportunity should pursue a complaint through the recognised procedures.'

(*Source:* Race for Opportunity website)

Policies such as these go beyond legislation in an attempt to offer equal opportunities to everyone. Of course, equal opportunities do not just apply in the recruitment and selection process. Employees should be treated equally throughout their period of employment. Employers should ensure that equal opportunities are offered in selection, pay and conditions, training and promotion.

Rights of employees

Under UK legislation, employees are given certain rights in relation to employment. We have already considered some of these rights when looking at equal opportunities legislation. Others relate to how any individual employee is treated by the employer. The main rights of employees are:

● the right to a **written statement of employment terms** – the law specifies what the statement should include. The statement forms the basis of the contract of employment. We will look at this in detail later in this section

● the right to an **itemised pay statement** – each employee should receive a payslip showing all earnings and deductions and the period covered (usually weekly or monthly)

- the right not to have **unlawful deductions** made from pay – employers can deduct items such as tax and National Insurance contributions from employees' wages. Most other deductions would require employees' agreement. An example might be a contribution to the cost of a vehicle provided for business and private use

- the right to **rest periods** and **paid annual leave.** The Working Time Regulations came into force in October 1998 as a result of a European Directive. They provide for maximum working hours, minimum rest periods and minimum amounts of paid leave. They apply to many, but not all, employees and can be varied by collective agreement of the workforce. Maximum weekly hours set by the regulations are 48 though this can be averaged over a 17-week period. Individual workers can agree to work longer hours. Employees are entitled to a daily rest period of at least 11 consecutive hours in each 24 hour period; a daily rest break of 20 minutes if working more than six hours a day; and a weekly rest period of 24 hours in each seven-day period (or 48 hours in 14 days). Every employee is entitled to four weeks' paid leave each year

- the right to **notice** on termination of employment by the employer. Employees are normally entitled to one week's notice for each year of employment, up to a maximum of 12 weeks. The employer may make equivalent payments to the employee and not require them to work during the period of notice. There are exceptions to this where the employee has acted unacceptably. For example, an employee caught stealing could be dismissed immediately, without notice or payment in lieu of notice. Employers can offer more favourable terms in contracts of employment – often employees are entitled to one month's notice after three months of employment. They are never allowed to offer less than the statutory minimum. (Employers

are also entitled to notice from employees of their intention to leave. The period is a minimum of a week which can be extended under the terms of the employment contract)

- the right to **written reasons for dismissal.** After two years with an employer, an employee becomes entitled to a written statement giving reasons for dismissal. Employees who are pregnant or on maternity leave when they are dismissed are entitled to a written statement of reasons, regardless of length of service

- the right to belong to a **trade union**, not to be **discriminated** against on the ground of trade union membership and to be given **time off** for trade union activities. Also the right **not** to belong to a trade union where one exists in the workplace. This last right arises from the so-called 'closed-shop' agreements that used to exist in some workplaces, where the unions refused to work with non-union employees and effectively forced every employee to become a member

- **maternity rights.** Women are entitled to time off for appointments in connection with pregnancy, to time off before and after the baby is born, to some payment during this time off work and to return to their job or an equivalent job following maternity leave. The amount of maternity leave and paid leave depends on length of service, though all women are entitled to the minimum of 18 weeks' leave, regardless of length of service. New European legislation introduced in 1999 makes allowance for parental leave of up to three months. Any parent (natural or adoptive) can take up to three months' unpaid leave with the right to return to work following that leave. The law also makes it unlawful to discriminate against people who take this leave

- **equal pay** for equal work (under the Equal Pay Act) – this was discussed earlier in this section

- not to be the victim of **discrimination** on grounds of race, gender or marital status (under equal opportunities legislation)

- the right **not to work on Sundays** and not to be discriminated against because of this. When Sunday shop opening was introduced, the government was concerned that employees might be forced into working on Sundays. It introduced legislation making it unlawful to discriminate against employees who did not wish to work then

- the right to receive **redundancy payments**. Any employee who has been employed for a minimum of two years by an employer is entitled to receive some payment if made redundant. The minimum amount is set out in legislation and depends upon the level of the employee's wages and length of service. Some employers will pay more than the minimum amount, particularly where they ask for volunteers for redundancy

 **Top Tips**

Businesses cannot just dismiss employees for no reason. Sometimes a business needs to reduce the number of employees – usually on economic grounds – so it makes people redundant.

- the right to **time off for job hunting** or to arrange **training** when facing redundancy. Employees who are to be made redundant are allowed to take time off to look for another job or arrange training for when they leave. A good employer will help employees by appointing outplacement consultants to help them find alternative employment

- the right to **time off** work for **public duties**. This includes time off for council duties, jury service and magistrates' duties. The employer does not have to pay employees for this time

- the right to receive wages at or above the **national minimum wage**. The government has set minimum wage levels which apply to most employees

- the right to receive **statutory sick pay** and to **return** to work following a period of illness. When an employee is absent from work due to sickness they are entitled to some pay and to return to work following their illness. Employees should not be discriminated against on the ground of illness

- **health and safety** legislation requires the employer to ensure that the workplace is safe for employees and that they are trained in aspects of health and safety. Safety representatives are entitled to **paid time off** in connection with their duties. Any employee who takes any action on health and safety grounds has the right not to be discriminated against. For example, an employee might report the employer for breach of health and safety legislation

- the right **not to be unfairly dismissed**. No employee should be unfairly dismissed. Employees who feel they have been treated in this way have the right to take their case to an industrial tribunal if they have been employed continuously for two years with the employer. In some cases, they can take the case to a tribunal regardless of length of service. These include cases where they have been dismissed for trade union membership or activities or non-membership of a trade union, for seeking to assert a statutory employment right, for taking action on health and safety grounds, for pregnancy or any reason connected with maternity, and for refusing or proposing to refuse to do shop work or betting work on a Sunday. These reasons for dismissal are **always** unfair.

Note that where a business is sold or taken over, employment is considered to be continuous. The new employer must take over employee contracts as if they were originally made with that new employer. Length of service is counted from the point they were originally employed – not from when the new employer took over.

Top Tips

More information about employee rights can be found on the Department of Trade and Industry website at www.dti.gov.uk/access.

ACTIVITY ㉑

Look at the employment rights detailed previously. For each one, explain why you think it was introduced and why it is important. Make notes for a discussion on this topic and discuss it with others in your group.

Key Skills C3.1a, C3.2

Contracts of employment

The agreement between employee and employer is a legal contract. Employees are entitled to a written statement of the terms of their employment within eight weeks of being appointed. Most employers provide statements much earlier than this, often requiring employees to sign them on taking up an appointment. The written statement can be very detailed and include anything that affects the relationship between employer and employee. The law requires that certain specific items are included. These items are:

- names of the employer and employee
- job title
- date of commencement of employment and a statement as to whether previous employment counts towards length of service.
- rate of pay and arrangements for pay (e.g. cash, direct to bank account etc.)
- required hours of work and any variations to these (e.g. shift work, overtime)
- entitlement to holiday and holiday pay
- pensions information, where relevant
- details about sickness, injury and sick pay
- notice periods for employer and employee
- grievance and disciplinary procedures.

Top Tips

The statement of terms of employment is not the same as the contract of employment. The statement sets out the main terms and conditions of employment. The contract is the agreement between the employer and employee. In a court of law, the contract might be held to include items such as the job description, and unwritten aspects of the relationship between employer and employee.

The flexible workforce

For many businesses, the workforce is one of the biggest costs. This is why it is important for them to employ the right people and the right number of people. If a business employs too many workers, it is wasting money. If it employs too few, or employs the wrong people, it will not be able to operate effectively. We have seen that employers cannot simply dismiss workers if they have too many. Businesses need to make sure that their workforce is flexible enough to cope with the changing demands of the business. Part of this flexibility comes from employing people on appropriate contracts of employment.

ACTIVITY ㉒

Can you think of any reasons why the following businesses might need flexibility in the workforce:

- a city centre public house
- a theme park
- a farm
- a bank (introducing a new computer system)
- a doctors' surgery whose receptionist is off work sick
- a toy shop.

Flexibility in the workforce can be enhanced by using appropriate contracts and terms of employment. The main ones are discussed here. Many people think of employment as involving a permanent, long-term contract. The expectation is that you will start work for a business, be employed full-time and probably work for them for a number of years. For many businesses their core employees are employed on this basis. These are skilled employees who carry out the mainstream tasks in the business. In fact, the pattern of employment is changing and many employees are now employed on part-time or short-term contracts.

In many businesses, the core workforce is supported by a large number of **part-time** workers. Full-time work is generally around 40 hours per week; part-time can be anything less than this. Part-time workers can work for a few hours each day, or on specific days. They can be used to cover specific tasks or busy periods. A shop might have additional part-time staff on Fridays and Saturdays when they are busier. Businesses typically employ cleaners on a part-time basis. Part-time contracts can be used to attract employees who might not otherwise work. For example, parents with school-age children might be attracted to jobs where they can work from 10 a.m. until 3 p.m. each day.

Fixed **short-term** contracts can be useful where businesses need more staff at specific times during the year. Seasonal businesses will need more staff during their busy season. For example, a ski school will employ ski instructors during the winter season. These contracts might be for only a few months. Businesses might also use fixed short-term contracts to employ additional staff for specific projects. For instance, a college of further education might employ a lecturer on this sort of contract to teach a specific course.

In times of recession, the use of fixed short-term contracts increases. This is because businesses do not want to commit themselves to long-term employment of staff. There has been a general increase in the number of employees employed on fixed short-term contracts. This is in response to rapidly changing business environments. The use of these contracts helps businesses 'keep their options open'. There is a down side to them in

that employees may feel less committed to the business and insecure.

Where businesses experience an unexpected busy period or staff shortage, they might employ **temporary** staff. These can be employed by the business on short-term contracts but more often come from agencies who specialise in providing temporary staff. In this case, the business pays the agency who then pays the person. Agencies provide temporary staff at short notice for a variety of tasks. Many office-based tasks, such as book-keeping, secretarial work and reception work, can be covered by temporary staff.

Businesses that operate for long hours may use **shift** workers. Some businesses run 24 hours a day. These include some manufacturing firms, some supermarkets and organisations such as hospitals. Others operate on hours that are longer than the normal working day. Some mail order companies keep their phone lines open from 7 a.m. to 11 p.m. each day. Obviously, employers can't employ staff to work such long hours so the staff work shifts. Shifts can be the same length as the normal working day (around eight hours) or may be shorter. Some workers' shifts might overlap to make the changeover between shifts run more smoothly or cover for busier periods. A supermarket might have overlapping shifts at lunchtimes to cover for the lunchtime rush of shoppers.

Some employees are contracted to work on a **job-share** basis. This means that two (or more) employees share one job. Each employee is part-time but together they cover the work of one full-timer. Job-sharing was really introduced to attract skilled women back to work after they had children. It does have problems in that there can be a lack of continuity. Where it works well, it can offer the employer some flexibility because there are two or more employees who know the same job. Often, job-sharers will cover for one another in holiday periods, or for sickness. They may also be persuaded to work additional hours when the workload is heavy.

As well as using different modes of working such as those described above, employers use different terms to increase flexibility of employees. Flexible working hours will increase flexibility. Instead of expecting employees to work the same hours each day, or even each week, the hours they work may be varied. **Annualised hours** systems contract workers to work a specified number of hours over the course of a year. Businesses can then vary the weekly hours to fit in with varying staff requirements.

Flexitime systems work on a weekly basis and allow workers to choose when they start and finish work each day as long as they work the required number of hours each week. Whilst the choice of hours is up to the employee, the system generally works to the employer's advantage. Some employees will want to start early and leave early each day and some will start later and leave late, so the business benefits from extended cover in the workplace. Any extra hours worked during busy periods can generally be taken as additional leave, which encourages staff to work when required. Employers generally set some limits such as core working hours of 10.30 a.m. to 3.00 p.m. to ensure that they have cover for the main part of the working day.

Employees can be offered additional payments to work overtime when required. **Overtime** is sometimes paid at higher rates to encourage employees to work. Overtime is useful to cover short-term additional staff requirements. It is not generally a good idea as a long-term solution as it can be expensive.

In some jobs, employees are expected to work additional hours without being paid overtime. They do this because it enhances their career prospects with the business. It is typically seen in professional service businesses such as accountancy and law practices. The staff who are prepared to put in extra time when the workload requires it are seen as being more committed to the business, and are more likely to be promoted. Businesses need to be careful not to take advantage of this and use it as a long-term substitute to employing more staff. Staff will leave or stop working extra hours if the expected promotions don't materialise.

Some types of businesses offer temporary, **piece work** to cover to cover specific tasks. Piece work is where the employee is paid per piece of work done. For example, a greetings card company might pay temporary workers to pack assorted Christmas cards into boxes of 20. The workers would be paid per box packed. Typically, this sort of work is offered as home-work and fairly low paid. Businesses can use this type of labour to cover seasonal jobs, such as packing Christmas cards.

As a final note, we will mention **volunteer** workers. Many non-profit-making organisations, and some public sector ones such as the Health Service, use volunteer workers to support their core staff. Many charities, for example, rely on volunteers to staff their shops. Volunteers are not contracted employees. Committed volunteers can add to a flexible workforce but cannot always be relied upon. They can decide to stop working at any time.

One unusual, but growing area, that uses an unpaid workforce is the Internet. For example, America Online (AOL) by 1997 had thousands of volunteers who provided guidance and advice to AOL customers. These guides were enthusiasts in their chosen fields, often working full-time managing customer communities. AOL rewarded the guides with nothing more than free AOL membership. AOL gained a flexible, committed and expert workforce at minimal cost.

ACTIVITY　**23**

Look back at the last activity. Write down what sorts of contracts and ways of working the different businesses might use to gain flexibility in their workforce.

ASSESSMENT　**3**
a c t i v i t y

Identify the main features of key recruitment documents and describe factors to be considered when planning to fill a vacancy. For your assessment, you will need to tailor this information specifically to your chosen business.
Key Skills C3.2

Section 3 *Training and development*

What you need to learn

In this section you will learn about:

- the reasons for business investment in training and development programmes.
- training methods and activities
- nationally recognised training structures and qualifications that can contribute to internal training programmes.

Training and development have become important in any business organisation. The economy is constantly changing and business organisations need to respond to the changes. One way in which they can respond effectively is by training and developing employees. Even the smallest organisations find that they need to train and develop employees.

Over the last 40 years, the UK economy has changed. There is now much less demand for unskilled workers. Much unskilled work is now carried out in Third World countries where the labour is cheaper. Also, the introduction of technology in many industries has meant that many unskilled jobs no longer exist. Employers found themselves faced with semi-skilled and skilled jobs and a largely unskilled workforce. One way to bridge this gap is by training and developing the workforce so that it can fill the new roles. The change has led to much government interest in training and development and the introduction of various schemes and incentives to encourage businesses to train and develop employees. The government has also set training targets to raise the general level of skills within the workforce.

Today's workplace is a constantly changing environment. Businesses need to respond to technological, social and legal changes. Technology changes rapidly. The desktop computers you use today have more computing power than was used to put the first man on the moon. New technology requires a workforce with new skills to operate it efficiently. It may also require a workforce that is organised differently which means managers and employees need new ways of working.

Social changes also lead to training and development needs. As young people enter the workforce, they need training to introduce them to jobs. Many women now return to work after taking time off to raise a family, and they need updating and retraining.

There are also legal requirements to train employees in some areas related to work. Perhaps the most widely spread is in the area of health and safety. The law requires that every employee receives some training on health and safety in the workplace. The aim is to reduce accidents in the workplace. It is the responsibility of the employer to provide this training. Another legal training requirement relates to employees who handle food. Anyone who handles food in the course of their work must be trained in food hygiene. This helps to prevent food-related illnesses. In both these cases, the employee must be given regular updates following their initial training.

The European Union also has an impact on training requirements. European law, as it is introduced, may affect businesses and employee roles, leading to the need for some re-training. Also, simply operating in a European Market instead of just the UK will require changes. Employees may, for example, need to work with different currencies such as the euro. Many business organisations have language training programmes to teach employees to speak another European language.

Businesses need to be flexible to respond to the changes and need to be prepared to invest in training and re-training of their employees.

Traditionally, management-level employees have always been offered training and development. To gain a competitive edge in today's markets, all employees need to be given the opportunity to enhance their skills and knowledge. Those businesses who do not respond to this challenge are unlikely to remain competitive.

ACTIVITY 24

Summarise the main reasons why employees need to be trained for a business to remain competitive.

Key Skills C3.2 C3.3

Business organisations find that the results of training employees are very positive. The positive effects are not just the most obvious ones relating to efficiency, but also improved morale and lower staff turnover. When employers undertake to invest in training and development, employees feel more valued and enjoy their roles more. The main benefits to businesses of investment in training and development are:

- motivation of employees – when employees are part of a training and development programme they become more confident, and feel valued. Training also, generally gives them better career prospects for the future
- better morale – when individual employees are happier, this leads to better morale in the workforce overall
- job satisfaction – where employees are trained in new skills and their job roles are widened, they can gain more job satisfaction. This tends to mean lower absenteeism and a lower turnover of staff
- efficiency – a better-skilled and satisfied workforce is likely to be more efficient
- increased productivity – greater efficiency will generally lead to increased productivity
- better-quality output – a skilled workforce is likely to produce a better-quality product or service

- competitiveness – an organisation that is more efficient and produces quality goods or services will be more competitive
- new ideas – as employees learn more about their own role and the business, they often come up with new ideas that can help to make the business even more competitive
- health and safety training – there are fewer accidents in the workplace
- more flexible workforce – a trained workforce will be more flexible and capable of responding quickly to change.

Later in this section we will look at the different methods that businesses use to train and develop their employees. First we will look at the aims of training and development.

ACTIVITY 25

Look at the following scenarios. Write down, in each case, why you think the employee may need some training:

- **Graham has just joined Tardis Cars as a salesperson. He has been working as a salesperson for another business for three years.**
- **Juliet has just joined Pearson's Solicitors as a receptionist. It is her first job since leaving college.**
- **Vivek has been working for Drysdale Components for 14 years on their production line. They have just made him foreman.**
- **Greg has been working at Freddy's Hamburger Palace for 10 months. They have just installed a new computerised till.**

Training is important for employees throughout their working lives. On joining the business they want to learn about it and learn new skills. During their working lives they will need to upgrade their skills to cope with changing job roles and promotions. Below we have listed the main aims that businesses might have in training and developing employees:

- **to introduce new employees** – when new employees join a business organisation, it will take them some time to settle in and learn about the business and their role within it. Training at this stage can help the 'settling-in' process. This is known as **induction** training. We will look more closely at what this might include later in the section

- to **improve skills of existing employees** – businesses might want to improve the skills of their existing employees, to make the workforce more efficient. For example, they may decide to send all computer users on a keyboard skills training course. This should help them to use their computers more effectively and become more efficient

- **to increase the range of skills of individual employees** – this is known as **multi-skilling** and can lead to the workforce being much more flexible. For example, employees in a department might be trained to do the jobs of other employees in the department. This would mean that, where someone was absent, another employee would be able to cover their role so that work could continue

- **to introduce new skills required** – this is usually in response to changes in equipment or processes. Employees may need re-training when their job roles change. For example if a new machine is introduced into a factory, employees will need to be trained in its use. New skills may also be required if the business reorganises departments, or roles

- to **prepare employees for promotion** or a **move to an alternative job role** – many businesses promote people within the firm. When a department manager leaves, for example, the assistant manager might be promoted to take their place. When an employee is given a new role, they may need some training to ensure they can carry out the job effectively

- to **increase employee awareness** – we mentioned earlier in this section the need to make employees aware of health and safety issues. There may also be other issues related to the business of which employees need to be kept informed.

Businesses use a variety of methods and activities to train employees. These range from formal training courses run by specialist trainers to watching and learning from someone doing the job. Most employees will see a mixture of different training methods used during their working life. Employers need to make the right choices of training methods and activities in order for training to be effective.

Formal training courses can be arranged within the workplace (in-house) or externally by a college or training organisation. These are training courses where the employee is taken out of the workplace to learn a skill or acquire new knowledge, or achieve a relevant qualification. To be most effective, training courses should allow trainees to transfer the skills they have learned to the workplace.

In-house courses are organised by the business for its employees, and may take place at or away from work premises. They are usually used where:

- there are several employees who need to receive the same training; or
- the topic is something specifically related to the business organisation; or
- there is in-house expertise to deliver the training.

Examples include induction courses where new employees are given introductory information about the company and their role. Health and safety training might be carried out in-house because all staff need training and regular updates. There may be a health and safety officer who can conduct the training. In-house courses can be cheaper than sending employees on external courses.

ACTIVITY   26

Imagine that you have just started work for a new employer. Write down what you would expect to learn on an induction course.

There are a large number of adult education colleges and training organisations that offer training in business skills and qualifications. These can be useful for training employees in specialist areas or introducing whole groups of employees to new technology or ideas. External training organisations will run regular courses in popular subject areas, but will also design courses for specific business organisations. Tailor-made courses have the advantage that they can be related specifically to the work of the business organisation.

Formal training can be offered in the form of technology or resource-based learning. This is where the trainee guides their own learning with the use of a computer- or paper-based learning programme. This sort of training is becoming more popular as trainees can fit it around other work and home commitments. A disadvantage to employees is that employers often expect the training to take place in the employee's own time. Traditionally, training courses are held in work time. Many national qualifications can now be achieved by 'distance-learning'.

Training can be carried out on the job. This is where an employee learns about the job while they are working. Usually this involves watching someone carrying out the tasks and being supervised and coached while carrying out the tasks themselves. Coaching involves giving the employee feedback on performance and advice on improving performance while they are doing the job. For some business skills and tasks, on-the-job training is the best way for the employee to learn. These tend to be when the tasks are relatively straightforward and mistakes are not critical. The disadvantages of training of this type are that the employee doesn't have the chance to think about the tasks in a wider context, and that

mistakes can be pop popd into costs for the business. In addition, on-the-job training has been criticised where it simply involves the trainee watching another employee carrying out tasks. Trainees learn better by 'doing' than by 'seeing'. To be successful, on-the-job training needs to be properly planned, so that the trainee gains the most benefit.

Training off the job might take place on formal training courses or informally perhaps on a one-to-one basis. Training needs to be designed in so that the trainee can transfer the skills they have learned to the real work environment. This might involve setting up simulations or using case studies. Off-the-job training is useful where it would be costly or damaging if the trainee made too many mistakes in the real work environment.

Perhaps the best way to train employees is with a mixture of on-the-job and off-the-job, formal and informal training. Trainees entering an apprenticeship will usually find this mixture of training methods and activities. Many trades and professions train new entrants through an apprenticeship scheme. These cover trades such as plumbing and joinery, and professions such as accountancy and law. Note that in the professions they are normally referred to as 'articles' rather than an apprenticeship, but are basically the same idea. The trainee will work during the period of their apprenticeship. They will start by completing very basic tasks but will move on to more complex work as their knowledge and skill increase. At the same time they will take a qualification usually at a local college. This provides them with theoretical knowledge to support their practical skills. Apprenticeships usually last three or more years.

In 1995 the government launched the Modern Apprenticeships scheme. This is a similar model to the one above except that the apprentice can be taken on by any employer. Training needs to be carried out over a three-year period and the apprentice will normally be employed and work towards a National Vocational Qualification (NVQ) at Level 3.

Some business organisations use a mentoring system to help in training employees. A mentor acts as a guide, coach and adviser to an employee. They will be someone more experienced in the business organisation than the employee. Mentors are particularly useful where an employee is new to the organisation. As well as knowledge, they can pass on organisational culture and help individuals settle in to their role and the organisation. Problems can arise where the mentor does not or cannot make enough time to meet the needs of the employee.

Training need not lead to a national qualification, but many employees will be keen to gain such qualifications. Nationally recognised qualifications generally improve an employee's career prospects within the business organisation. They also show that the person has reached a particular level of skill or knowledge which can be useful for employers appointing new employees. There are a wide range of qualifications related to every field of work. Many of these are offered by trade and professional bodies. In order to simplify the structure of vocational qualifications, the government introduced NVQs. These are work-based qualifications at Levels 1 to 5, 1 being the lowest and 5 the most advanced. NVQs are available in all vocational areas.

Before NVQs were introduced, employers had to recognise all the different qualifications that existed in a vocational area and try to assess their relative value. With NVQs, an employer knows that a Level 3 NVQ is at a specific level, whatever the vocational area. In addition, any other remaining vocational qualifications are linked to NVQ levels. This makes it easier for employers to compare candidates with different qualifications.

NVQs are specifically related to an employees performance on the job. They also provide a guide to the underpinning knowledge that the employee needs to be able to do the job effectively. This means that they can be valuable as a training tool for employers to ensure that employees are attaining an appropriate level of skills and knowledge.

We have seen that training can take a variety of different forms. A good training programme will use a variety of training methods and activities to train an employee. Training should be relevant to the employee and at an appropriate level. Training should be properly planned and programmes and individual training sessions should have identified aims and objectives. Trainees should be able to transfer the skills and knowledge they learn outside the workplace into real work situations. Training programmes should aim to develop the employee; to increase skills and knowledge. They should not simply confirm knowledge and skills that the employee already possesses.

ACTIVITY 27

Choose two vocational areas from the following list and make a note of what qualifications are offered in those areas. Include college/school-based qualifications as well as work-based and professional qualifications. Note the level of each qualification.

- **accountancy**
- **child care**
- **mechanical engineering**
- **leisure and tourism**
- **management.**

Key Skills IT3.1, C3.2

ACTIVITY 28

Write a checklist of the elements of a good training programme. This will help you evaluate training as part of your assessment.
Key Skills C3.3

The government recognises the importance of training for individuals and for businesses in the UK and had introduced various initiatives to help and encourage vocational training. National training targets have been set to try to raise the level of skills, training and qualification of the UK workforce.

The Investors in People initiative was launched in 1993 and set standards for employers to meet in relation to training and development of their employees. An employer who meets the standard is allowed to display the Investors in People logo on premises and communications. By achieving Investors in People status an employer shows a commitment to training and development; to regular review of training and development needs; to training employees throughout their employment; and to evaluating training.

ACTIVITY 29

Find a copy of the Investors in People Standard. Read through the Standard. What do you think the benefits are to:

■ **the employer**

■ **the employee**

of the business meeting the IIP standard? Write lists of the benefits and compare them with others in your group. You will find a copy on the Investors in People website, or can contact them for details.

Key Skills C3.2 C3.3, IT3.1

Another government initiative is the Individual Learning Account. This is a way of helping people in work pay for learning for their personal development. Individuals who register will be given discounts and benefits in relation to learning. A learning record will be maintained which could provide evidence of the individual's efforts and achievements.

ACTIVITY 30

Use the Internet or local library to find out more about Individual Learning Accounts. Write down how you think Individual Learning Accounts will benefit:

■ **individuals**

■ **employers**

■ **the country as a whole.**

Section 4 *Performance management*

What you need to learn

In this section you will learn about:

- monitoring individual and group behaviour
- the employment environment
- motivation theories and their influence in managing employees.

We have seen that, to be competitive, businesses need to select and recruit the right people. To remain competitive, the business needs to monitor and manage employee performance. By monitoring employee performance, the business will be able to identify any problems that arise and can then plan to address those problems. One way to address the problems will be through the training and development of employees.

Performance management is a continual process. Employee performance should be monitored and managed from the time they start with the business to the time they leave. In this section we will look at how businesses use formal appraisal systems to monitor and manage performance. You should be aware that the legal aspects of employment discussed in previous sections have an impact on the management of performance. In managing employee performance, businesses need to apply regulations relating to working hours, annual leave, maternity and paternity leave and minimum wage rates.

Performance reviews

Many businesses use a formal appraisal system to assess employee performance. Most systems use a variety of review techniques to assess performance. These include reviews by the employee's manager, by peers and by the employee themselves. A formal appraisal system will:

- measure employee performance against set targets
- provide feedback on performance to the employee and their manager
- identify training and development needs of the employee
- identify a future career path for the employee.

Employee performance can then be improved by meeting training and development needs.

A formal appraisal system involves setting clear objectives for individual employees and monitoring their performance against these objectives. A development plan can be created for each employee to help them to meet their objectives. Employee objectives should be clearly linked to the strategic objectives of the business. This ensures that all employees are working towards the overall goals of the business. It also means that each employee can see the contribution they are making to the business.

ACTIVITY ③①

What advantages do you think there are in employees having objectives to meet? Think about advantages to the employer and to the employee. Write down your answers and compare them with others in your group.

Key Skills C3.1a, C3.2, C3.3

Objectives will normally be set on an annual basis, but may need to be reviewed and revised at shorter intervals. The first objectives should be set when an employee joins the organisation. To be most effective, objectives should be set by the employees themselves with guidance from their manager or mentor. Employees will be more motivated by objectives where they have taken some responsibility for setting them.

ACTIVITY 32

Why do you think employees are more motivated by objectives where they help to set them? Discuss your ideas with your group. It may help you to think about how you feel when someone sets you a task; and how you feel when you set tasks for yourself.

Key Skills C3.1a

Objectives will need to be achievable by the employee. Objectives that set the targets too high, or depend on factors outside the employee's control, will simply discourage the employee. Objectives should not be too easily achievable. These might lead to complacency on the part of the employee.

Objectives need to be measurable. The appraiser needs to be able to assess whether the employee has met the target. The best objectives set clear and specific targets for the employee to meet. A salesman, for example, might have a target to increase his sales figures by 25 per cent. It would be easy for an appraiser to see whether this target had been met.

Next time you are at a railway station, a doctor's surgery, or a supermarket, look at some of the publicity material on the walls. Many organisations now tell customers what it is they are trying to achieve, or what they have achieved. Railways might say that in the last quarter, 90 per cent of their trains ran on time. A doctor's surgery might say that it aims to see patients within five minutes of their set appointment time. Supermarkets might say that they will open more checkouts when there are more than two customers in the queue at any checkout. These are all ways in which employees can be measured.

It isn't always that easy though. In some areas it may be difficult to find a quantitative (numeric) measure for performance.

ACTIVITY 33

Discuss with your group how you might set targets for the human resources department, for example. (You may like to split into smaller groups and each take a different function of human resources before discussing the topic overall.)

Key Skills C3.1a

Many business organisations will have a written set of standards for each department and individual and team targets can be set against these. A complaints department, for example, might need to respond to every letter within a certain time limit; to answer telephone calls within a certain number of rings; and to resolve customer complaints in a satisfactory manner. The first two of these will be relatively easy to monitor. The last might require some sort of customer survey to assess whether complainants are satisfied with how their case has been resolved.

Top Tips

Don't forget the labour productivity measure we looked at in Section 1, which might help in assessing team performance.

Good objectives will specify when they should be achieved. Objectives might be long-term, medium-term or short-term. Long-term objectives will be goals for the individual, their department, or the organisation which are achievable over several years. Medium-term objectives might cover a period of about two years. Short-term objectives are achievable within the year or period over which the employee is appraised. For appraisal purposes, any longer-term objectives should be split into short-term goals. Achievement of these short-term goals will show progress towards the longer-term objectives, but will be measurable within the appraisal period.

The objectives of employees in the same team or department should be complementary. To ensure the efficiency of the team, they need to be working towards the same general aims and objectives. Similarly, departments should be working towards the general objectives of the business as a whole. It follows then, that the starting point for setting objectives of individuals or teams, is the strategic plan of the business. The objectives of each team and each individual within the team should help the business to achieve its overall aims.

ACTIVITY 34

Make a checklist of the qualities of good objectives.

Key Skills C3.3

To evaluate employee performance, objectives will need to be reviewed on a regular basis. Most systems allow for an annual review by the manager or mentor. Many appraisal systems require more frequent informal reviews either quarterly or half-yearly. Reviews should also take place if the employee is absent from their normal role for an extended period, or if the employee role changes. The purpose of the review will be to assess the employee's performance over the period and determine whether set objectives have been met. Interim reviews are used to check progress towards meeting objectives and to revise objectives where they are no longer appropriate.

Each employee should have an annual appraisal meeting with their manager or mentor. At the meeting they should discuss progress made over the past year; set objectives for the coming year; and make or revise plans for training and development. The appraisal meeting is simply a formal discussion about performance. The monitoring of performance is a continuous task. Managers needs to be aware of how employees are performing throughout the year. If matters relating to employee performance arise during the year, they should be dealt with and not left to the annual appraisal meeting.

Top Tips

The appraisal meeting is a type of interview so all the points on good interview technique in Section 2 apply here.

For the system to work effectively, some planning and evaluation will have taken place prior to the meeting. Both the employee and their manager should be well prepared for the meeting. As part of the planning, managers should remind themselves of the employee's objectives and their performance during the review period. They should also think about appropriate objectives for the coming year. Employees should be encouraged to carry out a similar exercise. The employee's self-evaluation can be an extremely useful exercise. The employee is in a unique position to identify their own achievements, failures, strengths and weaknesses. Of course, the exercise involves the employee being honest with themselves and others.

Some organisations ask employees to carry out peer evaluation as part of the appraisal system. This involves asking the employee's co-workers about their performance during the year. This would usually be done by use of an anonymous questionnaire. A variation is the 360° appraisal where an employee's performance is rated by managers, subordinates and peers. Again this is usually done by the use of anonymous questionnaires. It is useful for managers and employees to see how the employee is rated by others in the organisation. If carried out effectively, the process will give a more objective and rounded view of the employee's performance.

The purpose of any evaluation of the employee's performance is to identify achievements, failures, strengths and weaknesses, and to measure it against the set objectives. Once this has been done, training and development can be planned and future objectives set. The link to training and development is important. There is no point in identifying strengths and weaknesses unless some plan is made to build on strengths and address weaknesses. Training and development based on these evaluations of employees will help to improve performance of individuals and teams.

One overriding quality that all appraisal systems should have is that they are not too time-consuming. The main objective of any business is not to appraise employees. This is useful, but incidental to the business. If the appraisal system becomes too demanding, it will start to affect the efficiency of operations. If the appraisal system is not taken seriously enough by management and employees, it can be de-motivating. It is a matter of finding the right balance.

As part of the performance management system, each employee should be interviewed on leaving employment. This should happen whether it is the employer or employee who has terminated the employment. The termination interview marks the end of an employee's time with the business organisation. Where employees have been dismissed, it is important to ensure that they understand the reasons for their dismissal. Where employees have resigned, it is useful to find out why they have decided to leave as this might help future human resources planning. When employees retire due to reaching retirement age or because of ill health, or they reach the end of their contracted time with the business, it may be useful to review their time with the business and simply wish them well for the future.

Performance management needs careful design to ensure that objectives of different departments or sections are not in conflict with one another or with the overall objectives of the business. For example, a manager might be given the objective of increasing profits. One way of increasing profits is to reduce costs. However, if costs are reduced by cutting spending on training and development, or new machinery, the long-term profitability and survival of the business might be threatened even though the manager meets short-term objectives.

ACTIVITY 35

Look at the following case study and identify any problems with the system.

A haulage firm employs maintenance staff and drivers. The drivers' main objective is to ensure that goods are delivered to their destination on time, while working within the legal and company driving limits. Maintenance staff are given the objective of maintaining the vehicles within the budget set by the management. A driver breaks down on the way to delivering a lorry full of fruit to a customer. Timing is critical as the customer won't accept the goods if they arrive late because they will be past their best. The driver rings the maintenance department and requests that someone is sent out to fix the vehicle. The maintenance department manager suggests that the driver stays somewhere overnight and says he cannot send out an engineer until the next morning. The maintenance manager is concerned that, because it is late in the day, he will have to pay overtime and for an overnight stay for the engineer. This will seriously affect his budget for the month.

Write down any problems you can identify. What should the business do to address these problems?

ASSESSMENT 4
activity

Note down the main purposes of a performance management system and explain how and why it is linked to training and development programmes. Keep notes from this Activity as they may help you with your assessment. For your assessment, you will need to relate this work specifically to your chosen business.

Motivation

Throughout this chapter we have mentioned the motivation of employees. In this section we will look at motivation in more detail. Motivation is what makes people behave in a particular way. Businesses want employees to work towards achieving the organisation's objectives. In other words, they want to influence the behaviour of employees to the benefit of the business. The best way of doing this is to ensure that the behaviour they want from employees benefits the individual employees as well as the business.

From as early as the nineteenth century, theorists have tried to find ways of improving the effectiveness and efficiency of workers. One early theorist who developed ideas about this was Frederick Winslow Taylor. Taylor developed the idea of scientific management. He was concerned with the job of the factory floor workers.

Taylor worked in the American steel industry in the late 1800s. As a supervisor, he was concerned that workers did not work at their most efficient. He thought that workers deliberately restricted possible output. The reasons he gave for this were:

- that the workers felt that if they each increased their workload, the company would need less workers and some of them would be out of a job
- that the workers were poorly controlled and allowed by management to work at a level below optimum efficiency
- that a lot of effort was wasted because they were simply not doing the job right.

Taylor thought that it was up to management to plan each job and tell the workers how to do it. Before this, how they worked had been left very much up to the workers themselves. Taylor wanted to make the workforce more efficient and the way he saw of doing this was to standardise tasks. By doing so he would also give more control over tasks and the rate at which they were carried out to management. He felt that the design of tasks and how they were carried out should be approached scientifically.

Taylor's first step was to analyse in detail all the different tasks that were carried out. He measured tools and workers and timed different tasks carried out in different ways. He split jobs into smaller repetitive tasks that could be carried out quickly. His aim was to find the 'one best way' of doing each task. He would then select the worker most suited to the task. (This, while not surprising today, was quite revolutionary in a time when jobs largely depended on who you knew rather than what you could do!) Finally, he devised an incentive system to encourage the worker to carry out the task in the way he set out. This incentive system was the piece work system of pay. Taylor paid workers for the number of 'pieces' they produced.

Whilst Taylor's overriding concern was efficiency and not what motivated workers, motivating workers to do things his way was essential to his theory. The way he motivated them was by using financial incentives. Taylor believed that this would motivate workers sufficiently to carry out the task in the 'one best way' that he devised. Taylor's methods did improve efficiency in the businesses for which he worked, but the workers hated them. In many cases the use of Taylor's methods resulted in conflict with management, and strike action. In some cases, his ideas had to be abandoned altogether.

ACTIVITY 36

Why do you think the workers did not like Taylor's methods? Think about how you might feel as a worker for Taylor. Discuss your ideas with other members of your group.
Key Skills C3.1a, C3.2

Taylor's ideas were developed by other theorists who made them more acceptable to workers and we can see some of them at work today:

- jobs split into smaller tasks, for example on the factory production line
- the selection of the best worker for the job
- time and motion studies of work tasks
- piece rates for some types of work.

Since Taylor, management theorists have identified that one problem with his theory was the assumption that workers would simply do as they were told if they were suitably paid. More recent research shows that workers respond to having some control over their own work and that there is more to motivation than just money. We need to look beyond Taylor for an explanation of what motivates employees.

Many theorists have written about motivation. They try to explain what it is that makes individuals behave in the way they do. The American Psychologist, Maslow, believed that humans have certain needs, which they try to satisfy in a particular order.

 **ACTIVITY** 37

Imagine that you have been left alone on an island with only the clothes you are wearing. The island is covered in tall coconut trees, has streams of fresh water and is populated by dangerous wild animals. It is the monsoon season and it is very wet.

You are allowed to choose two items from the following list. Which do you choose and why? Write down your answers.

- **hunting knife**
- **waterproof ground sheet**
- **rope**
- **radio**
- **book**
- **CD player with one music CD**
- **tins of food**

- **packets of seeds**
- **matches**
- **a friend**
- **money.**

You are now allowed to choose three more items. Write down your choices and your reasons for choosing those items.

Finally, choose three more items and note them down with your reasons.

Compare your answers with those of a colleague. Discuss what your priorities were when deciding which items to choose.

Maslow's hierarchy of needs set out different levels of needs, as shown in Figure 4.8.

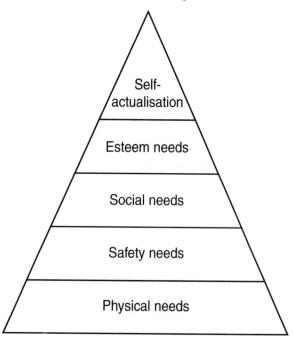

FIGURE 4.8 *Maslow's hierarchy of needs*

Let's look at what Maslow meant by these different categories of needs:

- physical needs – food, water, sunlight and sex: the basic requirements for survival
- safety needs – shelter, security, stability, an organised world
- social needs – belonging, contact, friendship, love and affection

- esteem needs – status, recognition, strength, confidence, respect from others
- self-actualisation needs – to develop one's full potential, self-fulfilment.

The first two categories are essential to our survival; the second two concern relationships with others and make us feel valued; the last category is the struggle to reach our full potential. Maslow believed that these needs were the motivators for human behaviour. He believed that, in ideal conditions, needs higher in the list would not act as motivators until those before them had been satisfied. For example, you would not look for friendship and love until you had food and shelter. The final need of self-actualisation, Maslow felt, could never be fully satisfied because it continually stimulated the desire for more.

ACTIVITY 38

Look back at the last Activity. Do your priorities on the island match Maslow's hierarchy of needs? Discuss this with your group.
Key Skills C3.1a

Maslow identified two further needs which he said were necessary for the other needs to be satisfied:

- freedom of inquiry and expression needs – freedom of speech, justice, fairness and honesty
- knowledge and understanding needs – curiosity, exploration, experimenting and learning.

Maslow believed that these two needs would help us to work up through the hierarchy and that we had an in-built desire to work up the hierarchy.

Maslow was writing in general terms about human motivation but we can look at how the needs he identifies can be satisfied for employees

at work:

- physical needs – met by good rates of pay, benefits and working conditions
- safety needs – met by job security, clarity of job role, clear organisational structure
- social needs – met by being part of a team, good lines of communication, social events
- esteem needs – met by job status, positive feedback, promotion
- self-actualisation needs – met by control over own work role, being given new challenges, development of new skills.

ACTIVITY 39

Write down how you think a business might help employees meet the other two needs identified by Maslow:

- **freedom of inquiry and expression**
- **knowledge and understanding.**
Key Skills C3.3

Maslow recognised that there were many factors affecting humans and their behaviour. His hierarchy was only put forward as an idea of what might happen under ideal conditions. He did not expect it to be applied rigidly. In reality, individuals may pursue some needs at the expense of others, or try to meet several needs at the same time. We can't use the theory to predict the behaviour of individuals but it does help us to recognise that there are a wide variety of motivators for that behaviour. Maslow's theory (developed in the 1940s) has been very influential on other writers in the field of human motivation.

Frederick Herzberg developed his two-factor theory from research he carried out in the 1950s in Pittsburgh. He interviewed around 200 engineers and accountants to find out what made them feel good about their work, and what made them feel bad about it. He developed two sets of factors:

- those that led to worker satisfaction – Herzberg called these motivators or content factors
- those that, if not properly met, caused worker dissatisfaction – these he called hygiene or context factors.

The motivators that Herzberg identified were: achievement, recognition, responsibility, advancement, growth, and the work itself. Hygiene factors were identified as: salary, company policy, supervision, status, security, and working conditions. He believed that improving hygiene factors would remove dissatisfaction and might encourage employees to stay with the organisation, but they would not motivate employees to work harder. To increase motivation and employee satisfaction, businesses would need to concentrate on the content factors.

Herzberg suggested the technique of job enrichment to improve employee motivation. Job enrichment involved re-designing jobs so that the focus was on the motivators or content factors. He suggested seven ways of achieving this:

- removing controls over employees
- increasing employee responsibility
- creating natural chapters of work
- giving direct feedback to employees
- giving employees new tasks
- giving employees special assignments
- giving employees more authority.

 **ACTIVITY** **40**

Look back at Taylor's theory. Compare Taylor's ideas with Herzberg's. Assuming that Herzberg's theory is correct, explain why Taylor's scientific management upset employees. Write down your answer.

Herzberg's theory has been applied in practice, but not very widely. However, it does give us some ideas about the importance of job satisfaction for employees. Many businesses today recognise that employees want some satisfaction from the work itself and not just from the things it brings, such as money, security and status.

 ACTIVITY **41**

Remember the two mountain bike businesses you saw in Section 1? Look back at the information about them. What conclusions can you draw about employee motivation in the two businesses by applying the motivational theories you have looked at here? Make notes and discuss your ideas with your colleagues.
Key Skills C3.1a, C3.2

In the 1950s Douglas McGregor carried out a survey of managers. He found that managers held two distinct views of workers in business organisations. He called these two views Theory X and Theory Y. Theory X managers believed that workers were generally lazy and not very bright by nature, and that they disliked responsibility. They also believed that workers had no ambition and no interest in the needs of the business. This led the Theory X managers to try to control and direct employees, using rewards and punishments as motivators. Theory Y managers believed that workers were creative and wanted to develop their potential and take responsibility in their work. These managers believed that their role was to create conditions where workers could achieve their own goals while working towards the objectives of the business.

McGregor's theory is one that addresses different leadership styles. It illustrates how managers may use different motivators, depending on their perceptions of employees. In reality, managers are not so easy to categorise. A single manager may use different management styles, depending on the situation and the individuals being managed.

McGregor believed that Theory Y managers were better at achieving the objectives of the business. Whilst most people would probably prefer the more democratic Theory Y style of management, Theory X-style management can be successful, for example in times of crisis. Think about crisis situations you have seen in television dramas, news or documentaries: a casualty department, a fire, a riot. In these situations, the people in charge don't start asking for ideas on how they should deal with the situation. They simply make decisions and give instructions. The same can happen in a business that is facing a crisis.

ACTIVITY 42

Discuss with your colleagues how the theories discussed above might be used to develop appropriate systems of performance management and employee development. Think about what factors management need to consider when designing these systems, bearing in mind the findings of management theorists. Make notes from the discussion as these may be useful for your assessment.

Key Skills C3.1a, C3.2

The theories we have considered here are basic theories of job design, motivation and management style. Since these theorists there have been many more who have developed different ideas on what makes individuals work more effectively and efficiently in modern businesses. We can identify, however, some general factors which appear to motivate employees and can be pop popd into practical incentives in the workplace. General factors include:

- the nature of the job
- trust between employee and employer
- the employees sense of achievement and employer recognition of that achievement
- a sense of belonging and job security
- status
- financial reward.

We can split the incentives into two broad groups: financial and non-financial. It is clear that the financial incentive is an important one. You only need to ask people what they would do if they won the National Lottery, to find out that many of them would give up work in favour of doing other things. It is interesting, though, that some will say they wouldn't give up work. This indicates that work provides something more than simply financial reward. Even where financial reward is important to individuals, this doesn't mean they don't also want other things from their work.

Non-financial incentives include:

- extending the scope of the employee's job in some way
- using team working
- better communication to increase employee understanding and involvement in the business
- board representation for employees.

Herzberg talked about job enrichment and research shows that the nature of the job can motivate the employee. We saw how he believed that giving workers more responsibility and authority to make decisions would improve job satisfaction. The empowerment of employees by giving them the freedom to make important decisions relating to their role, and letting them take responsibility for those decisions, can lead to job satisfaction. There is some evidence, though, that not all individuals want the additional responsibility and authority.

Employers do try to extend job roles in order to give employees more job satisfaction, though this is not always using the full job enrichment process that Herzberg envisaged. Job enlargement involves giving the employee a wider variety of work tasks but little more responsibility or authority. Employees can gain greater job satisfaction from the challenges offered by this variety of tasks. It also allows them to gain a wider picture of the organisation and their role within it. Job rotation involves employees swapping jobs with one another at regular intervals. It is usually used for repetitive jobs which can be boring for the employee. It avoids the monotony of carrying out the same tasks day after day. The employee gains a wider range of skills and a wider view of the organisation, which can give job satisfaction. It also has the advantage for the business of making employees more flexible.

Maslow identified social needs as one of his hierarchy of needs. Team working can increase employee satisfaction by giving them a sense of belonging. In addition, by allowing teams to organise workload and responsibilities among themselves, employees can be given greater control over their role within the business. Good teams will be more efficient as they work together to achieve shared goals. Weaker members of the team will be supported and motivated by the stronger members. Being part of a successful team is, in itself, motivating.

Quality circles are one type of team working. The circle members are given the freedom to organise and develop their own jobs. They meet on a regular basis to discuss work issues and suggest improvements to working methods or organisation. The circle has the authority to implement these improvements. Employees benefit from increased involvement in job design, which leads to job satisfaction. The business benefits from better quality work and quicker resolution of work problems.

Where good two-way channels of communication exist in the business, this leads to increased employee involvement in the decision-making of the business. Employees' sense of belonging and participation are enhanced by being kept informed about the policy of the organisation. Secrecy tends to lead to distrust and resentment, which are de-motivating. Good channels of communication will also help to fulfil the needs identified by Maslow of freedom of inquiry and expression, and knowledge and understanding.

Businesses can use a variety of methods to communicate policy to employees and find out their responses. Team briefings are used to pass on information to employees about business policy and operations. Team briefings are usually carried out on a regular basis by the line managers. Although this is one-way communication, it does give employees knowledge about the business and make them feel more involved.

Joint consultative committees allow workers to present their views to management. They will consist of representatives from management and employees who meet at regular intervals to discuss business policy and other business issues. They can then advise management. It is a way of workers participating in the day-to-day running of the business, though management usually reserves the right to make final decisions.

A few organisations appoint employee representatives to the board of directors or other high-level decision-making body. This rarely happens in the UK but is seen in other European countries such as Germany. It allows employees to take part in decision-making at the very highest level of the organisation.

An effective system of performance review and training and development within a business can help to motivate employees. Where performance review recognises the achievements and contributions of employees to the business, employees' esteem needs are met. Training and development can help employees feel valued by the business organisation and may allow them to meet their own self-actualisation needs.

ACTIVITY   **43**

Look at the range of non-financial incentives described before. Identify any links to the theories of motivation discussed earlier in this section. Write down which employee needs are met by each incentive.

Whilst it is recognised that non-financial incentives are important to motivate employees, financial incentives are still used as motivators. There are a wide variety of financial incentives including:

- piece rates
- performance-related pay
- profit sharing
- share ownership
- pension schemes
- medical insurance
- company cars
- preferential loans/mortgages
- discounts on company products
- staff benefits, such as subsidised staff restaurants and social clubs.

Taylor introduced **piece rates** to try to motivate employees. They are still used today, especially in smaller-scale manufacturing organisations and some farm work (fruit and vegetable picking). The employee is paid depending on output. The problem is that it does not encourage production at the highest quality. As long as the quality is satisfactory the worker will be paid, so there is no incentive to improve. In addition, it is difficult to change the pace of work to meet seasonal or other changes in business. Workers will tend to work at a pace that will pay them a reasonable, regular wage.

Performance-related pay systems reward employees on the basis of their performance during the past year. Those employees who have performed well will receive a higher pay rise than their colleagues who may not have performed quite as well. There is little evidence that this actually works as a motivator. It rewards individuals rather than teams and can put individuals in competition with one another. Most organisations operating the system put aside a set amount for merit rises, so that employees are competing for part of it. The linking of pay levels to appraisal systems can also

have a negative effect on performance review. Instead of being focused on the training and development needs of the employees, the appraisal becomes focused on achievement that might lead to merit rises in pay.

Profit sharing makes employees feel much more involved with the business. When staff know they will receive a share of the profits, they may start to take an interest in the business's profit levels. Profit sharing, unlike performance related pay, doesn't focus on the performance of individuals. The improvement of profit levels relies on all employees working towards the same goals.

Employees have a real involvement in the business where they **own shares**. Shares may be issued as part of profit related pay, or offered to employees on preferential terms. Employers may operate schemes where employees are able to save in order to purchase shares, or may offer share options. Share options allow employees to buy shares at a later date at a preferential price.

Pension schemes and **private medical insurance** are other financial incentives that are offered to employees. They are unlikely to encourage employees to work harder, but may persuade them to stay with the business rather than go elsewhere. **Company cars** have long been seen as a benefit to employees, though their attraction has reduced considerably in recent years due to changes in the tax system which make them less beneficial. Some businesses will offer **preferential loans and mortgages** to employees which can mean that they feel tied to the business in the longer term. Obviously if they leave the business, loans need to be re-paid or will revert to commercial interest rates. Many organisations offer employees **discount** on their own products or services, or **benefits** such as subsidised staff restaurants or social clubs. Again, these are not likely to make employees work harder but can form part of an financial package to attract suitable employees.

A more recent development in the financial packages offered to employees is the 'cafeteria benefits' system. Here, employees are offered a range of alternative financial benefits and individuals can pick and choose in line with their own requirements. Younger employees might choose to take more in cash and put less in pension schemes. Those with families might choose a subsidised mortgage and private health care. Older employees might want to put more money into investments or pension schemes. Employers recognise that employees are individuals with different financial needs, and attempt to cater for this.

In reality, employees work for a specific business for a variety of reasons. Successful employers will combine non-financial, and financial incentives in order to motivate employees. Employees are all individuals, and whilst theories of motivation might be applied broadly, individual needs are affected by many more things that simply the incentives the employer offers.

ASSESSMENT
activity 5

Explain how effective management of human resources can improve the competitiveness of a business. You should identify issues from the whole of this chapter. Note down any points you make, in preparation for your assessment.
Key Skills C3.2

In any business there is always the possibility that different functions and activities can come into conflict with one another. Human resources planning might show that the business needs to take on more staff to deal with the workload, but there will be other factors affecting the decision. For example, there may not be the money available for recruitment. Many organisations

undergoing cost-cutting exercises put a freeze on recruitment. This not only means they can't recruit new staff, but often that they don't replace staff who leave. This can have a very de-motivating affect on remaining employees who are left to deal with an increased workload.

Training and development, while important to maintain the skills of employees and motivate them, can often be neglected in the face of demanding work schedules. Most managers, when faced with the choice of completing their workload this month, or allowing an employee to attend a training course for a week, would cancel the training course. This achieves short-term aims, but in the long term performance will suffer because the employees have not had the training and development they need.

Performance management systems need to be understood and implemented by all managers or this can cause conflict within the business. For example, a performance management system might be designed to empower employees and enable them to become involved in the decision-making process. If managers are using autocratic management styles because they are unaware of the aims of the performance management system or are unwilling to subscribe to them, then the system will not work.

The sorts of conflicts that occur in any business between the human resources functions and other functions and activities of the business will depend on the individual business and the environment in which it is operating. The above examples are included as illustrations to help you to think about the sort of conflicts that can occur. As part of your assessment you will need to evaluate potential conflicts in your chosen business.

CHAPTER 5

Finance

What this chapter is about

Financial information is important for any business. It is the basis on which decisions about the business are made and business success or failure is judged. In this chapter you will learn about how businesses record financial information. You will also learn about how they use that information to construct statements of account and to manage the cash flow of the business. You will find out who uses these accounts to judge business performance and the techniques they can use to do this. ■

What you need to produce

The work covered by this chapter is assessed externally. Your tutor will give you a sample test to complete.

To complete the test, you will need to know:

■ why businesses need to keep accurate financial records, and the consequences of not doing this

■ why different stakeholders need financial information about the business and how they interpret this information

■ the different documents used to record financial information, how to complete them and why they are important

■ how financial recording documents are linked to one another and how information flows through the accounting system

■ how to identify assets, liabilities, expenses and revenues

■ how to construct a balance sheet and profit and loss account

■ how to use financial ratios to interpret accounts and the significance of this to different stakeholders

■ how businesses manage their working capital.

Section 1 *Recording financial information*

What you need to learn

In this section you will learn about:

- the purposes of financial information
- the users of financial information
- the documents used to record financial information.

Katie has started a new job in Manchester. She has moved away from home for the first time and has moved into a flat with an old school friend. She was very excited when she received her first pay cheque and went out to buy some new clothes and music CDs. She has been eating take-away food most evenings because she can't be bothered to cook, and she has been going out every night with her new friends. Two weeks before her pay is due, the bank manager sends her a letter telling her that her bank account is overdrawn. She also owes her flatmate some rent money and £20 that she borrowed one day when she didn't have time to go to the bank. Katie is really surprised: she didn't realise how much money she was spending.

 ACTIVITY

What has Katie done wrong? What should she do to make sure that she doesn't run out of money again?

Katie has spent more money than she has earned. She did not keep a record of the amounts she was spending and she did not put any money aside to cover regular expenses like her rent.

Katie needs to plan her spending more carefully. When she receives her pay cheque, she should put aside her rent money and the money she needs for food and travel expenses. Then she will know how much she has left to spend on clothes and CDs

and on going out with friends. She will also be able to see whether she can save some money, perhaps towards buying a car or going on holiday.

Katie needs to collect information about her finances and use it to plan her spending. In the same way, businesses need to collect financial information and will use it to make decisions about whether they can afford to buy new materials or equipment, or whether they need to borrow money. For businesses, the situation is slightly more complex because there are also legal requirements about keeping business records.

What is financial information?

Before we look at the financial information of businesses in more detail, let's consider what we mean by 'financial information' and what sort of financial information we are interested in for this chapter.

Katie's financial information is made up of:

- information about her income – how much she gets paid
- information about her expenses – bills and spending money
- the transactions on her bank account – what goes in and out, and the balance of the account
- money she borrows from other people and needs to pay back.

All of us come into contact with some sort of financial information every day, either about our own finances, about the finances of other people or businesses, or about government changes to taxes or benefits. You only need to listen to the news or open a newspaper to find financial information. Try the following exercise.

ACTIVITY   2

Write a list of the financial information you have come into contact with in the last few days. The list might include information about your own finances, things you have discussed with friends or items that you have heard on the news about businesses.

You may be surprised at just how much financial information you have heard or seen. Some of the information will be of particular interest to you, whilst other information will not affect you. Obviously businesses need to identify the information which is most relevant to them. They do not want to collect vast amounts of information about things that don't affect them!

ACTIVITY   3

Take another look at the list you made in the last activity. Identify any information that affects you directly.

You should have picked out from your list any information about your personal finances. You may also have identified information about other people's finances. For example, your friend Jason can't afford to pay you the £20 he owes you until next week! Finally, you might have identified some wider financial issues that affect you. If the government is increasing the price of petrol, or train fares have increased, for instance, this may have an impact on your personal finances.

The information which interests a business will vary depending on who is using the information and the purpose for which they want to use the information. In this chapter, we are particularly interested in the information the business needs to record on a day-to-day basis in order for the business to operate. We will be looking mainly at information that is generated from inside the business, about its own financial position, and considering the uses and users of this information.

Why do businesses need financial information?

There are three main reasons why a business needs to record financial information:

● so that the management knows the current financial position of the business – how much money it has and how much money it owes.

● so that management and other interested parties (stakeholders) can see how the business is performing and whether it is meeting its objectives

● to comply with legal requirements.

On a day-to-day basis businesses need to know that they have sufficient cash to survive. This short-term finance is known as working capital. Businesses need to know that they can pay the bills and buy the materials and equipment they need to continue trading, as well as making repayments on any loans they might have. If a business is unable to pay its debts, other organisations will not want to deal with it and it will not be able to remain in business. By recording financial information, a business can see how much money is owed to it by customers and follow up non-payment of customer accounts. It can see how much it owes to suppliers and keep track of when each bill needs to be paid. In addition, it can keep control of any bank accounts so it knows how much cash the business has at any time. This control of working capital will also help it to plan for future cash requirements of the business.

In the longer term, those interested in the business will want to know whether the business is meeting its objectives and that it is worthwhile continuing with it. One of the main objectives of most businesses is to make money, or 'profits'. This money is paid out to the owners or investors in the business. Business owners, and others who are investing in it, will want to know whether they will continue to receive a reasonable return from the business. Otherwise it might be better for them to close down the business, sell all the assets and put the money into an investment account in a building society or bank where it will earn interest. Anyone considering investing in, or loaning money to, the business will also be interested in its longer-term performance. They will want to know that that the business will be able to pay the interest they expect on the money they provide.

Businesses are required to comply with a variety of regulations set down by the government. The law relating to the management of limited companies and partnerships requires that certain records be kept. Financial records are also required for tax purposes. Every business has to pay tax on its profits and so needs to keep records in order to prove to the Inland Revenue how much profit it has made. Many businesses have to account for value added tax (VAT) on the goods and services they provide so records are needed to show how much VAT is due.

Peter has set up in business as an IT consultant. His business is going well and he is keeping busy. He doesn't really have time to keep proper financial records, but has a rough idea of how much his sales are worth and how much he spends. He needs an assistant but doesn't really know if he can afford to employ one. His bank manager has contacted him to tell him that his business account is overdrawn but Peter doesn't know why. He thinks one of his customers may be late in paying their bill. Also he has received a tax form from the Inland Revenue but he doesn't know how much profit he has made so cannot complete it.

ACTIVITY ④

Imagine you act as a financial adviser to Peter. Make notes for a discussion with Peter, explaining why he needs to keep accurate financial records and the possible consequences of failing to do this. Discuss your findings with the other members of your group.

Key Skills C3.1a, C3.3

Top Tips

Evaluate your performance in the discussion and keep this as evidence towards the achievement of key skills.

Who uses financial information about the business?

Having already considered the uses of financial information for a business, we can easily identify some of the users of that information.

ACTIVITY ⑤

Make a list of people you think might be interested in financial information about a business. You should be able to identify some of the users from your reading so far.

Top Tips

People who have an interest in the business doing well are known as stakeholders. They have a stake in the business. The business owners and managers are obviously stakeholders, but there are some less obvious groups, like the local community.

Your list probably contains some or all of the following :

● **Business owners.** We have already seen that the owners of a business want information in order to help them make decisions about the business and run it efficiently. For this they need detailed information about the business's financial transactions. They also want to know whether they are making a profit and whether it is worthwhile continuing their investment in the business in terms of money and time.

- **Senior managers.** Senior managers are responsible for the management of the business on a day-to-day basis and they will require detailed information to help them to manage effectively. In some cases, the senior managers of a business may also be the owners.

- **Investors.** These are people (or other organisations) who put money into the business but don't have anything to do with the day-to-day management. The reason people invest in businesses is to receive some return on their investment, similar to the interest you might receive on a savings account at your bank or building society. They need to know that their investment in the business is safe and that they will continue to receive the return they require on the money invested. They might also be interested in the value of a business if they consider selling their investment. Most investors buy shares in companies traded on the Stock Exchange and receive dividends in proportion to the number of shares they own. They are interested in the changes in share price of a company as well as the level of dividends paid. Investors don't require detailed information about the transactions of a business. They are more interested in an overall financial picture.

- **Employees.** Most employees will be interested in the financial position of the business to ensure that their position is secure and to determine the possibility of any increase in wages. They will be interested in whether the business can continue to operate – otherwise they may be looking at unemployment – and will also be interested in the profitability of the business to see whether or not they can expect, or demand, a pay rise. They will also be interested in more detailed information about the particular section of the business in which they work. It is possible for a business to close one section or department if it proves unprofitable.

- **Loan creditors.** These are people or organisations who have lent money to the business. They might be banks, or loan and hire purchase companies. They want to know that the business will be able to repay the loan and any interest due, so will be interested in the profitability of the business.

- **Suppliers.** Any person or organisation who supplies the business with goods or services will want to know that it will be paid for those supplies. Businesses usually buy on credit. They receive the goods and services and are invoiced for them later. No supplier wants to deal with an organisation which is unable to pay it for the goods or services it has supplied, so it may look at the financial position of the business before it agrees to supply it.

- **Customers.** If you walk into the corner shop to buy a loaf of bread, the profitability of the business probably won't concern you too much! If the corner shop did go out of business, you would just go elsewhere, which might be a nuisance but is hardly disastrous. However, if you were the owner of the corner shop and you bought all your supplies from a particular wholesaler who gave you some very good deals because you were a valued customer, you might be quite concerned if you thought the wholesaler was likely to go out of business. You might want to start building a relationship with another supplier, just in case you needed to change. You wouldn't need very detailed information but would want to know about the general financial position of the business.

- **The public.** The public has an interest in the business because it is part of the national economy. It may also be interested in the business as an employer and as a part of the local community. If a business is doing well, then the local economy will improve – more people will be working and they will have more money to spend. If the business does badly, particularly in areas where there is one main employer or industry, then the whole community can be at risk. The public is interested, in more general terms, in how well the business is performing.

● **The government.** Various government departments require financial information. We have already mentioned the Inland Revenue which needs to know how much profit a business makes for tax purposes. Customs and Excise needs information in order to collect any VAT charged by business on the goods and services they sell. At a more general level, the government needs to collect information about all taxes, National Insurance and levies it receives in order to plan the finances for the country.

We can split these users of information into two main groups: those people **inside** the business organisation – internal users – and those **outside** – external users. Internal users of information will include owners, managers and employees of the business. External users usually require less detailed information and will be more interested in an overall picture of the business. They include investors, loan creditors, suppliers, customers, the public and the government.

Accuracy and completeness of financial information

Before we go on to look at the financial recording documents used by businesses, let's consider the importance of the financial records being accurate and complete. It is not simply enough for a business to collect financial information. It has to ensure that the information it collects is accurate and complete. Consider the following situation.

Case study

Remember Peter, and his reluctance to keep any records? Peter has now set up a financial recording system which he tries to keep updated but doesn't see it as the most important of the tasks he has to complete. He is very busy trying to put together a business plan to take to his bank in support of a loan application. He receives an invoice from a company that supplies him with

computer software. The amount owed on the invoice is £9,465. Peter records the amount as £4,965 and files the invoice away. He will pay it at the end of the month. Peter spends much of his time out at clients' premises, giving them advice on their computer systems. Sometimes he forgets to record the time he has spent at a particular client.

ACTIVITY   6

What do you think the implications of these errors might be for Peter?

Peter will use the information from his accounting records for a variety of purposes:

● to make decisions about the business
● to pay amounts owed to suppliers
● to prepare invoices for clients
● to provide information to the Inland Revenue and Customs and Excise
● to provide information to his bank in support of his loan application.

The incorrectly recorded invoice means that his accounting records show that he is better off than he actually is, by £4,500. No doubt, when he comes to pay the account at the end of the month, his supplier will point out the error, but until then he is relying on incorrect information. If he needs to make any returns to the Inland Revenue or Customs and Excise, the figures on these returns may be incorrect. This could result in an investigation and even a fine, if considered to be a serious error. Also, the information he is supplying to his bank will be incorrect. This could result in him taking on a loan that he cannot repay. Finally, he will be making plans and decisions about the business using incorrect information which may lead him into spending more than he can afford.

If Peter fails to record all the services he provides to clients, he will not be able to send out correct invoices. This will result in him either under- or over-charging customers. If he under-charges, he is losing out on income for the business. If he over-charges, his customers may become disgruntled and even go elsewhere for the service. Also, if his records of work done are incomplete, it will mean that he will not be able to plan properly for the future. Future plans are based partly on past performance. If Peter does not know how long each job has taken, he cannot properly plan similar jobs in the future.

Peter has only just started his business and has not had time to make many errors. Imagine the problems where information is incorrectly recorded over a longer period. Managers need accurate, complete information on which to base business decisions. Fortunately, most businesses recognise the importance of accurate and complete financial information, and try to make sure that the recorded information is correct.

The stakeholders want to know that the managers of the business are maintaining proper control over the income and expenses of the business so that it continues to be successful. The financial recording documents discussed here help management to maintain proper control.

What documents does a business use to record financial data?

Businesses use a range of documents to record financial information. In this section we will consider the following documents related to purchase and sale of goods and to bank account transactions:

- purchase order forms
- delivery notes
- goods received notes
- invoices
- goods returned notes
- credit notes
- statements of account
- remittance advice

- cheques
- paying-in slips
- bank statements
- receipts.

You may have come across some or all of these before. If you have a bank account, you will probably have a cheque book and a paying-in book and receive a bank statement each month. Businesses use the same documents for their bank accounts. You will also probably know the purpose of an invoice and delivery notes, if you have ever had goods delivered to your home.

Let's look at each of the documents in turn, their purpose and how they are completed.

Case study

We will use two imaginary companies – Traditional Toys and Pendle Paints Limited – for the example documents. Traditional Toys is a company which makes traditional wooden toys and supplies them to a number of toy shops. It orders 100 tins of 'Guard Red' child-safe paint from its supplier, Pendle Paints Limited, and they are delivered. However, four of the tins are found to be damaged and are returned to the supplier. At the end of the month Traditional Toys pays its supplier for the goods received.

Purchase order forms

Businesses use purchase order forms to order goods from their suppliers. Using a purchase order form makes ordering more efficient as it ensures that the supplier is given all the right information, in writing, so that there is no misunderstanding. The supplier can also see that the order has been approved by the appropriate person. The information about goods being ordered will have been obtained from the supplier's catalogue or price list, over the telephone, or from previous orders made of the same item. The forms are often pre-printed with some information such as the name and address of the business, VAT reference numbers etc.; and will have columns for product reference numbers,

Traditional Toys
Purchase Order

Traditional Toys
Unit 14 Ketterley Mill
Enterprise Way
Bradhill
BR27 6EX
Tel: +44 1425 378728
Fax: +44 1425 378001

Number: 0769

To: Pendle Paints Limited
Hillside Road
Pendle
PE14 3ND

Date: 20th October 2000

Product Code	Quantity	Description
CS768	100 tins	"Guard Red" child safe paint

Authorised by: _____ *P. R. Mayton* _____   date: 20/10/00

FIGURE 5.1 *Example purchase order*

quantities and description of goods being order. The buyer just needs to complete the details of the order – what is required and how many – and sign it before posting or faxing it to the supplier.

Purchase orders show the following details:

- name, address and telephone number of the business which is ordering the goods
- delivery address, if this is different from the above address
- name and address of supplier
- order reference – each purchase order will be given a unique reference number which will help to identify it in the event of any problems or queries
- date of order
- details of the items being ordered – the supplier's reference, quantity and description. Sometimes the price will also be included where this is known or has been agreed with the supplier
- the signature of the person authorising the order. Most suppliers would not accept an order that has not been properly authorised
- a delivery date may be shown where delivery is required by or on a specific date.

Delivery notes

The supplier receives the order and dispatches the goods to the customer. With the goods, it will send a delivery note which will tell the customer what is in the parcel. The customer – in this case Traditional Toys – will sign a copy of the delivery note to confirm that the goods have been received. Again, most businesses will use forms pre-printed with some details and other information specific to the order will need to be completed before the note is sent out.

The delivery note will show:

- name, address and telephone number of the supplier
- name and delivery address of the customer
- dispatch date – the date goods were dispatched from the warehouse
- delivery details – how the goods were

delivered, for example by post or carrier

- delivery note reference – a unique reference by which the order can be identified
- order reference – where the customer has sent a purchase order, their order reference will be quoted which will help them identify the order
- details of the goods despatched – reference numbers, quantities and descriptions. No price is quoted on the delivery note
- the note will be signed and dated by the person receiving the goods.

Goods received notes

Once the goods are received by the customer, they may complete a goods received note. This is completed with details of the goods that have been received, for checking against the original order. The note is also used to identify any damaged or sub-standard goods. A copy of the form can then be sent to the accounts department as authorisation to pay for the goods. In this exercise, Traditional Toys notice that four of the tins of 'Guard Red' child-safe paint are post damaged. These are to be returned to the supplier.

Details shown on the goods received note include:

- name of the business; no address is normally shown because this is an internal document
- name and address of the supplier
- reference number to identify the document
- delivery note reference so that it can be matched back to this if necessary
- order number to match to order
- details of the goods received
- date received
- delivery method/carrier and carrier's consignment reference where appropriate
- signatures of persons receiving and checking the goods
- any comments about condition of goods or variances from original order.

Delivery Note

Number: 1201429

Pendle Paints Ltd

Pendle Paints Ltd.
Hillside Road
Pendle
PE14 3ND

Tel: +44 1356 487356

Deliver To:

Traditional Toys
Unit 14 Ketterley Mill
Enterprise Way
Bradhill
BR27 6EX

Purchase Reference	Invoice	Dispatch Date	Account
0769 (P R Mayton)	342645	25/10/2000	TT0122

Delivery	Quantity	Product ID	Description
Courier (SameDay)	100 Tins	CS768	CP(E) Paint - Guard Red

For [Traditional Toys]: *Steve Potter*　　　　　　date: 25/10/00

FIGURE 5.2 *Example delivery note*

Traditional Toys
Goods Received Note

		Number:	**1023**
Supplier:	Pendle Paints Limited Hillside Road Pendle PE14 3ND	Date:	25/10/00
Delivery note ref:	1201429	Purchase order ref:	0769
Carrier:	Sameday Deliveries	Consignment no:	9923760

Quantity	Description
100 tins	"Guard Red" child safe paint

Accepted by: *Steve Potter* date: *25/10/00*

Notes about condition of Goods:

Four tins damaged and to be returned to supplier.

FIGURE 5.3 *Example goods received note*

Invoice   Number: 342645

Pendle Paints Ltd

Pendle Paints Ltd.
Hillside Road
Pendle
PE14 3ND

Tel: +44 1356 487356

To:

Traditional Toys
Unit 14 Ketterley Mill
Enterprise Way
Bradhill
BR27 6EX

Purchase Reference	Invoice	Date/Tax Point:	Customer Account
0769 (P R Mayton)	342645	25/10/2000	TT0122

Quantity	Product ID	Description	Price	VAT	Total
100 Tins	CS768	CP(E) Paint - Guard Red	40:00	7:00	4000:00

Terms			
Net 30 Days		Amount	4000:00
		Plus VAT @ 17.5%	700:00
Free Delivery		Total Payable	4700:00

FIGURE 5.4 *Example invoice*

Invoices

The supplier will send an invoice for each order to request payment from the customer for the goods. The invoice shows all the details of the order, together with the price of the goods, any delivery charges and any VAT due.

Details shown on the invoice include:

- name and address details of the supplier
- name and address details of the customer, plus delivery address if different
- invoice reference number which uniquely identifies the invoice
- any customer reference which identifies the customer in the supplier's accounting system
- the customer's order reference to enable the customer to match the invoice to the original order
- details of the goods – reference, quantities, descriptions, price per chapter, any applicable discounts, and total price
- delivery charges where applicable
- VAT rate and amount; VAT is currently charged at 17.5 per cent on most items
- date of invoice
- terms of payment. Most suppliers will give one month's credit to customers, running from the invoice date. Sometimes suppliers offer a discount for prompt payment. This is usually about 2–2.5 per cent and can be deducted if the customer pays within the specified time.

Top Tips

Make sure you know how to calculate the various amounts required on the invoice:

Total price of goods = quantity × chapter price

VAT = total (including carriage where applicable) × 17.5 per cent

Invoice total = Total price of goods + VAT amount.

ACTIVITY

Look at the invoice in Figure 5.5 (page 238) and identify any errors. What do you think might happen if the errors went undetected?

Goods returned note

When returning goods to a supplier, the business may use a goods returned note. This gives details of the goods being returned and explains why they are being returned. It is sent with the goods.

Details on the goods returned note include:

- name and address of the business
- name and address of the supplier
- reference number to identify the document
- delivery note reference so that it can be matched back to this if necessary
- order number to match to order
- details of the goods being returned
- date of return
- reason for return.

Credit notes

Credit notes are issued by the supplier of goods for any goods that have been returned to it by the customer. The effect is to reduce the amount owed by the customer or, where the invoice has already been paid, to allow it credit against future orders. Information included will be similar to that shown on an invoice. Credit notes are often printed in red ink so that they are easily distinguished from invoices. In the exercise here, Traditional Toys is returning four damaged tins of paint. Pendle Paints Limited has issued it with a credit note for the paint.

The credit note details include:

- name and address details of the supplier
- name and address details of the customer
- credit note reference number which uniquely identifies the credit note

Invoice

:-) **Marsden Electronics plc.**

Marsden Electronics plc.
Bradley Road
Shipley
BD11 2AD

Tel: +44 1264 048270

To:

Tantalus Computing
Unit 7 Brough Hall Business Park
Watermill Road
Brough
York
YO32 6WE

Purchase Reference	Invoice	Date/Tax Point:	Account
	5467	03/08/2000	TC847

Quantity	Product ID	Description	Price	VAT	Total
50	GAAPI-3765	VDX 16 Graphics Adapter (API)	60:00	10:50	3000:00

Terms		Amount	2475:00
Net 30 Days		Plus VAT @ 17.5%	525:00
		Total Payable	3000:00

FIGURE 5.5 *Can you find the errors on this invoice?*

Traditional Toys
Goods Returned Note

Traditional Toys
Unit 14 Ketterley Mill
Enterprise Way
Bradhill
BR27 6EX
Tel: +44 1425 378728
Fax: +44 1425 378001

Return Ref: 1023/002

Supplier: Pendle Paints Limited
Hillside Road
Pendle
PE14 3ND

Date: 25/10/00

Delivery note ref: 1201429

Purchase order ref: 0769

Return	Description
4 tins	"Guard Red" child safe paint

Raised by: _Steve Potter_   **Return date:** _25/10/00_

Notes about condition of Goods:

Four tins damaged and to be returned to supplier.

FIGURE 5.6 *Example goods returned note*

Credit Note

Number: 15674
Date: 27/10/2000

Pendle Paints Ltd

Pendle Paints Ltd.
Hillside Road
Pendle
PE14 3ND
Tel: +44 1356 487356

To:
Traditional Toys
Unit 14 Ketterley Mill
Enterprise Way
Bradhill
BR27 6EX

Purchase Reference	Invoice	Invoice Date:	Customer Account	GRN Ref.
0769	342645	25/10/2000	TT0122	1023/002

Returned Quantity	Product ID	Description	Price	VAT	Total
4 Tins	CS768	CP(E) Paint - Guard Red	40:00	7:00	160:00

Terms		Amount	160:00
Net 30 Days		Plus VAT @ 17.5%	28:00
Free Delivery		Total	188:80

Return Reason

4 paint tins damaged and returned by customer

FIGURE 5.7 *Example credit note*

Statement of Account TT0122/10/2000

Pendle Paints Ltd

Pendle Paints Ltd.
Hillside Road, Pendle, PE14 3ND
Tel: +44 1356 487356
Fax: +44 1356 487100

VAT Reg: 873 283479

To:		Account:	TT0122
Traditional Toys Unit 14 Ketterley Mill Enterprise Way Bradhill BR27 6EX		Statement Date:	31/10/2000

Date	Document	Dr	Cr	Balance
01/10/2000	B/Fwd	256.80		256.80
05/10/2000	341902	1700.00		1956.80
06/10/2000	Payment - Thank You		256.80	1700.00
07/10/2000	341998	1800.00		3500.00
08/10/2000	342345	3000.00		6500.00
10/10/2000	15502		204:50	6295.50
17/10/2000	342645	700.00		6995.50
18/10/2000	342699	1345.23		8340.73
25/10/2000	342987	4700.00		13040.73
27/10/2000	15674		188.80	12852.73

FIGURE 5.8 *Example statement of account*

- any customer reference which identifies the customer in the supplier's accounting system
- the customer's order reference to enable the customer to match the credit note to the original order
- returned goods note reference
- details of the goods that were returned – reference, quantities, descriptions, price per unit, any applicable discounts, and total price
- VAT rate and amount; VAT is currently charged at 17.5 per cent on most items
- date of credit note
- reason for issue of credit note.

Statements of account

Businesses will usually settle accounts on a monthly basis and may have several invoices outstanding in respect of one supplier. To remind them of the amount due to be paid, suppliers will often send a statement of account. This summarises any invoices and credit notes that have been issued during the month and shows the balance now due for payment. In the case of Traditional Toys, its supplier, Pendle Paints Limited, has issued one invoice and one credit note during the month. Both of these will be shown on the statement of account.

Details on the statement include:

- name and address of company
- name and address of customer
- customer account reference
- date of statement issue
- details of any invoices and credit notes issued
- total amount now due.

Remittance advice

When the customer makes payment, a remittance advice may be sent to the supplier, showing details of the amount that is being paid. Often, the supplier statement will have a tear-off remittance advice for the customer to complete and return. Otherwise, the customer may have its own forms which it uses to send to advise suppliers of payment. In our example, Pendle Paints Limited has included a remittance advice with its statement.

Remittance Advice

Pendle Paints Ltd. Hillside Road
Pendle PE14 3ND
Tel: +44 1356 487356
Fax: +44 1356 487100

From:
Traditional Toys
Unit 14
Ketterley Mill
Enterprise Way
Bradhill
BR27 6EX
Account:
TT0122

Please indicate the amounts you are paying (✓) and return this advice with your payment

Reference	Outstanding	✓
341902	1700.00	✓
341998	1800.00	✓
342345	3000.00	✓
342645	700.00	
342699	1345.23	
342987	4700.00	

CHEQUE ENCLOSED   £ 6500.00

FIGURE 5.9 *Example remittance advice*

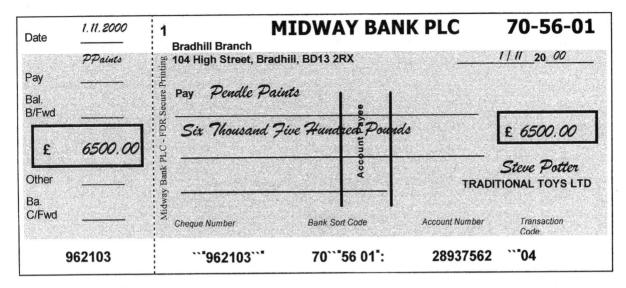

FIGURE 5.10 *Example cheque*

Note that before making any payment, the finance department staff at Traditional Toys will match up orders, delivery notes, goods received notes, good returned notes, invoices and credit notes. As long as there are no discrepancies, the payment will be authorised and the remittance advice and payment documentation prepared.

Details on the remittance advice include:

● name and address details of the supplier
● name and address details of the customer
● a note of the amounts outstanding
● an indication of which amounts are being paid
● an indication of the method of payment.

Cheques

Most businesses pay their bills using cheques, though an increasing number make payments electronically using the Banks Automated Clearing System (BACS) which transfers amounts electronically between bank accounts. Using the Traditional Toys payment as an example, Traditional Toys would advise its bank that a payment needed to be made to Pendle Paints Limited and its bank would transfer the amount from Traditional Toys' bank account to the account of Pendle Paints Limited at Pendle Paints' bank. The remittance advice would still be sent to Pendle Paints Limited to advise it that

payment had been made.

We are going to continue our example using a cheque payment but you should be aware of how BACS payments work as they will become much more common in the future. If you have a bank account of your own, you will be familiar with the details that need to be completed on a cheque.

A cheque will show the following details:

● the name and address of the bank
● the name in which the account is held
● the bank sort code which identifies the bank and branch in the central clearing system that all banks use
● the account number identifying the account on which the cheque is being drawn
● the cheque number which will identify that specific cheque
● details of the payment as completed by the business issuing the cheque: who is to be paid, how much they are to be paid (in words and figures), and the date of issue
● signature of the person issuing the cheque. Note that a business will normally have a number of individuals who are authorised to sign cheques on its behalf.

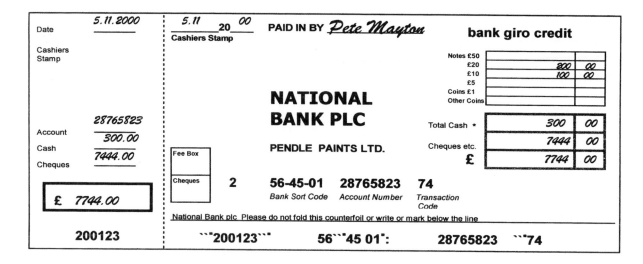

Reverse:

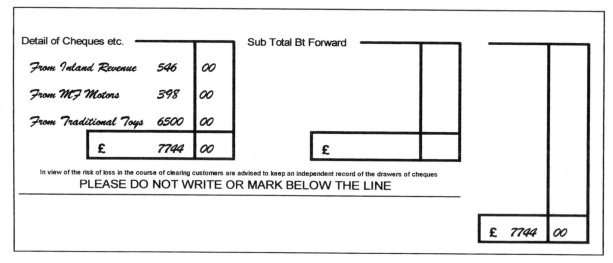

FIGURE 5.11 *Example paying-in slip*

Paying-in slips

When the supplier receives the cheque, it needs to pay it into its bank account. Again, if you have your own account, you will be familiar with a bank paying-in slip. The slip records the amounts being paid to the bank. In our example, in addition to the cheque from Traditional Toys, Pendle Paints is paying in two other cheques (for £398 and £546) and £300 cash (comprising £200 worth of £20 notes and £100 worth of £10 notes).

Details on the paying-in slip include:

- the name of the bank
- the name in which the account is held

- the bank sort code
- the account number identifying the account to which amounts are being paid
- a number which will identify that specific paying-in slip
- details of the amounts being paid in to the account as completed by the business. Cash is listed by denomination of notes and coins; cheque amounts are listed
- date of payment into the account
- signature of the person paying the amounts to the account
- the reverse side of the paying-in slip is used to list cheques paid into the account.

NATIONAL BANK   Account: 28765823
56-45-01
34 High Croft
Pendle
PE14 3GD

STATEMENT   Dates: **11 Oct**
                                                                 10 Nov
Pendle Paints   **2000**
No 342/3 - 10 November 2000

Balance at 10 November 2000 - £2415.83
O/D Facility 3000.00

Date	Details			Dr	Cr	Balance
10 Oct	B/Frwd					6895.80
11 Oct	Cheque	200567	CHQ	435.00		6460.80
12 Oct	Cheque	200568	CHQ	5787.00		673.80
15 Oct	BT		DDR	346.00		327.80
15 Oct	Cheque	200565	CHQ	3245.00		-2917.20
16 Oct	Pendle Brh		CHQ		5677.00	2759.80
18 Oct	Cheque	200554	CHQ	457.98		2301.82
18 Oct	MF Motors		PMNT		35654.76	37956.58
18 Oct	Pendle		CASH		436.78	38393.36
19 Oct	Cheque	200569	CHQ	346.23		38047.13
22 Oct	Cheque	200570	CHQ	644.67		37402.46
23 Oct	BT		DDR	456.90		36945.56
26 Oct	Cheque	200572	CHQ	356.00		36589.56
26 Oct	Cheque	200574	CHQ	874.00		35715.56
26 Oct	Cheque	200575	CHQ	864.57		34850.99
26 Oct	Cheque	200576	CHQ	5477.98		29373.01
31 Oct	Scarlan Ship		PMNT		4677.23	34050.24
31 Oct	Cheque	200573	CHQ	7698.90		26351.34
31 Oct	Traditional Toy		CHQ		4564.98	30916.32
1 Nov	Cheque	200582	CHQ	477.90		30438.42
1 Nov	HH Engineer		CHQ	4364.87		26073.55
2 Nov	Cheque	200584	CHQ	2464.87		23608.68
2 Nov	MND Bank		TRNS		3224.00	26832.68
4 Nov	Cheque	200579	CHQ	436.98		26395.70
5 Nov	Cheque	200581	CHQ	3456.09		22939.61
5 Nov	Pendle		SUND		7744.00	30683.61
8 Nov	AC 5387462		TRNS	20000.00		10683.61
8 Nov	Cheque	200587	CHQ	8909.09		1774.52
10 Nov	NET INTEREST PAID				768.31	2542.83
10 Nov	ACCOUNT CHARGES			127.00		2415.83
10 Nov	C/FWD					2415.83

FIGURE 5.12 *Example bank statement*

TJ Stationery

T Jones (Prop.) 13 High Street, Shipton, Yorkshire BD13 4YL

Receipt

Date: _25 Oct 2000_

Goods: _Staples *4_ Unit Price: _£5.99_ Total: _£23.96_

Payment: _Cash_

Signed: _Terry Jones_

FIGURE 5.13 *Example receipt*

Bank statements

Bank statements enable the business to keep track of amounts paid in and out of its bank accounts. The bank will issue a statement for each account on a regular basis. This might be monthly or weekly, to suit the business. On receiving the statement, the business can check all the transactions on the account and ensure that its own records of that account match with those of the bank.

The bank statement shows:

- name and address of bank
- name of account and name of business if this is different
- bank sort code and account number
- date statement was prepared
- statement number
- details of all amounts paid in or out of the account. These include cheque numbers or other references as appropriate
- balance of the account brought forward from the last statement
- balance of account at the statement date.

Receipts

There is one other document that you should be familiar with, though it doesn't appear in our example. Receipts are issued as proof that payments have been made. Traditional Toys could have requested that Pendle Paints Limited issue a receipt to show that it had received the payment, but the payment will show on Traditional Toys' bank account, and on its next statement from Pendle Paints, so it doesn't really need one. Receipts are more commonly issued for goods or services purchased and paid for immediately, or where goods or services are paid for in advance. If you walk into a shop and buy something, it will normally give you a sales receipt. They are often printed out automatically when the sale is entered in the till, though can be handwritten by the seller of the goods or service.

A receipt will show:

- name and address of the business making the sale
- date of sale
- description of goods or services sold
- price of each item sold

	Traditional Toys	Pendle Paints	National Bank
1	Order Form ⟶		
2			
3			

FIGURE 5.14

- total price
- method of payment – cash, cheque or debit/credit card.

ACTIVITY 8

Summarise in a flow diagram the movement of documents related to the order of paints by Traditional Toys from Pendle Paints Limited. Take an A4 sheet of paper and divide it into four columns. The first column simply numbers the stages of the transaction. Other column headings are: Traditional Toys, Pendle Paints Ltd and National Bank plc (Pendle Paints' bank). Under each heading you should show the documents prepared by that organisation and use arrows to indicate what happens to the document. The example in Figure 5.14 should help to start you off.

Key Skills C3.2, C3.3

Top Tips

Your flow diagram may be a useful revision guide for your external assessment.

ACTIVITY 9

Complete appropriate forms for the following transactions (your tutor will ask you to design a set of forms, or will provide you with blank forms):

- Traditional Toys orders 20 cans of 'Brick' colour paint for its dolls' houses, from Pendle Paints Ltd. The paint is priced at £34 per tin plus VAT. It is delivered 10 days later by Pendle's own delivery van and the whole order is checked and accepted by Jan Barton, the stock person at Traditional Toys. (Order No. 657, Order date 20th October, item reference CSP41 Brick, Delivery note no. 7631.)

- Yo-yo's, a toy shop, places an order with Traditional Toys for 25 wooden train sets at a cost of £18.25 each plus VAT. The order is requested on 14th August. The train sets are delivered on 31st August by Red Star Parcels, and are checked on arrival by Yo-yo's shop manager, Mr Greenway. He finds that three of the sets are damaged and returns these to Traditional Toys the next day. Traditional Toys issue an invoice to Yo-yo's on 12th September. A credit note is prepared and sent two days later. Yo-yo's pays its account, by cheque, on receipt of its statement dated 20th September. (Order no. 442, Item catalogue reference TS12, delivery note no. 4467, Returned goods note reference 58, Invoice no. 9/11, Credit note no. 9/3, Customer reference no. Y2.)

- Mrs Cayton buys a train set for her grandson from Yo-yo's on 14th October. The set costs £37.95 for which she pays cash. Later that day, Yo-yo's pays its day's takings into its account at Royal Bank plc. It has £160 in £20 notes, £90 in £10 notes, £105 in £5 notes, £32 in £1 coins, £7 in 50p coins, £3.20 in 20p coins, and £4.81 in 2p and 1p coins. It also pays in cheques of the following amounts: £24.95, £17.23, £87.61, £12.98, £15.94 and £42.96.

Key Skills C3.3

Self-Test Questions

1 Give the three main reasons why businesses benefit from keeping financial records.

2 Name two groups of stakeholders – one internal and one external – and explain their interest in the business.

3 Draw a flow diagram showing the flow of documents between a business and its customer for one sale of goods.

4 Bexhill Engineering sends out to one of its customers an invoice which has been prepared for the wrong amount – the invoice should be for £4,300 plus VAT but actually shows £3,400 plus VAT. The VAT has also been calculated incorrectly. What are the implications of this for Bexhill?

5 What information would be shown on a receipt and when would you be likely to receive one?

Section 2 *Constructing accounts*

What you need to learn

In this section you will learn about:

- the flow of information through an accounting system
- the different elements of the balance sheet and profit and loss account
- how to construct the balance sheet and profit and loss account.

At the start of this chapter, we read about Katie. Katie hadn't realised that she had run out of money until her bank manager told her. In the future Katie wants to avoid this situation, so she decides to keep a note of everything she receives and everything she spends. She also records any amounts she owes for expenses, like rent, and borrows from friends. This means that, at the end of each month, she can see how much she has earned and how much she has spent. She also knows what she has left, and how much she owes to other people.

The purpose of a business accounting system is simply to keep records in the same way that Katie does. It is a bit more complex than Katie's system because there are many more transactions to track; and because there are more transactions, it needs to be more formal than Katie's notebook of income and expenditure. The profit and loss account and balance sheet which are prepared from the information in the accounting system provide the business with a summary of income and expenses, and of what it has and what it owes. These statements are prepared on an annual basis for tax purposes, but can be prepared more frequently, for example monthly, for the business to monitor its finances.

Some organisations publish their annual balance sheet and profit and loss account, along with other documents, in an 'annual report'. This is available to investors and anyone else interested in the business as a record of its activities over the past year. These include public limited companies, any government controlled organisations and charities. The other documents

FIGURE 5.15 *Each plc publishes an annual report*

in the annual report explain the activities of the business during the year and may describe plans for the business's future.

The documents you are likely to see in an annual report are:

- **chairman's report.** Most annual reports contain a chairman's report. This is a report from the chairman of the board of directors and will probably review the business's performance over the past year, give any details of changes in directors or key employees and offer thanks to the company personnel for their efforts during the year.

- **directors' report.** This will talk about the business's activities and give details about the company directors, the auditors, any charitable donations the company has made, employment policy, any major changes in fixed assets and changes in share capital.

- **auditors' report.** Every limited company, government organisation and some other organisations, such as charities, are required to have their accounts audited. The auditors are an independent firm of accountants who check the accounts of the business to see if they are accurate and complete. Their report will be reproduced in the annual report.

- **balance sheet** and **profit and loss account.** These will include comparative figures from the previous year and notes to explain certain figures and changes between the two years.

- **promotional material.** Most businesses take the opportchaptery to talk about their products and services.

- **other reports.** Depending on the type of business and their aims, there may be other reports related to specific items. An example might be a report on how environmentally friendly the business had been during the year, if this was one of its aims.

  ACTIVITY   **10**

Obtain a copy of an annual report of a public limited company. There are a number of ways you can do this:

- **contact an organisation such as British Telecom plc, or one of the utility companies (Water, gas, electricity) and ask them to send you a copy of the last annual report. To choose an organisation, look at listings on the financial pages of the newspaper**

- **use the *Financial Times* Free Annual Reports Service – you can request copies of annual reports by telephone, fax or through the website. Details of the service are given in the *Financial Times* each day on one of the stock market pages**

- **visit a local branch of the company and ask for a copy – most banks and utility companies would keep copies at branch offices**

- **many large organisations publish their annual report on their website. Visit the corporate website of the organisation in which you are interested**

- **visit your local library who may keep some copies of annual reports (note that these are usually for reference purposes and cannot be removed).**

When you have obtained a copy of an annual report, try to identify the organisation's profit and loss account and the balance sheet for the last financial year. You should be able to see the income and expenses for the year, and what the organisation owns and owes at the end of the year. List the other documents that appear in the annual report and give a short explanation of the purpose of each document.

Key Skills C3.2, C3.3

 **Top Tips**

Keep the annual report you have obtained – you may use it again later in the chapter.

Date	Invoice No.	Account No.	Supplier	Goods Amount £	VAT Amount £	Total Amount £
3/10	567A	D12	DP Wholesalers	100.00	17.50	117.50
3/10	5679	G15	Green and Co. Ltd.	3420.00	598.50	4018.50
3/10	S/67	J1	Jennings	670.00	117.25	787.25
3/10	89076	H7	Henson Limited	120.00	21.00	141.00
3/10	5872	G15	Green and Co. Ltd.	1354.00	236.95	1590.95
				5664.00	991.20	6655.20

FIGURE 5.16 *Example purchase day book*

Before we look at how to construct a balance sheet and profit and loss account, let's look at the accounting systems that provide the information for them.

How does information flow through the accounting system?

In Section 1, we looked at various documents that are used in recording financial information. Here, we will look at what happens to the information on those documents when it is entered into the accounting systems of a business.

Purchases

Most businesses buy goods and services on credit. We have already looked at the invoices sent out by suppliers in respect of goods and services supplied. The business purchasing the goods needs to record the invoice amounts for payment. The invoice will first be entered in the **purchase day book**. This is the business record of all the invoices the business has received for goods and services purchased on credit. The book has columns to record and analyse all the invoice details. The columns are totalled on a regular basis. This is usually done daily or weekly, depending on the number of purchase invoices that the business receives.

No:G15   **Purchase Ledger Account**
Green and Co. Ltd.

Debit (Dr)   Credit (Cr)

Date	Details	£	Date	Details	£
			3/10	Balance b/fwd	243.75
3/10	Bank payment	243.75	3/10	Invoice 5679	4018.50
3/10	Balance c/fwd	5609.45	3/10	Invoice	1590.95
		5853.20			5853.20
			4/10	Balance b/fwd	5609.45

FIGURE 5.17 *Example purchase ledger account*

Top Tips

If you want to check that the totals of each column are correct, add up the totals of the analysis columns. They should equal the total in the Total amount column.

The business also needs to keep a record of how much it owes to each supplier. The easiest way to do this is to have a note or account of invoices outstanding to each supplier. These accounts are collectively known as the purchases or creditors ledger. The invoices from the purchase day book are posted to the appropriate purchase ledger account. All ledger accounts are divided into two sections. One side of the account records credits and the other records debits. A credit purchase will be entered on the credit side of the ledger account. When the account is paid, the payment will show on the debit side to balance the account. Figure 5.17 shows a purchase ledger account for one supplier.

At any time, the business can see from the ledger account how much is owed to that particular supplier by totalling each side of the account and calculating the difference. Amounts owed will always be credits. Each account will be totalled on a regular basis – usually monthly, so that it can be checked against the supplier statement – and the balances owing carried down for the next month. Note that total amounts including VAT are posted to the account.

The totals from the analysis columns of the purchase day book are posted to the general ledger.

A note about the general ledger

The general ledger is made up of accounts for different types of income and expenses. The layout is similar to that of the purchase ledger, with the accounts split to show debits and credits. Each different sort of expense and receipt will have a separate account in the general ledger. It is up to the business to decide which accounts it needs, and these will vary between businesses. For example, one business may have a separate account for window cleaning costs, whilst another includes these within general cleaning and maintenance. One business may have an account for motor expenses, whilst another doesn't have any motoring expenses. All businesses will have one or more accounts for their main source of income – usually 'Sales'. All businesses will have accounts for 'Purchases for Re-sale' (usually just called 'Purchases') or 'Cost of Sales'. These are items that the business has bought to re-sell, or costs that relate directly to the making and selling of their product or service. We will come back to these later when we look at the preparation of business accounts.

The totals from the purchase day book are posted to the debit side of the appropriate accounts. By looking at the general ledger accounts, the business can see how much it has spent on a particular expense item. Note that items are posted net of VAT. The VAT is posted to the VAT account in the general ledger.

General Ledger Account
Purchases

Debit (Dr)					Credit (Cr)
Date	Details	£	Date	Details	£
3/10	Balance b/fwd	14565.90			
3/10	Purchase Day Book	6655.20			

FIGURE 5.18 *Example general ledger account*

Date	Invoice No.	Account No.	Customer	Goods Amount	VAT Amount	Total Amount
3/10	13662	T3	B. Thorson	654.00	114.45	768.45
3/10	13663	Y1	H.T. Young Electronics	2987.00	522.72	3509.72
3/10	13664	T12	Trent Engineering	850.00	148.75	998.75
				4491.00	785.92	5276.92

FIGURE 5.19 *Example sales day book*

 ACTIVITY

Enter the following purchase invoices into a purchase day book and purchase ledger for Harrison Clothing Limited, a clothes wholesaler. Calculate the balance on each ledger account once you have made your entries. Transactions are for the week ended 24th November. You will need to divide your paper into the appropriate number of columns or use ruled accounts paper.

■ 200 ladies' T-shirts purchased from the Nash T-shirt Company. Purchase ledger account no. N43, Opening balance £567.98, Invoice no. H213, dated 20th November, amount £850 plus VAT of £148.75.

■ 100 pairs men's jeans purchased from The Jeans Company Limited. Purchase ledger account no. J4, Opening balance £ nil, Invoice no. 66741, dated 22nd November, amount £1,900 plus VAT of £332.50.

■ 250 pairs assorted socks purchased from Asgah Hosiery. Purchase ledger account no. A9, Opening balance £67.50, Invoice no. 4467, dated 22nd November, amount £187.50 plus VAT of £32.81.

■ Delivery of goods to customers by Redfern Haulage. Purchase ledger account no. R23, Opening balance £781, Invoice no. 00/876, dated 24th November, amount £546 plus VAT of £95.55 (distribution expenses).

■ Two boxes printed order forms from Grinley Printers. Purchase ledger account no. G14, Opening balance £ nil, Invoice no. 765, dated 24th November, amount £143 plus VAT of £25.02 (administration expenses).

Key Skills C3.3

Sales

A business issues sales invoices to its customers for the goods and services sold to them on credit.

No:T12

Sales Ledger Account
Trent Engineering

Debit (Dr)   Credit (Cr)

Date	Details	£	Date	Details	£
3/10	Balance b/fwd	654.37	3/10	Payment received	654.37
3/10	Invoice 13664	998.75	3/10	Balance c/fwd	998.75
		1653.12			1653.12
4/10	Balance b/fwd	998.75			

FIGURE 5.20 *Example sales ledger account*

General Ledger Account
Sales

Debit (Dr)   Credit (Cr)

Date	Details	£	Date	Details	£
			3/10	Balance b/fwd	38988.97
			3/10	Sales Day Book	5276.92

FIGURE 5.21 *Example general ledger account for sales*

As with the purchase invoices, the business needs to keep records of these invoices so that it knows the amount of sales made and how much is owed to the business by each customer.

Sales invoices are first entered into the sales day book. This is similar in layout to the purchase day book. The book may be analysed across different types of products or services if the business wants to record this information. In our example, the business are only interested in total sales.

As with the purchase day book, the columns will be totalled on a daily or weekly basis. Invoices for individual customers are posted to accounts in the sales or debtors ledger to provide a record of the amounts owed to the business by each customer. Invoices are posted to the debit side of the debtors ledger accounts. When a customer pays his account, the payment will appear on the credit side of the sales ledger account.

At any time, the business can see from the ledger account how much is owed by that particular customer by totalling each side of the account and calculating the difference. Amounts owed to the business by its customers will always be debits. Each account will be totalled on a regular basis – usually monthly, so that statements can be prepared for customers – and the balances owing

Cash Book
Sales

Debit (Dr)   Credit (Cr)

Date	Details	Bank £	Cash £	Date	Details	Bank £	Cash £
3/10	Balance b/fwd	7865.00	153.42	3/10	Electricity	567.00	
3/10	Cash Sales		543.00	3/10	Window cleaner		13.50
3/10	Trent Eng.	654.37		3/10	Jennings	157.60	
3/10	B. Thorson	234.09		3/10	Green and Co.	243.75	
				3/10	Stationery		43.88
				3/10	Balances c/fwd	7785.11	639.04
		8753.46	696.42			8753.46	696.42
4/10	Balance b/fwd	7785.11	639.04				

FIGURE 5.22 *Example cash book*

carried down for the next month. Note that total amounts including VAT are posted to the account.

The totals from columns in the sales day book are posted to the appropriate accounts in the general ledger. The totals from the sales day book are posted to the credit side of each account.

By looking at the general ledger accounts, the business can see the total of sales made.

ACTIVITY 12

Enter the following purchase invoices into a sales day book and sales ledger for Harrison Clothing Limited, a clothes wholesaler. Calculate the balance of each ledger account after you have made your entries. Transactions are for the week ended 24th November. You will need to divide your paper into the appropriate number of columns or use ruled accounts paper.

■ Tina's Ladies' Fashions, Sales ledger account no. T19, Opening balance £156.98, invoice no. 7456, dated 21st November, £356 plus VAT of £62.30.

■ The clothing warehouse, Sales ledger account no. C3, Opening balance £45.90, invoice no. 7457, dated 21st November, £788 plus VAT of £137.90.

■ Carters, Sales ledger account no. C1, Opening balance £ nil, invoice no. 7458, dated 22nd November, £514 plus VAT of £89.95.

■ Fashion Parade, Sales ledger account no. F12, Opening balance £141, invoice no. 7459, dated 23rd November, £120 plus VAT of £21.

Key Skills C3.3

Cash receipts and expenses

When the business receives cash or cheques, or pays out cash or cheques, these are entered into the cash book. The cash book is actually a record of two general ledger accounts – the cash account and the bank account – but because it has a large

number of entries is often kept as a separate book. Like all general ledger accounts, it is split into debits and credits.

All cash and cheque receipts and payments are recorded in the cash book. Each side of the book has cash and bank columns for total amounts received or paid. Each amount is posted to the appropriate general ledger account. Cash or cheques received are debits. Cash or cheques paid are credits. Note that any receipts or payments made directly to or from the bank account are also entered in the cash book. These might include transfers between accounts, bank charges, regular payments such as direct debits or standing orders that the business has set up to pay its bills, or amounts paid directly to the account from customers.

Note the following:

● the amount of cash held by the business and amounts held in the bank account can be established at any time, by totalling the brought forward balances, payments and receipts

● amounts received from customers or paid to suppliers are posted to the their personal ledger accounts

● cash sales and cash purchases never appear in the sales/purchase ledgers. They are entered in the cash book and totals posted straight to sales/purchases accounts in the general ledger.

Some businesses may keep a separate petty cash book for small expenses. The petty cash book is similar to the cash book but will only have columns for cash received and paid, not for bank receipts and payments.

Top Tips

Remember that every amount of cash or cheque received must be debited to the cash or bank account. Every payment made by cash or cheque must be credited to the cash or bank account.

If you do the entries to the cash book first, then it should be easy to see whether the corresponding entries in the ledger accounts are credits or debits.

Try the following activity which involves making entries to the cash book and ledgers.

 **ACTIVITY** **13**

Make the following entries in the cash book of Mick's Music, and post to the appropriate ledger accounts. Calculate the balances of cash and bank account and ledger accounts once you have completed your entries. Mick's Music is a small shop selling music tapes and CDs. Most of his sales are cash though he does allow credit to Des's Disco. You will need to divide your paper into the appropriate number of columns or use ruled accounts paper.

- **1st June: balances brought forward – Bank account £1,231.90, Cash £467, Sales account in general ledger £36,458.96**

- **1st June: shop takings: £231.87 cash, £26.99 cheques (includes VAT of £38.56)**

- **1st June: paid window cleaners – cash £25. (The window cleaner is not on the purchase ledger – he is paid cash each month when he brings in his bill. The amount is posted to the cleaning account in the general ledger on which the opening balance is £245. There is no VAT)**

- **2nd June: shop takings: £224.65 cash, £55 cheques (includes VAT of £41.65)**

- **2nd June: Des's Disco pays his May account by cheque, £156.98 (opening balance on ledger account £231.98)**

- **2nd June: Mick pays creditors by cheque: £132.48 to British Telecom (opening balance on ledger £132.48), £156 to The Music Company (opening balance on ledger £251.50)**

- **2nd June: Mick pays all the cheques and £750 cash into the bank**

- **3rd June: shop takings: £456.91 cash, £342.98 cheques (includes VAT of £119.14)**

- **3rd June: pays wages in cash to shop assistant £56 (opening balance on wages account £1,235)**

  Key Skills C3.2 C3.3, N3.2a

  **Top Tips**

You might see the purchase and sales day books, and sometimes the cash book, referred to as books of original or prime entry. Sales and purchases ledgers are also known as personal ledgers because they have accounts for different people/businesses. The general ledger is also known as the nominal ledger.

The trial balance and final accounts

When the business wants to prepare its final accounts, it will extract all the balances from the ledger accounts and the cash book. This is known as the **trial balance** and the total of debit balances should equal the total of credit balances. Note that the sales ledger balances are totalled and entered on the trial balance as debtors and the total of the purchase ledger balances is entered as trade creditors.

The columns are always equal because each entry to the accounts is made twice – to the credit side of one account and the debit side of another. Every time one accounts loses an amount, another account gains that same amount. The system is known as **double entry book-keeping**. Let's look at some examples:

- A purchase invoice is entered to the credit side of the purchase ledger account, and to the debit side of the purchases or expense account in the general ledger. The entry to the ledger account is made from the purchase day book when each invoice is posted to an individual account. Entries to the purchases/expense accounts are made by debiting the purchase day book totals at the end of the day or week.

Trial Balance for R Taylor Electrical Goods at 31st March 2000

Account	£	£
Capital account		45,000
Drawings	12,000	
Premises	38,000	
Fixtures and fittings	4,000	
Equipment	6,000	
Motor van	2,500	
Bank loan		3,500
Stock at 1st January	4,000	
Bank/cash	1,200	
Debtors	432	
Creditors		2,500
Sales		43,328
Purchases	14,380	
Wages	5,200	
Light and heat	1,200	
Printing and stationery	600	
Telephone	540	
Advertising	650	
Rates and water	2,400	
Motor expenses	850	
Interest paid on loan	376	
Totals	**94,328**	**94,328**

FIGURE 5.23 *Example of a trial balance*

- A sales invoice is entered to the debit side of the sales ledger account, and to the credit side of the sales account in the general ledger. The entry to the ledger account is made from the sales day book when each invoice is posted to an individual account. The entry to the sales account is made by debiting the sales day book totals at the end of the day or week.

- Cash or cheque receipts are entered into the debit side of the cash book, and to the credit side of the appropriate ledger account. Ledger account entries are made by posting the totals in the analysis columns of the cash book at the end of the day or week.

- Cash or cheque payments are entered into the credit side of the cash book, and to the debit side of the appropriate ledger account. Ledger account entries are made by posting the totals in the analysis columns of the cash book at the end of the day or week.

ACTIVITY **14**

Divide a sheet of paper into two columns. Head one 'Debits' and the other 'Credits'. For each of the following transactions, state which account should be debited and which credited:

1. invoice sent to a customer – Green and Company
2. cheque received from Green and Company, a customer, in payment of an outstanding invoice
3. window cleaner is paid in cash
4. cash sales
5. the business buys a new car, using a cheque
6. cash takings paid into the bank account
7. cash drawn from the bank account to replenish the petty cash tin
8. cash used to pay wages
9. bank charges charged to the account by the bank at the end of the month
10. invoice received from a supplier – Motson's Garage
11. payments to a supplier – Motson's Garage – by cheque
12. an amount paid directly into the bank account by electronic transfer from a customer – Maynard's Biscuits
13. Phone bill received from British Telecom.

There is no requirement for a business to use the system of double entry book-keeping, but most do because it gives them a useful check on the accuracy and completeness of their financial records. In fact, even computer-based accounting packages use the double entry system. If, when the trial balance is prepared, the totals of debits and credits are not equal, then an error has been made. This could be:

● an error in one of the ledger accounts – either in postings to the accounts or in calculation of the balance on the account
● an error in transferring the balance from the ledger account to the trial balance – either transferring the wrong figures, or putting the balance in the wrong column

● an addition error in totalling the debits and credits on the trial balance.

Figures from the trial balance can then be used to prepare the profit and loss account and balance sheet for the business. You may remember from the start of this section that these are the documents the business uses to summarise its performance.

Assets, liabilities, expenses and revenues

Before you can construct a profit and loss account and balance sheet for yourself, you need to be able to identify which of the amounts from the trial balance appear on each of these documents. The profit and loss account is a statement of how much money the business has made (or lost) over a year (or other financial period). If the business has received more money than it has spent, then it has made a profit. If it has spent more money than it received, then it has made a loss. The balance sheet is a statement of what the business is worth in financial terms at the end of a year (or financial period). Put simply, it shows what the business owns and what it owes.

In accountancy terms, expenses and revenues appear in the profit and loss account, and assets and liabilities appear on the balance sheet. Let's have a look at what each of these terms means:

● **expenses** are amounts that are paid out in order to run the business on a day-to-day basis during the year. This might include payments for goods to re-sell, wages, maintenance of machinery, petrol, electricity and telephone charges. They are all payments for goods and services used in trading for the year
● **revenue** is another term for income received by the business during the year. In most businesses, this will be amounts received from the sale of goods or services made in the year. Some businesses might have revenues from other sources such as interest from investments or rents from buildings owned by the business but used by other people

- **assets** are items owned by the business for use in running the business in the longer term. Assets would include such things as buildings, vehicles, machinery, computers and office furniture, all of which would be used over several years. They also include the balances of cash and bank accounts, the value of any unsold stock and the total of amounts owed on the sales ledger at the balance sheet date which will be used or collected in future years

- **liabilities** are amounts owed by the business. They include amounts outstanding on the purchase ledger, mortgages, loans and bank overdrafts at the balance sheet date. These are items that will be paid off in the future, so the balances are carried forward to the next financial year. Liabilities also include the amount invested in the business by the owner or shareholders because this is a bit like a loan to the business on which the owners or shareholders expect some return.

Top Tips

Imagine if the business were to end on the balance sheet date. All the assets could be sold or converted into cash, and all the liabilities would need to be re-paid. If an item can't be converted to cash or re-paid, then it shouldn't be on the balance sheet!

ACTIVITY 15

Divide a sheet of paper into four sections headed Revenues, Expenses, Assets and Liabilities. Put each of the following ledger accounts into the correct category:

- **sales**
- **bank charges**
- **rents received**
- **telephone charges**
- **loan interest**

- **delivery vans**
- **motor cars**
- **share capital**
- **petrol and oil**
- **insurance**
- **interest received**
- **purchase ledger balances**
- **sales ledger balances**
- **wages**
- **bank overdraft**
- **year-end stock**
- **owner's investment**
- **machinery**
- **purchases**
- **Buildings**
- **cash balance**
- **bank loan**
- **petty cash balance**
- **electricity charges.**

You should note that the bank loan appears on the balance sheet as a liability, but that any interest on the loan goes to the profit and loss account as an expense. The interest is the charge to the business for borrowing the money.

The assets on the balance sheet are split into fixed assets and current assets, and the liabilities into current and long-term liabilities. Balance sheet items are put into categories depending on the time over which they will be used. Assets that are used over several years in the business, like buildings, cars and machinery, are called fixed assets. Those that will change over the next financial year, such as cash and bank balances, stock and debtors, are known as current assets. Similarly, long-term liabilities are those that will last for a number of years, like bank loans, owner's investment and share capital. Current liabilities are those that will change in the next financial year, such as trade creditors and bank overdrafts.

Depreciation

Depreciation is an amount that the business charges to the profit and loss account for the use of the assets. Consider a business that buys a computer system for £6,000 that it expects to last three years. We have already mentioned that it would not be reasonable for the business to charge the whole of the cost of the computer to the profit and loss account in one year. The profit for that year would be reduced by £6,000 even though the computer is also used in future years. Nor would it be reasonable for the business to keep the computer at cost on its balance sheet forever, because after three years it will probably need replacing.

In order to give a fair reflection in the accounts of the cost of using the computer, the business makes a charge to the profit and loss account each year, based on the original cost and how long the computer will last. In our example, the business would probably charge £2,000 per year to the profit and loss account, in each of three years. It then reduces the balance sheet value by this amount of depreciation. All fixed assets are depreciated.

There are two methods of charging depreciation:

- the **straight line** method, where the same charge is made for each year of use
- the **reducing balance** method, where a higher charge is made in the earlier years of the asset's life. This is said to reflect the fact that assets are more efficient in the earlier years.

To calculate depreciation on a the **straight line basis**, the business would decide how long the asset was likely to be used in the business and whether it would have any re-sale value at the end of that time.

Case study

A business buys a motor car for £19,000 which it expects to replace after using it for four years in the business. It believes that, at the end of the four years it will be able to sell the car for about £6,000 (the residual value). The residual value is deducted from the original cost and the balance divided by the number of years over which the asset will be used.

$$\text{Depreciation per year} = \frac{\text{Original cost less residual value}}{\text{Number of years of asset use}}$$

For our example:

$$\text{Depreciation per year} = \frac{£19,000 - 6,000}{4} = £3,250$$

For each year of the asset's life, £3,250 would be charged to the profit and loss account and the balance sheet value would be reduced by £3,250.

Balance sheet values would be as follows:

Year 1: £19,000 − 3,250 = £15,750

Year 2: £15,750 − 3,250 = £12,500

Year 3: £12,500 − 3,250 = £9,250

Year 4: £9,250 − 3,250 = £6,000.

 **Top Tips**

The balance sheet value of fixed assets is known as the net book value because it is net of depreciation.

To calculate depreciation using the **reducing balance** method, the business would apply a percentage to the remaining balance each year.

Case study

A business purchases a motor car for £19,000 and decides to depreciate it at 25 per cent per year. Depreciation is as follows:

$$\text{Year 1: Depreciation} = \frac{£19,000 \times 25}{100} = £4,750$$

(or £19,000 × 25 per cent if you are using a calculator with a percentage key!)

Year 2: Depreciation is calculated on the original cost less last year's depreciation.

$$\text{Depreciation} = \frac{£14,250 \times 25}{100} = £3,562.50$$

(Businesses often work with whole numbers so would round this down to £3,562.)

$$\text{Year 3: Depreciation} = \frac{£10,688 \times 25}{100} = £2,672$$

$$\text{Year 4: Depreciation} = \frac{£8,016 \times 25}{100} = £2,004$$

Net book value at end of Year 4: £6,012.

As a general rule, under the straight line method, buildings are usually depreciated over 50 years, motor vehicles over three or four years and other fixtures, fittings and equipment over four years. For the reducing balance method of depreciation, buildings are usually depreciated by 2 per cent, and all other vehicles, equipment, fixtures and fittings by 25 per cent.

Some businesses write off computer equipment over a shorter period (or use a higher percentage) because it can become outdated very quickly. Some businesses do not depreciate buildings or premises because it is felt that they tend to increase in value rather than depreciate.

Remember the annual report you obtained? Have a look at it now. There will be a note on depreciation in the 'Notes to the Accounts' section. What methods and rates of depreciation are the business using for the different categories of fixed assets? Compare your answers with those of some of your colleagues who have looked at different annual reports.

Keep your copy of the annual report to hand as we will use it through the remainder of this section to identify certain items on the profit and loss account and balance sheet.
Key Skills C3.1a, C3.2

You should appreciate that the level of depreciation is a business decision, and should be based on a realistic view of the length of time the asset will be used in the business. In questions involving calculation of depreciation, you will normally be given the asset lifetime or percentage on which to base your calculations.

A business buys a computerised telephone switchboard system for £10,000. It believes that it will last three years and be worth £1,000 at the end of that time. Calculate depreciation using the straight line method and calculate the net book value at the end of each year.

A business buys a car for £22,000. Calculate the depreciation on a reducing balance basis at 25 per cent. Calculate the net book value at the end of each of the first three years.
Key Skills N3.2a

Constructing the profit and loss account

We have already learned that the profit and loss account shows the profit or loss made by the business during the year. In simple terms, sales made during the year, less purchases and expenses for the year, equals profit or loss for the year. All the profit and loss account does is set out this calculation in the accepted business format.

- **Heading** – the profit and loss account will always have a heading stating what it is and the period it covers. Businesses can choose their year-end date. Accounts don't have to be based on a calendar year. Many businesses choose the

R Taylor Electrical Goods Profit and Loss Account for year ended 31st March 2000

	£	£
Sales		43,328
Less: Cost of sales		13,880
Gross profit		29,448
Less: Expenses		
Wages	5,200	
Light and heat	1,200	
Printing and stationery	600	
Telephone	540	
Advertising	650	
Rates and water	2,400	
Motor expenses	850	
Interest paid on loan	376	
Depreciation	3,120	
		14,936
		14,512

FIGURE 5.24 *Example profit and loss account*

end of March as their year-end, to coincide with the tax year.

● **Sales** – this is the amount of sales made during the year, taken from the sales account in the general ledger.

● **Cost of sales** – the cost of sales figure includes amounts that the business has paid for the goods or services sold during the year. Items included here will depend upon the type of business. If the business is simply buying items and selling them, it will be the cost of the goods sold. For a business that is manufacturing goods, the figure will include costs of raw materials, labour and perhaps other factory costs. For a business that provides services, the figure will include the wages of employees delivering the service and any goods required to provide the service. Our example is a retail business that buys and sells electrical goods.

To calculate the cost of goods sold, we will first take the purchases figure from the purchases account in the general ledger. This figure will include all purchases made in the year. At the start of the year, a business would normally have some stock items left from the previous year. They will be sold in this year. At the end of any financial year, a business would

normally have some items left in stock that will be sold in the next year. We need to take account of these in our cost of sales calculation.

In our example, we calculated the cost of sales like this:

Stock at 1st April 2001	£ 4,000
Add: Purchases during the year	£14,380
	£18,380
Less: Stock at 31st March 2002	£ 4,500
Cost of sales	£13,880

● **Gross profit** – the gross profit is calculated by deducting the cost of sales from the sales value.

 **ACTIVITY** 18

Look at the annual report you obtained. Look at the profit and loss account and identify the figure for gross profit. You will probably find that cost of sales is not calculated on the face of the profit and loss account, as we have done, but there will probably be a note to the accounts explaining how it has been calculated.

- **Expenses** – amounts for most expenses are transferred from their respective accounts in the general ledger. Depreciation for the year will be calculated and entered as an expense.

- **Net profit** – to arrive at net profit, total expenses are deducted from gross profit.

 **ACTIVITY** **19**

Prepare a profit and loss account from the information given.

Martin Baker is a dealer in rare postcards and

stamps. He buys at auction and sells and stamp and postcard collectors' fairs around the country. His year-end is 31st December. The figures shown are for the year ended 31st December 2000.

Martin owns a van and display fittings for use in the business.

- The van was purchased in 1999 for £17,000. Depreciation to date is £4,250. He is depreciating the van at 25 per cent on the reducing balance basis.

- The display equipment was new at the start of this year so there is no accumulated depreciation. The equipment cost £3,000. He has decided to depreciate on a straight line basis over four years. There is no residual value.

R Taylor Electrical Goods Balance Sheet at 31st March 2000

	£ Cost	£ Depreciation	£ Net book value
Fixed assets			
Premises	38,000	0	38,000
Fixtures and fittings	5,600	2,600	3,000
Equipment	8,700	4,200	4,500
Motor van	7,500	5,620	1,880
	59,800	12,420	47,380
Current assets			
Stock		4,500	
Debtors		432	
Bank/cash		1,200	
		6,132	
Current liabilities			
Creditors		2,500	
Net current assets			3,632
Less: Long-term liabilities			(3,500)
			47,512
Financed by:			
Owners capital			45,000
Add: Net profit			14,512
			59,512
Less: Drawings			12,000
			47,512

FIGURE 5.25 *Example balance sheet*

Martin Baker financial information for year ended 31st December 2000

Sales	£54,000
Purchases	£28,000
Stock at 1st January 2000	£3,500
Stock at 31st December 2000	£5,500
Table hire at collectors' fairs	£4,300
Repairs to display shelves and lighting	£700
Stationery, printing and postage	£1,076
Insurance	£600
Telephone	£943
Bank charges	£349
Motor expenses	£3,122

Key Skills C3.3, N3.2a

Constructing the balance sheet

You should remember that the balance sheet summarises the assets and liabilities of a business at a point in time.

- **Heading** – the balance sheet always has a heading explaining what it is and the date for which it was prepared.

You will see that the balance sheet has two sections. One section includes all of the assets and liabilities, excluding owner's capital. The other sets out details of the owner's capital.

Top Tips

The two sections of the balance sheet are equal, i.e. the balance sheet should balance! If it doesn't, then you have made a mistake somewhere.

- **Fixed assets** – fixed assets are included in the total at net book value. You will see that the original cost and depreciation are also shown on the face of the balance sheet for information purposes. Many larger businesses include this information as a note to the accounts instead of on the balance sheet. The figure for depreciation on the balance sheet is a cumulative figure. It is the total of depreciation that has been charged against the fixed asset since it was purchased including the charge for this year. (Remember that the depreciation amount in the profit and loss account is just the charge for this year.)

ACTIVITY 20

Look at the balance sheet in your annual report. Find out where the fixed asset information is shown and identify the different categories of fixed assets that the business uses. Has the business bought or sold any assets during the year?
Key Skills C3.2

- **Current assets** – as we saw earlier in this section, these are short-term assets. The stock figure is the value of all items left in stock at the balance sheet date. Note that it's the same figure used to calculate cost of sales. The debtors figure is the total of sales ledger balances. Cash and positive bank balances will be taken from the cash book.

Top Tips

The bank balance can be an asset or a liability. If there is money in the bank, it is an asset. If the bank account is overdrawn, it is a liability.

- **Current liabilities** – this comprises trade creditors and bank overdrafts. The creditors amount is the total of purchase ledger balances at the balance sheet date. The bank overdraft figure is taken from the cash book at the balance sheet date. Where there are amounts owing to the Inland Revenue for tax or to Customs and Excise for VAT, these are shown separately under current liabilities.

● **Net current assets** – this is the total of current assets less current liabilities. It is also known as the working capital of the business because it is the amount that the business uses on a day-to-day basis. We will look at working capital further in Section 4.

 **Top Tips**

It is possible to have a negative figure when you deduct current liabilities from current assets. In this situation we would have a net current liabilities figure, and it could indicate that the business was having problems. You'll read more about this later in Section 4.

● **Long-term liabilities** – this section will include any longer-term loans (anything over five years) and mortgages.

The total for this part of the balance sheet is calculated by taking the fixed assets value, adding net current assets (or deducting net current liabilities), and deducting the long-term liabilities.

The bottom half of the balance sheet shows how the business was financed and, in our example, shows the capital account of the owner.

● **Capital account** – the owner's investment in the business is known as capital. The opening balance of capital is the balance at the end of the last financial year. We add the net profit to the opening balance because profits of the business are due to the owner. The owner may

---

R Taylor Electrical Goods Balance Sheet at 31st March 2000

	£ Cost	£ Depreciation	£ Net book Value
Fixed assets			
Premises	38,000	0	38,000
Fixtures and fittings	5,600	2,600	3,000
Equipment	8,700	4,200	4,500
Motor van	7,500	5,620	1,880
	59,800	12,420	47,380
Current assets:			
Stock		4,500	
Debtors		432	
Bank/cash		1,200	
		6,132	
Current liabilities			
Creditors		2,500	
Net current assets			3,632
			51,012
Financed by:			
Owner's capital			45,000
Add: Net profit			14,512
			59,512
Less: Drawings			12,000
			47,512
Long-term loan			3,500
			51,012

FIGURE 5.26 *Alternative presentation for a balance sheet*

choose to leave the profit in the business, but the capital account records what is owed by the business to the owner. We then deduct any drawings. Drawings are the amounts that the owner draws from the business during the year.

Top Tips

The total on this section of the balance sheet is the new balance of the capital account . It should be equal to the total of the assets and liabilities. The balance sheet should balance!

Sometimes the business will include long-term loans in the 'Financed by' part of the balance sheet, rather than in assets and liabilities. This is because they argue that the loan is being used to finance the business in addition to owner's capital. This is simply an alternative presentation of the same information and is quite acceptable. Figure 5.26 shows what our example would look like if presented in this way.

ACTIVITY 21

Prepare a balance sheet for Martin Baker, using the information from Activity 19 and the additional information given below. You will need to take the net profit figure from the profit and loss account that you prepared for Martin Baker. You will also need to use the depreciation figures you calculated.

Martin Baker Financial information for Balance sheet at 31st December 2000

Opening balance of capital account	£12,217
Debtors	£749
Creditors	£2,413
Cash in hand	£523
Bank overdraft	£982
Drawings	£10,500.

Key Skills C3.3, N3.2a

Where the business is a limited company financed by shares, the shares are shown under the 'Financed by': section of the balance sheet along with the total retained profits. Retained profits is the amount of profit that has been retained in the business. It is calculated by taking last year's balance, adding the net profit for this year, and deducting any dividends paid to shareholders.

ACTIVITY 22

Look at the profit and loss account in your annual report. You will probably see that, on the profit and loss account, after calculating net profit, figures for tax and dividends are deducted. The figure at the bottom of the profit and loss account may be called retained profit.

Look on the balance sheet. How is the business financed? There may be one or more different sorts of shares. There will be retained profit or profit and loss reserve. Any other funds you see – for example revaluation reserves – are really part of the retained profits but companies are required to show them separately.

Self-Test Questions

1 Explain the flow of a purchase invoice through the accounting system.

2 Give two examples of each of the following: assets, liabilities, revenues, expenses.

3 Explain, in your own words, the term 'depreciation'.

4 How would you calculate the following: gross profit, net profit?

5 Briefly explain what is shown by the profit and loss account, and the balance sheet.

Section 3 *Interpreting financial information*

What you need to learn

In this section you will learn about:

- how to calculate financial ratios for a business
- how to use those ratios in order to make judgements about a business
- other indicators that can be used in judging business performance
- which ratios and indicators would interest different groups of stakeholders.

In the last section we looked at the profit and loss account and balance sheet and saw how these presented information about the business's activities and its assets and liabilities. These statements are useful to the stakeholders in telling them what is happening in the business, but they don't give the full picture. The accounting statements only give information for one financial period and for one company. Stakeholders want to know about business performance – about the returns on their investment, about the security of their investment and about the efficiency of the business. They want to know about how the business performed this year compared to other years and how it performed compared to other businesses in the same industry.

One thing that stakeholders can do is compare accounts from different years and from different companies.

Case study

Look at the three sets of summarised accounts in Figure 5.29. The first two sets are from different years of Tracy Smith Computer Sales. Tracy runs a small business selling personal computers to the

public. The last set is for Orange Computers Limited, Luton Branch. Orange Computers runs a similar business to Tracy's but has several branches and much larger shop premises.

We can see from the accounts that the figures on Tracy's statements for the later year are higher than last year's, and that the figures for Orange are much higher than Tracy's figures. This may tell us something about size and price rises and levels of sales, but it is difficult to compare business performance.

Financial ratios look at the relationship between figures on the profit and loss account and balance sheet, and make it easier to do comparisons. By using ratios to analyse her business performance, Tracy will be able to make more useful comparisons across different years, and with other businesses. Let's have a look at some of the ratios that Tracy might use to analyse her business performance.

Top Tips

Ratios are only useful for making comparisons. One ratio doesn't really tell you anything.

Profitability ratios

The first group of ratios we will consider are profitability ratios. These will help Tracy to assess whether her business is trading successfully and giving a reasonable rate of return.

Gross profit margin

We saw from the profit and loss account that the gross profit is the profit before overhead expenses are taken into account. The gross profit ratio shows how much gross profit the business has made in relation to its sales figure. The ratio is

	Tracy Smith Computer Sales		Orange Computers Limited Luton Branch
	year ended 31.12.99	year ended 31.12.00	year ended 31.12.00
Profit and loss account	£	£	£
Sales	175,150	256,410	592,530
Less: Cost of sales	131,365	201,564	465,137
Gross profit	43,785	54,846	127,393
Less: Total expenses	20,435	30,438	66,955
Net profit	23,350	24,408	60,438
Balance sheet			
Fixed assets at net book value	87,486	102,175	269,331
Current assets:			
Stock	9,475	13,275	38,760
Debtors	10,095	28,585	24,688
Cash/bank	700	200	11,672
	20,270	42,060	75,120
Current liabilities:			
Trade creditors	10,947	20,797	48,451
Bank overdraft	976	2,417	–
	11,923	23,214	48,451
Net current assets	8,347	18,846	26,669
Total net assets	95,833	121,021	296,000
Financed by:			
Owner's capital	80,833	106,021	–
Shareholders' funds	–	–	296,000
Long-term loans	15,000	15,000	–
	95,833	121,021	296,000

FIGURE 5.27 *Summarised profit and loss accounts and balance sheets*

expressed in terms of a percentage. You can calculate the ratio as follows:

Gross profit margin % = $\dfrac{\text{Gross profit}}{\text{Total sales}} \times 100\%$

Using the figures from Tracy's profit and loss account for the year ended 31st December 1999, the calculation is as follows:

Gross profit margin =

$\dfrac{£43,785}{£175,150} \times 100 = 25\%$ (rounded up).

The higher the gross profit margin, the more profitable the business, but the gross profit margin varies between different industries. Something like fast food, for example, has a much lower gross profit than that on clothes. For an established business, the gross profit ratio should remain roughly the same from year to year. To make any sense of the ratio, you would need to compare it to those of previous years for the same business, and to those of other businesses in the same industry.

ACTIVITY 23

Calculate the gross profit margins for Tracy Smith and Orange for the year ended 31st December 2000. Compare Tracy's gross profit margin for the two years, and compare her margin for 2000 with that of Orange Computers Limited. What can you say about the figures?

(You should round your calculations to two decimal places).

Key Skills N3.2a, N3.3

You should have seen that Tracy's gross profit margin has dropped slightly in 2000, but is similar to the Orange Computers figure for the same year. For the gross profit margin to change, the sales revenue must change at a different rate to the cost of sales.

ACTIVITY 24

Tracy found the information in Figure 5.28 in her computer trade journal for January 2001.

Traders found that although costs of computers for re-sale rose in line with the general level of inflation, they were unable to raise their selling prices at the same rate. This was due to increased competition in the home computer market which saw traders offering discounts and free upgrades to attract more buyers.

FIGURE 5.28 *Additional information helps to explain changes in ratios*

Explain what you would expect to happen to the gross profit margin of businesses in the computer retail trade if the above article is correct. Do Tracy's figures indicate that her business has been affected by this? Do you think Orange Computers has been affected?

If, when comparing ratios, you find there has been a change from one year to the next, or there is a big difference between businesses in the same industry, it is important to look for reasons. Comparing ratios can indicate differences but don't tell us why.

Net profit margin

The net profit margin is a similar calculation to the gross profit margin, but takes account of the overhead expenses that have been incurred by the business. The net profit ratio shows how much net profit the business has made in relation to its sales figure. The ratio is expressed in terms of a percentage. You can calculate the ratio as follows:

Net profit margin % = $\dfrac{\text{Net profit}}{\text{Total sales}} \times 100\%$

Using the figures from Tracy's profit and loss account for the year ended 31st December 1999, the calculation is as follows:

Net profit margin % =

$$\frac{£23,350}{£175,150} \times 100 = 13.33\% \text{ (rounded down)}$$

Similar to the gross profit margin, the higher this figure is, the more profitable the business. The percentage should remain relatively stable from year to year, as long as the gross profit margin is also stable. If the gross profit figure remains stable from one year to the next and the net profit figure rises, this indicates that the business has cut its overhead expenses, perhaps by becoming more efficient. If the gross profit figure remains stable from one year to the next and the net profit figure falls, this may indicate a problem with overhead expenses. To analyse overhead expenses further and identify problem areas you could compare individual expense categories to sales.

Some care is needed when comparing the net profit margin of different businesses. Whilst they can often be similar, any differences may not be explained by inefficiency alone but may be due to differences in operating and financing arrangements. For example, we will consider two businesses, Trojan Toys and Kids Toys Limited.

The two businesses have similar gross profit margins, but the net profit margin of Kids Toys Limited is higher than that of Trojan Toys. Trojan Toys is a relatively new, small business which employs enthusiastic and dedicated staff. The business is partly financed by a large bank loan. Kids Toys Limited is a large chain and is wholly financed by shareholders' funds. In this case, the difference in net profit margin could be explained by the differences in financing arrangements. Included in the overheads of Trojan Toys are a large amount of finance charges. Kids Toys Limited has no such charges. If these are excluded, we may find that Trojan Toys has a similar or even higher net profit margin than Kids Toys Limited.

ACTIVITY   25

Calculate the net profit margins for Tracy Smith Computer Sales and Orange Computers Limited for 2000. Compare Tracy's net profit margin for 2000 with her margin for the previous year and with that of Orange. What conclusions can you draw from the comparisons? What differences in operating and financing arrangements do you think there could be that might affect the margins?

Key Skills N3.2a, N3.3

Top Tips

Published accounts show more than one net profit figure. Look at the annual report you obtained. The profit and loss account probably shows operating profit, profit before taxation and profit after taxation. The figure you should use is the profit before interest and taxation – operating profit – as this gives a better comparison between businesses.

Return on capital employed

Perhaps the best measure of the profitability of a business is return on capital employed. This compares the profit to the amounts invested in the business by the owners. It is useful because it can be compared to the rate that would be obtained from alternative investments. The business owner could invest in alternative businesses or put the money in a savings account. The return on capital employed is calculated as follows:

Return on capital employed =

$$\frac{\text{net profit}}{\text{capital employed}} \times 100$$

Note that net profit is profit before interest and taxation (or operating profit); and that capital employed is owner's capital or shareholders' funds plus long-term loans.

For Tracy Smith, her return on capital employed for 1999 was:

$$\text{ROCE} = \frac{£23,350}{£95,833} \times 100 = 24.37\% \text{ (rounded up to two decimal places).}$$

ACTIVITY 26

Calculate return on capital employed for Tracy Smith and Orange Computers for the year ended 31st December 2000. From a local bank or building society, obtain details of interest rates on long-term investment accounts. Compare Tracy's ROCE for 2000 with her ROCE for 1999 and with Orange's ROCE for 2000. What comments can you make? Would Tracy be better investing her money in a building society or bank account?

Key Skills N3.2a, N3.3

Liquidity ratios

Liquidity ratios give an indication of the short-term solvency of the business. This means whether it would be able to pay its debts in the short term. It looks at the assets that can quickly be turned into cash and compares them with the short-term or current liabilities. They are usually expressed as ratios, for example 3:1, rather than percentages.

Current ratio

The current ratio compares current assets with current liabilities. You will remember that current assets less current liabilities makes up working capital, and you might see this ratio referred to as the working capital ratio. Many businesses operate at a current ratio of around 1.5:1. This means that for every £1 of debt, they have £1.50 worth of current assets which is a good position for the business to be in. If the ratio is too low, this may mean that the business is unable to cover its debts. For example with a ratio of 0.7:1, it only has 70 pence worth of assets to cover each

£1 of debt. If it is too high, the business may be holding too much cash or have too much tied up in stock or debtors. It may be able to make better use of its working capital. The current ratio is calculated by:

$$\text{Current ratio} = \frac{\text{Current assets}}{\text{Current liabilities}}$$

Tracy Smith's current ratio for 1999 was:

$$\text{Current ratio} = \frac{£20,270}{£11,923} = 1.7$$

Expressed as a ratio, this would be 1.7:1 (Tracy has £1.70 worth of assets to each £1 of debt).

A ratio of lower than 1.5:1 may indicate that the business is having financial problems, but you should check it against other businesses in the same industry if possible. Some types of business do operate on a lower ratio – particularly those such as supermarkets where they don't have many debtors but take in large amounts of cash every day that can be used to pay creditors.

ACTIVITY 27

Calculate the current ratios for Tracy Smith and Orange Computers for 2000. Compare and comment on the figures.

Key Skills N3.2a, N3.3

Acid test

The acid test or quick ratio is probably a better measure of the business's financial position. It is similar to the current ratio but excludes stock from the ratio. This is because stock is generally harder to convert to cash than the other fixed assets. If stock were to be sold quickly to pay debts, it may well need to be sold off at less than its market value, whereas debtors and cash will most likely be equivalent to their balance sheet value. The ratio is interpreted in the same way as the current ratio, except that the usual ratio for businesses is about 1:1. This means they have £1 assets for each £1 of debt. The acid test ratio is calculated by:

$$\text{Acid test ratio} = \frac{\text{Current assets less stock}}{\text{Current liabilities}}$$

Tracy Smith's acid test ratio for 1999 was:

$$\text{Acid test ratio} = \frac{£20,270 - 9,475}{£11,923} = 0.91$$

Expressed as a ratio, this would be 0.9:1 (Tracy has 91p worth of assets to each £1 of debt).

As with the current ratio, a ratio of lower than the average may indicate that the business can't pay its debts, but for some types of business the ratio will be lower. A business that has a large amount of money tied up in fast moving stock, for example food, might have a lower ratio, or one that has few debtors. Always compare to other businesses in the same industry.

Top Tips

It is worth remembering that a business that is part of a larger concern could be supported by the main business and may be able to survive with lower ratios.

ACTIVITY 28

Calculate the acid test ratios for Tracy Smith and Orange Computers for 2000. Compare and comment on the figures.

Key Skills N3.2a, N3.3

Efficiency ratios

Efficiency ratios look at how efficiently the business has carried out its activities and managed its resources during the year.

Asset turnover

Asset turnover shows how efficiently the business has used its assets to generate sales revenue. The ratio compares fixed assets at net book value to sales as shown below:

$$\text{Asset turnover} = \frac{\text{Sales revenue}}{\text{Net book value of fixed assets}}$$

The figure calculated shows how many times the fixed assets are covered by sales revenue. The higher the figure, the more times they are covered, but this really needs to be compared with previous years. If the ratio is increasing from year to year, the assets are being used more efficiently. When comparing different businesses, it is important to recognise that different rates and methods of depreciation used for fixed assets might skew the results.

In 1999, Tracy's asset turnover was:

$$\text{Asset turnover} = \frac{£175,150}{£87,486} = 2$$

Tracy's fixed asset value is covered twice by her sales revenue in this year.

ACTIVITY 29

Calculate assets turnover ratios for Tracy Smith and Orange Computers for 2000. Comment on the results.

Key Skills N3.2a, N3.3

The other efficiency ratios that we will consider all relate to working capital, and show us how well this is being controlled by the management of the company.

Stock turnover

Stock turnover shows how many times the stock has been turned over in the year. The figure will vary between different types of businesses, so it is important to make comparisons between similar businesses. For example, a dairy will collect the milk each day and sell it, so will turn over its stock every day, whereas a company selling tractors might only turn over its stock 12 times a year. When comparing two businesses, if one has a higher stock turnover, then the business is more efficient because it is selling its stock quicker and not holding too much stock. A low ratio can indicate a problem with sales or with the amount of stock being held by the business.

$$\text{Stock turnover} = \frac{\text{cost of sales}}{\text{stock}}$$

(We take the stock figure from the balance sheet.)

In 1999, Tracy's stock turnover was:

$$\text{Stock turnover} = \frac{£131,365}{£9,475} = 13.86 \text{ times}$$

Debtor collection

The debtor collection ratio shows us how long, on average, the business is taking to collect payment from its customers. It is normally expressed in terms of days. You should be aware that where a business allows credit to its customers, it normally works on 30 days' credit. If the ratio is much higher than this, then the business could be taking too long to collect debts. Bear in mind, though, that some businesses may offer longer terms in order to attract customers. To calculate the ratio we need to compare credit sales with the debtors figure from the balance sheet.

$$\text{Debtor collection period} = \frac{\text{debtors}}{\text{credit sales}} \times 365$$

To calculate this ratio, assume that the profit and loss account figure for sales is equal to credit sales unless told otherwise.

Tracy's debtor collection period for the year ended 31st December 1999 is calculated below. In 1999, half of her sales were credit sales. (Credit sales = £175,150 ÷ 2 = £87,575). Tracy allows 30 days' credit.

$$\text{Debtor collection period} = \frac{£10,095}{£87,575} \times 365$$

= 42 days (answer rounded to whole days).

Although Tracy allows her customers 30 days' credit, she is taking an average of 42 days to collect payment from customers. This may not be a problem while her business appears to be doing well, but could cause cash flow problems in the future.

Creditor payment

This is similar to the debtor collection ratio, but tells us how long the business is taking to pay creditors. Again, most businesses work on 30 days, though you should check that longer terms have not been offered or whether there are longer credit periods specific to the industry. Even where a business appears to be in a strong position, if it doesn't pay creditors on time, it could be refused further credit. It generally makes sense for a business to have a creditor payment period that is the same as, or longer than, its debtor collection period. This means that it is collecting money from customers before paying it out to suppliers.

Note that you need to use the purchases figure, not the cost of sales figure for the calculation. The cost of sales figure is opening stock, plus purchases, less closing stock. If the cost of sales calculation is not shown on the face of the profit and loss account, there will generally be a note to the accounts. You can assume that the purchases figure given is credit purchases unless told otherwise. In fact most businesses buy most of their purchases on credit.

$$\text{Creditor payment period} = \frac{\text{creditors}}{\text{credit purchases}} \times 365$$

Tracy's purchases all her stock on credit terms. The calculation for cost of sales in 1999 was as follows:

Opening stock	£8,654
Purchases	132,186
	140,840
Less: Closing stock	9,475
Cost of sales	131,365

$$\text{Creditors payment period} = \frac{£10,947}{£132,186} \times 365$$

= 30 days (answer rounded to whole days).

Tracy is paying her creditors within 30 days. This is generally an indication that the business doesn't have a cash flow problem and can pay its debts.

ACTIVITY 30

Analyse the working capital efficiency of Tracy Smith Computer Sales for the year 2000, by making comparisons with the previous year, and with Orange Computers Limited for the same year. Explain the possible implications of your results. You are given the following further information to help you with your calculations.

Credit sales for the year 2000:

■ Tracy Smith – Tracy gained a new business client in 2000, who buys on 30 days' credit. The proportion of credit sales therefore increased to two-thirds of total sales.

■ Orange Computers offer credit of 30 days to half of its customers.

Cost of sales information for 2000 is as follows:

	Tracy Smith	Orange Computers
Opening stock	£9,475	£29,888
Purchases	205,364	474,009
	214,839	503,897
Less: Closing stock	13,275	38,760
Cost of sales	201,564	465,137

Key Skills N3.2a, N3.3

Tracy's new business client is keeping her very busy and she has not had time to carry out normal administrative tasks for the business, such as sending out statements to customers and paying supplier accounts. Her new client takes about six weeks to pay its account, though doesn't appear to have any difficulty in paying. She is reluctant to chase it for payment in case she loses its business. The new client is replacing all its computers with a specific model that Tracy orders and sends straight out to it.

Orange computers buys all its stock from Orange Warehousing Department and is expected to pay for it within 20 days of receipt. Customer statements for Orange are sent out from the central accounts department, who ensure that all bills are paid on time.

You should now be able to calculate and interpret the ratios to give more information about the financial position of a business. Where possible, you should always look for further information to explain changes in ratios for a business from year to year, or differences between the ratios of similar businesses. If you are working with financial statements from the annual report of a company, you may find the explanations elsewhere in the report, or in the business press.

Top Tips

Always look for further information to support or explain the ratios you have calculated.

ACTIVITY 31

Calculate ratios for a public limited company from the information given in its annual report. Comment on the financial health of the company.

Key Skills N3.1, N3.2a, N3.3

You should understand that ratios alone will not provide sufficient information to understand a business's financial position. You need to make comparisons and take account of other information about the business and the industry in which it operates.

Investors ratios

Investors and potential investors in a public limited company are interested in the following indicators:

● share prices – the price at which shares are traded on the Stock Exchange

● dividends – the payments made to shareholders in return for their investment

● the price/earnings ratio – the share price as compared to the earnings of a company.

These all give some indication of the financial success and stability of the business and whether or not it is a good investment. Shareholders have two chances to make profits on their investment. First, they should receive a regular return – dividends paid from the profits of the company – for as long as they own the shares. Second, they can sell their shares in a company and make a profit if the share price is higher than when they bought the shares.

Share prices depend on investors' perceptions of a company. If a company is thought to be doing well, or likely to do well, there will be a demand for shares among investors and the share price will increase. If investors believe it is not performing very well, then its share price will fall as existing investors in the company try to sell their shares. As you have seen with the interpretation of ratios, it is not easy to analyse the financial position of a company. All investors have their own thoughts on the success or otherwise of companies and will buy and sell shares based on these. Also, some shareholders will buy for long-term gain, whilst others want short-term profits. So share prices will rise and fall every day as the demand for individual shares changes.

Let's look at some of the things that can affect investors' perception of a company and, therefore, share prices.

- **Takeovers.** When a take-over of one company by another is expected, the share prices of both companies usually change. Usually a take-over means that the shareholders in the company being taken over will receive a generous payout for their shares, so the share price of the company will generally increase as investors try to buy shares. Obviously, the money for this payout will come from the other company, so its share price is likely to fall because the shareholders believe there will be less profit for payment of dividends, and will try to sell their shares. Note that even a rumour of take-over is enough to affect the share prices.

- **Annual results.** If annual profits of a company are higher than expected, share prices will rise because investors believe that dividends will be high. If the profits are lower, investors may sell shares in the company because they think dividends will be low, and the share price will fall.

- **Sector-specific events.** Sometimes the share prices within a whole sector can be affected. If, for example, one of the major banks were to go out of business, the share price of all banks could fall as investors lost confidence in the sector. If there is confidence in a sector, then the share prices can rise out of proportion with the real worth of the companies as investors try to buy in to the sector. This can be seen currently with the e-commerce businesses – those that trade over the Internet. A number of these companies have been sold at large amounts of money, so many investors are trying to buy into the sector.

ACTIVITY 32

Look through the financial pages of a current newspaper. Pick out three articles that you think might affect share prices. (The *Financial Times* has the most business information – your local library will have copies.) Discuss the articles with your group.

Key Skills C3.2

Top Tips

The change in share price doesn't necessarily depend on an actual event. A rumour will do!

Dividends can be a good indication of the wealth of a company. An established company will pay out similar or rising amounts in dividends each year. If the dividends are falling, investors might want to re-consider their investment in the company. You should note, though, that the level of dividends doesn't just depend on the profits of the company. The directors will decide how much to pay out in dividends and will consider how much profit needs to be retained in the company. If they are planning a large project in the near future, they may pay out a dividend that is the same or even less than last year's.

ACTIVITY 33

Obtain two annual reports and look at the dividend levels of the companies over the last two years. Have the dividends changed or stayed the same? What explanation can you find for this?

Key Skills C3.2, N3.1

Investors will look at levels of share prices and dividends when making investment decisions, but a more useful way of comparing companies is to use the price earnings ratio. To compare the market price for shares is difficult, because it depends on so many factors. Dividend levels are also difficult to compare because, as we have seen, different companies will have different policies, depending on their current and future activities. The price/earnings ratio compares the share price with the earnings of the company. The price/earnings ratio is calculated as follows:

$$\text{PE ratio} = \frac{\text{market price per share (in pence)}}{\text{earnings per share (in pence)}}.$$

To calculate earnings per share, you take net profit after tax and divide it by the number of shares as shown on the balance sheet or in the notes to the balance sheet.

You will not normally need to calculate the PE ratio as it is quoted in the financial press, along with share prices and dividend levels, and will be shown in the annual report of a company. In general, the higher the ratio, the better, but you will need to compare the ratio with those of other companies and with those from other years for the same company.

ACTIVITY 34

Using the two annual reports you obtained for the last Activity, and information about current share prices from the financial press, decide which of the two companies you would invest in. Explain your choice. You should show that you have considered share prices, dividend levels, PE ratios and any other relevant financial information in making your decision.

Key Skills C3.2, N3.1, N3.2a, N3.3

In this section, we have considered a number of ratios which can help in interpreting the financial health of a business. Different stakeholders will be interested in different aspects of the business, and may use some of these ratios to help them. Try the following exercise which asks you to identify useful ratios for different stakeholders.

ACTIVITY 35

For each of the following stakeholders, select two main ratios or other indicators which may help them, and give reasons for your choice:

- **a new supplier to a business**
- **a bank which is considering making a loan to a business**
- **a manager who is trying to reduce the level of overhead expenses**
- **a potential customer of a business who will be using the business as its main supplier**
- **An investor looking for long-term income from a company.**

Self-Test Questions

1 The gross profit ratio of a business is increasing, but the net profit ratio is decreasing. Give reasons why this might happen.

2 Explain the difference between the current ratio and the acid test ratio. Which do you think is a better measure of the business liquidity and why?

3 What do the efficiency ratios tell us about the business?

4 Explain why share prices change. Give examples of three events that may affect share prices.

5 A company claims its profits have increased by 25 per cent on last year, but has paid out a lower dividend to investors. Explain why this might be the case.

Section 4 *Cash flow management*

What you need to learn

In this section you will learn about:

● budgeting and why it is important
● how businesses control and manage their working capital.

Business survival is not just about making a profit. Look at the following case study:

Case Study

Marton Farm Machinery is a small, but well-respected company, making machinery for use in farming. It is a family-owned company and its profits have been increasing steadily over the last few years so the family has been able to pay itself large dividends. However, it is having some problems. The main metal cutting machinery has broken down. This has happened a lot over the last two years. When the machine was purchased, it was felt that its lifespan was six years. It is now 10 years old. In addition, the company is not very good at collecting money from its debtors. It knows that the cash flow for farmers is erratic and doesn't like to push its customers for payment. Consequently, there is not much cash in the business and it is finding it difficult to pay creditors and employees. It has exceeded its overdraft limit at the bank and the bank manager has asked for immediate repayment. Its major supplier has demanded full payment of its account before it will deliver any more materials. February is always the busiest month for orders, as farmers order new machines in preparation for that year's harvesting. Every year the production manager has problems because he has not ordered sufficient materials to meet the increased production.

Though the name and some other details have been changed, this describes a real company. It went out of business even though it had plenty of orders for future work, and had been profitable. It went out of business for two main reasons: lack of planning and poor cash flow. It failed to plan for future expenditure and failed to control working capital. It didn't manage the cash in the business properly in order to meet the business's needs.

Many businesses, particularly smaller ones, go out of business for these reasons. It has nothing to do with the success of the business idea or the profitability of the business but comes down to a lack of planning and control. In this section, you will look at how businesses can achieve these factors.

Budgeting

At the start of this chapter we met Katie, who had just left home and started work, and who needed to control her finances so that she didn't run out of money at the end of the month. Katie could have used a budget to plan and control her expenditure. It might have looked like Figure 5.31.

From her budget, Katie can see how much money she will receive in wages, and how much she will need to spend on essentials such as rent, gas and electricity bills, and food. When she has put aside the amounts she needs for essentials, she can choose to save or spend the rest of the money. She has used the budget to plan her expenditure for the next six months. The budget also now acts as a target for Katie. She can try to keep her spending in line with the budget.

Having prepared the budget, Katie can use it to control her expenditure. If she compares what

	Feb	March	April	May	June	July	Total
	£	£	£	£	£	£	£
Wages received	876	876	876	876	876	876	5,256
Regular expenses:							
Rent	350	350	350	350	350	350	2,100
Electricity/Gas	30	30	30	30	30	30	180
Telephone	20	20	20	20	20	20	120
Food	50	50	50	50	50	50	300
Travel expenses	120	120	120	120	120	120	720
Total expenses	570	570	570	570	570	570	3,420
Money left:	306	306	306	306	306	306	1,836
Savings	150	150	150	150	150	150	900
Left to spend	156	156	156	156	156	156	936
	306	306	306	306	306	306	1,836

FIGURE 5.29 *Katie's budget*

she actually spends each month with her planned spending, she can identify where there are any differences and make any necessary adjustments. If she is spending more than she planned on one item, she might decide to spend less in future, or to adjust her budget to take account of the extra amount.

Figure 5.30 shows the amounts Katie actually spent in February, March and April.

 **ACTIVITY**

Compare Katie's actual total spending for February, March and April with her budgeted total spending. Identify individual items where differences have occurred.

Key Skills N3.2a

In March, she invited some friends for a meal and spent a bit extra on food. In April, she went to

	Feb	March	April	Total
	£	£	£	£
Wages received	876	876	876	2,628
Regular expenses:				
Rent	350	350	400	1,100
Electricity/Gas	30	30	30	90
Telephone	20	20	20	60
Food	50	70	45	165
Travel expenses	120	120	120	360
Total expenses	570	590	615	1,775
Money left:	306	286	270	862
Savings	150	67	150	367
Spent	156	219	120	495
	306	286	270	862

FIGURE 5.30 *Katie's income and expenditure for February, March and April*

stay with her parents for a few days so spent a little less on food. In March, Katie spent more on clothes than she had planned, and wasn't able to put any money into her savings account. She decides that she won't do this in future because she is saving for a car. In April, Katie's rent increased. Unfortunately, there is nothing Katie can do about this, so she needs to adjust her budget to take account of the increase.

A budget is a forecast of future income and expenditure that can help to control and monitor finances. To be of any value, budgets need to be monitored. They need to be matched with actual income and expenditure, and differences need to be identified and resolved. Budgets are not fixed because they are only estimates of what will happen in the future. If circumstances change, then the budget may need to be revised.

Budgeting is useful for businesses because they can help to make sure that a number of individuals are working towards the same targets. Each department is likely to have its own budget, and these are collected together into a master budget for the whole of the business. The main elements of a business budget are sales, purchases or production costs and expenses. If you think about the profit and loss accounts we looked at in Section 3, each item of revenue and expenditure on the profit and loss account needs to appear on the budget.

Case study

Figure 5.31 shows the budget for Carrington Coaches' 2001 summer season. Carrington runs coach tours around the Lake District.

Carrington's sales revenue comes from the sale of tour tickets. The cost of sales is made up of coach running costs which include petrol, maintenance, insurance, road tax and wages for coach drivers and tour guides. It also has general expenses for advertising the tours and running the booking office.

Figure 5.32 shows a budget for the whole of the business but is actually made up of the sales budget, tour costs budget and booking office budget.

The sales have been estimated using last year's figures as a guide. Sales for each month consist of the revenue from tours taking place in that month. Carrington has increased the amounts from last year to allow for an increase in prices and because it expects a few more customers in the coming season. Carrington knows that its business is seasonal, so it has allowed for this in its budget. It knows that it will sell more tour tickets in the summer months than in spring and autumn.

	April	May	June	July	Aug	Sept	Total
	£	£	£	£	£	£	£
Sales of tickets	3,500	5,000	10,000	12,500	15,000	6,750	52,750
Cost of sales:							
Coach running costs	450	650	1,250	1,550	1,850	850	6,600
Drivers' wages	1,500	1,500	1,500	1,500	1,500	1,500	9,000
Guides' wages	500	750	1,500	1,875	2,250	1,000	7,875
Total cost of sales	2,450	2,900	4,250	4,925	5,600	3,350	23,475
Expenses:							
Advertising	200	400	400	400	200	100	1,700
Stationery	100	100	100	100	100	100	600
Office staff wages	1,000	1,000	1,000	1,000	1,000	1,000	6,000
Office expenses	500	500	500	500	500	500	3,000
Telephone	100	100	150	150	150	100	750
Total expenses	1,900	2,100	2,150	2,150	1,950	1,800	12,050

FIGURE 5.31 *Budget for Carrington Coaches*

	April	May	June	July	Aug	Sept	Total
	£	£	£	£	£	£	£
Sales of tickets	3,500	5,000	10,000	12,500	15,000	6,750	52,750
Less: Cost of sales	2,450	2,900	4,250	4,925	5,600	3,350	23,475
Gross Profit	1,050	2,100	5,750	7,575	9,400	3,400	29,275
Less: Total expenses	1,900	2,100	2,150	2,150	1,950	1,800	12,050
Net profit/loss	−850	0	3,600	5,425	7,450	1,600	17,225

FIGURE 5.32 *Budgeted profit and loss accounts*

Once it has estimated sales for the season, it can look at the tour costs. You can see on the budget that drivers' wages are the same each month but coach running costs and guides' wages change. Carrington employs full-time drivers and knows that it will need to pay these drivers whether or not it runs the tours. Guides are employed on a casual basis for each tour that takes place, so the level of wages depends on the number of tours. Coach running costs are made up of some expenses that depend on the number of tours – such as petrol and maintenance – and some that are the same for each month – such as insurance and road tax.

Lastly, Carrington will estimate its general overhead expenses. Some of these – like telephone expenses and advertising – will vary depending on the time of year and whether the booking office is very busy, while others will be the same each month – like office rent and wages for office staff.

Once it has prepared all the budgets, Carrington can put them together and prepare a forecast profit and loss statement for each month.

In order to prepare a budget, a business has to consider each revenue and expense item. It will need information about how these vary depending on season, or level of activity, and need to estimate amounts. Many businesses use last year's results as a guide for next year's budget. The budget will be used to monitor expenses and revenues throughout the year. Any differences between actual and budgeted figures are calculated and the reasons for the difference ascertained.

	April £
Sales of tickets	4,000
Cost of sales:	
Coach running costs	530
Drivers' wages	1,500
Guides' wages	560
Total cost of sales	2,590
Expenses:	
Advertising	200
Stationery	100
Office staff wages	1,000
Office expenses	500
Telephone	130
Total expenses	1,930

FIGURE 5.33 *Actual income and expenses for April*

During the year Carrington will compare its budget to actual revenues and expenses and identify any differences. Figures 5.33 and 5.34 show the actual receipts and expenses, and the actual profit and loss account of Carrington Coaches for April 2001.

	April £
Sales of tickets	4,000
Less: Cost of sales	2,590
Gross profit	1,410
Less: Total expenses	1,930
Net profit/loss	–520

FIGURE 5.34 *Actual profit and loss account for April*

ACTIVITY 37

Calculate the total differences in sales, cost of sales and expenses. Identify the items that do not agree with the budget and calculate the difference.

In April, a Japanese travel company unexpectedly booked a number of its customers on to Carrington's 'View of the Lakes' tour. This accounts for the increased sales. Can you explain why some of the cost and expense items have changed?

Calculate Carrington's actual profit or loss for April and compare this with the budgeted figure.

Key Skills N3.2a

The differences between actual and budgeted figures are known as variances. Where a revenue or expense item is better than expected, the difference is known as a **favourable** variance. Where it is worse than expected, it is called an **adverse** variance.

ACTIVITY 38

You are given some information about actual revenues and expenditure for Carrington Coaches. In each case, compare the figure to the budget, calculate the variance and state whether it is favourable or adverse, and calculate the effect on profit for the month:

- **in May, ticket sales were £47,00**
- **in May, coach running costs were £614**
- **in June, advertising was £500**
- **in July, ticket sales were £12,950**
- **in August, coach running costs were £2,200.**

Key Skills N3.2a

Top Tips

A favourable variance will increase profit; an adverse variance will decrease profit.

Where the information is available, you should always look for explanations for variances. You can only control variances if you know why they have occurred.

ACTIVITY 39

Your friend Asif has just taken over as manager of the local supermarket. Head office has told him that he needs to plan his revenues and expenses for the next year. He is not quite sure how or why he should do this. Write a letter to Asif, explaining the benefits of budgeting and how the budgeting process works.

Key Skills C3.3

Management of working capital

Working capital is the finance that is available for running the business on a day-to-day basis. The amount of working capital required depends on the size and type of business and on how it is set up and financed. Every business, therefore, will be different.

To manage working capital efficiently, it is important to understand how changes in each element affect the business. We saw in Section 2 that the amount of working capital can be ascertained by calculating current assets less current liabilities. In this section we will look at each of the categories of current assets and liabilities and how they can be managed effectively.

Stock

Effective stock management is particularly important for businesses that buy or manufacture products for re-sale. If they have too much cash tied up in stock, they could risk not being able to pay bills. If they have too little stock, they may run out and risk interruptions in production or sales. If a company does have too much stock and needs to raise cash, it may consider selling stock at a discount – having a sale. If it needs more stock, and cash is not available, it may need to arrange overdraft facilities or negotiate longer credit terms with suppliers.

Debtors

The debtors collection period can be calculated to assess how efficient the business is at collecting payments. Usually, payment will be required within 30 days, though many UK businesses actually wait much longer for payment from their customers.

In businesses where customers are given credit, the management can try to speed up collection of the amounts owed. This might simply mean making sure that the bills are paid on time by sending out reminders and chasing up non-payments. In some cases it may be possible to negotiate shorter credit terms with customers or offer discounts for early payment.

Businesses can also use a debt factoring company. A business can present its invoices to such a company which will pay it 80 per cent of the invoice value. The debt factoring company then collects the debt from the customer. It will keep a fee – usually about 5 per cent – and pay the remainder to the business.

Where the business is cash-rich, it may wish to offer longer terms as an incentive to customers.

Trade creditors

The longer the credit period, the longer cash will remain in the business before payment has to be made. The creditors collection period can be calculated to see how long the business is taking to make payments.

The business may be able to negotiate longer credit terms with its suppliers. This is usually possible only where the supplier has confidence in the business's ability to pay. If businesses simply take longer to pay, without proper negotiations, they risk a loss of confidence by the supplier which could result in it refusing future supplies.

Where the business is cash-rich, it may be able to take advantage of special offers or discounts offered by suppliers for early payment.

Cash

The most useful tool in managing working capital is the cash flow forecast. We can see how much working capital the business has by looking at the balance sheet but this only tells us about one moment in time, and about a historic moment! It doesn't give us an indication of what is happening now or in the future. The cash flow forecast looks at when cash will be received from debtors and paid to creditors.

In the case study at the start of this section, you saw how Marton Farm Machinery failed because it hadn't budgeted for the new machine it needed or properly managed the cash in the business. One of the things it could have done to improve control was to prepare budgets; this would have helped it plan for the February flood of orders. Its main problem, though, was a shortage of cash. To avoid this, it could have prepared a cash flow forecast.

Consider the case study on Carrington Coaches. Carrington's budget shows the level of sales and expenditure for the summer season, but doesn't

	April	May	June	July	Aug	Sept	Total
	£	£	£	£	£	£	£
Receipts:							
Sales of tickets	2,500	4,000	8,000	12,500	15,000	9,750	51,750
Loan received				25,000			25,000
	2,500	4,000	8,000	37,500	15,000	9,750	76,750
Payments:							
Coach running costs	300	600	1,050	1,450	1750	1,210	6,360
Drivers' wages	1,500	1,500	1,500	1,500	1500	1,500	9,000
Guides' wages	500	750	1,500	1,875	2,250	1,000	7,875
Advertising	0	200	400	400	400	200	1,600
Stationery	100	100	100	100	100	100	600
Office staff wages	1,000	1,000	1,000	1,000	1,000	1,000	6,000
Office expenses	500	500	500	500	500	500	3,000
Telephone	0	0	350	0	0	350	700
New coach	0	0	0	31,500	0	0	31,500
	3,900	4,650	6,400	38,325	7,500	5,860	66,635
Opening bank balance	13,467	12,067	11,417	13,017	12,192	19,692	13,467
Net receipts/payments	−1,400	−650	1,600	−825	7,500	3,890	10,115
Closing bank balance	12,067	11,417	13,017	12,192	19,692	23,582	23,582

FIGURE 5.35 *Cash flow forecast for Carrington coaches*

tell it how much cash it will receive or need to pay each month. While the sales of tickets for April tours may be £3,500, this doesn't necessarily mean that Carrington will receive this much cash in the month. Some customers will have paid for their tickets in advance – in February or March, perhaps – and others, for example hotels making block bookings, may be offered credit and not pay until June. Some customers will buy tickets in April for the April tours.

Similarly, with expenses, Carrington will pay some of the expenses in the month they are incurred – such as wages. Other expenses will be paid later because they have been given credit. For example it may have a fuel account at the local service station. Some expenses, like the telephone account, will only be paid quarterly, even though they have been included in the budget on a monthly basis.

At the end of the six months Carrington expects to be owed £1,000 by customers. It will owe £300 for fuel bills, and £100 for advertising costs. Carrington is planning to purchase a new coach in July. It has included this expenditure in its cash flow, together with the loan it intends to obtain to cover part of the purchase. To complete the picture, the opening bank balance is shown, and the closing balance calculated taking account of the information in the cash flow forecast. Note that some businesses will prepare a separate capital budget which shows planned purchases of any new fixed assets and how they will be financed.

In order to manage cash flow better, larger items of expenditure such as buildings and cars may be avoided by renting or leasing instead of buying. This means that instead of paying out a large sum of money now, the business is paying on a monthly basis.

Cash flow forecasts need to be monitored in the same way as budgets. The figures are only estimates and if the actual figures are different, then cash flow will be affected. Businesses need to plan for some margin of error by considering what they would do if cash comes in later than expected, or payments need to be made earlier. The measures discussed for managing stock, debtors and creditors will help cash flow but sometimes there will be a cash shortfall and more cash will be required in the business.

There are a number of ways to introduce more cash into a business. For small businesses, it may be that the owner has private funds to introduce, but most businesses will use loans and overdraft facilities to cover cash shortages. Overdrafts are usually very quick and easy to arrange and so can help cover day-to-day fluctuations in cash flow. They should only be used for short-term cash flow because they can be re-called by the bank at any time, and usually work out quite expensive in the long term. For longer-term cash flow, a business might use a loan. These are usually suitable for buying fixed assets, but not for the day-to-day running of the business. Some businesses actually sell their fixed assets and then lease them back from the buyers in order to release cash into the business.

ACTIVITY 40

Look back at the case study on Marton Farm Machinery. What measures could it have used for better working capital management?

Key Skills C3.21

Self-Test Questions

1 Explain why budgeting is important for businesses and how it works.

2 Explain the difference between a budget and a cash flow forecast.

3 Explain the term 'debt factoring' and describe how it can help a business.

4 Give four examples of how a business might improve its working capital position.

5 Explain what a variance is and how it is calculated.

6

Business Planning

What this chapter is about

All businesses need to carry out some planning. For new businesses, planning helps the owners or managers to establish whether the business idea is viable and to identify resource needs. The plan can also be used to support any applications for loans or to show potential investors expected returns on their investment. Once the business is established, planning is essential to monitor the success, or otherwise, of the business and to identify changing resource requirements. This chapter is about producing a business plan. You will learn about the planning process and how to prepare a business plan. The chapter draws on all the other work you have covered in the compulsory chapters. Throughout the chapter you will find ideas of places to look for information that might be useful to you. Detailed information about these is included in the resource list at the end of the chapter. ■

What you need to produce

You will need to produce a business plan for a new product or service. The plan will include:

■ a market analysis for the product or service that you have prepared using primary and secondary market research data and an analysis of the competition

■ a marketing plan that describes the product or service, explains your choice and details prices, promotional methods and distribution

■ a production and quality assurance plan

■ a financial plan based on the market analysis, identifying sources of finance and including a budget, break-even analysis, cash flow forecast, projected profit and loss account and start-up balance sheet. You should use a spreadsheet or similar programme to produce your financial plan

■ a description of and justification for the approach you took to constructing your business plan and any alternative approaches you considered

■ an evaluation of your plan, including an assessment of viability.

You may be able to complete some of the planning work with your colleagues as a group, but your plan must be written up individually.

Section 1 *Choosing your business idea*

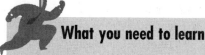

What you need to learn

In this section you will learn about:

● how to choose a business idea
● protecting your business idea
● how to write your business objectives
● how to write a mission statement.

Finding a good idea

Before you can write your business plan, you need to decide on a business idea. You need to decide whether your plan will be for manufacturing goods or providing services. There are several issues to consider when choosing a business idea on which to base your plan.

If you are intending to start a business, it makes sense to choose something related to an area in which you already have some knowledge and interest. If you decided to open a video store, but had no at all interest in films, you might soon be very bored. Also, your customers could be put off by your not knowing anything about the films. You might also find that, for areas in which you are interested, you find it easier to identify a gap in the market.

For your business to be successful, you need to choose a product or service that will sell. It needs to be something that customers want. The most successful businesses identify a gap in the market and try to fill that gap. A gap in the market is where there is something the customer wants, that they are unable to buy. The gap might be national (or even international) where the product or service is not available anywhere, even though there is a demand. The Body Shop, for example, recognised that people wanted to buy environmentally friendly cosmetics, and there were very few generally available. There might be

a gap in the local market. For example, people might like to buy organically grown vegetables. These may be available in other areas but there may not be a local supplier. Finally, it may be that there are products or services on the market, but that they are not exactly what the customer wants. Perhaps they don't have all the features the customer would really like, or are not of the right quality. For example, a washing machine manufacturer might recognise additional programmes that people require on their machines. A fast food restaurant might identify that people want a better quality of burger.

Consider the following situation:

Fred is selling shirts from a market stall and making a reasonable amount of money. You think you will do the same. You buy the same shirts, from the same supplier, and sell them at the same price, on the same market. Why would customers buy from you, rather than Fred?

Of course the answer is that they wouldn't necessarily buy from you rather than Fred. You might sell shirts to customers who happen to pass your stall first and are not regular customers of Fred. There is no reason, though, why customers would prefer to buy from you.

If you can't identify a gap in the market, you should think about whether you can provide an existing product or service better than your competitors can. This might mean providing better quality; or the same product or service at a cheaper price; or giving better customer service. You will need to think about why you will be able to 'do it better'. Ask yourself the question: if it is possible to do it better, why aren't the competitors already doing it? You may be able to offer products or services at a lower price because you are working on a smaller scale and have lower overheads. For example, a large contract window-cleaning business will have many staff and lots of equipment. If you start off by yourself, with a ladder, bucket and cloth, your costs will be much lower and you may be able to charge much less for the service. You may have some special knowledge or skill that will enable you to provide better products or services. You might be a prominent member of the local surfing club, and be very skilled at making surf boards. This could mean that local surfers would prefer to buy their boards from you. Looking back at Fred on his market stall, if you can sell better-quality shirts than Fred, at the same price; or can sell the same shirts at a cheaper price, then you might have a successful business!

You should consider the general economic climate for the business you choose. This will give you some clues as to its potential success. If the general market is in decline, consider why. Is it because people no longer want the product, or because it is being produced cheaper elsewhere? For example, the manufacturing industry in the UK has been generally declining for a number of years. Many items can be produced more cheaply using cheaper labour in Third World countries. Could you really compete with this? You may find that there are more opportunities in expanding markets.

Top Tips

The issues discussed here are issues that you would consider if you were starting a real business. For the purposes of your assessment you should also consider the following:

■ **For a hypothetical business, choose something on which information is easily available. This will make your research easier and your plan more detailed. This doesn't mean you can't still choose something that fills a gap in the market. Make your plan realistic. Most businesses start small. For example, you wouldn't aim to set up a national chain of video stores all in one go. You would start with one shop.**

■ **If you are linking the assessment to a Young Enterprise activity, or similar, don't be over-ambitious with your ideas. If you need actually to set up and run a small business, make sure it is something manageable on the limited resources you may have available.**

ASSESSMENT *activity* ①

In small groups of three or four colleagues, think about some business ideas. To begin with, spend 10 minutes writing down every idea that each person suggests. Aim to list as many ideas as you can, however unrealistic they seem at first. Then go through the ideas, and try to pick out ones that meet some of the criteria discussed above. Finally, agree on one idea and note down why you think it is a viable business idea. Present your findings to the whole of your group.

Key Skills C3.1a, C3.1b

Top Tips

'Brainstorming', the technique used above where you begin by writing down every idea, is a useful one when you are working in groups. It can produce some imaginative and unusual ideas.

Before you decide on your business idea, you might want to do a little research to establish the potential market, competitors and viability. This is not like the detailed planning you will carry out to prepare your business plan. It is simply an initial assessment to check whether your idea is feasible. You might even consider a couple of ideas at this stage. You might discuss the idea with a few friends, a relative who has business experience, or your tutor. A real business might have initial talks with the bank manager. You could use local business directories or *Yellow Pages* to find out about local competition, or search the Internet to find out information. Local reference libraries will have information about local businesses, resources and organisations who can give advice and support to new businesses. The government often has initiatives – either national or local – to support them. These might take the form of free advice, training or help with business planning, or cash help in the form of subsidies or grants. Banks can also be useful sources of advice on how to start business planning. As well as providing business start-up packs in their High Street branches, many banks now have websites to help people carry out business planning. There is a resource list at the end of this chapter.

ASSESSMENT activity 2

Decide on your business idea. Write a description of the product or service you would like to provide. Carry out some initial research to check whether the idea is realistic.

Key Skills C3.2

Protecting your business idea

If the product or service you choose is a totally new idea, you may need to consider protecting your idea. This should be done at the earliest possible stage. The following are different forms of protection available:

- patenting inventions – registering a new invention with the Patents Office protects your idea. It can be quite expensive and will need renewing regularly. Information is available from the Patents Office.

- registering trade marks – if you have a particular trade mark or product name that you want to use, you can register it with the Trade Marks Registry. You can obtain information from the Patents Office.

- registering a design – the design for a product or service can be registered with the Design Registry. This applies to fashion items, for example, where you may have designed the style or fabric for an item of clothing. Information is available from the Patents Office.

- protection of copyright – books or music can be protected by copyright. If you have written the work then the copyright automatically belongs to you. To protect yourself, you need to be able to prove when the material was written. There is no registry for copyright. You can post a sealed copy of the work to yourself and keep it in a safe place. The date of posting is proof of when the material was written. Alternatively, you could lodge the material with a solicitor.

Remember that registering patents, trade marks or designs, or lodging copyrighted material with your solicitor, will add to your costs of starting the business.

ASSESSMENT activity 3

Decide whether your idea, product or service, needs protecting in any of the ways described. If so, find out how to register and the costs involved.

Key Skills C3.2, IT3.1

Writing your business objectives

When you have thought of a business idea, it is a good idea to think about your general objectives. Your main objective in setting up a business may be to make money, but you need to pop pop this into more specific targets. Your aim might be to break-even in your first year, for example. The break-even point of a business is the point at which its income just covers its costs. Costs should include owners' wages at a level to meet their financial needs. Until you have completed your financial planning, you will not know how much costs for the business will be. You should be able, though, to assess your personal financial requirements. You will need to consider any personal expenses that will need to be covered from the business income. How much you need will depend on your circumstances. If, for example, you have another source of income that covers living expenses, you might be happy for business income to cover the business costs. If the business will be your only income, you may need money to pay for rent, food etc. You will need the business income to cover these expenses as well as business costs. You may aim to make a profit in the first year. You will be better able to judge the amount when you have done some financial planning.

You may want to limit your risk from the business by restricting the amount of money you invest or borrow. For example, you might want to put no more than £10,000 investment into the business because you have this amount to invest, or because you know that you can borrow on reasonable repayment terms. If you decide to put this sort of restriction on your business from the start, you need to consider it during the planning process. It is one of your general objectives.

You may want to achieve a certain level of sales or take a particular share of the market. You may have objectives that relate to the product or service you are offering, such as to offer the best quality product you can, or the most efficient service. Other objectives may relate to the way you operate. You might want to make sure your business is environmentally friendly, or is particularly child-friendly.

In considering your objectives, you should also think about the sort of person you are and how you are likely to run your business. You might need to include some objectives to remind yourself of things you shouldn't do! If you really care about your products and your customers, to the point that it might cost you more than you are making, you should consider whether you need to modify your views slightly. Your objective might be to provide a product or service which satisfies customers and is profitable, rather than to please customers at all costs! If you are not very attentive to detail, you might want to introduce an objective which addresses this issue.

You should think about all the different aspects of your business and consider the issues which are important to you. If a particular aspect does not have any important issues for you, then you do not need to set an objective. By writing down the important issues to begin with, you can work your plan around these. If you don't come up with any important objectives, then your business plan and your business will not work because you don't have any reason for doing it.

Once you have carried out the detailed planning for your business, you might need to revise these initial objectives slightly or add some new ones. You may even find that you have an objective which needs to be abandoned because it's just not possible. At that stage you will be able to decide whether your important objectives are achievable.

ASSESSMENT activity 4

Work in a small group to identify general issues for consideration when identifying business objectives. Use the brainstorming technique you used at the start of the chapter to generate ideas.

Individually identify and write down all the issues that will have an impact on your business. This should include why you want to start the business, and the things that are important to you.

Key Skills C3.1a

If you are working in a group to complete the assessment, you will need to consider the needs and preferences of each group member. You may need to resolve any conflicts between the needs and preferences of different people.

Top Tips

Although your business idea may be purely hypothetical for your assessment, try to approach it as if you were really setting up in business. Your plan will be much more realistic and you will have a better chance of achieving good results.

Objectives can be divided into short-term, medium-term and long-term objectives. The detail in your business plan will relate mostly to short-term objectives. These are things that need to be done or can be achieved within the first months or first year of the business. You need to be realistic in regard to these objectives, especially those relating to sales targets and profits. Remember, for example, that generating lots of sales might also lead to lots of expenses of advertising and marketing. Consider anything outside your control that might affect the business. Many new businesses make the mistake of over-estimating income and under-estimating costs.

Medium-term objectives look into the next two years of the business. You need to consider these when you are carrying out your planning. Whilst it is difficult to know what might happen in the future, you need to anticipate as many problems as you can and include these in your planning.

You will also need to think about medium-term business developments and consider these at the planning stage. For example, you may wish to take on a staff member after the first year.

You need to consider the impact this will have on the business. Thinking about medium-term objectives will help your business to survive the first few years, which are usually the hardest.

The further into the future you look, the harder it is to make firm plans. It is difficult to take account of long-term objectives at the initial planning stages of the business.

This doesn't mean that you shouldn't have any. These long-term objectives are often your vision for the future and your whole reason for setting up the business. Everything you do should take you one step closer to these objectives.

ASSESSMENT   ⑤
a c t i v i t y

Write short- and medium-term objectives for your business, taking into consideration the issues you identified in the last activity. Think about your longer-term goals. Write these down and make sure that your short- and medium-term objectives are working towards these. Business objectives were covered in Chapter 1.

You might like to look back at that chapter to see what sort of business objectives other businesses set. This might give you some ideas for writing your own objectives.

Key Skills C3.3

Top Tips

Don't worry too much about long-term goals. Because the plan is for your assessment, you may not have real, long-term aims for the business.

You should plan, though, for your business to be viable in the medium term. It would be unrealistic for a business to plan only for the short term.

Writing a mission statement

A mission statement highlights and summarises your key business objectives and might include any wider social goals of your business.

Try thinking about your own values and attitudes as these might highlight the things that are important to you. Even if you don't actually write a mission statement, your mission will be communicated to your customers, colleagues and staff in what you do and how you do it. If you write it down, it can help you keep in mind your business philosophy.

ASSESSMENT activity 6

Write a mission statement for your business. If you look back at Chapter 1, you will see some mission statements for other businesses. You could also look in the annual reports of businesses to see the sorts of issues they cover in their mission statements. This might give you some ideas for writing your own statement. Remember that your mission statement should reflect your own views and business philosophy.
Key Skills C3.3

Choosing a business name

Many businesses simply trade under the owner's name, but you may want to choose a name that says something about your product or service.

Think about some High Street names: Prontaprint, Burger King, Superdrug. They give you an impression about the businesses' products and services before you even enter the shops. You will need to take account of the Business Names Act 1985 which regulates the names that businesses use and requires them to display the business name and details of its owners on business premises.

A summary of the Act can be obtained from Companies House in London, or from its web page (see Resources List), or try the local library. The guidance lists some words that businesses are not allowed to use in their names, as well as some general rules.

ASSESSMENT activity 7

Think of a business name. Look at business directories and *Yellow Pages* to see what sorts of names other businesses use. This might give you some ideas. Obtain some guidance about the Business Names Act to make sure your choice of name is legal.

Key Skills C3.2

Section 2 *Market analysis and marketing planning*

What you need to learn

In this section you will learn about:

- how to identify target consumers
- how to identify potential competitors
- how to position your product or service in the market
- how to make judgements about the likely level of sales.

You may find it useful to refer to the notes at the end of Chapter 3, about producing a marketing strategy.

Your marketing plan will help you to identify your customers and competitors, price your product or service and judge the likely level of sales. Your marketing plan will form the basis for your business plan. There are three main tasks to be completed in preparing the marketing plan:

- carry out some analysis of the market and your potential customers. For this you will need to use primary and secondary research techniques
- make some decisions about your marketing strategy, including identifying your marketing objectives, positioning your product or service in the marketplace, and establishing sales targets
- make specific plans for implementing your marketing strategy and monitoring its effectiveness.

Analysis

Your marketing plan will be based on your research and analysis. There are a number of areas you will want to consider, and we will look at these in more detail. In each area you will need to decide the most appropriate method of research. In most cases you will need to use an appropriate mix of primary and secondary research.

Defining the market

A useful first step is to define the industry and market in which you intend to operate. This will give you a focus for your analysis of the market. Identify the industry sector and find out some general statistics about the sector. You will be able to find some information in published government statistical reports and some in industry-specific journals and reports. Look at market size and market growth. Market size is the total value of sales of all businesses in that industry. Market growth can be measured by comparing market size in different years. Market growth or decline will give you some idea of market potential. Consider the number of businesses already in the market. Are there are large numbers or is the market dominated by a few large businesses?

 ASSESSMENT
activity

Identify and define the industry sector of your business.

Analysing the market environment

It is important that you understand the environment in which your product or service will be produced and sold. In Chapter 3 you looked at the use of PEST analysis and this is a useful way of approaching the analysis of the market environment. You will need to investigate the following in relation to your product or service. Remember that you are interested in the impact that these factors have on your business.

- **Political.** A good place to start is by finding out which government agencies have an interest in the industry and then finding out which of their policies might affect you. This will include the Department of Trade and Industry which has an interest in all business. It may also include other government agencies which have a more specific interest in the industry in which your business is involved. For example, the Food Standards Agency may have an impact on businesses making and marketing food products.

Local government bodies may also have some impact, for instance in relation to licensing of various activities. Look on the Open Government website for information (see Resources List). The business press might also be a useful source of information about how government policy impacts on specific industries. Try the *Financial Times*.

Lastly, look for information about any public interest groups or current public issues which might impact on your business. Public interest groups will lobby government to bring about changes in policy or legislation. The government will also respond to public pressure on important issues. Look at the government response to the issue of car prices, for example. The government commissioned a report into the car sales industry because of the disparity between prices charged in the UK and those charged in the rest of Europe for the same models. This was in direct response to public pressure. These sorts of issues might not have an impact on your business now, but you need to think about their possible future effects.

- **Economic.** You will need to analyse general economic conditions. Consider whether there is currently a recession or a boom. This might be general to all markets, or specific to your own industry or geographical area. Look at government statistics relating to the economy for general trends, geographical and industry-based information. A general recession may seriously affect consumer spending power and spending patterns. In times of recession, people tend not to buy luxury items. Interest and tax rates will affect consumer spending power. They may also directly affect the business where money is borrowed, or where taxes or duties relate to specific products.

You need to establish the general levels of demand in the industry and their stability. In some industries – such as the fashion industry – demand for different products may fluctuate dramatically. Some industries will experience seasonal fluctuations. Others, such as markets for basic food items, might be fairly stable. Depending on your product or service, you might need to consider the impact of credit availability. Look at the business press and specialist trade journals.

- **Social.** Look for changes or potential changes in fashion and taste, attitudes and population structure that might have short- or long-term impact on your market or the industry in general. Industry-specific publications might help you look at trends relating to your particular product or service. The more general press might give you indications of changes in public attitudes. For example, the attitude towards genetically modified foods has been well documented in all news sources. More long-term changes, such as changes in population structure, are covered by government statistics.

- **Technological.** You will need to look at the technological changes that may affect your business. You should also consider the pace of change in the relevant technology. If technology is developing rapidly, you could find your product or process is obsolete before you've finished the planning! Remember that technology can also offer opportunities to business. If you can operate with the most up-to-date equipment, while your competitors can't afford to replace their old machines, you may gain a competitive advantage. Trade or industry journals might give information about these issues.

- **Environmental issues.** The Green movement puts ever-increasing pressure on industries to be environmentally friendly with their products and processes. You should consider general issues such as using recycled and recyclable materials, and more specific issues like disposing of waste products from your business. There may be regulatory issues to consider here too. The government is increasingly concerned with environmental issues and monitors levels of pollution and emissions to make sure they are within acceptable limits. There can be opportunities here for businesses who want to market themselves as environmentally friendly.

Other impacts of environmental issues might be shortages of raw materials where the business uses materials from a non-renewable source, and high energy costs. You need to consider whether these will substantially affect your business.

● **Legal and regulatory.** Throughout your course, you have considered the various laws that affect businesses. You need to re-consider these laws in the light of your business and decide which ones will have an impact on your business and its market. You should also look at laws specific to the industry sector. For example, there are lots of rules and regulations relating to food safety.

You should also consider guidance and support offered by trade or industry associations. Many trades or professions have representative bodies which offer guidance to members and the industry in general. Whilst their guidance does not have the force of law, it is often sensible to work in line with recommendations they may make. Look for any bodies or associations specific to your industry sector. Note that they are often the same bodies that offer qualifications for the sector.

ASSESSMENT activity ❼

Analyse the market environment your business faces. Summarise the opportunities and threats presented by the environment, and any constraints it places on the business. Consider how your plan might address these issues.

Key Skills C3.2

Customer needs

You need to understand your customer needs and expectations so that you can successfully position yourself in the market. You will need to find out about your potential customers and build a customer profile. The customer profile will need to describe potential customers in terms of the variables described in Chapter 3 (under Market segmentation). These variables are categorised as demographic, ethnographic, geographic, behaviour, socio-economic and psycho-graphic variables.

The guidance at the end of Chapter 3 will help you decide what you need to find out about customers. Consider also:

● What benefits does the customer expect from the product or service?

● Are there any related needs? For example, if the customer purchases a computer, do they need help setting it up?

● What affects the customer's purchase decision? For example, delivery, after-sales service.

● How do customers choose where to buy?

● Where do they look for product information?

● How important is brand identity to customers? For example, do they always buy Heinz Beans?

You will need to use a mixture of primary and secondary research. Secondary research may help you define the type and numbers of potential customers who may buy the product. To find out customers' opinions and preferences, you may wish to use questionnaires, observations, testing, tastings, surveys, panels, interviews or focus groups. You should choose methods appropriate to your product and the questions you are trying to answer. You may wish to look back at Chapter 3 to remind yourself about sampling. Try to validate the data you collect by checking its accuracy against other sources.

You will need to organise your research results in an appropriate manner. You should keep notes from interviews, observations etc. together and file them in a logical manner so that you can easily refer to them. Always note sources of information – especially secondary research – as you may need to refer to it. Large numbers of similar responses, for example questionnaire results, might be best stored in a database.

Interpret your results:

- summarise your findings
- what did you find out about customers?
- did you answer all your questions about customers?
- what key issues can you identify that might affect your marketing strategy?

ASSESSMENT activity ⑧

- **Plan your market research.**
  - **identify the questions you want answered about customers and their behaviour**
  - **identify appropriate research techniques**
  - **design any questionnaires, surveys etc.**
- **Carry out your research and record your results.**
- **Interpret your results and check that you answered all your research questions.**
- **Identify key issues which will inform your marketing strategy.**
  Key Skills C3.2, C3.3, N3.1, N3.2c, IT3.1, IT3.2, IT3.3

Competitors

Before identifying specific competitors, you will need to decide whether you are operating in a national or a local market. If your market is a national one, you may be competing with many large businesses. In a local market you might have one or two main competitors. You will also need to find out whether there are substitute products because these could mean additional competition. For example, if the price of butter goes up, the sales of margarine may well increase as customers switch products. If you are selling

butter, you need to look at the potential competition from margarine companies.

You can identify your specific competitors using business directories and *Yellow Pages*, and perhaps industry and trade journals which might give information about market share. You will need to try to find out the market share of each business. You might want to consider the possibility of other competitors entering the market. When video recorders became easily available, a large number of video hire shops opened. When mobile phones became more commonplace, the number of phone shops increased. Consider whether there are ways to prevent competitors entering the market by, for example, patenting or registering your invention or design.

Analyse information about each competitor. You may want to collect information about the number of different products or product options they offer and their prices. Request brochures and price lists from competitors. Look at their marketing literature and see how they position themselves in the market. Look at the strengths and weaknesses of each competitor and their products or services. You can use this information to decide how to position your own product in the market. It might be appropriate, at this stage, to identify your own business's strengths and weaknesses and those of your product or service for comparison with competitors.

ASSESSMENT activity ⑨

- **Identify and analyse your competitors.**
- **Assess the probability of new competitors entering the market.**
- **Analyse your strengths and weaknesses.**
  Key Skills C3.2, N3.1, IT3.1, IT3.2

Reviewing the product or service

The information you have collected about the market, your customers and your competitors may have changed your ideas about your product or service. Before you start making strategic decisions about marketing, look back at your product or service description in Section 1. Are there any changes that you would like to make to your product or service to bring it in line with customer requirements?

ASSESSMENT *activity* ❿

Write a new description of your product or service, including any additional features.

Marketing strategy

Once you have carried out your research, you can begin to develop a marketing strategy which will be the basis of your marketing plan. At each stage in the process, you should identify and consider all the alternatives. You should justify the decisions made at each stage by giving reasons for your choice, and note why alternative strategies were not used.

A mission for the marketing function

A good start point for marketing strategy is to write a short summary of the overall purpose of the marketing. You will need to consider the business's mission statement that you prepared in Section 1. The marketing mission should contribute to the business's mission. The statement should state the main role of marketing for the business. This might be profit, customer service or market opportunities. You will need to decide which are most important in order to focus your marketing strategy. As well as the product or service, think about the customer needs and the benefits the product offers. Consider the strengths of the business which might be the foundation of the marketing strategy.

ASSESSMENT *activity* ⓫

Write a statement of no more than half a page which describes the focus of your marketing strategy; what that means in terms of the product or service; and the strengths of the business that will enable the achievement of marketing aims.

Key Skills C3.3

Identifying the markets

You have carried out research into the market and should now have a much clearer idea of its activities and requirements. You should now be able to define the market(s) in which you will operate.

ASSESSMENT *activity* ⓬

Describe your market in terms of customer requirements, size and characteristics. Explain why you have chosen this as your target market over alternative markets.

Key Skills C3.3, IT3.1

Competitive advantage

As part of your analysis, you looked at the strengths and weaknesses of competitors and their products, and at customer perceptions of competitors. Consider this analysis together with the information you gathered about customer needs. Can you identify what it is that you can offer customers, that your competitors can't? Consider issues that are important to customers, such as the range of products, quality, innovation, value for money, features and customer support. In which areas can you offer customers something better than the competitors? You should be able to identify the competitive advantage for your business and its products or services. Ask the question 'Why should the customer buy my product/service in preference to others on the market?' What is the product's or service's unique selling point?

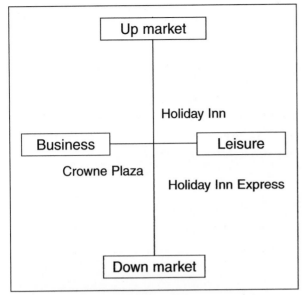

FIGURE 6.1 *Perceptual map for Bass Leisure Retail Group*

It is useful to look at where you might position your product in the market compared to competitors' products. You can do this using the perceptual mapping discussed in Chapter 3. The example used in Chapter 3 looks at the hotels of the Bass Leisure Retail Group.

The map uses the variables business and leisure, plotted against up-market and down-market hotels. You should choose variables that have been identified by your research as important to customers. Often these will be price, plotted against quality. Your perceptual map should be based on customers' perceptions of competitors' products. Plot each of your competitors' products on the map. Look for any gaps in the market which you might be able to fill with your product.

Draw a perceptual map to help you position your product or service in the market. Explain the basis of your competitive advantage. Describe the issues on which you are competing and why you have chosen these. Identify the USP for your product or service.

Key Skills C3.3

Objectives

You should now be in a position to set some objectives for your marketing activities. These are much more specific than the mission statement you wrote at the start of this section. They should have a measurable element. You might decide to try to achieve X per cent of market share, to sell Y number of units, or to achieve sales of £Z. These objectives should be defined in terms of values, volumes and market shares. You will also need to specify the timescale within which they should be achieved. These objectives will form the basis for your production plan and financial forecasts. Your objectives should be realistic, based on what you have learned from the market.

Write specific marketing objectives for your business. Explain why you have chosen these objectives and how you calculated sales volumes etc.

Key Skills C3.3, N3.2a,b

Implementation

Now you have decided your marketing strategy, you need a plan to implement it. Implementing it will involve finding the right marketing mix, identifying and allocating tasks, estimating costs and preparing budgets. You will also need to decide how the success of your plan will be monitored.

The marketing mix

You will need to consider the following components of the marketing mix:

● **product.** You need to think about the whole concept of the product or service, not simply the product or service itself. You are selling customers much more than a product. You might be selling reliability, quality, concern for the environment, customer service and any number of other features that the customer

FIGURE 6.2 *BMW: The ultimate driving machine*   *Source: © Kim Sayer/CORBIS*

requires. Take BMW cars. If you buy one, you are buying much more than a car; you're buying a whole image.

- **promotion.** Promotion is the way you bring your product or service to the customer's attention. You will need to decide on an appropriate mix of promotional activities. Look back at Chapter 3 to see what these might include. You might want to think about advertising, image, brand awareness and trials. You should refer to your analysis of customers before selecting the most appropriate promotional tools.

Your action plan for determining the promotional mix should include:

- reminding yourself about what your target market is

- listing customers' values and requirements

- looking at your product positioning; determining a timetable, bearing in mind your marketing objectives

- selecting promotional tools to be used in line with your analysis of markets and customers

- identifying specific media and formats to be used

- determining the costs involved so that they can be included in your financial plan.

- **place.** You will need to decide on the most appropriate way for your product or service to be distributed. This will depend on the product or service. It might involve direct selling, or selling to wholesalers or retailers. You will also need to establish actual distribution methods, i.e. how goods are to be transferred to the selling outlet. Determine the costs of distribution.

- **price.** Chapter 3 discusses various price strategies that you might use. You will need to think about your objectives. Do you want to penetrate the market quickly, using an initial low price, for example? Consider the price that the market will bear, and look at competitors' pricing. You should be able to set a price for your product. You may want to revise this when you complete your financial analysis. Think about any credit terms that you may need to offer. Larger purchases might require hire purchase arrangements, for example, and business customers will expect 30 days' credit.

● **People.** Think about the staff you need – if any – to meet the customers' expectations.

Determine your marketing mix.

Action plan

You should identify the tasks to be carried out and the timescale for achieving each task. Consider each task and determine the costs involved. This will form the basis of your marketing budget.

Draw up an action plan for marketing. Determine the costs involved in each task.

Section 3 *Production and resource requirements*

What you need to learn

In this section you will learn about:

- relating product decisions to the marketing plan
- designing the production process
- judging resource requirements
- identifying constraints in the business environment.

The production plan will look at the premises, machinery, labour, raw materials and processes required and how they can be organised to produce quality goods or services. You should have already established the level of sales you expect to achieve, in your marketing plan. The production plan will need to meet these sales levels and so needs to be linked to the marketing plan. This will help you to establish the levels of different resources required to provide the product or service.

The production process

The production process will depend on the type of product or service that is to be provided. Let's look at three main methods that you might consider:

- **job production** is used for products or services that are individually tailored to the customer. The production process is based around meeting the specific requirements of one customer. Services such as hairdressing or car maintenance/repairs would be done on this basis.
- **flow production** is used where a large number of identical products are manufactured. The process is organised around producing a continuous flow of items. If you decided to

make and sell tennis balls, for example, you might use a flow production process.

- **batch production** is used where batches of identical products are made for a specific order. A printing company might use this to meet specific printing orders for individual customers.

The production process will help to determine the type of resources that you may require for the business.

Quality assurance

Poor quality products and services result in unnecessary costs to the business as they need to be discarded or replaced and can risk loss of customers. You should think carefully about how you can assure product or service quality. You may wish to refer back to the section on quality in Chapter 1. A good start is to set a standard for the product or service and then think about ways in which you can monitor units against the standard.

 ASSESSMENT
a c t i v i t y

Decide what sort of production process is appropriate for your business idea and the quality assurance process you can implement.

Resource requirements

The resources required may include some or all of premises, machinery and equipment, labour and raw materials. Of course, businesses also require financial resources, but these will be determined once the other resource requirements have been estimated. Let's look at each of these resources in turn:

- **premises.** The requirement for premises will very much depend on the nature of the business. Many small businesses operate from the home of the business owner. This is normally suitable only where the business simply needs an office base, where administrative tasks can be completed. A window cleaner, for example, may only require space to store equipment, and somewhere to write up business records. A taxi firm may just need somewhere where calls can be taken. It is unlikely that you would want to run a manufacturing or retail business from your home. In fact, it is unlikely that you would be allowed to do this under local planning regulations.

For a small business that requires premises, the most attractive option is usually leasing suitable premises. To find premises to lease, and costs of leasing, you will need to approach local estate agents. These might be agents who deal with both residential and commercial property, or specialist business agents. If you know where you would like the business to be based, then it may be worth having a look around the business park, industrial estate or other area, to see if anything is being advertised as available. The size of the premises will depend on the scale of your business operation and the machinery and equipment it requires. It is a good idea to draw a floor plan of your chosen premises with the layout of machinery and work areas. Note: you will

FIGURE 6.3 *You need to find suitable property from which to operate your business*

Source: © London Aerial Photo Library/CORBIS

need to work within health and safety requirements relating to numbers of employees in a work area. See later in this section on legal constraints.

- **machinery and equipment.** You will need to decide what machinery and equipment the business requires. This includes everything for production of the goods or services you will be selling, as well as items like computers that may be required for administrative work. You will need to think about each task that the business will need to carry out, and how this will be achieved. You will also need to consider the level of sales as detailed in your marketing plan as this will determine the number or size of machines or tools required.

You will need to find suitable suppliers for the machinery and equipment. You may find these in local business or telephone directories, in specialist journals relating to the business area, or on the Internet. You will need to decide whether machinery and equipment will be purchased, hired or leased, and establish the costs of your chosen method. You should also consider the level and timing of costs related to maintenance, servicing and replacement of consumable items and parts. You will need this information for your financial plan.

- **labour.** You will need to decide the numbers and types of employees required. Of course, many small businesses start off with only the business owner working for the business. This, again, will depend on the level of production and sales. You will need to think about the functions within a business – as discussed in Chapter 1 – and decide how you will cover the different areas. It may be that you intend to carry out all tasks yourself to begin with, or simply need help in one area. For example, you might employ a sales person, because your expertise is in making the product. Alternatively, you may need someone part-time to cover administrative tasks because you are providing a service which requires you to deal with clients.

For sources of information about local labour availability and rates of pay, try your local Jobcentre. If there are lots of businesses in your area competing for the same sort of employees, then you may need to consider paying higher wages in order to attract the right sort of staff, or be prepared to train staff in the skills required. All staff will need training in health and safety. You will probably find local colleges or training organisations who offer training for employees. Sometimes this can be funded or subsidised by the goverment.

Note down likely levels of wages and training and development costs as well as the number and type of staff that you require. You should also find out about employer's National Insurance contribution levels. You will need to pay these for each employee and so will need to calculate amounts for your financial plan. Contact the local tax office for information, or look on the Inland Revenue website (see Resources List), or find a tax guide in your local library that will give you the information you need.

Top Tips

You don't need to worry about employees' tax and National Insurance contributions because they are simply deductions from the employees' wages. Just include employees' gross wages in your financial plan, plus employer's National Insurance contributions.

ASSESSMENT 18
a c t i v i t y

Draw an organisation chart for your business, showing all the employees and their job titles.
Key Skills C3.3, IT3.3

Find suitable premises for your business and draw a floor plan showing the layout of work areas. Remember to note all costs of premises – deposit required, rents, service charges, business rates etc. and when they need to be paid. You will need this information to prepare your budget.

● **raw materials and stock.** Raw materials includes the materials you need to make a product or provide a service. You will need to find suitable suppliers who can supply sufficient materials at the right time and at the right price for your business. If you are setting up as a hairdresser, materials would include shampoos, conditioners, hair colours and hairsprays. You could buy these from the local chemist, but it is likely that you will get a better deal buying them from a specialist wholesaler. You might also find that some suppliers are prepared to give you a special deal if you use just their products.

You will need to consider 'lead times' for ordering raw materials and the levels of stock you will need to keep. The lead time is the time between ordering a product and receiving it. You don't want to risk production being interrupted, or not being able to provide a service to a client, because you have run out of the required raw materials. Idle staff and machines cost businesses money. You will need to decide how much of each raw material you will need to order and how often. The amounts will depend on your level of production and sales. How often you order a product will depend on how quickly you use it, and the time it takes to arrive following an order. Holding stock costs the business money because it ties up finance and uses up storage space. There is also a risk that, if there is a downturn in the market, the materials will be wasted. Stock levels should be kept to a minimum. Many businesses order materials on a monthly basis – you would need to decide how much you need for one month's worth of production. If materials are perishable, such as fresh foods, they may need to be ordered daily or weekly.

You will need to note the costs of the materials and any delivery and storage costs for your financial plan. You will also need to think about timing of payment for goods. Many suppliers are reluctant to give credit to new businesses, and you may find you have to pay up-front for the first few months. If you are offered credit, it will usually be on a monthly basis. Note that suppliers may offer discounts for prompt payment of accounts. One way of obtaining credit for your raw materials is to use a business credit card. You would need to negotiate with your bank for one of these. They are usually payable in full on a monthly basis, but would at least give you the month's credit normally offered by a supplier.

ASSESSMENT ⑲
activity

Calculate the amounts of raw materials you require, and stock levels. Find suitable suppliers and note the costs of the materials you require. Look at trends in prices – you might need to allow for a price rise later in the year.
Key Skills C3.2, N3.1, N3.2a,b, N3.3

The business environment

Businesses do not operate in isolation. The production process and other operations of the business take place within a specific business environment. You will need to consider the implications for your business of legal, financial, social, environmental and technological issues. You may find that these place certain constraints on your business within which you need to work. You may already have identified some or all of these issues in your market research. Now you need to consider the practical implications of these for your production activities.

Legal issues

You will need to have an appreciation of the laws and regulations that will apply to your business. Some of these are general liabilities. They are outlined in Chapter 1 in the section on business ownership. Laws and regulations relating to employment are covered in the Chapter 4.

You will need to consider the following laws and regulations:

● employment law, including equal opportunities legislation, industrial relations legislation, regulations relating to leave and rest breaks, minimum wage restrictions and rules about maximum working hours

● health and safety law, including laws and regulations about health and safety at work, working conditions, accident policies and fire and emergency regulations

● environmental regulations which cover pollution levels. This might be noise or chemical pollution

● consumer protection law, including laws relating to weights and measures, trade descriptions, contracts of sale, consumer safety, trade marks and competition policy

● data protection laws relate to the control of information kept on computer. If you are intending to keep databases with details of individual customers, suppliers and employees, you may need to register with the Data Protection Registrar. There will be a cost related to this registration, of which you will need to take account for your financial plan

● specific laws and licensing regulations that may relate to your particular business. These include things such as licensing of taxi-cabs, and licensing to sell alcohol, which are controlled by local government, and also Sunday trading laws which may affect opening hours on Sundays.

For most of the general legal issues, you will find sufficient information for your plan in the other chapter. You will need to research any specific legislation that applies to your business. For your business plan, you are not interested in just the existence of these laws, but the practical implications that they have for your business. These implications might be constraints – where you may not be allowed to do something or are required to take a particular action – or costs – where you need to pay to register or license something. For example, pollution controls may mean that you need to adjust your production process or find a way of disposing of any waste safely. Health and safety laws require you to train employees in health and safety, allow a certain amount of work space per employee, and provide protective clothing where required. A taxi firm needs to license its cars to carry passengers. All these have design and/or cost implications for a business. When you set up the business, you will need to operate within these restrictions. At the planning stage, you are interested in the design and cost implications.

ASSESSMENT *activity* 20

Identify the laws and regulations that will have design and/or cost implications for your business. Estimate any costs you will incur as a result of these.

Key Skills C3.2, N3.1, N3.2a

Financial issues

We will look at detailed financial planning in the next section, but you may need to consider some financial elements at this stage. It is no good, for example, designing a production process around machinery and equipment costing £30,000 if you know you are only likely to be able to borrow £10,000. If you know of any financial constraints or restrictions at this stage, you should plan around these. This will save you having to make too many adjustments to your plan after you have completed financial projections.

You should, at this stage, also consider any insurance requirements which will protect the business against any losses or claims. The main insurance cover that businesses need are:

● **protection of assets against fire, damage and theft.** This insurance covers the assets of the business. If there is any loss or damage to assets such as premises, machinery, equipment or stock, the insurance will cover its replacement. The level of cover will depend on the value and replacement value of the assets.

● **disruption of trading.** Where assets are damaged or lost, this might affect production

and cause loss of earnings. This type of insurance compensates the business for loss of earnings.

● **public liability.** This insures the business against claims by members of the public who may have been injured as a result of their business activities, and claims for damage to customers' property. If a customer trips over a loose carpet tile in your offices, or a staff member damages the customer's furniture while making a delivery, the customer may make a claim against the business. The public liability insurance should cover the cost of this claim.

● **product liability.** This insures the business against claims for damage or injury caused by its products. If the toaster you sold a customer blows up and causes damage to the customer and their kitchen, this insurance should cover the claim.

● **employer's liability.** This insurance covers claims made by employees for compensation where they have been involved in accidents at work.

Note that the first two of these insurance types are not required by law, but are a sensible precaution on the part of the business. The last three are required by law for businesses where they are appropriate. Most banks offer an insurance package for small businesses that provides appropriate levels of cover for all the above. Contact branches or check websites for details.

ASSESSMENT *activity* 21

Identify any financial issues which might place constraints on your business.

Key Skills C3.2, N3.1, N3.2a

Determine the insurance requirements for your business and find out about suitable insurance cover. You will need to estimate the value of the assets you need to insure. Calculate the likely cost of insurance for your business.

Social issues

Any business needs to take account of the society in which it operates. Businesses need to consider changes in population structure, changes in customer preference, and the ethics of their business operations. You will have considered these issues in your marketing plan and product design but they may also have implications for the business operations and structure. Recently, the reputations of some fashion clothing companies suffered when it was revealed that they were taking advantage of cheap, child labour in the Third World. This wasn't acceptable to the general public and the businesses concerned suffered some loss of custom. This puts a constraint on the business because businesses may need to switch to using more expensive labour. The fashion industry is one that constantly needs to respond to customer preferences and this may have an impact on the way the business is structured or operated.

ASSESSMENT **22**
a c t i v i t y

Identify any social constraints that may affect your business.
Key Skills C3.2, IT3.1, N3.1, N3.2a

Environmental issues

As public awareness of environmental issues increases, businesses need to take account of these issues in their business strategies. Environmental constraints on your business might include restrictions on disposing of waste or on emissions from any manufacturing process. This might have a cost in finding alternative disposal methods for waste, or having to introduce expensive filtering systems. These are regulated by law, in order to protect the general public.

Other environmental constraints may arise as a result of public opinion. It may not be illegal to cut down the rainforests in pursuit of your business aims, but it may not be wise if there is a large body of public opinion opposed to it. This might mean that your supply of raw materials needs to change, which could have cost or availability implications.

ASSESSMENT **23**
a c t i v i t y

Identify any environmental constraints that may affect your business.
Key Skills C3.2, IT3.1, N3.1, N3.2a

Technological issues

Technology is constantly changing and being updated. Technology affects production processes and products. Production processes will change with the use of new technology. Products will be replaced by improved models and alternative technologies. Technology offers opportunities and imposes constraints on businesses. Businesses at the forefront of new technology may have the opportunity to introduce new or improved products. Businesses using new technology for production may gain a competitive advantage because they can now produce more efficiently.

New technology can be expensive, and businesses may not be able to afford to invest in it. If you cannot afford to invest in new technology, you may need to find alternative ways to make production effective in order to remain competitive. If your products are replaced by new technology, you may need to look at switching production to alternative products.

The technology you use may itself place constraints over your production. If you have a machine that, for example, fills 40 bottles of milk per hour, you would need to take account of this in your production budget. It is no good estimating production at 60 bottles of milk an hour!

ACTIVITY **3**

Identify any technological issues which will affect your business idea. You should consider the technology used by your competitors and the technology available to you.
Key Skills C3.2, IT3.1, N3.1, N3.2a

Section 4 *Financial analysis and planning*

What you need to learn

In this section you will learn about:

● how to estimate the financial requirements of your business idea

● how to identify suitable sources of finance

● how to decide on appropriate legal status for your business

● how to prepare a break-even analysis

● how to prepare a projected profit and loss account and a start-up balance sheet.

Financial requirements of the business

Your financial plan will bring together all the other aspects of your planning and pop pop them into financial terms. By completing your marketing and production plans, you should have sufficient information to estimate costs and revenues. Your first step is to prepare budgets for:

● sales – using estimates of sales volume and price from your marketing analysis

● marketing expenditure – from your planning of the marketing mix. You need to consider packaging, promotions and distribution

● production – based on the volumes to be produced, and the cost of materials, labour and premises and equipment where these are leased or hired

● capital – cost of equipment purchased for use in the business.

Your next step is to prepare a cash flow forecast showing the timing of all payments and receipts. Remember to include your own financial requirements as discussed in Section 1. Remember to consider timing of payments and receipts by taking into account credit terms offered by

suppliers and to customers. At this stage, the cash flow will show a deficit. This is because you haven't yet added your initial sources of finance. The reason for preparing the cash flow at this stage is to establish how much funding is initially required. If you use a spreadsheet package to prepare your cash flow, you will find it easier to add and amend figures.

Prepare budgets for the areas listed above, and a cash flow forecast. Identify the business's initial funding requirements.

Key Skills C3.3, N3.1, N3.2, N3.3, IT3.1, IT3.2, IT3.3

Sources of finance and legal status

You need to consider the most appropriate source of funding for your business. You also need to decide on the legal status for your business. The two may be linked. If, for example, you feel that selling shares is the best way to raise money, you would need to become a limited company. The sources of finance you might access include the following:

● loans – you will find information at banks about business loans and interest rates

● private loans or investment – from friends and family. Find out what return they require on their investment

● your own resources – you will know how much money you can afford to put into the business

● share capital – if you become a limited company. Remember that only public limited companies can sell shares on the Stock Exchange

- hire purchase or credit agreements – linked to the purchase of specific goods or equipment. You should be able to find details of interest charges from suppliers of equipment or banks.

ASSESSMENT 25
activity

Investigate sources of finance and establish the most appropriate source(s) for your business. Calculate the costs of that finance. Add your initial injection of cash and your finance costs to your cash flow.

The legal status you choose may depend on a number of factors:

- your intended source of finance – if shares, you need to become a limited company
- how many people are own the venture – if more than one then you cannot be a sole trader
- image – will limited company status give you more credibility?
- the advantages and disadvantages of each type of ownership, as discussed in Chapter 1.

You will need to estimate any costs involved in setting up, for example to a solicitor for setting up a partnership agreement.

ASSESSMENT 26
activity

Decide on an appropriate legal status for your business. Are there any costs involved in setting this up? Add these costs to your cash flow forecast.
Key Skills C3.2, N3.1, N3.2a, N3.3

Break-even analysis

Break-even analysis is used to establish the volume of sales required at a specific price for a business to cover costs. At the break-even point, the business makes neither a profit nor a loss.

Revenues exactly cover costs. As long as you know the total business costs and the price for each unit, you can calculate break-even volume.

To calculate the cost per unit, you will need to identify direct variable costs per unit. For a product this will usually be the costs of raw material for one unit, plus any cost of packaging for one unit. If production workers are paid using piece rates, this would also be included. For a service, the cost would be the cost of labour in providing that one unit of service. There may also be the cost of consumables to add. For example a washing machine repairer would cost his labour on one job plus the cost of parts. Cost per unit is easy to calculate where all units of a product or service are exactly the same. Where goods or services are provided to the specification of individual customers, this is not so easy. In this case, for the purposes of your assessment use an average cost per unit. Do not include any other costs in cost per unit, except for those related directly to the unit. The cost per unit is known as the variable cost because it varies in line with the number of units produced. All other costs are fixed costs or overheads.

Example

Jane has a business making and selling boxes of luxury biscuits. Each box of biscuits costs £2 to make in terms of raw materials and £1 for packaging. Her fixed costs amount to £50,000 per year. The boxes of biscuits sell for £10 each. We can calculate the quantity (Q) she needs to sell in order to break even:

Total costs = fixed costs + variable costs

TC = £50,000 + (£3 × Q)

Total revenue = Price × Quantity sold

TR = £10 × Q

Q is the number of boxes sold.

At the break-even point, total costs equal total revenues: TC = TR

or 50,000 + (3 × Q) = 10 × Q

NUMBER OF UNITS	SALES REVENUE (@ £10 PER UNIT) £	VARIABLE COSTS (@ £3 PER UNIT) £	FIXED COSTS £	TOTAL COSTS £	PROFIT/LOSS £
0	0	0	50,000	50,000	–50,000
2,000	20,000	6,000	50,000	56,000	–36,000
4,000	40,000	12,000	50,000	62,000	–22,000
6,000	60,000	18,000	50,000	68,000	–8,000
8,000	80,000	24,000	50,000	74,000	6,000
10,000	100,000	30,000	50,000	80,000	20,000

TABLE 6.1 *Break-even chart*

You need to solve the equation to find Q:

$$50,000 = (10 \times Q) - (3 \times Q)$$

$$50,000 = 7 \times Q$$

$$\frac{50,000}{7} = Q$$

$$Q = 7,142.9 \text{ boxes}$$

We would normally round this to the nearest round figure. Jane will need to sell 7,143 boxes in order to break even.

You may find it easier to use a break-even chart or graph. This plots costs and revenues against quantities. The first step is to calculate the total costs and total revenues for different levels of output. We have done this for Jane's biscuit business in Table 6.1.

Total revenue figures and total cost figures are plotted on the graph in Figure 6.4. Where the two lines cross is the break-even point.

If costs or prices rise, the lines can be re-plotted to see the effects on break-even. Most businesses would build in a margin of safety to their budgets. Jane might aim to sell 10,000 boxes of biscuits to ensure that she covers all costs.

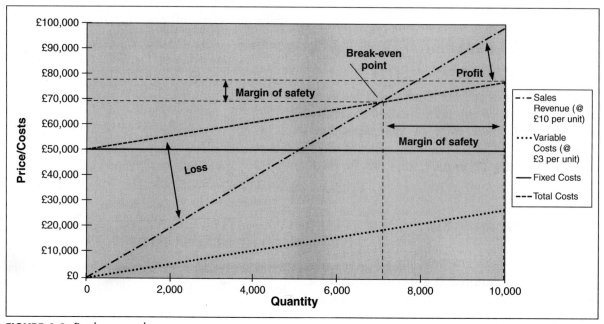

FIGURE 6.4 *Break-even graph*

For your assessment, you should compare the break-even quantity with your sales target quantities to ensure that you will at least break even. You will be able to use the break-even analysis to see how much costs could increase or prices could fall before the business made a loss.

ASSESSMENT activity 27

Carry out a break-even analysis for your business. Draw a break-even chart. Establish how much costs could rise or prices be reduced before losses were made.
Key Skills C3.3, N3.1, N3.2a,d, N3.3, IT3.1, IT3.2, IT3.3

Projected profit and loss account and balance sheet

Your projected financial statements will be prepared in the same way as actual statements would be prepared. You should look back at Chapter 5 to remind yourself of this. Your projected profit and loss account will show the profit or loss you expect to make in the period covered by your plan (usually one year). You should include all your revenues and expenditure.

You should prepare an opening balance sheet and a projected balance sheet at the end of the period. The opening balance sheet is drawn up for the first day of trading. It will show assets of equipment purchased, any stock purchased and cash. It should also show liabilities such as bank overdrafts, loans and trade creditors. You will not have any debtors at this point.

Your projected balance sheet will show:

● fixed assets less depreciation for the year

● stocks – you will be able to estimate the value of stock from the stock levels in your production plan

● debtors and trade creditors – your cash flow forecast will help you identify year end debtors and creditors

● cash and bank overdrafts – identify these from your cash flow forecast

● owner's drawings – from your estimation of your needs

● net profit – from the projected profit and loss account.

ASSESSMENT activity 28

Prepare start-up balance sheet and projected profit and loss account and balance sheet for your business.

Key Skills C3.3, N3.1, N3.2a,b, N3.3, IT3.3

Section 5 *Putting the plan together*

What you need to learn

In this section you will learn about:

● how to put your business plan together
● how to present your business plan.

You will need to present your business plan as a coherent document to support your business case. Throughout this chapter you should have carried out assessment activities which form the basis of different sections of your plan. You will now need to put all these together. You may need to re-write some bits and add linking paragraphs and introductions.

Putting it all together

The sections you should include in your business plan are:

● introduction and summary – a brief overview of the business, including business name
● description of the business
● mission statement and objectives
● ownership
● key personnel – experience and qualifications
● marketing plan
  – mission and objectives of marketing strategy
  – product description
  – summary of marketing environment and trends
  – profile of target customers
  – analysis of competitors
  – core markets
  – competitive advantage

  – product positioning
  – marketing mix
  – marketing action plan
● production plan
  – processes
  – quality assurance
  – resource requirements (include staff training and development where required)
  – organisation chart
  – constraints on production and how they will be minimised
● financial plan
  – budgets
  – cash flow
  – break-even analysis
  – projected financial statements.

In all sections you should justify your actions by explaining why you have made certain decisions. Detailed analysis and market research should not be included in the plan. Overviews should be written, picking out the main points. Where you feel it is necessary you may include summaries of data in an appendix to the report.

Presentation

You should present your plan in a professional manner. This will normally mean that you should word-process your work. You may wish to present it in a binder.

Write your business plan.

Key Skills C3.3, IT3.3

Section 6 *Evaluating your business plan*

What you need to learn

In this section you will learn about:

● how to analyse and assess the viability of your business plan.

You should be able to use the following techniques to analyse your business plan:

● return on capital employed and profit margins – calculate using figures from your projected financial statements. Look back at Chapter 5 to remind yourself how to calculate and interpret these ratios

● the ability to reward or repay investors – look at investors' expectations and profit levels to establish whether they can be paid some return

● percentage of market share gained – calculate your total projected sales value as a percentage of the total market ($\frac{\text{total sales}}{\text{total market}} \times 100$).

From your analysis you should be able to draw conclusions as to the viability of the business.

ASSESSMENT **30**
a c t i v i t y

Carry out an evaluation as described above and draw conclusions about the viability of your plan. Write a summary of your findings, to be presented with your report.

Key Skills C3.2, C3.3

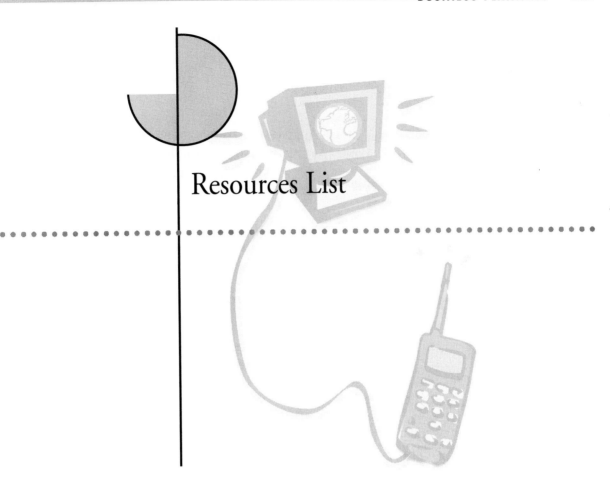

Resources List

The reference library

Your local reference library will be a useful source of local information. It can usually provide you with directories of local businesses, copies of *Yellow Pages* and telephone directories, and information about local advice centres for businesses. It will be able to give you information about the local TEC (Training and Enterprise Council) and its services. It may also have copies of any trade journals which might be relevant to your business area.

Estate agents

Local estate agents – look them up in *Yellow Pages* – will be able to give you details of rent levels and availability for business premises in the area.

Banks

The High Street banks are a good source of information about business planning and finance. Most produce business packs for new businesses, and you may be able to obtain a copy

by calling in to your local branch. Alternatively, try the following websites:

Lloyds TSB   www.lloydstsbbusiness.com
Barclays   www.barclays.co.uk/business
HSBC   www.banking.hsbc.co.uk

Follow the links to information for small businesses.

Patent Office

The Patent Office can provide details of how to register inventions, designs and trade marks, and give information about copyright.

The Patent Office
Harmsworth House
13–15 Bouverie Street
London EC4Y 8DP

Website: www.patent.gov.uk

Companies House

Companies House can provide information about choosing a business name (for all businesses, not just limited companies). It will also give you information on how to set up a limited company and the regulatory requirements related to this.

Companies House
PO Box 29019
21 Bloomsbury Street
London WC1B 3XD

Website: www.companies-house.gov.uk

Data Protection Registrar

Contact for details of how to register a business and on whether you need to register your business.

The Office of the Data Protection Registrar
Wycliffe House
Water Lane
Wilmslow
Cheshire SK9 5AF

Website: www.dataprotection.gov.uk

Though we have given postal addresses above, the quickest way to find the information you want is often through the websites. Other useful websites are:

Department of Trade and Industry

Useful information for businesses and support that DTI can provide: www.dti.gov.uk

Inland revenue

Information about the tax and National Insurance implications for employers: www.inlandrevenue.gov.uk

Customs and Excise

Information for businesses involved in imports or exports, and for those likely to register for VAT: www.hmce.gov.uk

Training and Enterprise Councils

Links to all local training and enterprise councils and information about the services they provide: www.tec.co.uk

Government

Central government information site. Provides links to all government departments and local authorities: www.open.gov.uk

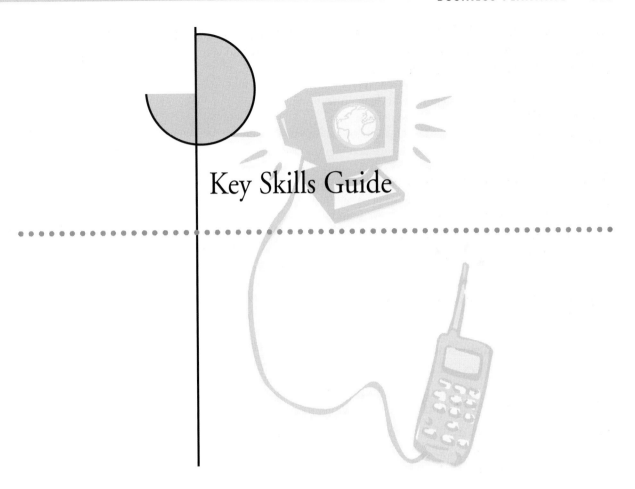

Key Skills Guide

The following is included as a brief guide to the key skills referenced in the text. To complete your key skills work, you will need more information about key skills. Your tutor will provide you with this.

Communication

C3.1(a) Contribute to a group discussion about a complex subject.

C3.1(b) Make a presentation about a complex subject using at least one image to illustrate complex points.

C3.2 Read and synthesise information from two extended documents about a complex subject. One of these documents should include at least one image.

C3.3 Write two different documents about complex subjects. One piece of writing should be an extended document and include at least one image.

Application of Number

N3.1 Plan and interpret information from two different types of sources, including a large data set.

N3.2 Carry out multi-stage calculations to do with:

a amounts and sizes

b scales and proportions

c handling statistics

d re-arranging and using formula

Work with one large data set on at least one occasion.

N3.3 Interpret results of calculations, present findings and justify methods. Use at least one graph, one chart and one diagram.

Information Technology

IT3.1 Plan and use different sources to search for, and select, information required for two different purposes.

IT3.2 Explore, develop and exchange information and derive new information to meet two different purposes.

IT3.3 Present information from different sources for two different purposes and audiences. Include at least one example of text, one example of images and one example of numbers.

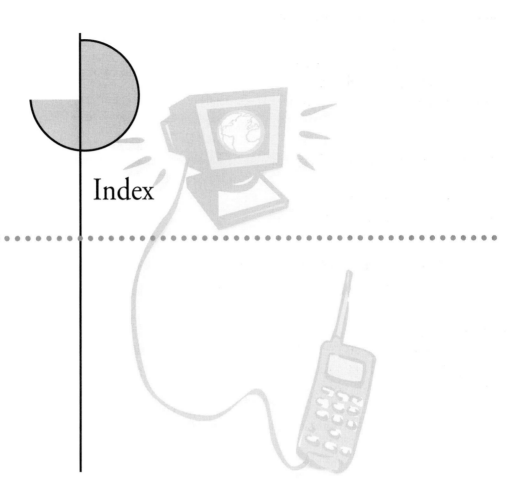

Index